The Author

Dr. Yeager has had a broad and varied background in education. He has been superintendent of city school systems, head of the Department of Education in a Pennsylvania teacher's college, and member of the State Department of Public Instruction in Pennsylvania. For the past fifteen years he has been Professor of Education and director of the course in School Administration at the University of Pittsburgh.

ADMINISTRATION

AND THE PUPIL

EDUCATION FOR LIVING SERIES

Under the Editorship of

H. H. REMMERS

Administration
and the Pupil

WILLIAM A. YEAGER

Professor of Education
Director of Courses in School Administration
University of Pittsburgh

HARPER & BROTHERS · NEW YORK

To

ALICE CATHRALL YEAGER

CONTENTS

Part III. Providing for All Pupils

Part VIII. The Organizing Function

TABLES

xiii

FIGURES

FOREWORD

There have not been wanting critics of public education who note with concern tendencies that they observe in American public education to be patterned upon big business organizations with a disregard for the differences in objectives in business and in education. These critics contend that this tendency is harmful in that it depersonalizes education and tends to lose sight of the major concerns of education—concern for the welfare of the individual and concern for the common good.

Whatever the degree of validity of these criticisms, it is gratifying to present a book on educational administration that by title and content keeps its focus upon both of these major concerns. Professor Yeager has written a book solidly bottomed upon a sound educational philosophy, broad scholarship, and authoritative familiarity with the problems of school administration in our society.

The reader will note with interest the titles and content of certain chapters not generally found in books on administration—e.g., "Guidance as an Adjustment Service," "Psychiatric and Clinical Procedures and Research," "Problems of Social and Personality Adjustment," and the like.

While the book is primarily intended for prospective and practicing school administrators, much of its content might well be read by anyone concerned with education either in a professional capacity or as a citizen. Both professional educators and lay persons will profit from reading it.

H. H. Remmers

PREFACE

Most significant of all movements in education is the broadened conception of the school's responsibility for adequate preparation of children and youth for full participation in social and economic life according to the American way of living. No longer are the school's functions confined to the four walls of the classroom in which the child's intellectual progress is the principal goal. Education is now concerned with the growth and development of the whole child, his physical, mental, moral, social, emotional, and spiritual nature. Indeed, one should not think of each of these several natures as a thing apart. The concept of the integrated personality contemplates a maturing process in which each aspect is meshed into the completed whole.

The child is a living creature, pulsating in a larger world, the home, the community, the group life; he is even now a citizen of the world. He must be taught to live as these environments are manifested to him. To this end he must develop potentialities in many directions; and in becoming a rich and many-sided individual he needs an education and understanding of greatly enlarged scope and vision. Potentialities dormant or perhaps undiscovered must be developed in him to meet the larger concept. Here is the opportunity for a great cooperative enterprise for public school leadership.

The development of adequate educational services to meet the needs of boys and girls along these lines is now conceded to be a principal function of educational administration, and has been designated as the pupil personnel function. In this respect it contrasts with a parallel function in educational administration designated as the staff personnel function.

It is the purpose of this book to comprehend the nature and scope of the pupil personnel services as an essential administrative function. This is a professional task of a high order, requiring specialized types of services under trained personnel in order that the larger purposes of education may be better realized and complete child welfare may result.

The scope of the pupil personnel services and their administration herein discussed are greatly broadened over earlier and narrow concepts of the pupil personnel function. At the outset it is essential to understand its nature and social basis, comprehended within a fitting educational philosophy of childhood and youth as set forth in earlier paragraphs. The first task of the school is to enroll and keep in school all children of school age. There are many problems of admission, classification, and promotion not only of the pupil who makes "normal school progress" but especially of those who are in any manner exceptional. The central philosophy of the whole text is geared to the continuous pupil-growth concept.

As a broad and satisfying educational program is now adapted to these children of such varying capacities and concerns, numerous problems in facilitating growth, adjustment, and articulation must be met and solved and procedures developed. The school organization is the framework within which the child develops. All relevant services should be made available to aid in that development. Of great significance is the organization and administration of those adjustive and evaluative services which are essential to the maturation process. These include in part the school environment, school control, the health program, the guidance service, clinical procedures, and the evaluation program. In all of these services the best available practice in recording and reporting each pupil's progress should be an essential characteristic.

The outcome of the pupil personnel services and their administration is the adequate social and personality adjustment and maturation of each individual youth as he enters into full and complete membership in varying social groups. Not only are the home and community essential to this process but they in turn contribute immeasurably to the outcome. As each youth leaves school, he must become a contributing member of society fitted adequately to the social whole and an essential part of it. This is a cooperative task and involves educational leadership at many turns.

The text closes with a discussion of the relationships which desirable school organization bears to the pupil personnel services. Finally, principles of organizing the pupil personnel function are outlined and applied to school systems under varying conditions.

It is the hope of the author that he may contribute to a more wholesome educational program for childhood and youth.

In writing this book, the author desires to acknowledge many valuable suggestions received from writers in the field. These are too numerous to mention specifically. Especially is he indebted to his many students who have contributed through materials and ideas. Suggestions have been received from friends and associates. Acknowledgment is made to numerous publishers of textbooks and magazines who permitted quotations from their publications. These are indicated in the body of the text. Finally, thanks are due to the author's wife, to whom the book is dedicated, for stimulating encouragement. Whatever shortcomings the book possesses are entirely his own.

W. A. Y.

Pittsburgh, Pennsylvania
November 1, 1948

PART I

The Nature and Social Basis

of the

Pupil Personnel Function

CHAPTER I

Social and Educational Status of Childhood and Youth

THE approach to the proper administration of the pupil personnel is a full and complete understanding of the social and educational status of childhood and youth. The lifeblood of a democratic society is a sound educational system, free to all, in which the rights of every child are recognized and adequate opportunity is given to the development of his individual capacities in accordance with his needs, interests, and inborn abilities. Social attitudes toward the child affect in no small degree the fulfillment of these rights. The attitudes must be understood in their proper perspectives. All must be in accord with sound educational objectives. It is the purpose of this chapter to create the setting for effective pupil personnel administration in the light of these approaches.

EDUCATION AS A FUNCTION OF GOVERNMENT IN A DEMOCRACY

The Nature of Democracy. Democracy in America was born under circumstances of great political, economic, and social stress. Escape from conditions which they found difficult to endure, or the hope of better things abroad prompted the founders of America, our forefathers, to seek new homes in a new world. Removed from the restraints of more stable governments, new governments had to be formed and new ideals molded to suit new, evolving patterns. The imprints of varied racial and social stocks and the traditions of many cultures checkered the problems of the new social order about to be formed.

Democracy as conceived under these conditions has become a great

3

social principle. Its ideas and ideals have left their impressions upon the earlier periods of our history and have become the warp and woof of American social thinking. Democracy then may be said to be a way of social living. The democratic process enables each one of us to develop his personality in the light of these American ideals, and to attain a full measure of individual, family, and group development through the protection of freedoms and rights guaranteed him by tradition and legal procedure. However, to attain this development, the individual must fulfill his due responsibility to the group and to the government which he selects. The function of the state is to serve the interests of all the people who compose it. That democracy may be said to serve best wherein a proper balance is achieved between the personality of the individual and the state of which he is an integral part.

Education in a Democracy. For the preservation of democracy and for the creation of a suitable environment for the growth and perpetuation of democratic principles, education in the United States may be said to have been instituted. As the physical races must be reproduced, so the social and cultural process must be recreated. In fact some writers speak of education as social reproduction. With education "one generation can stand upon the shoulders of its predecessor." With education racial and cultural progress can be reasonably assured, democratic institutions reasonably preserved and enhanced, and the rights of individuals, families, and other groups reasonably maintained. Such is the spirit of education in a democracy.

Yet education conceived in this sense is a far broader term than schooling, that is, the formal education commonly provided in a school. Indeed, if one considers man's entire experience toward social betterment since the dawn of time, the school, more particularly the public school, has not had a particularly large part in his advancement. Other institutions, such as the home, the church, and community activities of all kinds, have played and are playing an enormous part in the educational process. More recently the moving picture, the radio, the newspaper, the magazine, and other cultural-social agencies have influenced the American mind to an extraordinary degree.

The student of education then should have an awareness of the scope and variety of educational influences in American social life.

The learning processes of the child may be subject to a constant bombardment of experiences during his waking hours, which mold or counteract unformed or previously formed experiences. Whatever we are may be said to be the sum total of our experiences, good, bad, or indifferent.

The Place and Function of the Public School. The public school is America's peculiar contribution to the cause, continuance, and preservation of democracy. Wherever in colonial or early national life the public school appeared, its establishment and continued existence and support were predicated upon democratic principles. Systems of state education were established in harmony with this great ideal. To the average American, education is associated only with the public school. This he supports; to it he sends his children willingly, although he knows that a penalty will be enacted if he fails to do so; to it he looks for such educational leadership as his community may exert.

Although the public school is but one of many influential institutions, it performs for society a unique function. This function is one of formal education in contrast with the incidental educational nature of other social institutions. Thus, the public school may be said to be an educational supplement for all childhood designed to perform those tasks which no other social institution is performing or which are being performed inadequately. Since democratic society tends to be dynamic, the school must be ready to assume desirable educational functions which have been abandoned by other social institutions, and to inaugurate new activities as conditions require which may in time be assumed by other social institutions or absorbed by a new educational process.

The public school then has been conceived as fundamental to the democratic state. Its purposes have expanded and receded with the needs of the democratic state and community life through the generations. *All that our citizens wish for their children which may be in harmony with democratic principles and ideals and are not otherwise adequately provided in the social order should be the work of the public school.* Thus, the cause of democracy is the cause of public education—each is essential to the other. The strength of one is the strength of the other, as the weakness of one is the weakness of the other. If eternal vigilance is the price we pay for liberty, no less is this statement true of the cause of the public school.

State and Local Responsibility for Public Education. By virtue of the Constitution of the United States and numerous court decisions and common acceptance, public education is a function of each state, which must provide every child with an educational opportunity. Public education must be conceived as a service to the community for the benefit and welfare of the state. Although the individual may receive this benefit as a free gift, many courts have ruled that to attend a public school is a duty and not a privilege. The implications of this principle are of much importance in pupil personnel administration.

The provision for education, with its control and support, rests primarily upon the state legislature. Under its constitution, all that the state desires for its children is here resident. The legislature determines the minimum educational program, creates or employs agencies to carry out its educational policies, and authorizes local units to organize and maintain schools in its behalf. Complete authority is vested in the legislature over the agencies it creates. At the same time, it acts through these agencies, which it clothes with sufficient powers to achieve the ends sought.

The local unit legally provided to administer public education generally through the United States is the school district. It is a creature of the legislature and as such enjoys the powers and functions which may be delegated to it. These powers are intended to provide the means whereby the people may accomplish adequately the tasks essential to the operation of the public schools. Under the constitution and the legislature, these powers may be vested in (1) the local electorate, (2) various officials or persons associated with the conduct of the schools, and (3) specified powers and duties permitted or denied to the school district.

Local school organization with some measure of state control has proved to be the best means of protecting the democratic nature of public education. Here parents can participate effectively in the operation of the schools, the local educational authority being the agent of the community as well as of the state. Ideally, education should be divorced from local partisan political domination. Each unit should operate in a socially coherent area large enough to provide for a system of education sufficient to meet the needs, interests, and desires of the people for their children during their pre-adult years. The educational function should extend to adults as well, so that the physical, economic, social, and cultural development of all may lead to greater social efficiency.

The local unit of organization is undergoing significant reconstruction in many states. Every effort is being made to organize a unit which will be of sufficient scope and size to provide adequate educational opportunities for all.

The Federal Government and Education. Despite the fact that no mention of education is to be found in the federal Constitution, the federal government has participated in American education to a marked degree. For a century and a half it has followed almost consistently the policy of encouraging the several states to develop their educational systems, acknowledging at the same time no direct responsibility for education. During the years this encouragement has taken the forms of (1) grants of land, (2) grants of money for special types of education, notably in the vocational field, (3) maintenance of certain types of schools and colleges for specialized training, as West Point and Annapolis, (4) maintenance of schools in the District of Columbia, the territories, and for the Indians, and (5) the United States Office of Education.

Recently, the federal government has entered into a more direct relationship to education. Federal funds have been expended for constructing school buildings, beautifying school grounds, establishing school lunch programs, providing funds to keep financially distressed school systems in operation, guaranteeing minimum educational opportunity to all children, and providing vocational opportunities for many youth. In addition to these advantages of federal support, attention should be called to the far-reaching benefits rendered by national organizations and foundations engaged in research, educational services, and support.

The benefits of these federal services are ultimately felt by every school child, although they were primarily intended to insure adequate educational opportunity for less fortunate children. The problem in federal participation is how to maintain a proper balance in relation to state and local control while attempting to insure educational opportunity.

SOCIAL ATTITUDES TOWARD THE CHILD

One interested in administering the pupil personnel function should have an understanding of social attitudes toward the child, both past and present. In fact many present-day attitudes toward child life have their roots deep in the past. Until within the past fifty years, the history of child life has been strangely neglected by most, if indeed not all, of the historians of human experience. This fact is most significant, for in striking contrast to the higher regard in which modern society holds its children, societies of earlier years held an equivalent lack of regard. The more wholesome attitudes toward childhood correspond quite accurately with the history of the rise of humanitarianism, morality, justice, order, and civilization in its best sense. This section will sketch briefly the nature of these attitudes.

Pre-Christian Conception. "To increase, to multiply, and to replenish the earth," the Biblical command to the early Jewish people, found literal fulfillment in the large families of the pre-Christian era. A high birth rate and corresponding high death rate, especially among little children, laid emphasis upon the survival of the fittest. As races grew in numbers, there came about many migrations of peoples, owing largely to the fluctuating food supply and endless wars for territory and aggrandizement. Under such conditions it is natural to assume that the continuous struggle for bare existence subordinated any humanitarian conception of childhood to racial survival.

Social practices affecting children took many forms. Some form of infanticide has been prevalent in every age and under all forms of civilization, being conditioned not only by the economic struggle but also by taboos and tradition. Seemingly, the female child suffered most. Human sacrifice and cannibalism are closely related to infanticide. Mutilation and abuse of children has been common among many peoples. Many countries and ages have permitted the punishment and mutilation, even death, of children for their parents' or families' crimes. Slavery of children can be traced over long periods of time. Industrial slavery may at its worst reveal a far more depraved and corrupt society than chattel slavery. The economic order of a people seemed to make its children economically useful. Some exceptions to these practices are to be found in the upper and middle classes, where childhood was treated with greater respect.

The Christian Concept. The most leavening force in all history in regard to childhood has been the Christian concept. Perhaps the greatest appeal of Jesus centers around His infant birth, which we have solemnized in our Christmas. He taught the family life concept: the Fatherhood of God, the brotherhood of man, and the sanctity of childhood. To enter into the Kingdom *as a little child* introduced a new conception of humility and social relationship untaught before His day. All through the ages, the Christian concept has been slowly spread by means of the missionary spirit. Modern education as a great social force has been profoundly influenced by it.

Naturalism in Education. The wretched economic and social conditions of the eighteenth century and after, and the conflicting educational panaceas which were offered as a means of solution, were clarified through the remarkable contribution of Jean Jacques Rousseau (1712–1778). He revolted against the severe discipline of his day, the poorly suited methods of instruction, the pitiful conditions surrounding childhood, and society's apathy toward them. Revealing the influence of John Locke (1632–1704), he emphasized the importance of the natural development of the child and contended that the three great teachers of man were nature, man, and experience, and that the second and third tended to destroy the value of the first. He urged that nature should develop the child's body and character properly, that at eighteen, with his plan, a boy would still be natural and unspoiled by the social, artificial life about him.

Rousseau had many followers who developed the various aspects of his philosophy. The influence of these thinkers and their ideas can be definitely traced in the social, psychological, economic, and moral uplift of childhood. There was now to be a new estimate of the value of child life. These principles were written into statutes in the form of child labor legislation and became the basis of state systems of education, compulsory school attendance, care of the poor and the handicapped child, and health and medical inspection; they have profoundly influenced the philosophy and practice of education.

Modern Attitudes. The complexity of modern society with its vast social and economic changes has made the adjustment of the child to his environment seemingly a greater task for education. Perhaps never before in the history of the world has a higher value been placed upon child life than during the twentieth century. We have seen how the roots of this marked change in childhood values may be found in the Christian concept and in the contributions of Rousseau; they are also apparent in Pestalozzi, Herbart, Froebel, Luther, and many others. There arose at the turn of the century an individual who sensed this complexity of modern social and economic life and the enormous problems confronting the child in his adjustment to it. John Dewey (1859–   ) discovered that the child has, in reality, a life of his own to live, that perhaps the best assistance we can give him in making his adjustments is to seek to enable him to live adequately the life he is now living.

Dewey may be said to have thus thought out and stated a new educational philosophy, suited to changed and changing conditions. This philosophy, both theoretical and experimental, has given new meaning to both the psychology and the sociology of education and the relation of childhood to it. Dewey gave to education a practical content along scientific and industrial lines, and has sought to interpret to the child the new social and industrial conditions of modern society by connecting the activities of the school closely with those of the community.

Other individuals and movements have helped to clarify this modern attitude toward childhood. Mention has been made of child labor legislation. The Society for the Prevention of Cruelty to Children in the United States was organized in 1875 and has had a remarkable history. The directed public playground had its inception in Boston in 1868 and influenced the growth of boys' clubs and similar organizations. Books and studies of childhood appeared, notably those of G. Stanley Hall, whose first studies were begun in 1880 and whose *Adolescence* was published in 1904 in two volumes. Journals of psychology and child study appeared between 1887 and 1900 and reported the results of movements and experiments. Books and magazines for parents appeared. The beginnings of the parent-teacher movement can be traced back to 1855, although the National Congress of Mothers, the parent organization, first came into being in 1897. Educational sociology has had its most rapid growth since 1920. Mention should be made of the child welfare conference called by President Roosevelt in 1909 and the White House Conferences of 1919, 1930, and 1940.

The federal Children's Bureau established in 1912 has awakened a national recognition of the worth-whileness of the study of childhood. Research laboratories have been sponsored by foundations, universities, and colleges, and by many other agencies and associations. Our courts have been aroused to a new responsibility in the formation of juvenile courts and a more sympathetic attitude toward misunderstood children. Clinics and child study groups participate in the movement. Attention is now given to the handicapped child, the feeble-minded, delinquent, crippled, blind, and deaf. And what may we add of books and pamphlets, journals and monographs, newspaper syndicated articles, societies and conferences, all of which contribute to the study of the child and his proper adjustment to life as he finds it about him.

No discussion of changing social attitudes toward childhood would be complete without a brief statement on the progressive education movement. It had its roots in the philosophy and experiments of Francis Parker and John Dewey in Chicago. Formed during the winter of 1918–1919 by Stanwood Cobb in Washington, it sought to awaken and foster the natural impulses of the child through child study and a proper school environment. To its earlier principles— natural development, the interest motive, teacher-training, study of the physical and mental growth of the child, cooperation with the home, and a stimulating environment—has been added a consideration of socio-economic problems in their relation to this educational process. Without doubt its influence has been of great significance.

Just at the time when the rights of childhood seemed to have been universally recognized and assured, a sinister influence recently emerged in Germany. Termed bio-political, this new philosophy had two objectives: (1) to increase the population of Germany by forcing healthy Germans to have more children, legitimate and illegitimate, and (2) to decrease and debase the future populations of other European countries by starvation, sterilization, and downright mass slaughter. Childhood was thus subordinated to a bio-political policy of the supremacy of an ideology. In the wake of this policy came immorality, divorce, slave labor, starvation of children, removal of children from their homes, and cruel and fantastic regulations designed to achieve the master purpose. It is utterly out of accord with the rights of childhood under democratic principles. The children of suppressed nations may suffer for years to come.

It should be evident from this review that those concerned with administering the pupil must do some right thinking as they approach their tasks. The fact that communities and individuals within those communities differ markedly in their attitudes toward childhood must be recognized. The primary task of all engaged in administering the pupil personnel is to maintain the proper attitude toward the child, to study his interests, needs, and abilities, and to provide for them adequately in the light of his development and the achievement of democratic ideals.

Specific Objectives of Public Education

Objectives Varying with Time and Community Attitudes. The specific objectives of public education have naturally varied with time and popular attitudes. The religious motive in education was dominant in colonial times, especially within groups who had settled and lived under a controlling religious influence. The political motive gradually superseded the religious, as the need for a participating citizenship for the protection of the state and the general welfare became paramount in an evolving democracy. The economic motive was a resultant of great material expansion in the United States. This motive is still readily discernible. More recently, the social motive is assuming increasing importance. Throughout there has been an emphasis upon the cultural and the useful; at times these seemed mutually exclusive.

Cardinal Principles of Secondary Education. In times of great social crises we have been led to redefine the nature and purposes of education. World War I excellently illustrated this thought. In 1918 the Commission on Reorganization of Secondary Education in its Cardinal Principles of Secondary Education[1] indicated the following as major objectives: (1) health, (2) command of the fundamental processes, (3) worthy home membership, (4) vocation, (5) citizenship, (6) worthy use of leisure, and (7) ethical character. These cardinal principles have had a tremendous influence upon the nature and purposes of secondary education in the United States. With the omission of *vocation* as an aim, they have been accepted by many as the objectives of elementary education. Many writers have formulated general aims of education based on them and have profoundly influenced the educational process thereby.

The Children's Charter. It is believed that America wants for her childhood the highest standards of living and achievement compatible with her resources and ways of living. Perhaps nowhere have

---

[1] "Cardinal Principles of Secondary Education," *Bulletin No. 35*, Washington, Bureau of Education, 1918.

these goals been better expressed than in the Children's Charter set forth below. It is quoted at length because of its importance to the subject under discussion. It may easily be accepted as the base of operation for this discussion. Is it possible to achive it and to what degree?

THE CHILDREN'S CHARTER

I. For every child spiritual and moral training to help him to stand firm under the pressure of life.

II. For every child understanding and the guarding of his personality as his most precious right.

III. For every child a home and that love and security which a home provides; and for that child who must receive foster care, the nearest substitute for his own home.

IV. For every child full preparation for his birth, his mother receiving prenatal, natal, and postnatal care; and the establishment of such protective measures as will make childbearing safer.

V. For every child health protection from birth through adolescence, including: periodical health examinations and, where needed, care of specialists and hospital treatment; regular dental examination and care of the teeth; protective and preventive measures against communicable diseases; the insuring of pure food, pure milk, and pure water.

VI. For every child from birth through adolescence, promotion of health, including health instruction and a health program, wholesome physical and mental recreation, with teachers and leaders adequately trained.

VII. For every child a dwelling place safe, sanitary, and wholesome, with reasonable provisions for privacy, free from conditions which tend to thwart his development; and a home environment harmonious and enriching.

VIII. For every child a school which is safe from hazards, sanitary, properly equipped, lighted, and ventilated. For younger children nursery schools and kindergartens to supplement home care.

IX. For every child a community which recognizes and plans for his needs, protects him against physical dangers, moral hazards, and disease; provides him with safe and wholesome places for play and recreation; and makes provision for his cultural and social needs.

X. For every child an education which, through the discovery and development of his individual abilities, prepares him for life;

and through training and vocational guidance prepares him for a living which will yield him the maximum of satisfaction.

XI. For every child such teaching and training as will prepare him for successful parenthood, homemaking, and the rights of citizenship; and, for parents, supplementary training to fit them to deal wisely with the problems of parenthood.

XII. For every child education for safety and protection against accidents to which modern conditions subject him—those to which he is directly exposed and those which, through loss or maiming of his parents, affect him indirectly.

XIII. For every child who is blind, deaf, crippled, or otherwise physically handicapped, and for the child who is mentally handicapped, such measures as will early discover and diagnose his handicap, provide care and treatment, and so train him that he may become an asset to society rather than a liability. Expenses of these services should be borne publicly where they cannot be privately met.

XIV. For every child who is in conflict with society the right to be dealt with intelligently as society's charge, not society's outcast; with the home, the school, the church, the court and the institution when needed, shaped to return him whenever possible to the normal stream of life.

XV. For every child the right to grow up in a family with an adequate standard of living and the security of a stable income as the surest safeguard against social handicaps.

XVI. For every child protection against labor that stunts growth, either physical or mental, that limits education, that deprives children of the right of comradeship, of play, and of joy.

XVII. For every rural child as satisfactory schooling and health services as for the city child, and an extension to rural families of social, recreational, and cultural facilities.

XVIII. To supplement the home and the school in the training of youth, and to return them those interests of which modern life tends to cheat children, every stimulation and encouragement should be given to the extension and development of the voluntary youth organizations.

XIX. To make everywhere available these minimum protections of the health and welfare of children, there should be a district, county, or community organization for health, education, and welfare with full-time officials, coordinating with a state-wide program which will be responsive to a nationwide service of general information, statistics, and scientific research. This should include:

(a) Trained, full-time public health officials, with public health nurses, sanitary inspection, and laboratory workers;

(b) Available hospital beds;

(c) Full-time public welfare service for the relief, aid, and guidance of children in special need due to poverty, misfortunate, or behavior difficulties; and for the protection of children from abuse, neglect, exploitation, or moral hazard.[2]

The Purposes of Education in American Democracy. Perhaps the most comprehensive statement of the purposes of education in American democracy has been made by the Educational Policies Commission appointed by the National Education Association and the American Association of School Administrators.[3] Education has arisen to fulfill the essentials of democracy. In fact, democratic schools arose as a response to the evolutionary processes of American life. Democracy and education are inextricably related. The success of one implies the preservation of the other. To achieve the minimum essentials of democracy, namely, (1) the general welfare, (2) civil liberty, (3) the consent of the governed, (4) the appeal to reason, and (5) the pursuit of happiness, four groups of objectives are identified, namely, (1) self-realization, (2) human relationship, (3) economic efficiency, and (4) civic responsibility.

Each of these major purposes of education is broken down into specific objectives. Included in self-realization are the inquiring mind, speech, reading, writing, public health, recreation, intellectual interests, aesthetic interests, and character. These enable the individual to realize himself.

In achieving the objectives of human relationship there must be respect for humanity, friendship, cooperation, courtesy, appreciation of the home, conservation of the home, homemaking, and democracy in the home. These enable the individual to be homemaker, friend, and neighbor.

---

[2] "The Improvement of Education," *Fifteenth Yearbook,* Department of Superintendence, Washington, National Education Association, 1937, pp. 18–19.

[3] *The Purposes of Education in American Democracy,* Educational Policies Commission, Washington, National Education Association, 1938.

The citizen is both producer and consumer, which implies individual and group economic efficiency. To realize this objective, there is need for work, occupational information, occupational choice, occupational efficiency, occupational adjustment, occupational appreciation, personal economics, consumer judgment, efficiency in buying, and consumer protection.

The objectives of civic responsibility look outward toward an ever widening political and social humanity. Their attainment depends on social justice, social activity, social understanding, critical judgment, tolerance, conservation, social applications of science, world citizenship, law observance, economic literacy, political citizenship, and devotion to democracy.

The burden of realizing these objectives is shared by various fields of life and endeavor. Education has a definite place in the achievement of all, but more particularly in the field of civic responsibility. Yet its responsibilities are being constantly extended. All are shared through the interworkings of the great social processes.

THE WIDENING BASES OF PUBLIC EDUCATION

The nature of public education, conceived in terms of such goals as are expressed in the Children's Charter and in *The Purposes of Education in American Democracy,* is of far broader scope than was dreamed of by the founders of the public school system. The student of education should reexamine these goals and activities in order to grasp their comprehensive significance for the administration of pupil welfare. Here it is important to understand that the bases of public education are widening and that those responsible for the public school enterprise, recognizing these broadening bases, should at the same time recognize the need and opportunities for some measure of their realization. Whatever the problems and conditions of society, education should be prepared to assist in their solution and adapt its program to that end.

In view of the increasing number of institutions and agencies within the community which are developing programs around certain aspects of child welfare, there is ample evidence of social recognition of the new goals, as well as some progress toward their achievement. The widening objectives and programs of public education tend in the same direction. What is now most needed is a cooperative relationship on the part of all those associated in any manner with the welfare of childhood and youth.

Education, War, and Peace. Education has passed through the war experience tempered by many vivid experiences, such as rationing, drives of all sorts, curricular curtailments and adjustments, and teacher shortage. The schools have been brought closer to the community life. Through them boys and girls have been enabled to participate constructively in the war effort. They have learned about other nations, their ideals, problems, and relationships. As a result, education should emerge as a stronger and more fundamental institution, better adapted to the democratic way and the more abundant life.

The chief goal of the modern world is international peace and amity. Education has a tremendous role to play in bringing about an enduring peace among all nations. In UNESCO we have an organization working toward this end; yet it needs the hearty cooperation and understanding of all peoples. Undoubtedly the public schools of the nations must develop a sensitivity in all youth for the brotherhood of man and exercise leadership in the direction of a united international citizenry.

Those responsible for the administration of public education should keep in mind that the purposes of public education must be focused on the welfare of the child. In some school systems there is little evidence that such is the case; in others, the whole educational process is definitely child centered. The supreme purpose of education should be conceived as the development of rich and many-sided personalities fitted for participation in a social pattern of right living, involving high ideals and adequate corresponding knowledge and skills. The child then becomes the focal point of good school administration. Pupil personnel administration becomes the process whereby these purposes, in large part, may be achieved.

QUESTIONS AND PROBLEMS

1. What aspects of present-day American social life are not in harmony with the principle that democracy is a great social ideal?
2. What proportion of American citizens accept the point of view that public education is essential to a more abundant way of living?

3. Wherein is education in conflict with the forces of tradition and the forces of democratic process?

4. Give specific examples of the "usurpation" by the school of functions formerly performed by the home, church, or other institutions of society.

5. What specific reasons can be assigned for different points of view as to education in any community? Is the present school system a correct expression of the will of the people?

6. Do you agree with Professor Beard's statement that the assurance of democratic society can no longer be taken for granted? Where does public education enter this picture?

7. Make a list of the different attitudes toward childhood which you have met in your readings. Attempt some form of classification.

8. What present conceptions toward childhood can you discern which have their origins in tradition or taboo? Try to locate these in their historical perspective.

9. What countries of the world have been the most enlightened toward childhood? The most unenlightened? Explain your answer.

10. What influences in modern educational procedure are directly traceable to Rousseau?

11. In what ways has John Dewey influenced those school activities having to do with the administration of the pupils? Illustrate your answer.

12. Comment on the observation: "The most leavening force in all history in regard to childhood has been the Christian concept."

13. Comment on and compare definitions of education as suggested in this chapter with any others that you may find.

14. Wherein are the seven cardinal principles of education inadequate for modern education? What new principles are advanced in "A Bill of Rights for the New Age" and the Children's Charter?

15. Read carefully the "Quotation Problem" in Patterson, Choate, and Brunner, *The School in American Society*, p. 56. Defend your choice of the three paragraphs.

16. What international educational problems must be solved in order to secure world peace?

SELECTED REFERENCES

1. Bear, Robert M., *The Social Functions of Education*. New York: The Macmillan Company, 1937, chaps. iii, iv.

2. Beard, Charles A., *The Unique Function of Education in American Democracy*. Educational Policies Commission. Washington: National Education Association, 1937.

3. Bossard, James, *The Sociology of Childhood*. New York: Harper & Brothers, 1948.

4. Chamberlain, A. F., *The Child and Childhood in Folk Thought*. New York: The Macmillan Company, 1896.

5. Counts, G. S., *Education and the Promise of America*. New York: The Macmillan Company, 1945.

6. Educational Policies Commission, *The Purposes of Education in American Democracy*. Washington: National Education Association, 1938.

7. Gillette, John M., and Reinhardt, James M., *Problems of a Changing Social Order*. New York: American Book Company, 1942.

8. Glover, Katherine, and Dewey, Evelyn, *Children of the New Day*. New York: D. Appleton-Century Company, 1934.

9. Judd, Charles H., *Education and Social Progress*. New York: Harcourt, Brace and Company, 1934.

10. Mangold, George B., *Problems of Child Welfare*. New York: The Macmillan Company, rev. ed., 1936.

11. Mort, Paul R., *Principles of School Administration*. New York: McGraw-Hill Book Company, 1946, chap. ii.

12. Mursell, James L., *Education for American Democracy*. New York: W. W. Norton and Company, 1943, chap. iii.

13. "Paths to Better Schools," *Twenty-Third Yearbook,* American Association of School Administrators. Washington: National Education Association, 1945.

14. "Schools for a New World," *Twenty-Fifth Yearbook,* American Association of School Administrators. Washington: National Education Association, 1947, chaps. iii, iv, v.

15. Strang, Ruth, *An Introduction to Child Study*. New York: The Macmillan Company, 1938.

CHAPTER II —————————————————————

The Nature and Scope of Pupil

Personnel Administration

THE fundamental principles of democracy as a way of social living and the objectives of education in achieving them have been set forth in the previous chapter. It is essential that the administration of education be in harmony with the attainment of these objectives, especially in the light of the primary importance of the worth and dignity of the individual and the full development of his personality. It is the purpose of this chapter to outline the nature and scope of the administrative responsibility in this process.

THE INDIVIDUAL AS A PERSONALITY

Each year nearly four million babies are thrust across the threshold of life and begin their earthly existence as individuals. After an important period of personality development in the home, they spend the greater part of their young lives, until they are approximately eighteen years of age, subject to the molding influences of the school. Education as a developmental process proposes to free them so that they can better express their natural interests and abilities, enjoy life more abundantly, and gain that self-reliance which is hardly less important to them than it was to their pioneer forefathers. Education proposes to develop in them an appreciation of the expanding forms of civic responsibility and a better understanding of the nature of social living with its satisfactions of cooperative enterprise. These become the tasks, not only of the school, but of all those social institutions associated with the rearing of youth.

Once emancipated through educational opportunity, each individual owes to society his earnest endeavor for the common good. For our society to succeed, there must be *mutual* concern for the democratic way of life. The preservation of the eternal verities plays an important part in this process, not only through indoctrination, but through individual internal control or self-discipline. This social orientation should be realized in the light of immediate problems understandable to the child, rather than in the light of past glories and decadent civilizations, without meaning as yet to his immature mind. Proper education is an imbuing as well as a transforming process.

Concern with these principles is now basic to the administration of the schools. The logical conclusion of the matter is the development of rich and many-sided personalities fitted for entrance into an evolving democratic social pattern, involving the achievement of high American ideals, and fortified with adequate knowledges and skills. Viewed in this light the focal point of efficient school administration should always be located nearest to those vital purposes for which the public school exists. This means the boys and girls. Every act of teaching and every aspect of the organizing, administering, and supervising functions should contribute directly to the end that the boys and girls in each stage of their development receive a full measure of attention. In all this the welfare of the whole of society is paramount. There should be no point of issue between individual and social good.

The School Population

Age and Sex Distribution. The primary responsibility of education is to America's youth—theoretically all individuals from birth to young adulthood. The formal processes of education begin with children about five years of age and extend until they are seventeen or eighteen. Because of the perplexing problems of vocations, school facilities are frequently made available on a full- or part-time basis to youth beyond those ages. A few children, usually in urban areas, have the advantage of nursery schools and kindergartens at ages as low as two years.

The scope of the educational responsibility is revealed in Table 1. It is noted that 34.5 per cent of the nation's population is under twenty years of age, roughly one in three. Exclusion of those under five years of age leaves 26.5 per cent between the ages of five and twenty, roughly one in four. Although the population of the United States has increased 7.2 per cent over 1930, there has been a decline of 4.3 per cent in the under-twenty age group, indicating both a declining birth rate and greater longevity. This temporary decline has been halted by the increased birth rate since 1940.

TABLE I.　DISTRIBUTION OF YOUTH BY AGE GROUPS (1940 Census)

	Per Cent Total Pop.	Per Cent Male	Per Cent Female	Ur- ban	Per Cent Rural Non- Farm	Rural Farm
Under 5 years of age	10,597,891	8.0	50.6	49.4	47.5	24.1	28.4
5–9 years of age	10,725,873	8.1	50.8	49.2	47.6	22.9	29.5
10–14 years of age	11,790,934	9.0	50.6	49.4	49.8	21.4	28.8
15–19 years of age	12,346,481	9.4	50.1	49.9	52.7	22.2	25.1
Total under 20 years	45,461,179	34.5	—	—	—	—	—
Total 20 and over	96,208,096	65.5	—	—	—	—	—
Total United States	131,669,275	100.0	50.2	49.8	56.5	20.5	23.0

Boys slightly exceed girls in number. Nearly half of all youth live in urban areas. The rural farm areas now contain less than 30 per cent of all youth, the percentage remaining about stationary since 1930. Of significance is the rapid growth of rural non-farm areas (largely suburban), the total population there increasing 14.5 per cent over 1930. This has made necessary recent provision for many new school facilities in these areas.

Population Characteristics. In view of the need to provide proper educational facilities for those of school age, the student of pupil personnel administration should be concerned with several important characteristics of the population. First, the population of the United States has been gradually aging. In 1880, the average age was 20.9 years; in 1940, 29 years. The urban population is older and has fewer children than the rural farm population. There are great variations as to characteristics by regions. Average ages are affected by both birth and death rates. Second, the birth rate has been declining since 1800, when it was 55 births per 1000 white population. In 1880, it was 35; in 1930, 20; in 1940, 17. Recently there has been a slight rise due to war and economic conditions. Third, the death rate has been de-clining, now standing at 10.6 per 1000 population. The life ex-pectancy at birth of a white child born in the United States is about sixty-four years. Negroes average about ten years less. This change has come about through our great advances in matters that affect health. Especially are we concerned with the marked decline in the death rate of infants. In 1915, out of 1000 babies born alive, 100 did not survive the first year of life. The number has now been reduced to 50.

A fourth characteristic of the population of interest to education is the net reproduction rate. This represents the average number of daughters that would be born per 100 females starting life together if present birth and death rates at different age levels remained un-changed. In 1940 the net reproduction rate was 96, compared with 111 in 1930. This indicates that we are failing to reproduce ourselves by 4 per cent, a fact of tremendous significance, since the birth rate af-fects education at so many points. A rising birth rate will offset this. A fifth characteristic is the fertility ratio, i.e., the number of children under 5 years of age per 1000 women of ages 20 to 44. This has dropped from 579 in 1920, and 488 in 1930, to 410 in 1940.

Since there is great regional variation in the United States, all such data must be studied in that light. On the whole, the trend over the years has been toward fewer births and fewer deaths. Our natural increase comes principally from American stock since immigration is now negligible. It must be borne in mind, however, that an edu-cational problem still remains with a not inconsiderable percentage of foreign born.

We should not close this discussion without calling attention to the recent significant shift in population due to the war effort and other factors of mobility. New communities have been established in many places bringing problems of housing, school facilities, and social service. Many of these communities are temporary; many more will remain.

School Enrollments. Since the public school is the characteristic institution for the education of children in the United States, school enrollment should be studied. Table 2 shows a distribution of en-rollments in elementary and secondary schools during the period 1930 through 1944. The elementary school population in 1944 showed a marked decline over 1930 owing to the falling birth rate. This has now been reflected in all elementary grades. However, the secondary school population shows a considerable increase during the same period except for a decline for 1942 and 1944. This was due, especially among the upper age groups, to selective service and occupational demands for youth, and may continue for some time and eventually be reversed with the return of nearly normal economic conditions.

TABLE 2. TRENDS IN THE ENROLLMENTS OF PUBLICLY CONTROLLED ELEMENTARY, SECONDARY, AND HIGHER SCHOOLS OF THE UNITED STATES (1930–1944)

Year	Elementary[a]	Secondary	Higher Schools[b]	Total
1930	21,278,593	4,426,708	525,376	26,230,677
1932	21,182,472	5,164,894	528,168	26,875,534
1934	20,880,120	5,715,608	552,001	27,147,729
1936	20,495,767	6,020,268	638,336	27,154,371
1938	19,842,744	6,269,723	713,714	26,826,181
1940	18,934,382	6,635,337	823,867	26,393,586
1942	18,267,335	6,420,544	760,571	25,448,450
1944	17,803,770	5,584,656	449,743	23,838,169

[a] Includes kindergarten.
[b] Includes Indian schools.

In addition to those pupils attending public elementary schools, data reported to the U. S. Office of Education in 1944 showed 2,087,-861 pupils enrolled in private nursery, kindergarten, and elementary schools (Table 3). There are also about 3600 private secondary

TABLE 3. TRENDS IN ENROLLMENTS OF PRIVATELY CONTROLLED ELEMENTARY, SECONDARY, AND HIGHER SCHOOLS IN THE UNITED STATES (1930–1944)

Year	Elementary[a]	Secondary	Higher Schools	Total
1930	2,309,886	373,159	749,613	3,432,658
1932	2,384,181	427,978	694,730	3,506,889
1934	2,382,251	380,880	601,669	3,364,800
1936	2,274,584	415,435	670,336	3,360,355
1938	2,263,703	477,951	737,662	3,479,316
1940	2,172,273	487,672	796,672	3,456,617
1942	2,150,896	512,721	968,307	3,631,924
1944	2,087,861	445,961	751,993	3,285,815

[a] Includes kindergarten.

schools in the United States enrolling nearly a half-million pupils. If college enrollments, schools for Indians, and other specialized types of education were added, total enrollments in all types of schools would approximate twenty-seven million boys and girls, about 20 per cent of the total population.

The Pupil Personnel Function

The Quantitative Approach. In the schools of a half-century or more ago there was little need to keep strict account of all the children of the school district.[1] Only a little schooling was essential for one to be able to take his place in the economic and social life of the community. When compulsory education came to be established, it was difficult for many parents to comprehend its significance in even the most loosely administered form. However, now that society had demanded mass education for all of its children, Massachusetts being the first to do so in 1852, it was essential for the school authorities to know the whereabouts of all children and provide a means of insuring a semblance of regular school attendance for the legal period specified. Once the children in school the teacher's task was to keep them orderly and busy.

It was to this quantitative approach that earlier writers gave principal attention. Records and reports were simple. One record book sufficed for all. Ayres[2] was probably the earliest writer to use the term "child accounting," emphasizing the quantitative approach. Moehlman[3] followed in 1923 with a study bearing a similar title. Although Heck[4] continued to emphasize the quantitative aspect of pupil personnel administration, he is probably the first writer to sense qualitative approaches. Thus earlier definitions of pupil personnel administration referred to it as "keeping track of pupils" and "child accounting." These aspects are still of the utmost importance. We must keep track of all children through the school census, attendance departments and officials, records and reports, and the legal stipulations, as child labor laws, more especially where attendance is associated with state appropriations for education. We

---

[1] Personnel procedures in the traditional schools are described in Chapter III.

[2] Leonard P. Ayres, *Child Accounting in the Public Schools,* Philadelphia, William F. Fell Company, 1915.

[3] Arthur B. Moehlman, *Child Accounting,* Detroit, Friesema Brothers Press, 1923.

[4] Arch O. Heck, *Administration of Pupil Personnel,* Boston, Ginn and Company, 1929.

must study the causes of non-attendance as well as the means of serving greater regularity. These quantitative aspects are constantly being improved as school systems give more and more attention to the qualitative aspect, since they are essential to it.

The Qualitative Approach. The qualitative approach to pupil personnel administration emerges at that moment when one begins to study and interpret the quantitative records and materials in the light of individual pupil betterment and understanding. The methods and materials of social case workers have stimulated attendance workers and teachers to give attention to problem children and do something about them. Thus the qualitative approach begins with the discovery of the individual and his problems.

Unfortunately, many writers in this field have used the terms "guidance" and "pupil personnel" synonymously. The result has been confusion as to the scope of each. The pupil personnel function is much broader in scope, the guidance service being an essential part of it. Warters,[5] who made a careful analysis of definitions, came to the conclusion that one element common to all personnel work contributes to the student's personal development. Other writers use such terms as "understanding," "baffling problems," "interests and opportunities," "adjustment," and "self-discovery."

If one accepts such modern educational mandates for childhood development as the Children's Charter, new guides are offered to the study of childhood which have a direct bearing on pupil personnel administration. These guides may be taken as the basis for ministering to the pupil and his needs; they identify the services which become necessary to this end. The school cannot attain these objectives alone, or provide all the necessary services, but must reach out for assistance into the total social environment.

Definition. Pupil personnel administration may be defined as the provision for all those services and activities pertaining to the welfare of childhood and youth, within both the school and the community, to the immediate end that the abilities, interests, and needs of each child are increasingly realized and his greater development and good achieved, and to the ultimate end that he can become a happy, useful, contributing member of ever larger social groups. This means that the educational program must be as broad as life

---

[5] Jane Warters, *High-School Personnel Work Today,* New York, McGraw-Hill Book Company, 1946, chap. ii.

itself and the services rendered in accord with it. A high degree of cooperation, more particularly with the home and the community, is essential in achieving this objective, especially in the light of the broadening aims of education. Thus the simpler features of a quantitative administration must be followed by the more comprehensive and individualized program when the qualitative approach is emphasized.

The Scope of Pupil Personnel Administration

Growth and development are inherent in human nature and no less so in every child. Since a suitable environment is so essential to growth, the school should aim to provide it and the necessary instructional procedures, all adequately administered, to the end that the progress of each child becomes regular and complete. This administrative function must be conceived (1) as providing every means conducive to this end and (2) as removing every obstacle which impedes that normal progress in any manner.

The administration of the pupil begins at the first point of contact which the school makes with the home through birth records, health and child care clinics, the school census, and the administration of the attendance function. When the child enters school it is as a member of a suitable organization immersed in a suitable environment which best accelerates his educational progress and most adequately meets his specific needs and abilities. Such an organization, procedures, and environment should be so coordinated as to bring about uninterrupted progress. Whenever adjustment takes place it should always be *childward* rather than toward the organization. Far from being confined to limited areas, the study of each child must be thorough and continued if this aim is to be achieved. As an end result, the responsibility of the school for his educational progress would seem to have ceased when he has made reasonable personal, social, economic, and spiritual growth and adjustment, as measured by a reasonable achievement of social and educational goals for his age, as he takes his place in society as a contributing citizen. However, this book takes the position that education can never cease. The formal processes of the school tend to be extended upward and outward. In addition, there are many means at hand in the life beyond the school which truly educate. The ultimate happiness and well-being of each individual and nation may well depend upon the degree of coordination of those formal and informal processes which are educative.

While this book may point out certain principles and procedures of general application, the administration of pupil personnel requires close study and modification to circumstances. Care must be exercised not to apply *in toto* a successful pattern found in existence elsewhere without the desired modification. Like a suit of clothes made for another, it never quite fits.

IMPORTANCE OF ADEQUATE PUPIL PERSONNEL ADMINISTRATION

If desirable educational administration places the proper emphasis where it naturally belongs, namely, upon pupil development, a new spirit of cooperation and understanding must prevail among administrative officers and teachers. Especially is this necessary if we are to focus administration as well as teaching *childward,* in the light of such objectives as are found in the Children's Charter. Administrators and teachers need to have an intelligent and sympathetic attitude toward the whole social process especially in relation to the place of education in general and the public school in particular. Both should have an awareness of the changes in the attitude of society toward childhood through the years.

The administrator should realize that those aspects of the educational process over which he has immediate oversight—buildings, matériel, the budget, his office, supervision, and many others—must contribute to the achievement of the principles set forth above. He must see that the facilities for desirable pupil personnel administration are provided and adequately supported. He can do much to interest the board of education in boys and girls. Facts and figures should not be viewed apart from child values. These observations apply equally to other school personnel: clerks, janitors, attendance officers, bus drivers, the business department, in fact everyone associated with the undertaking. The function of the administrator is to infuse his personnel with a concern for human values. He must avoid any tendency on the part of education to become "big business," in which the individual child is lost but the system saved.

The teacher has the principal part to play in developing happy, well-modulated boys and girls. The youth should be imbued with a sense of balance. The right to complete fruition within himself is countered by the right of every other person to the same thing, which seemingly difficult but obvious balance can be achieved only by a sense of harmony through government, culture, science, religion, and varied associations. To this end the teacher should have an abundant understanding of social values and the social responsibility of the school. Each child must become a personality to him, that is, a developing personality. There must be less and less of the pernicious and all too prevailing attitude that pausing to understand the individual child and helping him with his problems interferes with teaching. Real teaching is measured in terms of the total growth of all the pupils.

QUESTIONS AND PROBLEMS

1. Find definitions of the personality concept in education. How does it apply to the administrative function?
2. Study the latest population data in order to find as many different characteristics as possible.
3. What trends can you discover in school enrollments over the years? Check back to 1870 when the first school enrollment figures appeared.
4. Study the definition of pupil personnel administration in this chapter and compare it (*a*) with that of other writers in the field; (*b*) with your own conception. Try to improve upon this definition.
5. To what extent is Heck's classification of the quantitative and qualitative aspects of pupil personnel work satisfying?
6. Why is it true that the administration of pupil personnel becomes essentially a matter for local study and application?
7. Comment on the importance of pupil personnel administration. What further values can you point out?

SELECTED REFERENCES

1. Bent, Rudyard K., and Kronenberg, Henry H., *Principles of Secondary Education*. New York: McGraw-Hill Book Company, 1941, chap. i.
2. Bode, Boyd H., *Democracy as a Way of Life*. New York: The Macmillan Company, 1937.
3. Educational Policies Commission, *The Purposes of Education in American Democracy*. Washington: National Education Association, 1938.
4. Educational Policies Commission, *The Unique Function of Education in American Democracy*. Washington: National Education Association, 1938.

5. Heck, Arch O., *Administration of Pupil Personnel*. Boston: Ginn and Company, 1929, chap. i.
6. Moehlman, Arthur B., *Child Accounting*. Detroit: Friesema Brothers Press, 1924.
7. *Recent Social Trends in the United States*. New York: McGraw-Hill Book Company, 1933, chaps. xxiii, xxiv.
8. Riebe, H. A., Nelson, M. J., and Kittrell, C. A., *The Classroom*. New York: The Cordon Company, 1938, chap. i.
9. Scott, Walter D., Clothier, Robert C., and Mathewson, Stanley B., *Personnel Management*. New York: McGraw-Hill Book Company, 1931, chaps. i, iv, v, vi, vii.
10. Warters, Jane, *High-School Personnel Work Today*. New York: McGraw-Hill Book Company, 1946, chaps. i, ii, iii.
11. Watkins, Gordon S., and Dodd, Paul A., *The Management of Labor Relations*. New York: McGraw-Hill Book Company, 1938, chaps. i, iv.

NOTE: The student should be familiar with the several pamphlets of the *Biennial Survey of Education,* Office of Education, Washington.

CHAPTER III ─────────────────────

The Development of the Pupil
Personnel Function

THE emergence of the pupil personnel function
has been slow. Its growth has been retarded, for instance, by the
force of tradition and inertia which allows educational procedures
to persist sometimes through generations. The acceptance of a
worthy educational concept is usually a difficult process. So strong
is the influence of the conservative attitude that new ideas may be
greatly changed in form and appearance before they reach the classroom. Sometimes educational progress is retarded because of just
plain laziness. This does not necessarily mean that everything ancient
is bad, or that everything new is good. If one wants a true insight into
the nature of the educational process, he must delve into its more
practical aspects.

There are many contributing factors outside the field of education
to the development of the pupil personnel function. These include,
for example, the concept of individual differences and contributions
of business, industry, and social work. It is the purpose of this
chapter to discuss briefly some of these influences.

Typical Schools of the Nineteenth Century

Educational Objectives. Educational objectives of the nineteenth
century were highly practical. For most children they consisted of
(1) the means of communicating and the acquisition of certain
mechanical skills, as the three R's, considered the most fundamental
of all educational aims; (2) the process of acquiring knowledge
classified by its critics as "rote learning and wordmongery"; (3) a

31

narrow partial culture, with emphasis on faculty and moral development; and (4) the attainment of worldly success and consideration as an outcome of education.

However, it would seem that these were ideals scarcely understood, much less generally believed in, or indeed attainable, in the typical one-room school of the nineteenth century. It was the exceptional teacher who understood their significance and practiced them. Teachers were too busy teaching the three R's, with moral suasion to the "tune of the hickory stick." One is struck with the emphasis laid on maxims, mottoes, and stories with a moral, the evil to be avoided for its dire consequences, and the good to be cherished and emulated.

In 1850, only one person in ten of the total population attended any school whatever for any part of the year. Most of these children attended a one-room brick, frame, or stone structure heated by a wood-burning stove located in the middle of the room. Thus, it was usually too hot for those seated near by and too cold for those seated in the corners. The jacketed stove had not yet made its appearance.[1]

Opening the School. Little previous preparation was made by the new teacher, who approached his school the first morning with much solicitude. The chances favored his being either without teaching experience or new to the district. If he came just about in time to call school, he probably found forty or fifty children who had gotten there early, eager to size up the new teacher and to appropriate the "best seats." Everyone seemed to need his attention immediately. The decisions of the first hour often determined his control and usefulness for the term. His smiles or his gruffness, his rules about to be read and posted, the number and conspicuousness of his ferules or other methods of punishment, his walk, dress, umbrella, the sound of his voice, and many other details noticed and remembered by every child were the drama of that first hour. Could he sing? Was he strict? What would he do with the big boys bent on trying out the new scheme hatched that morning behind the school-

---

[1] The reader is referred to the following for interesting accounts of schoolroom practices and procedures in the nineteenth century: George Brewster, *Lectures on Education*, Columbus, John Bailhache, 1833; Warren Burton, *The District School As It Was*, New York, Orville Taylor, 1838; Clifton Johnson, *Old-Time Schools and School Books*, New York, The Macmillan Company, 1904; Alonzo Potter and George Emerson, *The School and the School Master*, New York, Harper & Brothers, 1842; Samuel S. Randall, *First Principles of Popular Education*, New York, Harper & Brothers, 1869; J. P. Wickersham, *School Economy*, Philadelphia, J. B. Lippincott Company, 1865.

house? What class would come first? Would they have to work hard?

Class Organization. The early schools were ungraded. Since compulsory attendance was yet to come and many older pupils came later to school when the fall work was done, classes were composed of large and small. Much of the teaching was individual, the pupil coming up to the teacher's desk on the raised platform, his lesson to be recited. This suggests the high degree of memory work with its accompanying punishments for unlearned lessons. Where any attempt was made at grading, children were known as the ABC class, primers, first readers, second readers, or third readers, depending upon the reading book to which they were assigned. In the same classes were five- and fourteen-year-olds. When the graded schools came later in the century, there was some difficulty in deciding on the proper bases for grading. Some suggested the pupils' attainments and capacities; others warned against the whims of parents and the caprices of the children themselves. In some schools the "loose" method of permitting pupils to recite different studies in different classes was used; in others, the "close" method which required all members of a class to study the same thing.

Considerable progress, however, was made in grading pupils after 1850. Custom seemed to fix three general grades in the school system: primary, grammar, and secondary, the latter being either the academy or the emerging high school. In rural areas or small towns the primary school still remained ungraded, while in larger districts it was again divided into from six to eight grades. The grammar school usually had from three to four grades. With the usual enrollment of fifty pupils in the typical one-room school, it was difficult to classify them by any rule that would provide for their real needs and abilities, if one would believe that these were well understood. Hence the school remained largely ungraded. As the number of children increased above fifty, the primary and grammar schools made their appearance, with an assistant teacher assigned to the primary room adjoining the main room. As the high schools came into existence, the more advanced pupils were there assigned, the ratio of pupils in the high school, grammar school, and primary school being one, three, and eight respectively.[2]

---

[2] James Pyle Wickersham, *A History of Education in Pennsylvania,* Lancaster, Inquirer Publishing Company, 1886, pp. 15–16. The student will find in Wickersham an excellent description of grading systems in operation, pp. 19–22.

Schoolroom Management. Interruptions were constant: Please mend my pen, please may I sharpen my slate pencil on the stone, please may I get my book, please may I go out (usually one or two fingers upraised), please may I get a drink (three fingers); questions on the meaning of words, forbidden whisperings, merited or unmerited punishments, as shakings or floggings, of which there were not a few in the course of the day, shufflings of feet, dropping of books, marbles, or knives; and above everything else, perhaps, the stern, raucous, even yelling voice of the teacher. If tardiness added to the confusion of an ill-managed room, there was the usual forfeiture of recess or other privileges. Fifteen-minute recesses occurring twice daily were often looked-for releases from dull routine. The scant playgrounds afforded room only for the big boys or girls in their games of ball or tag, the little ones being crowded into a corner or behind the school to play marbles or house. Always there were some kept in, which gave the teacher little time for his own relaxation, especially if he was called upon to settle a disputed game or a fist fight on the playground.

School was called by the ringing of the schoolhouse bell, usually at eight-thirty or nine o'clock in the morning, although some schools started as early as eight o'clock. The reading of Holy Writ was the first exercise of the morning. Then came reading, followed by the spelling and writing lessons. After a ten- or fifteen-minute recess, arithmetic, geography, grammar, natural law, and occasionally some singing and drawing, with reading usually repeated, became the work of the morning. A noon intermission of from one to two hours found the children eating cold lunches out-of-doors in nice weather or around the stove in the winter. Few children went home unless the distance was short. Another recess broke the afternoon monotony of a partially repeated program. By four o'clock (sometimes as late as five) children were eagerly waiting for the dismissal bell, except, of course, those "kept in" for lesson failures or infractions of the rules. Time schedules were seldom adhered to. Classes came and went, thirty to fifty a day; periods were as short as four minutes because of the number to be heard, and if time was taken for disciplinary occasions, visitations, or the like, perhaps classes became a procession.

Welcome were the Friday afternoon literary societies which broke the dull routine of the week, unless, of course, one's piece was not well memorized, or one's essay was badly written. The gazette was the climax of the afternoon's program. On debate days, interest in controversial subjects, such as "Resolved that the country is better than the city," would keep the boys and girls busy arguing on the way home from school. Many a boy or girl rose to later distinction because of the training afforded by the Friday afternoon debates. Preparation for holiday and birthday anniversaries not infrequently interrupted the daily schedules. The teacher who wanted the visiting parents and board members to carry away a good impression of his exercises drilled his pupils in their "pieces" when perhaps reading or grammar was the order of the moment. More conscientious teachers foresaw the inevitable examinations and drilled accordingly.

School Environment. In these earlier schools, few teachers paid attention to the school environment as a factor in teaching. Ceilings were low and the air in winter was usually foul. In localities where the Saturday night bath was not yet a ritualistic procedure, unwashed bodies did not help much in this respect. Dangling legs indicated seats unadjusted to the size and comfort of their owners, and desks were poorly adapted to the eye or arm demands of writing lessons. Often there were no backs to the desks, which were sometimes so placed that the pupil faced the open window. In later years, the desks were placed in rows so that the pupil faced a windowless north wall, with light coming in on either side. Outhouses were usually filthy; some schoolhouses had none at all, the near-by woods or a fence seeming to be sufficient cover for the occasion. Too often the school was placed on an undesirable site, usually useless for any other purpose. Adequate playground space was considered unnecessary, since chores at home would provide sufficient exercise for every child.

School Government. There was little "soft pedagogy" in the management of either town or rural schools prior to the Civil War and indeed long after. Corporal punishment, already referred to, was provided for as many as fifty different offenses,[3] including failure to recite. The "rod of correction" was sometimes accompanied by prayer to overcome the depravity of the offender. A whipping at school was usually followed by one at home if the culprit was found out;

---

[3] Compare Cubberley's account of the disciplinary records kept by the Swabian schoolmaster, Häuberle, typical of German school discipline which without doubt influenced disciplinary attitudes in earlier American schools: Ellwood P. Cubberley, *The History of Education,* Boston, Houghton Mifflin Company, 1920, pp. 455–456.

brother or sister usually saw to that. Yet even in these schools there were kindly teachers like Christopher Dock who advocated a judicious combination of love and fear. Certain types of school organizations, the monitorial and infant schools, for instance, looked with disfavor upon the use of the rod. Mid-century textbook writers urged moral suasion using sterner measures. Toward the latter part of the nineteenth century, the trend was definitely away from harsher practices.

At the same time, freedom and activity were scarcely known. Silence was the rule of the school if it could be enforced. Even the freedom of the monitorial schools shocked the conservatives of the time. If corporal punishment had to be given, many preferred that it be given in private. All the while the teacher hoped that a mutual feeling of cooperation would eventually characterize the management of the school. To know the right and do the right was the extent of desired school government; but always there were rules to be obeyed, and who didn't become careless sometimes? And yet the gap between theory and practice remained rather wide.[4] One wonders how well we have now succeeded in closing it.

Attendance. Universal public education, as we now know it, did not exist in the middle nineteenth century. Three classes of children never attended school: children of foreign-born parents, colored children, and children of indifferent parents. Children of migratory workers seldom had the opportunity. Then, too, there were many children of tender age working, indeed exploited, in the factories, mines, and mills. For example, it was estimated that over 5000 boys were employed on the Erie Canal eight months of the year, few of whom ever attended school at all. More than 30,000 children in New York City did not attend school. It was estimated that more than 200,000 females were employed in manufacturing establishments in the United States in 1840, many of school age. Child labor regulations, as we know them, were yet to come.

Recording of attendance was an inaccurate procedure prior to 1840. No distinction was made between total and average attendance. In fact, little attention was paid to absence at all. About 1840, some im-

---

[4] The reader will find an interesting and thorough account of schoolroom management based on sources in Samuel M. Neagley, *An Analysis of Early American Pedagogical Textbooks,* Doctor's Dissertation, University of Pittsburgh, 1939.

provement was noted, largely through legislation, in recording absences, pupils who left school, or those who reentered. Attendance averages varied from 60 to 75 per cent. Where state appropriations were based on attendance, many districts wasted needed amounts through lax attendance administration. In those districts where the parent paid for the actual number of days his children attended, a premium was thus actually placed on irregular attendance.

Pupils were admitted to school from the ages of three to seven, or even younger, especially when they accompanied an older brother or sister, usually the latter. The upper limit was generally twenty, although young men and women above that age not infrequently attended. By 1865 some attempt had been made to fix the entering age at five or six years. Once admitted, the children usually chose their own seats, being moved only for some infraction of the rules. In schoolrooms where desks or benches were of varying sizes, the larger ones being placed toward the rear of the room, the children sat accordingly, boys on one side, girls on the other.

Visitations. Periodic visitations by the prudential committee or the minister, in vogue before 1840, could scarcely be termed supervision of instruction. However, after Buffalo elected the first city school superintendent in 1837, superintendents of schools multiplied in rapid succession. County superintendents were provided by law in Pennsylvania in 1854. Horace Mann and Henry Barnard, arguing for educational reform both in and out of New England, did heroic work in stimulating the new movement for universal education and its proper supervision. Naturally, the effects were felt in the classroom and led to improvement in methods and management and the extension of the district system to areas which heretofore had not enjoyed any form of educational opportunity.

Influence of Early Educational Procedures

The American public school has made tremendous progress during the past century. Where once the church was pointed out as the outstanding building in any community, the public school may now be said to have achieved that distinction. Its increasing use as a place of community activity is noteworthy. Conversely, public school activities extend into the community life. The school bus is a familiar American institution. More children are going to better schools having better school programs for more school days under better trained and better prepared teachers than ever before in our educational history.

In spite of these forward-looking movements, the reader will note the persistence of many of the schoolroom procedures described on the preceding pages. It is entirely possible to point out duplications of many of these situations in whole or in part in many rural and village schools. This persistence may be indicated in the following: (1) the graded school is still characteristic of the elementary schools; (2) numerous characteristics of earlier classroom management may be found in many elementary and secondary schools, indicating perhaps a certain soundness in, and practical knowledge of, educational procedures; (3) the one-teacher school remains the typical schoolhouse in the United States, despite great advance in school buildings, especially consolidation—it is still regarded with reverence by an unusually large number of persons; and (4) in numerous sections of the United States supervision is still an inspectional procedure.[5]

One distinguishing but unenviable characteristic of the American public schools which still persists is the great variation in educational opportunity afforded children among states and in school districts of the same state, owing partly to early educational lag. The many unusual opportunities for education now available in towns and cities do not generally extend to all rural boys and girls, nor indeed to many of those living in villages and small towns, except where consolidation and transportation have been provided. Perhaps the greatest single problem confronting American education is how to provide an adequate measure of educational opportunity to all youth without regard to location, financial ability, race, or any other factor.

Influences of Advances Made in Business and Industry

Wherever there has been the employment of hired labor, or any type of work involving wages, there has existed the relationship of master and servant. Even the Bible speaks of the keeper of the vineyard and the laborers in it. While the lot of the worker was not a particularly happy one, his relations with his employer were, to a large degree, personal in character. There were many opportunities for close personal understanding. With the industrial revolution re-

---

[5] The careful reader may be able to point out many other characteristics of the earlier schools which persist.

sulting in grouping workers together in large numbers by standardizing their activities, civilization entered the machine age. The individual was submerged. Labor came to be viewed en masse. Unrestricted privileged classes were enabled to build their kingdoms upon the backs of the underprivileged group, the laboring class.

Gradually, the human concept of labor began to emerge. It held that all men are equal in the sense that they have the same impulses and reactions as all other men and are entitled to a reasonable measure of life's benefits. It held that business and industry had a moral obligation, not only to permit their workers to achieve these benefits, but to encourage and help them make as much of their own lives as possible. Unionized labor came into national prominence. Studies were made of employees, their capacities, interests, and opportunities, also of working conditions, production, consumption, social conditions, and class-consciousness. Efforts were made to bring about a greater harmony in employer-employee relationships.

Out of this movement there has gradually emerged a social conscience which has demanded that the lot of the worker be made happier. Abundant illustrations prove its effectiveness: safety and first-aid provisions, lunch and rest rooms, visiting nurses, improved working conditions, frank and open relationships, recognition of individual differences of workers, opportunities for advancement, a voice in industrial affairs, part ownership through stock or other means, bonuses, shorter hours, child labor regulations, unions, relationships of employees to one another, and many others.

The point to be kept in mind throughout this discussion is that personnel management, to a considerable extent, has pointed the way to better relationships between employer and employee and has thereby influenced, more than we realize, conditions within the public schools. Its influence has extended to staff members as well as pupils. What is desirable for fathers and brothers in the shop and factory may be equally desirable for pupils in the schools, especially as they learn about them in the schoolroom and home, and through community discussions.

Changing social conditions have been much intensified as a result of war. The necessity for the selection and placement of men for specific tasks in time of war has given psychologists and personnel officers a task as well as an opportunity of enormous proportions. Tests have been developed and complete records of training, experience, capacities, and aptitudes made. Personnel techniques such as these have eventually been utilized in the administration of both staff and pupil personnel.

CONTRIBUTIONS OF SOCIAL WORK

The Movement. The amelioration of conditions among socially disorganized individuals and groups through some form of organized effort has had a direct influence upon child welfare and its relations to the public school. In small communities and rural areas where most of our people lived before the growth of large cities, the satisfactory adjustment of an individual or a family to his social environment was achieved through the efforts of the church, relatives, and neighbors. As communities increased in size and became great urban centers, individuals, families, and social groups became lost in the urban matrix; relationships became impersonal, with seemingly none to care or be concerned. Children were involved in many instances.

Although possibly many ancient cities had some form of relief for distress, modern alleviation can be traced to legislative measures enacted between 1550 and 1642 for the relief of the poor on the Continent and in England. The movement spread. Private agencies took up the work, being moved by attitudes created by the humanitarian movement on one hand and by the beginning of scientific thought on the other. Added to these were rising political and social theories championing the rights of man and democratic concepts of government.

Definition. Social work may be defined as "the development of personality and of group life through adjustments systematically effected between persons or groups and their social environment."[6] Early efforts at amelioration of the conditions of unfortunates were usually in the direction of group rather than individual adjustment. Gradually, there came about a changed emphasis in that it became necessary to study the individual, or client as he came to be called, in relation to his environment. Thus, early concepts of social justice and social responsibility for the group gave way to stress upon the rehabilitation of the individual as a personality, with an adequate adjustment to his family life or other social milieu.

---

[6] Warner, Queen, and Harper, *American Charities and Social Work,* New York, Thomas Y. Crowell Company, 1930, p. 556.

Outcomes of Social Welfare Work. Some outcomes of the social welfare movement have been the reform of the almshouses and institutions for the insane, the removal and care of children who may be implicated in these conditions, aid to the delinquent child, provision for play and playground and other recreational centers, introduction of prenatal care and care of mothers and young children, nursing and health education, condemnation and alleviation of child labor, infusion of social work into medical treatment and public health, elimination of malnutrition of children, a more enlightened attitude toward venereal diseases with resulting emphasis on social hygiene and sex education, introduction of decent standards of living and relief among poorer classes, even removal of children from homes and conditions in which such decent standards do not give promise of being met. Then too, there is increasing emphasis upon social group surveys, community appraisals, pensions for mothers and the aged, social insurance, and safety legislation, all of which may affect childhood directly or indirectly.

Social Case Work. Social work activities are usually classified into four main groups. These, according to Queen, are case work, institutional work, group work, and organization and administration.[7]

The whole field of social work has reached probably its highest development in social case work. As indicated above, the individual emerged as most in need of study and assistance. He might have been enmeshed in various forms of social disorganization, including poverty, disease, illness, death, prostitution, illegitimacy, family disorganization or conflict, mental and nervous instability, economic distress, crime and delinquency, and many others. Children who might have been directly or indirectly concerned had to be provided for in some manner.

Individual differences and conditions made treatment of the individual all the more necessary. A suitable combination of techniques appropriate to his peculiar problem of maladjustment had to be applied. An underlying knowledge of these techniques drew heavily from the fields of economics, law, biology, psychiatry, psychology, and sociology. Above all, knowledge of people and a human touch were necessary. Causes of maladjustment had to be understood and proper measures undertaken for their relief.

[7] *Ibid.*, p. 554.

In treating the client, social case work generally recognizes certain steps: social study, preparation of social history, diagnosis, planning, treatment, and recording. Social case work is carried on principally by agencies employing professional personnel, rarely by independent practitioners. There has been an increased emphasis upon the training of these workers, especially as to observation, interviewing, recording data, and establishing a proper confidential relationship. Appropriate to the training in these techniques is an adequate knowledge of sociology and psychology.

Educational Outcomes. Family case work and child welfare work are the natural outcomes of these social treatments. It is with them that the student of pupil personnel administration is more directly concerned. Agencies and professional workers come in direct contact with the school authorities. Among the agencies are juvenile courts, orphanages, children's aid societies, correctional schools, municipal and county welfare agencies and institutions, and protective agencies for boys and girls. Almost every community has its dependent, neglected, and mistreated children in need of social treatment, its broken homes, illegitimate children, those in foster homes, waifs, problem children, truants, and delinquents. Education is concerned with all of these.

Cooperating Media. Many media have been developed through which the activities of social workers are conducted and with which public schools can cooperate. These include child guidance clinics of all sorts; mental hygiene classes; juvenile court facilities, including detention houses; foster homes; probation, parole, and follow-up service; day nurseries; and hospitals. In many cities the services of these agencies are highly coordinated—for example, associated charities. The public schools themselves are developing media for making contacts, among them being guidance counselors, visiting teachers, home visitation on the part of regular teachers, and health, psychological, and psychiatric services in public schools, colleges, and universities.

Children who are city dwellers have had the greatest advantage of social case work. Comparatively little has been done in the rural areas, probably because of less need, unless it be in small towns with serious economic problems, such as "company" towns. The cost of these services has been met largely by voluntary contributions. Little support has developed from state and municipal sources. More recently, the federal government has recognized the need in a more substantial manner. Education should utilize every agency and activity devoted to this work and, wherever possible, develop its own plan and facilities in accordance with the needs.

INFLUENCE OF THE CONCEPT OF INDIVIDUAL DIFFERENCES

The scientific movement in education made one of its principal advances in the systematic study, originating in the psychological laboratory just prior to 1900, of differences between persons. These variations were not at first considered educationally important. As more and more became known through discoveries and experimentation, the principle of individual differences came to assume such an important place that no educational procedure is now possible of arrangement or research dealing with instruction unless certain variations among children are first taken into consideration.

The emphasis upon individual differences came to have greater meaning as the doors of the public school opened to admit larger and larger proportions of children of both elementary and secondary school age. Truly now the public school ministers to all the children of all the people. As more and more children of each age group have found their way into the schools, those enrolled in any one age or grade group have manifested greater dissimilarity of intellectual, physical, and emotional traits than did the former more highly selected groups. This rapidly changing character of both the elementary and the secondary school population has created new problems of administration and instruction. Measures of individual differences have been developed and a wide variety of ways of meeting the situation have been tried. These have included semi-annual and quarterly promotions, double-track curricula, aids to teachers, enrichment plans, remedial sections, and a variety of special classes for exceptional children. The educational importance of individual differences has come to have greater meaning with the development of the testing movement.

This rapidly changing character of the public schools with its attendant experimental activities is of the utmost importance in pupil personnel administration. It would now seem to be the school's problem to assume educational responsibility for all the children as it finds them, administering a program to meet individual needs, interests, and capacities. To accomplish this objective individual consideration for each child is a large order. If respect for his personality is evident throughout the educational experience, he will thereby be enabled to make social and economic adjustment as a "personalized individual," prepared both to contribute and to be contributed to.

This chapter should not be closed without calling attention to the fact that world-wide events of the past decade have brought about a deeper realization of the importance of the fundamental rights of all citizens in a democratic society. In achieving them for some we must be careful not to deny them to others, both at home and abroad. The conception of the whole world as a universal brotherhood, adults as well as children, will affect the educational pattern more than is commonly realized.

QUESTIONS AND PROBLEMS

1. Make a list of classroom management practices which may be traced through two or more generations. Evaluate these.

2. Are textbook writers of a given period a reliable guide to contemporary educational practices? Give reasons for your answer.

3. Can you evaluate your own experiences in relation to a "typical school of the nineteenth century" or later?

4. What is meant by the term *educational lag*? Explain further by means of specific examples.

5. In which fields of pupil personnel administration do we seem to have made the greatest progress? What early administrative practices might better have been retained, if any?

6. Cite specific examples of great variation in educational opportunity within your own state or county. Comment on the term *equal educational opportunity* as compared with *adequate educational opportunity*.

7. Evaluate the section on influences of personnel management in business and industry. Wherein, if at all, do its statements concern the public schools?

8. What techniques used in social case work are finding useful application in the public schools? How?

9. Find data to show the extent of social case work generally; in your community.

10. Compare the preferred education of a social case worker with that of a home and school visitor or visiting teacher.

11. Make a list of techniques used in wartime which have been found useful in administering the pupil.

12. To what extent has public school administration been influenced by the concept of individual differences? Be specific.

SELECTED REFERENCES

1. Brown, Elmer Ellsworth, *The Making of Our Middle Schools.* New York: Longmans, Green and Company, 1902; rev. ed., 1926. Read selected chapters.
2. Cubberley, Ellwood P., *The History of Education.* Boston: Houghton Mifflin Company, 1920, chaps. xxv, xxvi, xxvii.
3. Elsbree, Willard S., *The American Teacher.* New York: American Book Company, 1939, chap. xvi.
4. Gillin, John Lewis, *Poverty and Dependency.* New York: D. Appleton-Century Company, rev. ed., 1939.
5. Gist, Noel P., and Halbert, L. A., "The Organization of Social Welfare," *Urban Society,* Second Edition. New York: Thomas Y. Crowell Company, 1946, chap. xix.
6. Martin, George H., *The Evolution of the Massachusetts Public School System.* New York: D. Appleton-Century Company, 1923.
7. Neagley, Samuel M., *American Pedagogical Textbooks,* University of Pittsburgh, Doctor's Dissertation, 1939.
8. Reisner, Edward H., *The Evolution of the Common School.* New York: The Macmillan Company, 1930, pp. 365–388.
9. Scott, Walter D., Clothier, Robert C., and Mathewson, Stanley B., *Personnel Management.* New York: McGraw-Hill Book Company, 1931, chaps. i, iv, v, vi, vii.
10. "Social Work," *Encyclopaedia of the Social Sciences,* 1934, XIV, 165–187.
11. Turnbull, Agnes Sligh, *The Rolling Years.* New York: The Macmillan Company, 1936.
12. Warner, Amos G., Queen, S. A., and Harper, E. B., *American Charities and Social Work.* New York: Thomas Y. Crowell Company, 1930.
13. Watkins, Gordon S., and Dodd, Paul A., *The Management of Labor Relations.* New York: McGraw-Hill Book Company, 1938, chaps. i, iv.
14. Wickersham, James Pyle, *A History of Education in Pennsylvania.* Lancaster: Inquirer Publishing Company, 1885.
15. Yeager, William A., *Home-School-Community Relations.* Pittsburgh: University Book Store, 1939, chap. iii.

PART II

The Attendance Function:
Problems and Procedures

CHAPTER IV

Foundations of School Attendance

THE compulsory school attendance of every child of school age is a necessary accompaniment of the democratic process. As one naturally turns to legal sources for light concerning school attendance, he finds laws deeply rooted in social patterns which serve as the foundation of the whole school attendance structure. The meaning of this foundation must be sought in the family, the individual, great leaders, democratic processes, evolving legal patterns, and social responsibility. Unfortunately, educational opportunities and facilities are in no wise equal, or even adequate, for all children, being influenced by community attitudes, limitations of time, space, and support, and legal exemptions as a result of social pressures. Thus the literacy as well as educational attainments of a nation become important criteria of the success of its educational philosophy and facilities. Complete success can only be reached through acceptance of a full measure of social responsibility for universal school attendance. This chapter seeks to place all of these facts and principles in proper perspective.

SOCIAL RESPONSIBILITY AND SCHOOL ATTENDANCE

School Attendance Essential to Social Existence. Many centuries ago Aristotle in his *Politics* established a fundamental principle that the adaptation of education to its form of government probably contributes most to the permanence of a society's institutions. This principle has found universal acceptance among most, if not all, nations. Whatever the form of education, it becomes necessary that its recipients be placed in a position to receive the instruction to be provided. This means that provision must be made for attendance upon the means of instruction. Over the years the public school has come to be recognized as the best agency for popular education. It is now accepted as an institution which should be tax supported, non-sectarian, and publicly controlled. To achieve its possibilities, there must be compulsory attendance, free tuition, free textbooks, and, above all, equal educational opportunity.

Variance of Claims of Church and State. In the practical application of these principles, the claims of the state and the church are quite at variance. Modern compulsory education originated in the Protestant Reformation. Luther and the Calvinists urged universal education under state control. The Calvinistic state was dominated by the church, involving union of church and state. The Roman Catholic Church has held that education is essentially a religious prerogative, as illustrated in the encyclical letter of Pope Pius XI in 1930 on the "Christian Education of Youth." This letter, while recognizing the concern of the family and civil society in education, states that the right of the church is "absolutely superior to any other title in the national order."

A denominational basis is recognized in many countries, as in England (Church of England), Holland, and Italy, and among certain Protestant groups in America. Sectarian control over education may be said to be based upon (1) the superior claims of the church over the child, (2) primacy of family claims, (3) provision for minority interests, (4) claims of better provision for social heritage and religious needs, (5) resistance to standardization of the public school, (6) freer scope to experimentation and allowance for individual differences, and (7) removal of the burden of support from public school taxpayers.

Education as a Parental Responsibility. In addition to the claims of the state and the church, there is ample support for the principle that the education of children is primarily a parental responsibility, to be performed as the parent sees fit either in the home or in a private school, provided, of course, that it is properly and adequately maintained. This theory can be traced back to the English common law, under which a father had almost unlimited control over the education of his children. It was held in America until modified by statute. While the state may go far toward limiting the rights of individuals on behalf of the general welfare and to improve its citizens, as in establishing public schools, it cannot exercise its police power to interfere with the liberty of parents and guardians to direct the upbringing and education of children under their control, nor can it prohibit private schools altogether. This was shown in the famous Oregon case.[1] The theory here is that liberty must never be interfered with through any form of standardization implicit in universal public education. If the parent insists on providing his children with educational facilities outside the regularly organized school, the courts have held that he may be called upon to show that these facilities are equivalent to those furnished by the state.[2]

Earlier Administrative Concepts. In the development and administration of education in the United States following these principles, certain varying attitudes have emerged, traces of which still remain. Three earlier attitudes are clearly discernible: (1) the compulsory-maintenance attitude of the Puritans, calling for a combined religious and civil government in control of education; (2) the parochial school attitude, as in Pennsylvania, schools usually established in connection with the church thus leaving the educational function to private or parochial schools; and (3) the pauper school non-state-interference attitude, as in Virginia and the South, where tutors, small private schools, pay schools, pauper schools for poor children, and the apprentice system became the means of education. These attitudes have materially affected subsequent administration. Although generally the compulsory-education-under-state-control concept came to replace them, their resistance to it was strong and even today stubbornly remains in some sections. State control of education meets strong opposition from the church and from parents in some quarters.

Recent Administrative Concepts and Problems. The theory as to whether the child belongs to the state or is an individual and as such has certain inalienable rights remains in conflict as between different countries. Yet there would seem to be unanimous agreement that education is a state function. Hence the state must provide the means for education and require the child's attendance upon it. The general tendency all over the world is to accept and require com-

---

[1] *Pierce* vs. *Society of the Sisters of the Holy Names of Jesus and Mary,* 268 U.S. 510, 45 S. Ct. 571, 69 L. Ed. 1070, 39 A.L.R. 468.

[2] The reader should be familiar with the reasoning of the courts in these instances. See especially Newton Edwards, *The Courts and the Public Schools,* Chicago, University of Chicago Press, 1933, chap. xvii.

pulsory education from an initial age of six to eight years up to the age of about fourteen. That age has been widely accepted as the terminus of elementary education, in large part because the non-employment of children under fourteen is generally agreed to. Even while this principle is universally accepted, there is a varying lag in its enforcement due to: (1) economic conditions, (2) lack of sufficient financial support, (3) lack of school facilities, (4) lack of a school program, (5) parochial or private school influence, (6) lack of enforcing facilities, and (7) inertia of parents, many of whom have had little or no education themselves.

The compulsory public school attendance of the child is now recognized as a parental responsibility. The state may fine or imprison the parent for his neglect, and even bring the *body* of the child to the school. While his compulsory attendance universally covers that period designated as elementary, the state may insist upon a minimum standard of efficiency and achievement before the child leaves school. More recently, the age limits of school attendance are being extended both upward into the secondary education field and downward into the pre-elementary field, although in these instances attendance may not always be compulsory. The changing compulsory age limits are affecting the public schools with regard to (1) vocational education, (2) provision for individual differences as exemplified in the atypical child, (3) child labor, (4) part-time education, (5) reorganization of the secondary school, (6) teacher education, (7) provision for dependent children, and (8) methods of enforcement of attendance.

Emergence of the Compulsory Education Concept

Origins. The Protestant Reformation furnished the beginnings of the concept of universal public education and compulsory school attendance. Under the new theory of individual judgment and responsibility for one's own spiritual welfare, it became very important that everyone should be able to read the Word of God, to participate in the worship services, and to order his own life with understanding. This undoubtedly called for the education of all. Moreover, the close association of the church with secular government and the rise of democratic government gave birth to a new conception of public education for all children under the control of the state. To accomplish it took many years. The nineteenth and twentieth centuries were to roll around before it was fully realized.

There were many important personages associated with this movement. Martin Luther wrote a long sermon as early as 1530 to be preached in Lutheran churches throughout Germany admonishing parents to send their children to school. He advocated compulsory school attendance, basing the right to compel attendance on the general right of the state to protect itself and advance its welfare.[3] Eight years later, John Calvin at Geneva outlined, in the vernacular for all, a system of elementary education which had a far-reaching influence, especially since Geneva in Calvin's day became the refuge of persecuted Protestants from many countries. These ideas were carried to France, the Dutch and Belgian Netherlands, Palatinate Germany, Presbyterian Scotland, and Puritan England, whence it crossed the Atlantic Ocean with the stanch Calvinists to the American colonies.

In ascribing the beginnings of universal public education to continental origins, one should not forget the educational contributions of England. The Puritans were Englishmen first, with a heritage through which they had come to know the meaning and value of education for themselves and their children. The prevailing systems of education, providing well for those who could pay, did not quite reach down into the masses. As England became more and more industrialized, the philanthropic movement of the eighteenth century brought about the emergence of a new concept,[4] that of providing industrial education for the children of the working classes by statute, making it compulsory and calling for its support by public taxation.[5] The English poor laws at the turn of

---

[3] Martin Luther, Sermon on the Duty of Sending Children to School, quoted in Ellwood P. Cubberley, *Readings in the History of Education,* Boston, Houghton Mifflin Company, 1920, p. 244.

[4] Compare the contention of Motley and others that the people of New England were principally indebted to the Dutch for their school systems, that these came to New England by way of New Amsterdam. Martin seems to dispose of these contentions by a careful handling of the facts: George H. Martin, *The Evolution of the Massachusetts Public School System,* New York, D. Appleton-Century Company, 1923, pp. 33 ff.

[5] See Forest Chester Ensign, *Compulsory School Attendance and Child Labor,* Iowa City, Iowa, The Athens Press, 1921. See Chapter I for an excellent discussion of English foundations.

the sixteenth century revealed the idea of the education of the apprenticed child as a social obligation. This concept was to take fast hold on the people of America and continue as an educational principle for more than two centuries. To it can be traced many colonial and state statutes for the education of pauper children and those whose parents or guardians were unable to pay the rates or the tuition.

Early New England Laws. And so the system of public education in America came to be dominated by two fundamental concepts: (1) universal public education with its religious and civic implications and (2) the compulsory education of the apprenticed child, later extended to include all children of the working groups. Many poor children were apprenticed so that some educational advantage might accrue to them.

By 1640 there were more than twenty thousand people, all of English birth, settled around Massachusetts Bay. These were Englishmen in their own right. Most of them were well bred and well educated, at first largely church members and property holders. To their ranks were later added servants and laborers. Children of all classes were employed to work in emerging industries. These became objects of public solicitude and undoubtedly were the occasion for the passage of the Law of 1642. This law reaffirmed the English conception of the productive employment of children, and further enjoined upon the towns and parents and masters that these children should learn to "read and understand the principles of religion and the capital laws of this country."[6]

Thus, although no penalties were attached, here appears the first compulsory education law in America, and with it, as Ensign[7] points out, the first child labor law. The act was in operation for two years, then was reenacted with strengthening changes in 1648, 1710, and 1771. Its principles appeared in later codes of Massachusetts and Connecticut and undoubtedly influenced public attitudes toward the education of children in other colonies.

The celebrated compulsory school law of 1647 supplemented certain features of the Law of 1642. Probably because no schools were legally provided or because the original act was not enforced, the

---

[6] *Records of the Governor and Company of the Massachusetts Bay in New England,* Boston, 1853, II, 6–7.

[7] Ensign, *op. cit.,* p. 20.

new act provided for a master to teach reading and writing in every community of fifty families, a grammar school in every town of a hundred families, teachers to be paid by parents or masters or a general tax (community support), and a penalty upon any community failing to meet the terms of the law.

Thus were laid down the principles upon which our modern public school system was largely based. Martin indicates these as follows:

1. The universal education of youth is essential to the well-being of the state.
2. The obligation to furnish this education rests primarily upon the parents.
3. The state has a right to enforce this obligation.
4. The state may fix a standard which shall determine the kind of education and minimum amount.
5. Funds may be raised by a general tax to support such education.
6. Education higher than elementary may be supplied by the state.[8]

Later Principles. With these principles already established, there remained but two more to come. The first of these concerned some form of attendance definition and requirement, with an enforcing basis and agency. The evolution of this principle has been most interesting. The second concerns the restriction upon the labor of the child, so that attendance at school would be possible. The development of this phase of public education is even more interesting and dramatic, culminating, through a variety of state laws, in a proposed child labor amendment to the Constitution.

School Attendance in the South Compared. It will be noted throughout this discussion that compulsory public school attendance was largely characteristic of the northern colonies. The South, holding to a different philosophy, did little to establish the principle. In the North education, at least in the fundamentals, was deemed necessary to the democratic way of living. The South, while democratic in political complexion, was not so in spirit. Compulsory education based upon a concept of human equality was accepted generally in the North, but not in the South because of its purely social lines. At the same time, it must be remembered that economic conditions played an important part. The North being wealthier could afford

---

[8] Martin, *op. cit.,* p. 23.

universal public education of the masses for longer and longer periods. In part this was denied to the South because of lack of funds. As an outcome, the South developed two systems of education, one a private undertaking for those who had the means, and the other public, for those who had not, both being built upon educational principles strangely contrasting.

Emerging Purposes. As one reviews these developments of the compulsory aspects of school attendance, he perceives certain purposes which stand out with some clearness. The first of these is educational. Children should develop habits of good citizenship, be taught moral and religious truths, and have an understanding of the laws of the land. The second is economic. Children should be fitted to make a living and become useful self-supporting members of society. The third is definitely social. Society desires to eliminate pauperism as much as possible by providing for the maintenance and compulsory education of the apprenticed child who is likely to become a public charge.

What the State May Do. In these early developments appear the first evidences of state responsibility for education. The state may act toward education in a threefold way: (1) It may make direct provision for its control and management; (2) it may force it upon a given community or individual; and (3) it may provide for its support or see that support is provided by the local district. Once established, compulsory education, from the state's point of view, may include these features: (1) age limits of attendance, varying widely in the states; (2) an annual period of compulsory attendance, also widely varied; and (3) certain exemptions from attendance, which include illness, certain types of employment, a substitute educational program, upper or lower age limits, and conditions over which there is no control, as geographical or climatic factors. The courts have been called upon from time to time to clarify the nature of the state's responsibility as it affects not only the state but also local and parental responsibility. More recently, there has emerged a new emphasis as to compulsory education. This has come largely from leading voluntary movements which have stressed the physical, moral, and intellectual welfare of the child. Thus, the adequate development of the whole child is now the primary purpose of compulsory public education and would seem to be an all-inclusive reason for its existence.

Establishment of Compulsory School Attendance in all States.
Table 4 summarizes the development of modern compulsory education in the forty-eight states. Massachusetts was the first to pass a
compulsory attendance law, and not until after the Civil War, in
1867, did another state, Vermont, follow suit. Then closely followed
New Hampshire, Michigan, and Washington in 1871 with a succession of northern and western states through the next three
decades. Kentucky was the first southern state to pass a compulsory
attendance law, in 1896. Other southern states, with the exception of
West Virginia, delayed until the twentieth century, the last being
Mississippi in 1918.

Development and Present Status of Compulsory School Attendance in the Several States

Origins. Thus public opinion brought about the establishment of
free schools. The compulsory features have been many years in developing. Public authorities had difficulty at first in taking care of
those who wanted to go to school without bothering too much about
those who did not want to go. Various laws gradually extended upward requirements for the universal education of children. Especially
after 1800, state regulations took a variety of forms governing provision for destitute children, enumeration, manner of distributing
state funds, employment of children, manner of enforcing attendance, and the like.[9] As the principle of stimulation of universal attendance developed, the several states enacted laws compelling children of certain ages to attend school, placed legal prohibition upon
the employment of children of specified ages, and provided a state
school fund to be distributed to local districts to make further provision for the education of children.

Present Status. A study of the compulsory attendance laws in the
several states reveals wide variation. The ages most common for
compulsory attendance are 7–16 years (24 states). In other states the
ages are 8–16 (9 states) and 8–17 (3 states). For ages 14–16 or 14–18
there are, except in four states, regulations covering both school attendance and employment. Meanwhile, there are many forms of

---

[9] "School Census, Compulsory Education, Child Labor, State Laws and Regulations," *Bulletin No. 1,* Federal Security Agency, Washington, United States Office of
Education, 1945. See also "Development of Compulsory School Attendance," *Bulletin*
(1940) No. 6, Monograph No. 5, Washington, United States Office of Education,
1942, part i.

exemption which will be discussed in a later section.

Several trends are apparent in the earlier attendance laws: (1) The parent is to be held responsible for compliance with the compulsory education law. This has been a continuous and universal practice. Where irregularity of attendance occurs, parental blame must be attached along with laxity in enforcement which may be its concomitant. (2) There is a definite trend to increase required school

TABLE 4.   YEARS IN WHICH MODERN COMPULSORY EDUCATION LAWS
WERE ADOPTED IN THE 48 STATES[10]

Years	States	Years	States
1852	Massachusetts	1889	Colorado, Oregon
1867	Vermont	1890	Utah
1871	New Hampshire, Michigan, Washington	1895	Pennsylvania
		1896	Kentucky
1872	Connecticut, New Mexico	1897	West Virginia, Indiana
		1899	Arizona
1873	Nevada	1902	Iowa, Maryland
1874	New York, Kansas, California	1905	Missouri, Tennessee
		1907	Delaware, North Carolina, Oklahoma
1875	Maine, New Jersey		
1876	Wyoming	1908	Virginia
1877	Ohio	1909	Arkansas
1879	Wisconsin	1910	Louisiana
1883	Rhode Island, North Dakota, South Dakota, Montana, Illinois	1915[a]	Florida, South Carolina
		1916[a]	Texas
		1917[a]	Alabama, Georgia
1885	Minnesota	1918[a]	Mississippi
1887	Nebraska, Idaho		

[a] Does not appear in the United States Bureau of Education publication.

attendance to cover the full term of school in keeping with the importance of reaching established educational goals and making for long-range economy. (3) There is a growing trend to make more specific the conditions under which children may attend non-public schools or receive other educational advantages in lieu of public school attendance. (4) Rapid progress is being made in shifting emphasis from penalties imposed for violations to preventative measures. (5) There is a definite attempt to tighten up exemptions from com-

[10] United States Bureau of Education *Bulletin No. 2*, No. 573, Washington, 1914, p. 10.

pulsory school attendance allowable under previous laws, and to provide for greater continuity of school attendance.

LIMITATIONS UPON SCHOOL ATTENDANCE

The well-being and safety of the state are the determining factors in the compulsory aspects of education. While compulsory education laws apply generally, there are certain limitations to the authority of the state in their administration. A few of these will be pointed out.

Attendance in Other Than Public Schools. The Supreme Court of the United States has held that no state has the authority to require children to attend public schools exclusively.[11] Laws requiring compulsory attendance must be reasonably enforced. Where instruction is provided outside the public schools, proof may be demanded that it is substantially equivalent to that afforded by the state. Legal age limits must be adhered to and certain scholastic achievements attained.

Domicile. The residence of children has been a matter of considerable controversy. Usually it is held that to attend school the child must have a legal domicile within the district. There are exceptions to this general rule. However, where circumstances make it necessary for the child to attend school from the home of a relative or guardian, or when the child is an inmate of an institution, he may be admitted as a non-resident under certain conditions, as on a tuition basis or through the establishment of a temporary residence.

Exclusion. Under some conditions a school board may exclude children from school attendance. One of these conditions is failure to meet the school's entrance requirements, scholastic, physical, or moral. The school is generally conceded to have the authority to classify pupils on the basis of scholarship or by other methods of gradation. It has the right to exclude pupils for failure to pay tuition or incidental fees which are within statutory provisions. Pupils may be excluded from school because of mental or physical defects, where adequate provision for his needs cannot be made, or where his continued presence may be detrimental to the welfare of other pupils, as for disciplinary or moral reasons.

---

[11] *Pierce* vs. *Society of the Sisters of the Holy Names of Jesus and Mary,* 268 U.S. 510, 45 S. Ct. 571, 69 L. Ed. 1070, 39 A.L.R. 468. The reader will find an excellent treatment of the legal limitations upon school attendance as held by the courts in Edwards, *op. cit.,* chap. xvii.

Race Segregation. Race segregation has proved a troublesome attendance problem, the Fourteenth Amendment being invoked in several instances. Statutory provisions of the several states are usually the basis of varying court decisions on this subject. In general, it is held that boards of education have the right to classify pupils in such a manner as seems best adapted to promote the interests of the schools, subject of course to state statutes.

Distance from School. The distance a child lives from the appointed school is a factor of considerable importance in his attendance. Regularity of attendance and school progress in relation to distance has been the subject of much study. Naturally, the rural child is the chief sufferer. Climate, conditions of roads, the weather, age of children, and other factors enter into consideration. Irregularity of attendance usually begins when the child has to walk more than two miles. Relief has lately come about through provision for the transportation of pupils. Statutory enactments or state regulations have outlined specific procedures in most states. Discretion is necessary in laying out bus routes and in planning types of transportation and schedules. Safety is becoming a larger factor. Great difficulty arises where the child is exceptional in any way—crippled, blind, or tubercular. Studies have shown that when rural children are transported at public expense, they make a much better attendance record than when no transportation is provided. An emerging issue is whether public funds can be used legally for the transportation of non-public school children.

EXEMPTIONS FROM SCHOOL ATTENDANCE

In reviewing the features of compulsory attendance laws and court interpretation, we note that certain significant types of exemptions have become established. As was pointed out in a preceding section, efforts are being made to remove exemptions which interfere with a continuous educational program for each child.

Minimum Amount of Education. Although the completion of the elementary course of study has been generally recognized in times past as the minimum educational requirement, a number of states require the completion of the twelfth grade. Nearly all variations from this standard include a combination of age and grade achievement.

Church Observance. Exemption from school attendance for certain church observances is provided in eight states. This is especially true where special provision is made for some form of religious instruction. Usually age limits and number of hours are specified.

Children of Indigent Parents. The matter of excusing children from school attendance on account of poverty is recognized as legitimate in some states unless there is some form of financial or other relief. Many states provide for relief under certain conditions and for dependent and neglected children. There is an increasing tendency in this direction, so that a greater measure of equality of educational opportunity can prevail. It is just as important for poor children to attend school regularly as for the children of the financially well favored.

Work Permits. The benefits arising from the labor of children in cases of indigence of parents has become a matter of issue and concern, especially in large families where the father may be unemployed, or on farms. In every state, however, children between certain ages, usually fourteen and sixteen, may be excused from attending school if legally employed. Certain educational requirements generally have to be met. Work permits are subject to review of circumstances, as type of occupation, working hours, necessity for the employment, and sex of worker.

Attendance at Private or Parochial Schools. The compulsory school attendance laws of each state express or imply that children may attend private or parochial schools instead of public schools at the discretion of their parents. Usually these schools are neither supervised nor approved, although in some states such control is exercised. The Oregon case definitely establishes parental rights in this respect. Children who attend other than public schools must do so regularly, the public school authorities being responsible for their attendance. It is presumed that the program of study is equivalent to that of the public school, although it may not always be so.

Administrative difficulties often arise at transfer points. Many public schools require examinations for admittance from private or parochial schools. The pupil is sometimes unable to adjust himself because of a different type of instruction. Then again, the fact that some private school pupils attend public school simultaneously for particular subjects—vocational, music, or health instruction—creates problems of scheduling and control.

Indefinite Exemption. The board of education may exempt the child from attendance if he is physically or mentally incapacitated. Several states are now making provision for such handicapped children. Other reasons for exemption are arrival at the age limit specified by law, farm labor, and whatever else the proper authorities may deem legitimate. As indicated previously, there is a definite trend to limit exemptions in the interest of a more continuous education for more and more children of school age.

ATTENDANCE AND SCHOOL OPPORTUNITY

Unfortunately, we do not have a complete record of school attendance prior to 1870, when reliable statistics were first compiled by the then National Bureau of Education. We do know that in that year only 57 per cent of the children between the ages of five and seventeen were enrolled in school. This has gradually improved through the years until, in 1940, 85 per cent were enrolled. In 1870, of those enrolled, each pupil attended seventy-eight days; by 1940 the number of days had doubled. The percentage of pupils in high school had increased from 1.2 to 26 per cent in 1940. Other interesting and significant data can be gleaned from Table 5.

Although the table shows the definite progress made over the years in school attendance, it does not point out the marked inequalities in educational opportunity. For example, in 1940 schools were in session 175 days on a national average. The range was from 185 days and over in Maryland and New Jersey to 153 in Alabama and 145 in Mississippi. Children in Ohio, Connecticut, and Montana in 1940 attended over 90 per cent of the period the schools were open, while children in Georgia, Mississippi, South Carolina, and Oklahoma attended but 79 per cent of a school term of considerably fewer days.

COMPULSORY SCHOOL ATTENDANCE IN RELATION TO LITERACY

The benefits of democratic government as well as individual responsibility for its development and maintenance are dependent upon the literacy of its people. This has been recognized since the earliest days of the republic. Compulsory education of all children has brought us steadily closer to our goal of making literacy as nearly complete as possible.

Extent. In 1870, about 20 per cent of the total population were classified as illiterates (about 5,658,144 persons). These were largely in the south Atlantic, southern, southwestern, and mountain states, where nearly 50 per cent of the total population were so classified. Less than 10 per cent in the eastern and north central states were illiterates.

TABLE 5. SIGNIFICANT FACTS CONCERNING THE EDUCATIONAL FACILITIES PROVIDED FOR AND ADVANTAGES TAKEN BY CHILDREN OF SCHOOL AGE (1870–1940)

	1870	1880	1890	1900	1910	1920	1930	1936	1940
1. Percentage of children 5–17 (inc.) enrolled	57	65	68	72	73	78	81	83.4	85
2. Average number days attended by children 5–17 (inc.)	45	53	59	72	83	94	116	122	129
3. Average number days attended by each pupil enrolled	78	81	86	99	113	121	143	146	152
4. Percentage of pupils in high school	1.2	1.1	1.6	3.3	5.1	10.2	17.1	22.7	26
5. Average number days schools were in session	132	130	134	144	157	162	172.7	173	175
6. Percentage of children enrolled attending every day	59	62	64	68	72	75	83	85	87

The extension of the means of education and the development of compulsory school attendance laws have served to reduce the illiteracy problem sharply. One is struck forcibly by the following facts: From 1870 to 1915 (1) The average school term increased 19 per cent; (2) the annual attendance of school children 5–18 years old increased 55 per cent; (3) the percentage of illiteracy among persons 10 years of age and over decreased about 50 per cent.

The fact that 20 per cent illiteracy in 1870 has now been reduced to approximately 4 per cent indicates, in reality, splendid progress. Conditions in some states have served to augment the problem continually. Among native whites the percentage is about 1.5; among Negroes, about 16.

Important Aspects. In considering the problem of illiteracy through these years, there are important aspects to be noted. First, for the most part it has been a problem peculiar to certain geographical sections where the native adults were themselves illiterate and where the educational facilities were meager or almost non-existent. Second, there were sharply contrasting differences, as between urban and rural areas and between racial stocks. These affected state attitudes and policies. And third, the problem of illiteracy was being continually augmented by waves of illiterate immigrants, bringing with them different concepts of government and proving difficult to assimilate.

In spite of the fact that every state had adopted a compulsory school attendance law by 1918, revelations of the continued presence of illiteracy during World Wars I and II and through the federal census reports were discomfiting. Lengthened school terms and extended educational facilities have served to lower it sharply. Immigration, especially of illiterates, has been reduced to a minimum. Federal emergency agencies have assisted in the solution of the problem. Night classes for adult illiterates have been established and other means provided for acquiring the essentials of a common school education.

The educational statistical summary now uses the term "educational attainment" of the population. In 1940 this was found to be 8.4 years (grades in school). At the same time a relatively high proportion of the total population (13.7 per cent) had less than a fifth-grade education. With continued effort illiteracy may be reduced to its irreducible minimum, about 1.5 to 2 per cent, which represents that portion of our population over ten years of age who have a mental incapacity for literacy in any degree.

QUESTIONS AND PROBLEMS

1. Analyze the school attendance legislation of Pennsylvania (or your own state), and compare with any state of your choice. (Consult U. S. Office of Education publications for comparative data.)

2. Compare the justice of the claims of state and church concerning the education of children.
3. Locate the relative places of the parent and the state as to responsibility for the education of children.
4. Trace the thread of compulsory education from the Protestant Reformation to the passing of the Massachusetts Law of 1862.
5. Balance the relationship of the state and local school authorities as to the compulsory education principle.
6. What historical conditions affected the dates of passage of compulsory education laws from 1862 to 1918? Illustrate by reference to several states.
7. Justify each of the limitations upon school attendance.
8. Are the exemptions for school attendance equally justifiable? Illustrate.
9. To what extent should the federal government attempt to equalize facilities provided for school attendance? Examine procedures by means of which this has already been done.
10. What factors other than education have assisted in making more American people literate? Account for variations in literacy in the several states and sections of the country.

SELECTED REFERENCES

1. Bohlinger, Joseph H., "Other Twelve Per Cent," *Journal of Education,* September, 1946, pp. 203–204.
2. Cook, W. A., "A Brief Survey of the Development of Compulsory Education in the United States," *Elementary School Teacher,* March, 1912, pp. 331–335.
3. Cook, W. A., *Federal and State School Administration.* New York: Thomas Y. Crowell Company, 1927, chap. xii.
4. Cubberley, Ellwood P., *The History of Education.* Boston: Houghton Mifflin Company, 1920, chaps. xv, xxv, xxvi, also pp. 519–527.
5. Deffenbaugh, Walter S., and Keesecker, Ward W. (eds.), "Compulsory School Attendance Laws and Their Administration," *Bulletin No. 4,* United States Office of Education. Washington: Government Printing Office, 1935.
6. Edwards, Newton, *The Courts and the Public Schools.* Chicago: University of Chicago Press, 1933, chaps. i, xvii.
7. Ensign, Forest Chester, *Compulsory School Attendance and Child Labor.* Iowa City, Iowa: The Athens Press, 1921.
8. Heck, Arch O., *Administration of Pupil Personnel.* Boston: Ginn and Company, 1929, chaps. ii, iii.
9. Liebler, C. C., "Court Decisions Affecting the Enforcement of Com-

pulsory Education," *American School Board Journal*, October, 1928, pp. 49 f.

10. Martin, George H., *The Evolution of the Massachusetts Public School System*. New York: D. Appleton-Century Company, 1923.

11. "School Attendance Laws," *School Life*, October, 1935, p. 47.

12. "School Census, Compulsory Education, Child Labor, State Laws and Regulations," *Bulletin No. 1*, Federal Security Agency. Washington: United States Office of Education, 1945.

13. Wagner, J. E., "Fifty Years of Compulsory Education in Pennsylvania," *Pennsylvania School Journal*, November, 1945, pp. 71–73.

14. Wanger, Mina, "Attendance 88 Per Cent," *Journal of Education*, April, 1946, pp. 122–123.

CHAPTER V

The Administration of School Attendance

FROM an examination of the historical background and legal basis of school attendance, we now turn our attention to its administration. This becomes one of the first and most important administrative functions of a school system. If it is properly conceived and adequately carried out, it should result not only in regularity of school attendance on the part of every child but in a certain happiness therein. Adjustive services in the school should be so developed as to meet problems of irregularity, both without as well as within the control of the pupil.

Although education is essentially a state function, the very nature of school attendance make it primarily a local administrative problem; the school census locates the school child as defined by the law. This chapter discusses the attendance problem itself, the attendance officer and his duties, the attendance department and its functions, changing concepts of the attendance service, school transportation, and related factors.

THE PROBLEM OF SCHOOL ATTENDANCE

Nature. The problem of school attendance is to locate every child of school age and keep him in school regularly within the limits and under the conditions specified by law. In Tables 2 and 3, distribution of these children by public and private schools has been indicated. Table 6 summarizes these enrollments, which represent approximately 20 per cent of the total population. This means that on each morning of the school year, one person out of five in the

United States leaves his home, unless ill or otherwise not attending legally, for some public or private educational institution, to engage in a learning activity.

During a four-year period (1940–1944) the percentage of the entire population enrolled in the public schools decreased from 19.3 to 16.9 per cent. During the same period the percentage of the total number of children five to seventeen years old inclusive enrolled in public

TABLE 6.   TRENDS IN ENROLLMENTS OF PUBLICLY AND PRIVATELY CONTROLLED SCHOOLS IN THE UNITED STATES (1930–1944)

Date	Public	Private	Total
1930	26,230,667	3,432,658	29,663,325
1932	26,875,534	3,506,889	30,382,423
1934	27,147,729	3,364,800	30,512,529
1936	27,154,371	3,360,355	30,514,726
1938	26,826,181	3,387,886	30,214,067
1940	26,393,586	3,456,617	29,850,203
1942	25,448,450	3,631,924	29,080,374
1944	23,838,169	3,285,815	27,123,984

schools fell from 85.3 to 80.4 per cent. These were war years, and our figures indicate certain war effects on the schools. With a returning normal condition and eventual increased birth rates, ratios may approximate those of 1940.

Reeves[1] has pointed out that the trend of the school population in any given city has been difficult to predict because of migrations of people from cities or regions having no war industries to those having war industries. Many of these persons will never return to their former homes. One of the principal problems is the housing of the children in such areas; another is the declining population and increased costs in other areas. Decreased high-school enrollments are expected to continue through 1952, depending somewhat upon industrial conditions.

Ratios.   The ratio of children of school age to the total population varies in the states and is reflected in the total enrollments. For instance, in one year 15 per cent of the total population of New Hampshire were enrolled in the public elementary and secondary schools

[1] Charles E. Reeves, "Outlook for School Population of the Future," *American School Board Journal*, February, 1943, pp. 40–41.

of that state, while in the same year in Mississippi 30 per cent were enrolled. In thirty states, the ratio of enrollment to the total population was 20 per cent or more, and in five states, it was 25 per cent or more. These ratios are directly affected by the birth rate and other factors. These extremes in ratios of children attending school to the total population are of importance in understanding the problems faced by other states and those within each state.

In considering ratios it should be recalled that three out of four children attend elementary schools. With a heightened birth rate the number of little children will increase. Slightly more girls than boys are now enrolled, especially in the secondary schools, corresponding to the slightly higher proportion of females in the total population. Recently, these sex ratios among older age groups have been accentuated owing to war and economic conditions.

Percentage of Attendance. If every child attended school regularly, there would be no problem of attendance or need for compulsory attendance laws and their enforcement. The percentage of the pupils enrolled in the public elementary and secondary schools in the United States who attend school each day is approximately 85. This means that, out of 20 pupils, 3 are absent from school every day. By states, the percentages range from 94.4, that is, 19 present out of 20, to 76.4 (15 present out of 20), with 38 states attaining or bettering the 85-per-cent record and 5 holding a higher than 90-per-cent record (1942). Within the same state there are many variations due to climatic and economic conditions and parental attitudes. Many states stimulate better attendance through state appropriations based on attendance and rewards of various kinds.

Local Administration of School Attendance

Need for Local Administration. The administration of the school attendance of children, although essentially a state function, must depend for its efficiency, for the most part, upon local management. We have noted varying attitudes toward compulsory education in the several states as well as in different communities and geographical areas of those states. Difficulties in the way of securing regular school attendance locally have resulted from many obstructions and objections, the latter charging infringement of parental rights over the child, interference with business by the elimination of child labor, and un-Americanism on the part of the school in arrogating a new power to government, and citing the needs of parents in agriculture and the home.

Nevertheless, an efficient public school system in any community is predicated on the regular attendance of its children. The school district as the subdivision of the state becomes at once the locus of the attendance problem. Here state laws must be enforced in the interest of every child.

Locating the Responsibility. Laws requiring attendance of children at school are not self-enforceable; nor can the state depend upon haphazard methods of enforcement through parental willingness, neighbors' complaints, or the local police. Responsibility must be definitely placed somewhere to locate the child and his parents and to make it possible for him to attend school. Authority must be vested in regularly constituted attendance officers. There must be certain recognized procedures to be followed in obstinate cases, such as the collection of information, investigation of the case, issuance of the complaint, and bringing legal action where necessary. In other words, it is necessary to establish the competence to carry out the provisions as well as the spirit of the compulsory attendance law in the interests of a better-educated citizenry.

The current trend is to make more specific the conditions under which children may attend non-public schools, or be provided with private tutorage, to meet the requirements for compulsory education. State laws and practices are being strengthened relative to accrediting non-public schools. Qualifications of teachers for these schools are being written in terms of the qualification and certification practices required for public school teachers. Other trends extend to similar courses of study, educational experiences and reports, and inspection requirements.[2]

The School Census

Need. An accurate census record of every child of school age is the first step in providing for the attendance of eligible children. Achievement of the democratic principle of universal education is predicated upon the known whereabouts of every child and assurance that he is in attendance on the educational means provided.

---

[2] "School Census, Compulsory Education, Child Labor, State Laws and Regulations," *Bulletin No. 1,* Federal Security Agency, Washington, United States Office of Education, 1945, p. 24.

Universal acceptance of this principle is shown in that all but three states now provide for a school census.

Purposes. While it would seem that the school census is primarily to assist in the enforcement of the compulsory school laws, originally its purpose was to afford the basis for the distribution of state school funds. It is still so used in some states where these funds are allotted on the basis of the number of children of school age. More recently, other important purposes of the school census have been developed. These are (1) to ascertain the nature and scope of educational service that a school district must provide; (2) to provide a basis for the developing of a school building program; and (3) to provide the basis for the enforcement of compulsory school attendance.[3]

Within the school district, the census has many more purposes. These are to (1) ascertain essential facts as to beginning children; (2) locate those children who move into, out of, or about the district; (3) provide for new groups of children specified by law; (4) check enrollments and absences in public as well as private and parochial schools; (5) locate parental responsibility; (6) discover the employment of the child; (7) discover home conditions and improve home-school relationships; (8) provide a means for disseminating information about the school; (9) discover the causes of non-attendance; and (10) check truancy.

Procedures. A state-controlled school census is provided for in forty-two states, being required by law in forty. Of the remainder, three states have permissive legislation and three others do not mention it. It is usually taken annually, but sometimes biennally, at four- or five-year periods, or continuously.

The age spans most popular are 6–21 years (11 states), 6–18 (10 states), and 5–21 (5 states). There are 14 different age ranges, being combinations of from birth through 21 years. Likewise, there is a great variation of the census ages with the compulsory attendance ages.

The school census is prescribed in most states for some period (usually about a month) between the first of April and the end of September, with many variations of dates in the remaining states.

Usually, the local school board or some individual person or agency

---

[3] "Compulsory School Attendance Laws and Their Administration," *Bulletin No. 4,* United States Office of Education, Washington, Government Printing Office, 1935, p. 22.

is designated to take the census, with power to employ enumerators. In some states teachers are asked to take the census as a part of their regular work; more often, other employees, clerks, or occasionally police officers in large cities are the census takers. The language of the state laws and the regulations as to who shall be accounted for and what information shall be sought vary widely. A good beginning has been made with regard to the census of handicapped children. Usually definite accounting forms are prescribed along with the manner of the report.[4]

Local districts often provide additional census data. There is a tendency in some sections to register children on the school record immediately after birth or as soon thereafter as possible, or in connection with pre-school education or health clinics.

Variations as to census ages naturally suggest variations in educational opportunity among the several states. They also suggest the advisability of making the census ages identical with the compulsory attendance ages. Many districts are lax in administering the law; others, if stimulated by some state policy pertaining to support, make every effort to account continuously for every child. Halfhearted administration of the school census with meager census data should be replaced by an adequate plan providing for the known whereabouts of every child of school age together with all the data essential to his school progress.

Preferred Census Data. A continuous school census should be based upon an initial, careful house-to-house canvass. The names of all children up to the age of twenty-one years should be recorded on suitable cards approximately 4″ × 6″ or 5″ × 8″ in size. The cards should make available the following information: full names of all children living in the school district, complete street or other address with identifying locations (wards, blocks, or communities), nationality of child, names of both parents or guardians or others responsible for them, date of birth, school attended (public, private, or parochial) with name and location of school, employment data if any, reasons for non-attendance if any, and record of any physical or mental handicaps. Other data might include home conditions (possibly involving racial, language, or economic problems), parents'

---

[4] "School Census, Compulsory Education, Child Labor, State Laws and Regulations," *Bulletin No. 1*, Federal Security Agency, Washington, United States Office of Education, 1945, pp. 6 ff.

occupation or nationality, health and vaccination record, present grade in school. Specific information should be given in the case of children who are wards of the court or institutionalized, or concerning whom there may be other extenuating circumstances.

Although numerous cards are available which might easily serve as patterns for a school census card, it is important to point out that the card should be constructed and adapted to the specific needs of the school district. A commercially constructed card, while sometimes convenient, never quite fits.

A Continuous School Census. Using the suggestions indicated in the preceding paragraphs, the basis is laid for a continuous census of every child, that is, one that is kept up to date throughout the entire year, not necessarily periodically. A continuous system has several characteristics. First, a master census card is filed for each child of school age as he is located within the district, and follows him throughout his school career. Then, various methods are used to locate the child—house-to-house canvass, teachers' enrollments, birth records, private school records, and records of movings in and out of the district. It must be kept up to date by (1) removal of cards of pupils who leave the district or are beyond the census age; (2) inserting cards of transfer pupils; (3) inserting cards of new pupils; (4) making corrections in such data as age, grade, address, etc.

The cards of all children who come within the census ages should be placed in the *live file;* those removed for any reason, in a *dead file* arranged alphabetically. Further, distribution of the live file may be made by schools, compulsory or non-compulsory ages, enrollment in non-public schools, or in other ways indicated by the administration of the attendance service. Many schools are now using the *visible index* system, which enables them to ascertain quickly any child's status. It is important to point out that census data must be accurate in order to be useful. A desirable school census is adequately integrated with every other phase of attendance administration.

Enumerators of the Census. In large cities, the department responsible for the enforcement of the attendance laws and regulations should likewise be responsible for the school census. Usually the staff is well qualified for the work. In smaller districts attendance officers who look upon their position as one of locating and preventing truancy are scarcely qualified for these important home-school contacts. The by-products of census taking, as well as attendance enforcement, are highly important in school administration, as Mosher pointed out when he said, "Taking the census is no job for anyone who is physically unfit, who is illiterate, or who lacks tact or judgment."[5]

A highly recommended plan for smaller communities is to have the school census taken by the regular teachers, previously trained for the task and under constant and competent supervision. Under this plan the community is divided into blocks or districts, and the census is taken by all teachers working simultaneously on a certain afternoon or on a Saturday. By this means teachers are brought into direct contact with homes. Moreover, more effective use of the census can be made by the school in developing its program. Where the project is directly organized and supervised by the superintendent and principals, the latter can be made aware of the community's educational problems and may thereby secure the greater cooperation of the teachers. Additional compensation for this service may be provided at the discretion of the board of education. Perhaps there will be a better attitude toward this important service if it is provided, especially if additional demands are made on the teacher's time.

In larger communities the school census should be the responsibility of professionally educated personnel, directly related to the attendance department and having direct contacts with individual schools and teachers as well as with others entitled to this information. The importance of census takers as public school relations intermediaries should be readily apparent.

School Attendance and Its Enforcement

After the child has been located through the census, the second step in the administration of school attendance is to get and keep him in school during the period prescribed by law or local regulation. This function, as commonly administered, varies widely.

The Attendance Department. In larger cities, administration is integrated within the structure of the school organization. Such integration becomes more and more necessary as the scope and function of the school enlarge and as its social service aspects are related to the

[5] Charles L. Mosher, *Bulletin No. 928,* Albany, New York, University of the State of New York, 1929, p. 9.

attendance administration. Schultz[6] has isolated four types of organization for the management of the attendance service.

Type I. Attendance service is a major division of the school system embracing all of its special pupil adjustment services in one department and in charge of an assistant superintendent (Jersey City cited as an example).

Type II. Similar to Type I but in charge of a director of the department (Gary, Indiana).

Type III. The director of attendance is responsible, not to the assistant superintendent, but directly to the city superintendent (Louisville, Kentucky). Superiority is claimed for this type in its more direct contacts through the department from superintendents, principals, and teachers. The absentee and problem child are dealt with more expeditiously.

Type IV. The attendance department is one of a number of separate special service departments or divisions of the school organization, each under a different director. The virtue of this type is in the equality of the services of the departments and their proper coordination, as medical science with psychological science.

Within these departments, certain special services have been isolated. They may be classified, according to Schultz,[7] into three forms of organization as follows: (1) the integrated attendance department, with all special pupil-adjustment services merged in one department; (2) the attendance department with a limited range of special pupil-adjustment services, which requires close coordination with other departments; and (3) the attendance department which is a coordinating agency rather than an integrated department. Types of special services to be included for the treatment of specific needs of pupils are: medical, dental, psychological, and psychiatric; those involving the visiting teacher, special class assignment, and behavior problems; those providing for parental schools, care of delinquents, home instruction, and hospital instruction.

Further discussion of these special services will be given in a later section. Whatever the nature of the attendance department or the extent of the service given, care must be taken that the work does not become merely routine in character. After all, the education and

---

[6] Joseph LeMart Schultz, *An Analysis of Present Practices in City Attendance Work*, Doctor's Dissertation, University of Pennsylvania, 1938.

[7] *Ibid.*

adjustment of the child should be an individual concern. He may become lost in a maze of routine which will identify him in relation to the system itself, but fail in the end results achieved. Even with the best of systems, some children are lost while the system is saved, as illustrated by the seventeen-year-old-boy whose parents thought him about to graduate from a large city high school, but upon investigation it was discovered that he had never even attended the high school. This city had an efficient attendance department, yet that one boy was lost for four years. Perhaps in that same city there were others.

The Attendance Officer. At the state level, departments in eight states have some specified responsibility regarding the appointment of attendance officers.[8] Such oversight usually pertains to appointment of local officers in case of neglect or the setting of desirable standards for attendance workers; in states where the county is the administrative unit for school affairs, provision is made for appointment by the county boards. In several states the county superintendent is required either to appoint or to serve personally as attendance officer.

Where the function of school attendance enforcement becomes a local matter, the attendance officer may be appointed in either of two ways. His appointment is (1) required in some twenty states in accordance with varying regulations as to specific district, and (2) permissive in as many states, also in accordance with similarly varying regulations.[9]

Only ten states have set up any educational qualifications for the office represented by some form of certification, usually state controlled. These qualifications include, for the most part, preparation in the teaching and social service fields and experience in teaching, or its equivalent. Pennsylvania's provision for certification of the home and school visitor (optional) and California's advanced requirements indicate forward steps in securing a trained type of attendance officer.

Some cities have set up certain educational standards for attendance officers. These include (1) civil service examinations; (2) high-

---

[8] Connecticut, Delaware, Maryland, New Hampshire, New Jersey, Oklahoma, Pennsylvania, and West Virginia.

[9] See *Bulletin No. 1,* 1945, p. 11.

school diploma; (3) high-school diploma and two years' additional training; (4) baccalaureate degree; (5) additional social service training; and (6) optional state certificate for attendance officers based on specific course requirements.

Changing Concepts of the Attendance Service. Formerly, the attendance service rested almost entirely upon the idea of compulsion, thus emphasizing the police power of the attendance officer. There was little or no suggestion as to the social service these officials might render. The police power, while still necessary, is now less emphasized, more importance being attached to corrective and curative measures.

The type of service rendered can be no greater than the type and character of the attendance officer himself. Liebler[10] found these men selected from various occupations; they were police officers, real-estate dealers, meatcutters, glass blowers, painters, and electricians. Only 14 per cent could be classified as professionally trained; 36 per cent were fifty-one years of age or older. The White House Conference Report points out this condition rather forcibly.

Attendance service has suffered as the place to which political appointments are made. It is also utilized to care for superannuated personnel from other fields as well as other school departments. In one city it was explained that one of the attendance officers had been a teacher for a number of years, but finding teaching too strenuous she had been asked to be transferred to a less arduous assignment. In the places visited (17, including 7 large cities), with one exception the majority of attendance officers were over 45 years of age. In most cases, moreover, those in their fifties and sixties had not had an extended period of attendance service but had entered the field late in life.

With possibly four exceptions, there are attendance officers in the places visited who have not completed an elementary education. From material on school attendance secured from the county study it was found that in some counties all the attendance work is done by the marshal, members of the school board, the sheriff, the constable, or the policeman on his regular beat. By and large a definite educational standard is not required of those selected to do attendance work.[11]

---

[10] Charles C. Liebler, "Qualifications and Compensation of Persons Charged with the Enforcement of Compulsory Education," *Elementary School Journal,* May, 1927, p. 705.

[11] "The School Health Program," *White House Conference on Child Health and Protection,* New York, New Century Company, 1932.

Higher state standards for attendance officers indicate newer concepts of the office in terms of a better selected and prepared personnel. The office is now conceived as that of the social worker. Helping the child, his home, his environment, has taken the place of the compulsory (bring the body) concept. The attendance service is now concerned with keeping the child in regular attendance, ascertaining the causes of absence, studying the home and home conditions affecting attendance, taking the school census, and developing everywhere a friendly, helpful attitude toward the child and his problem.

In-Service Improvement. The in-service improvement of thousands of attendance officials has necessitated an intensive in-service program. In many states, notably New York, Indiana, and Maryland, conferences have been held and talks given on child welfare problems. States are preparing pamphlets and other helpful material. The National League to Promote School Attendance, an organization for education, pupil adjustment attendance, and social welfare service organized in 1911, has been doing outstanding work in developing the social service concepts of school attendance work. A review of its annual *Proceedings* reveals the remarkable progress which has been made in its consideration of attendance as an educational and social problem. Some of the problems discussed in relation to attendance are poverty and pauperism, low intelligence and indifference of parents, the broken home, over-ageness, undisciplined children, role of social agencies, role of psychology and sociology, and standards of efficiency of attendance officers.

Number of Attendance Officers. The White House Conference Report suggests that attendance officers for every 1500 or 2000 children enrolled in public, private, or parochial schools should be provided. With this number it would be possible to do more intensive work in every case in which such work is needed. This seems a fair statement to accept. However, in considering any ratios, one must bear in mind at the same time the preparation of the officer, the area to be covered, the attitude of the parents, and the many difficulties involved.

THE VISITING TEACHER MOVEMENT

The visiting teacher movement seems to be a definite outcome of a happy coalition of two other great movements: (1) the child-centered school movement based on the Dewey philosophy which began to make its appearance at the turn of the century and (2) the social work movement which developed about the same time. Problems of attendance, truancy, juvenile delinquency, tardiness, and the many emerging social conditions within the home and community affecting the school and the child seemed to demand a newer type of attendance contact, a special type of training to understand and deal adequately with these problems.

Beginnings. The beginnings of the visiting teacher movement can be traced to the years 1906–1907 when the cities of New York, Boston, and Hartford initiated programs of better understanding between the school and the home. As with vocational guidance, the drive to initiate the movement was not located in the schools, but in private agencies. The New York Settlement Houses assigned two visitors to three schools in 1906. Similar associations in Boston sponsored the plan in 1907. School boards, sensing the worth-whileness of the movement, began to adopt the idea as one of the mandatory provisions of the school administrative setup.[12]

Oppenheimer[13] has pointed out three stages in the development of the visiting teacher movement: (1) 1906–1914, the period of beginning; (2) 1914–1921, the period of adoption by boards of education; and (3) 1921 to the present time, the period of national expansion. Nudd[14] attributes its growth to three factors: (1) newer concepts concerning the education of the child; (2) increasing enrollment, brought about by compulsory education and child labor laws; and (3) recognition of vast differences in abilities and interests among children.

Recent Development. The movement spread.[15] Rochester in 1920 created a department of visiting teachers. In November, 1921, the Commonwealth Fund undertook a program to prevent delinquency

---

[12] The reader is referred to the following for early accounts of the visiting teacher movement: Howard Nudd, *The Purpose and Scope of Visiting Teacher Work,* New York, Division of Publications, The Commonwealth Fund, 1928; Jane F. Culbert, *The Visiting Teacher at Work,* New York, Division of Publications, The Commonwealth Fund, 1929; Elizabeth Lingenfelter, "The Visiting Teacher," *Journal of Education,* July 21, 1930, p. 56; Julius John Oppenheimer, *The Visiting Teacher Movement,* New York, Joint Committee on Methods of Preventing Delinquency, 1925.

[13] Oppenheimer, *op. cit.,* pp. 1–18.

[14] Nudd, *op. cit.*

[15] Frank M. Miller, *Development, Present Status, and Administrative Relationship of the Visiting Teacher in the United States,* Doctor's Dissertation, University of Pittsburgh, 1942.

and proposed the development of the work and training of visiting teachers in New York City. Through the Public Education Association of New York, it organized a National Committee of Visiting Teachers, whose purpose it was to establish demonstrations in thirty communities throughout the United States, communities which presented a wide variety of geographical, social, and educational situations. These demonstrations were continued by the Commonwealth Fund until June, 1927, when they were turned over to local boards of education. It was reported by the Commonwealth Fund that at the close of the demonstration period, twenty-five of the thirty projects were continued by the local boards. Returns from a recent survey reveal that out of twenty of the above communities reporting, only five now have the visiting teacher service. The chief reason advanced for its discontinuance was lack of funds. Despite the fact that so many communities have been forced to give up this service, the years from 1927 to 1939 saw its inauguration in twenty-five new communities; in thirteen it was established in the period from 1934 to 1939. Today the visiting teacher service is scattered over virtually the entire United States,[16] the southern states having the smallest representation. The size of the school district employing the service ranges from approximately 2500 population to our largest cities. In over 90 per cent of the communities using it the service was inaugurated and is financially supported by the local school board.

Administration. The administration of the visiting teacher service varies with the community. In the smaller districts the visiting teacher is directly responsible to the superintendent of schools. In the larger cities of 100,000 or over, the visiting teacher service is usually located in the attendance department, psychological clinic, or guidance department, or is under the direction of a coordinator of all the child welfare departments. The latter type of organization gives every indication of being particularly effective. The coordinator usually acts as a clearinghouse for information gathered by the various departments on all pupil cases. In all communities the superintendent of schools outlines the policies and gives general initiative to the visiting teacher work. The relationship between the visiting teacher and the school staff is unique. The success of her efforts depends upon the degree of cooperation given by principals, teachers,

---

[16] *Ibid.*

and the other members of the school staff. Her position is that of a specialist assisting in the prevention and solution of pupil maladjustments. As a social case worker, she supplements the school personnel and offers another point of view on the problems of the child. As an intermediary between home and school she becomes a coordinator of the efforts of all in the interest of the individual child. Yet in the performance of these duties she has no authority over any of the staff with which she works. Superintendents having the visiting teacher service declare themselves in favor of some training in social case work *for the classroom teacher* in order to establish a more effective coordination of effort between the two.

Education. The educational training of the visiting teacher ranges from graduation from normal school to a master's degree, the median being a bachelor's degree. Training in social work ranges from occasional, part-time, or summer school courses to completion of a two-year graduate course, the majority of visiting teachers having a one-year graduate course in a school of social work. Visiting teachers are professionally organized in the American Association of Visiting Teachers. This organization began in 1919 and at the present time is active in dispensing information to develop standards for the training of visiting teachers, improving working conditions, and aiding local boards of education in establishing the service.

Qualifications. A visiting teacher should, first of all, have completed the education of a teacher and have had some experience in that capacity. Preferably a college-trained person, she should have had courses in sociology, social service, and related fields. Personal qualifications are of prime importance and should include good health, sincerity, patience, tact in dealing with people, maturity and judgment, trustworthiness, and leadership in community life. She should possess right attitudes toward children and home life, believing in the school and its work; she should be unprejudiced, and have respect for the judgment of others, a cooperative nature, and a willingness to accept irregular hours of work.

Functions. The primary function of the visiting teacher is to bring about a healthier, happier relationship among the child, his home, and his school. Her work is concerned with the adjustment of the child and his problems, information about and interpretation of the school to the home, and, wherever possible, an adjustment in the home as well as in the child. To accomplish these purposes, contacts must often be made with, and assistance secured from, the courts, social service agencies, relatives, and other groups. Oppenheimer lists a total of thirty-two different functions, which include a study of the child and his environment; study of the home and of the parents, information and adjustment of each to the other aiding the child in his health, physical, and social needs; bringing information secured to the school; helping the family secure assistance through employment, hospital service, and with food and clothing; securing cooperation of necessary social agencies and the courts or the churches; and lending a hand in any manner which will secure the adjustment needed. The worth of this service to the school is invaluable. It is not difficult to perceive its great superiority over the usual administration of attendance.

State Administration of School Attendance

State Functions. The scope of state administration of school attendance may be noted from the following list of functions performed in many of the states. It should be pointed out that efficient state administration requires close cooperation with local school districts.

1. Distribution of attendance registers and other forms for attendance reporting and recording.
2. Requirement of attendance and other reports from the school district.
3. Stimulation of perfect attendance records through various forms of recognition.
4. Direct supervision of local administrative attendance procedures.
5. Preparation of attendance data for appropriation or other financial purposes.
6. Administration or supervision of the school census and other forms of enumeration.
7. Field service through state supervisors or other representatives.
8. Preparation of age-grade tables.
9. Preparation and dissemination of bulletins, circulars, reports, and other information on school attendance, child labor, and child accounting statistics.
10. Provision for qualified local professional attendance officers, as home and school visitors, including an educational program leading to improved qualifications for local attendance workers, certification, and reimbursement on salaries.

11. Stimulation of the use of approved social service techniques.
12. Direct or indirect state oversight of child labor regulations.
13. General supervision of employment certificates and farm and domestic permits.
14. Institution of court action under certain conditions.
15. Administration of medical inspection and health regulations.
16. Collaboration with other divisions of the state and local administrative divisions in related services, i.e., tuition, transportation, health, special education, and relief.

Procedures. A number of prescribed forms are needed in the administration of the compulsory attendance laws. These include official notices of violations, for recording essential information and for reporting action on cases and services rendered. A considerable number of the states require all or most of the forms to be used. This service develops uniformity of practice within the state and undoubtedly increases the effectiveness of local administration. For example, a uniform state attendance register enables a state department to secure comparable data for child accounting. State departments of education need reports not only on the census, enrollments, and average daily attendance but also on the work of enforcement. Even though some departments have little or no specific authorization for control over attendance, they can and do exercise a form of control through information which reveals conditions and services and may build up public opinion supporting effective enforcement.

Distribution of School Funds and Attendance. Rewards for better attendance by increase in state school funds to local communities have been an added incentive to improve the administration of school attendance. Approximately half of the states use a formula in apportioning funds to each community which takes into consideration the pupil basis, such as the school census, average daily attendance, or membership in each district. Where attendance is the basis, a day's absence of any pupil results in an appreciable financial loss. Local districts may increase state appropriations through careful administration of attendance and the school census. Schultz has shown how in Los Angeles, by increasing the average daily attendance 1 per cent, the district gained $150,000 per year from state funds.[17]

Using average daily membership as a measure, such states as New York and Pennsylvania measure the school load of the district (num-

[17] Schultz, *op. cit.,* p. 31.

ber of pupils per teacher) and appropriate funds to school districts accordingly. This technique serves as an incentive to employ better-qualified attendance officers, which in turn reflects improved pupil personnel administration in general.

Qualifications. Qualifications for state supervisory officials vary greatly. Usually a master's degree is required and preparation and experience in education and social work are specified. Positions are held by men with salary ranges for directors from $4500 to $5400, and for other employees from $1400 to $3500 (salary ranges show increases since these data were prepared). Probably the most encouraging feature of state supervision of school attendance is its emerging cooperative relationship with other child welfare agencies and functions of government, both state and local.

Compulsion vs. *Social Service Concepts.* Education should develop its child accounting procedures the way business operates in the field of personnel, in order to provide data for a proper review of its efficiency and progress. It would seem to be the duty of the state to lead in the development of these procedures so that adequate educational facilities may be provided for the needs, interests, and capacities of individual boys and girls. Attendance service formerly rested almost entirely upon the idea of compulsion, with the emphasis on the police power of the attendance officers and the state. More and more, the states are recognizing another important purpose in the administration of attendance, that of social service. The latter principle is slowly permeating and mellowing older concepts based entirely on compulsion, which, however, must always remain for the recalcitrant.

THE TRANSPORTED PUPIL

Directly related to the administration of school attendance is the administration of school transportation. Because of the growth of consolidation, especially in non-urban areas, and the enlargement of school facilities to meet the varied needs of more and more children, transportation must be provided for many of these children. The problem has thus become not only an attendance one but also one involving greater educational opportunity. This section will deal with the scope of transportation. A later section will discuss the enlarged opportunities growing out of it.

Scope. Large numbers of children now ride where formerly every child walked, through sunshine, rain, and snow, to the district school.

Latest available figures estimate that more than 4,500,000 pupils are being transported in some 92,500 school busses and similar vehicles, and thousands by other means, at an estimated cost of nearly $100,-000,000. Parents take or send their children to school in the family automobile or the business truck; in streetcars, taxis, and steamboats; on bicycles, motorcycles, horseback; and in horse-drawn vehicles of every description. Farley[18] reports such unusual means as snow-mobiles, dog sleds, a cable basket in Idaho, a trailer schoolhouse in Montana, motorboat transportation in Oregon and Florida. Perhaps there are cases of transportation by air not yet made a matter of record. No one knows exactly how many children ride to school each day.

The development of school transportation is just about a hundred years old, being first started in Massachusetts about 1840. All states now transport pupils in some manner. In North Carolina, for example, nearly 40 per cent of the pupils are transported. In most states transportation is mandatory under certain conditions. Legal objection that this is class legislation has been met by court decision favorable to transportation. Most transported children live in rural or not densely populated areas. Not over 10 per cent of urban children are transported at public expense to school, although many do, of course, ride by means furnished largely by their parents. On an average about 20 per cent of all pupils are transported at public expense.

Transportation costs have become a major current expense item in many states—more than 10 per cent in such states as Louisiana (10.3), Mississippi (16.7), Montana (10.8), New Mexico (12.2), and Wyoming (11.6), with per-pupil costs ranging from $7.00 to almost $51.00 (Montana). It is logical to expect, too, that the transportation of school children will continue to increase in volume as well as cost, as consolidation and large administrative units develop.

Transportation in Urban Areas. As indicated above, transportation of school children in urban areas is limited. About 70 per cent of cities of 25,000 population or more provide some facilities for it.[19] Its principal purpose is to provide for exceptional children, although about half of the cities provide for all groups.

---

[18] Belmont Farley, *Willingly to School,* Washington, National Education Association, 1938.

[19] M. C. S. Noble, Jr., *Pupil Transportation in the United States,* Scranton, International Textbook Company, 1940. This is a comprehensive treatise on school transportation.

Factors leading to transportation of normal children in cities are state laws, distance, poverty, racial segregation, safety, and consolidation. Distance is the most important factor. Special means must be provided for exceptional children owing to the nature of their needs; more children with physical defects than with mental deficiency are transported. In this group crippled children lead, followed by mentally deficient, partially blind, and hard-of-hearing groups. Transportation facilities are necessary for the special classes for exceptional children, including cardiac and epileptic cases, fresh-air groups, disciplinary groups, and the undernourished. Transportation of gifted children is negligible. Bus transportation ranks first, followed by streetcars, taxicabs, and subsidy to parents for such plans as they wish to use.

The transportation of children is then definitely a problem in pupil personnel administration. Indeed it has far-reaching implications which have to do with the school schedule, school program, school control, school activities, and the school day in general. Through it educational opportunities are opened up to more and more children, which in turn makes further demands upon the administration of pupil personnel.

Consolidation of schools has undoubtedly been a major factor in the development of transportation. One of the principal issues is whether public school funds shall be used to transport children of school age to non-public schools. Other issues pertain to transportation of school children for extra-curricular activities, such as athletics, evening affairs, or trips to museums. Decisions on these and similar issues should be made in the light of the scope of the future educational program and its support.

QUESTIONS AND PROBLEMS

1. Consult the most recent U. S. Office of Education school enrollment statistics, in order to show variations in school enrollments in the several states.
2. Evaluate the purposes of the school census indicated in the text. Can you add others?
3. Make a list of the facts which should be collected about each child at the time of taking the census. Compare with those in the text.
4. Account for the great variation in census ages in the several states.
5. Outline a desirable school census procedure.
6. Compare in parallel columns state and local responsibility for the

administration of school attendance, using selected states as examples.

7. Evaluate the functions of a desirable state attendance service as indicated in the text. Are there others?

8. Comment on the practice of certain states in distributing state school funds on a census basis; on A.D.A.; on other bases. Defend the best plan.

9. Set up desirable qualifications for a school attendance officer; for a school attendance department.

10. Work out a plan for the administration of school attendance in a small school district in which the desirable aspects of the services in larger cities are made available.

11. Compare two plans for the administration of school attendance based on the compulsion as compared with the social service concept.

12. Make a list of the problems associated with school transportation in (*a*) a county, (*b*) a city, (*c*) a state.

SELECTED REFERENCES

1. Bender, J. F., *The Functions of Courts in Enforcing School Attendance Laws*. New York: Bureau of Publications, Teachers College, Columbia University, 1927.

2. Book, Herbert E., *A Study of Compulsory Education in Pennsylvania Through the Interaction of the Legislature and Judiciary,* Doctor's Dissertation, University of Pittsburgh, 1943.

3. Deffenbaugh, Walter S., and Keesecker, Ward W., "Compulsory School Attendance Laws and Their Administration" *Bulletin No. 4.* United States Office of Education, Washington: Government Printing Office, 1935.

4. Edwards, Newton, *The Courts and the Public Schools*. Chicago: University of Chicago Press, 1933.

5. Ensign, F. C., *Compulsory School Attendance and Child Labor*. Iowa City, Iowa: The Athens Press, 1921.

6. Ginrich, Leah, "Special Education—Progress in the Relation Between the School and Society Viewpoint of the Attendance Officer," *Twenty-Second Annual Schoolmen's Week Proceedings*. Philadelphia: University of Pennsylvania, 1935.

7. Heck, Arch O., *Administration of Pupil Personnel*. Boston: Ginn and Company, 1929.

8. Heck, Arch O., "How May State Departments of Public Instruction Plan Pupil Personnel Services to Secure for All Children the Educational Opportunities Contemplated by School Attendance Laws,"

Twenty-Second Annual Schoolmen's Week Proceedings. Philadelphia: University of Pennsylvania, 1935.

9. Heck, Arch O., and others, "School Attendance," *Review of Educational Research,* April, 1936, pp. 157–163.

10. Larson, Emil L., "Migration and Its Effect on School," *Elementary
School Journal,* December, 1940, pp. 283–295.

11. Lawing, John L., *Standards for State and Local Compulsory School
Attendance Service.* Doctor's Dissertation, Teachers' College,
Columbia University, 1934.

12. Peterson, R., "Administration of Attendance," *Bulletin of the National Association of Secondary School Principals,* April, 1945, pp.
105–109.

13. "Progress in Rural Education," *Research Bulletin,* National Education Association, September, 1940.

14. "School Census, Compulsory Education, Child Labor, State Laws
and Regulations," *Bulletin No. 1,* Federal Security Agency. Washington: United States Office of Education, 1945.

15. Schultz, Joseph LeMart, *An Analysis of Present Practices in City
Attendance Work.* Doctor's Dissertation, University of Pennsylvania, 1938.

16. "The State and Sectarian Education," *Research Bulletin,* National
Education Association, February, 1946.

17. Wright, Marion Thompson, "Cooperation with the Attendance Officers," *Educational Administration and Supervision,* January, 1944,
pp. 32–39.

NOTE: The student should examine the several pamphlets of the Biennial Survey of Education (United States Office of Education)
and the Children's Bureau (United States Department of Labor)
in regard to school attendance.

CHAPTER VI

Non-School Attendance and Its Improvement

THE regularity of each child's attendance is a problem of major concern in educational administration. Absence for any length of time, even a school period, disrupts the continuity of the educational process. To keep the child in regular attendance is the primary duty of all associated with his educational interests and control. This statement is true even with regard to those school systems which have developed plans of individualized instruction. Regularity of attendance is desirable in developing proper habits, the feeling of mastery through success, interest in school, a sense of responsibility, and those important character-building aspects of the molding process on the young life which have a definite effect in later life. Irregularity tends to cause the pupil to achieve less than he is normally capable of. Every break in educational continuity leaves its record. Lost school time can scarcely be made up satisfactorily through any tutorial scheme. The latter denies the intangible values of regular classroom instruction. Coaching at home by parents or a tutor, or at school by the teacher or another pupil, is usually little more than an educational makeshift, being of lessened value to the child and frequently time-consuming to the teacher. Moreover, even if the child "makes up" the work and is promoted with his class, what might he have achieved if he had attended regularly? Will gaps in his educational progress sooner or later appear?

In order for the state to fulfill its obligations to society, it must see that the child of school age is present in school regularly. By putting a premium upon regularity through appropriate stimulation, state enforcement agencies, and attendance laws, the state demands an accounting for every child's absence from school, or for that matter, while in school, from the means of instruction provided.

This chapter seeks to inquire into the causes of non-attendance of school children, methods of improving school attendance, the truancy problem, and tardiness as an attendance problem, with special emphasis on practical means to secure regularity in the school attendance of every child of school age.

THE INCIDENCE OF NON-SCHOOL ATTENDANCE

Ideally, all children of elementary and secondary school age should go to school, while in school be in regular attendance upon the means provided, and attend every day school is in session. This ideal has never been attained. According to the 1940 census, nearly 15 per cent of the children 5 to 17 years of age were not attending school. Of this number about 40 per cent were of elementary school age (5 to 13 inclusive) and about 60 per cent were of high-school age (14 to 17 inclusive).

These percentages, of course, do not take into consideration the average daily attendance of those who are now enrolled in the schools. Considering attendance in relation to enrollments, using 1940 figures, and including public school (25,433,542) and private and parochial school (2,611,047) enrollments, 3,729,927 or 13.3 per cent of the 28,044,589 enrolled children were absent each day. Adding this number to the number of children not in school at all (4,311,704), we get the grand total of 8,041,631 children not in school on any one day during the school term in that year. While sufficient for general purposes, this figure does not take into consideration children attending special schools or children classified as exceptional who are not enrolled in any school.

In reviewing these figures, one must subtract a small number of school children who are under the age of six years or eighteen years or over. With those omitted, approximately eight million or 20 per cent of the school population six to seventeen years of age are out of school each day of the school year.

The careful student of the problem of non-attendance will consider the great variations in school absence among the several states. There are the differing limits of the compulsory attendance ages, the varying length of the school term. Geographical sections of the country show wide differences in school attendance reflected in parental attitudes, factors of distance, wealth or poverty of the people, occupations, and industrial conditions. Many absences from school are entirely legal and excusable, as when caused by illness and climatic conditions. The child himself is always a factor to be considered, as well as the school to which he is sent.

TYPES OF NON-ATTENDANTS WITH SPECIAL EMPHASIS ON TRUANCY

Classification. Compulsory education laws provide, theoretically, for the school attendance of every child within the prescribed age limits. In an earlier chapter we have noted certain legal exemptions. Public school facilities should be made available to all other children. Besides those few adequately provided for in other, equivalent educational environments, a goodly number of children are "lost" entirely to the educational process as related to the public school. These children may be classified as (1) educable and (2) non-educable. The former group includes all those who by reason of their fitness could profit by public school offerings; in some instances, however, it would seem that other educational facilities or circumstances offer better training. The latter group includes those who for one reason or another are not able to profit by a public school or equivalent education, such as institutional cases, idiots, imbeciles, or others who for physical, mental, or moral reasons cannot or should not be educated in that environment.

Educable Children. Among educable children there are several groups who either are not enrolled in the public school, or although enrolled, become attendance problems.

First, some children regularly enrolled in the public school seek, for many reasons, to evade attendance. Evasion may be their own idea or due to parental connivance. Every illegal absence is a form of truancy, although that term is usually applied to willful or continued absence. Where truancy is associated with incorrigibility in any form, the term *juvenile delinquency* is usually applied.[1]

Second, there are the children who should be enrolled in the public school, but who have been "lost" in the census enrollment because parents were absent at the time the census was taken, because

---

[1] The student should review statistics as to the ratio of enrolled children to the total school population. Since 1870 this has been gradually rising, from 61.5 to 85.5 per cent. Unenrolled children must be classed as truants.

of moving of families (as migrant workers), or for other reasons involving both school and parental omission or neglect.

The third group includes those children who are legally excused from school attendance owing to child labor exemptions, temporary conditions of health, home, or other factors. Upon the cessation of employment or when the conditions which have brought about the temporary absence have been removed, the child sometimes fails to return to school. Means of adequate follow-up may be faulty or non-existent.

In the fourth group are those children whose education is already provided for, ostensibly at least, in some other acceptable manner. They may be taught at home, or in private or other types of schools. Responsibility lies with public school authorities to see that equivalent education is provided for them and that they are regular in attendance. In practice, many difficulties attend this responsibility. There is usually little or no check on content, equivalence or adaptability of the instructional processes, or regularity of attendance. Then, too, the increasing migratory tendency of winter vacationists and for economic reasons offers serious hazards to children's education.

Truancy and Delinquency. A truant child, then, is one who is unlawfully absent from school for a period longer than is legally permissible, or who otherwise disregards the school attendance laws of the state in which he lives, through his own or his parents' neglect. Truancy is usually associated closely with delinquency, because it is the first overt act toward that end. The delinquent child is one who violates any state law, who is disobedient or unmanageable, or whose behavior is such as to injure or endanger the morals, health, or general welfare of himself or others. Although all truants do not become delinquent, it may be said that habitual truants tend to become so. Many of the characteristics of truants, particularly habitual ones, are similar to those of juvenile delinquents.

Characteristics of Truancy. Truancy is a symptom, not a disease, since, unless corrected, it leads to further complications. It is principally a problem of adolescence—of the junior high school and the lower years of the senior high school. Ordinarily, it does not arise in the elementary school, unless possibly in the seventh and eighth grades. Boys are more guilty (80 per cent) than girls. The mean age of truants is about 15½ years. The mean grade is the ninth and halfway through it. More than half of all truants have some physical defect. Most truants are single offenders; second or third offenders tend to become habitual. Truancy has considerable relation to retardation. It occurs mostly in the spring, on circus or similar days, and is related to report card periods (poor marks). Weather is not generally to blame except perhaps fine spring days. There is usually a progressive rise in truancy, beginning with a new semester, reaching a peak, and steadily declining toward its end. Truancy may be related to economic cycles, being less common in periods of depression when job hunting is more or less fruitless. Minimum age requirements for employment tend to reduce this cause. Love of adventure plays a part, especially when the circumstances are favorable, as balmy days, a chance for a ride, decisions of dominant companions, or escape from unpleasant school or family situations or a poor school report. Other conditions in the school directly related to truancy are inadequate facilities for recreation, inelastic school systems, poor attendance laws and poorer administration of them, unsympathetic principals and teachers, and other environmental conditions not conducive to the child's interests or needs.[2]

CAUSES OF NON-ATTENDANCE

The Approach. Approaches to problems of non-school attendance naturally suggest inquiries into causes. Numerous studies have been made of the problem.[3] Illness is still given as an important cause as reported by parents and attendance officers, common colds being the principal illness. However, Kincaid[4] believes that illness is given as an excuse to cover other causes which, in many instances, include parental negligence or indifference, parental stupidity or ignorance, weather, economic conditions of the home, parental greed, and the failure to adapt the school to the child. Gardner[5] went further and concluded that absence is rarely the result of any one cause, but rather

---

[2] The reader is referred to T. Earl Sullenger, *Social Determinants in Juvenile Delinquency,* New York, John Wiley and Sons, 1936, for a good discussion of this problem.

[3] The reader is referred to a report of these studies set forth in "Pupil Personnel, Guidance, and Counseling," section on "Causes of Non-Attendance," *Review of Educational Research,* April, 1939, pp. 162 ff.

[4] New York (State) University, *Problems of School Attendance and Pupil Adjustment,* Albany, State Education Department, 1932, 74 pp.

[5] John Ralph Gardner, *Truancy and Non-Attendance in the Salt Lake City Junior High Schools,* Master's Thesis, University of Utah, 1935.

of several associated factors. Lawing[6] traced poor school attendance to lack of legislation defining which children must attend, length of time they must attend, and penalty for non-attendance. Lack of enforcing agencies are also in large measure responsible.

Factors Related to Non-Attendance. In addition to these there are many other factors related to non-attendance. Pupils who are often absent tend to receive the lowest grades, the reverse of this being similarly true. Many studies have sought to show the relation between intelligence, achievement, and attendance, in which there seems to be a lack of agreement.[7] Young children of a given grade were found to have a better record of attendance than older children of the same grade. Girls are usually slightly more regular than boys, although isolated studies differ on this observation. Accelerated pupils usually attend more regularly than others. Pupils whose parents are unemployed tend to be absent more often than those whose parents were employed. Distance from school is a factor, as are tardiness and penalties for absence. Transportation of children has undoubtedly increased regularity of attendance.

Lawful and Unlawful Absence. The causes of non-attendance may be classified as (1) lawful, the chief being illness of child, illness in family, lack of clothing, death in family, and work at home; and (2) unlawful, the chief being truancy, parental neglect, work at home, illegal employment, and out-of-town visits. Bermejo[8] classifies twenty-seven different causes with some disagreement as to their lawfulness or unlawfulness. One might also include, as a separate classification, that group of children of school age who are not enrolled in any school for lawful or unlawful reasons.

Home and Community Environment. In addition to those indicated in the previous section, one must look further for certain causes of truancy within the home environment. Some of these causes and conditions as developed by Abbott and Breckinridge[9] are (1) family emergencies, (2) poverty, (3) lack of clothing, (4) parental carelessness in sending the child to school, (5) lack of parental discipline,

[6] John Leslie Lawing, *Standards for State and Local Compulsory School Attendance Service,* Doctor's Dissertation, Columbia University, 1934.

[7] *Review of Educational Research,* April, 1939, pp. 162–163.

[8] F. V. Bermejo, *The School Attendance Service in American Cities,* Menasha, Wisconsin, George Banta Publishing Company, 1923.

[9] Edith Abbott and Sophonisba Breckenridge, *Truancy and Non-Attendance in the Chicago Schools,* Chicago, University of Chicago Press, 1917.

(6) working mothers, and (7) broken homes and parental rifts. Causes of truancy within the community may be (1) bad companions, (2) poor cultural environment, and (3) lack of recreational or other facilities.

All of these statements indicate that the causes of truancy are numerous and complex. They lie in the combinations of factors which affect the child's life. In every instance the truant child presents an individual problem; the causes must be studied and understood before the remedy is applied.

Responsibility for Non-Attendance. The facts of non-attendance being known, responsibility must be placed for their alleviation. To this end, an analysis was made of all available studies of causes of non-attendance. A classification was then made with a view to locating some responsibility, in whole or in part. It was found that responsibility may be divided among (1) the home, (2) the school, (3) the pupil, and (4) the community.

Single causes of non-attendance in which the *home* is primarily responsible are:[10]

Both parents employed
Church services
Domestic social maladjustments
Emergencies at home
Family moved out of the district
Funerals
Geographical location of the home, as distance
Illness of others in the home
Lack of proper or adequate clothing
Malnutrition
Parental apathy
Poverty and economic mismanagement in the home
Private lessons
Pupil accompanying parents on vacations
Pupil belonging to a migratory family
Quarantine of the home
Weddings

Causes of non-attendance traceable to the *school's responsibility* are:

---

[10] In these lists of causes, the arrangement is alphabetical, rather than by order of importance.

Age 14 and has passed highest grade offered
Age 15 and is employed as domestic or as farm hand
Age 16 (or legal age) and holds employment certificate
Allowable transfer to other school district
Emergencies of the school plant and equipment
Exempt by completion of secondary school
Inability to secure a teacher
Instruction at expense of teaching (certification *vs.* qualification)
Lack of orientation or guidance
Lack of school facilities (sanitation, overcrowding, etc.)
Quarantine of school building
Regular school vacations
Strikes of pupils or teachers or similar occurrences
Too few pupils in district (legal limits)
Transportation deficiencies
Unattractive school program
Unwise location of school

Causes of non-attendance for which the *pupil* himself must assume some responsibility are:

Forged excuses from school
Immorality
Pupil-pupil controversy
Pupil strikes
Shame (or pride) of pupil in which may be involved probation, parole, immorality, alcoholism, crime of parent, self, or relation
Temporary unconfining illness of pupil
Transportation by individual pupil
Truancy of group of pupils
Truancy of individual pupil

Causes of non-attendance traceable to the *community* are:

Explosions
Fires that disrupt community routine
Impassable highways and detours
Strikes affecting the community
Transportation emergencies (traffic accidents or tie-ups)
Wars and insurrections

Added to these causes should be *acts of God* which include inclement weather, earthquakes, floods, and violent storms which prevent the pupil from getting to school.

Multiple Causes. Many causes of non-attendance are multiple, that is, the responsibility must be placed in more than one location. Illustrative of these are community celebrations, transportation difficulties, mutual dislikes affecting pupil-teacher-parent and community, incorrigibility, mental unfitness, laxity of enforcement, school excursions, and enforced vacations due to religious, social, political, economic, parental, or other reasons. We may add communicable diseases, fear of examinations or other school assignments, pupil suspension or expulsion, moving of family, entertainments in which the pupil through participation or non-participation is kept out late, part-time occupation of pupil, child labor, malingering, seasonable activities involving both employment and non-employment, visitors in the home, and court routine, as detention and parental indifference to pupil connivance.

In rural school districts farm work is responsible for many absences. Country schools are often almost emptied of their pupils during the busy season. Cotton picking extends from late summer to after Christmas, so that many young cotton pickers do not enter school until after the season is over. Children in the sugar-beet districts frequently do not even enroll until after the middle of November, when the season is over. Truck farming has much the same effect on children's schooling. Both the planting of crops in spring and their harvest in the fall take their toll of school attendance in all northern states. The migrant child who follows the season's crops seems the most seriously affected. In fact, farm work of one sort or another is almost universally the chief cause of absence in rural areas.

IMPROVING SCHOOL ATTENDANCE

Contrasting Approaches. Since the basis of school attendance is compulsory, the first suggested approach to its improvement is through legislative enactment or adequate law enforcement, or both. There is great need for this approach in many states and in individual districts of those states. However, we are led to agree with Heck's statement as to the proper approach when he writes: "The remedy for non-attendance is understanding, not force. If society demands regularity of attendance of all children, then society must equalize the burdens which such compulsion to attend places upon individuals. All data compiled which show the existence of such inequalities must be utilized in an attempt to eliminate them. Steps thus taken, backed by knowledge of conditions, certainly have more chance of lessening non-attendance than a policy of force alone."[11]

Improving Health Conditions. Illness, either of the child or in the home, suggests the need for an adequate health program involving the child, the home, the community, and the school itself. Colds, the chief cause of non-attendance due to illness, may be the result of unhygienic conditions within the school or the home, overheating, low vitality, lack of nourishment, overeating, or lack of exercise. Proper health instruction, adequate school medical service, improved health conditions within the community as well as more sanity with regard to health in the home and the school will help. Epidemics should be made a matter of concern before they occur. Health regulations must be strictly enforced, i.e., vaccination and quarantine. Local boards of health should take their responsibilities far more seriously than they usually do. The medical profession should realize that the obnoxious fee system is depriving thousands of people, including many children, of adequate medical attention. They should be alert to these needs and opportunities and seek the proper way to meet them.

Economic Conditions. Remedies should be provided for those economic conditions which cause laxity in attendance laws and their enforcement. Everyone is entitled to a childhood free from that form of oppressive labor which deprives him of his educational birthright. We need a uniform child labor law adequately enforced. All types of acceptable home and farm work should be subordinated to the child's right to an education; at the same time we must remember that the dignity of work is also his birthright. Lack of economic means depriving the child of attendance at school must be society's responsibility, also provision for suitable clothing and suitable food. Perhaps the excessive tendency in high schools to exact fees for this and that activity keeps some children out of school. Those causes of non-attendance due to seasonal economic conditions or depression, or still others seemingly chronic with certain racial or social groups, should be studied and provision made for the educational release of the children concerned.

Responsibility of the Home. Those causes of non-attendance due to the home need to be studied where they exist, that is, *in the home.* The home should be brought, first of all, to see its expanding pur-

---

[11] Arch O. Heck, *Administration of Pupil Personnel,* Boston, Ginn and Company, 1929, p. 114.

pose in the educative process. To bring this about should be the primary obligation of the school, perhaps through the visiting teacher or organized forms of parent-teacher cooperation. Parental interest should supplant parental indifference. Greater cooperation with the home is needed in matters involving absences due to private lessons, weddings and funerals, movings, religious and social activities, family vacations, and concerning those all too common causes in which parental or pupil pride hides a condition beyond their control. Social agencies can offer their services. Teacher visitation will yield many dividends. Those districts which encourage friendly home visitation to the school may find many of their problems melting away. Whatever means is provided to secure rapport is commendable.

Responsibility of the School. Within the school itself reside, to a considerable extent, the control and elimination of non-attendance of many children. A study of causes traceable to the school which have been set forth in a previous section reveals many conditions in the school that cannot but have a melancholy effect upon the child himself. Pupils will use every excuse to evade the monotony of an unattractive program, a dull routine, or an unanimated or irascible teacher. Perhaps the administration of attendance itself is made a perfunctory rather than a social service. School should be a happy place where the child wants to be and where he feels the lift of a wholesome environment. A closer study should be made of state laws and school regulations in order to ascertain if they are impeding educational progress.

Place of the Teacher. The teacher has a definite role in securing better attendance. First of all, he has a legal responsibility to keep such records and administer absences as may be required by statute or regulations. But his duties do not end there. As one directly responsible for good teaching, he should make that process interesting and vital on every child-level. Adequate restorative procedures should be adapted to those legally absent without slowing up the whole class. It cannot be said that much progress has been made in this direction. An attractive school environment enhanced by the pleasing personality of an understanding teacher will do much to attract children to school and to eliminate non-attendance before it occurs.[12] Learning should be a delightful experience, even through mastery

---

[12] Compare William A. Yeager, *Home-School-Community Relations,* Pittsburgh, University Book Store, 1939, chap. vi, for a discussion of the place of the teacher and school environment in the educational process.

of difficult subject matter. To learn should be a challenge. Problem cases should be studied, and every effort made to coordinate the special services in the school system to the desired end of pupil adjustment. Good teachers teach children rather than subject matter.

Place of the Administration. Suggestions indicated for the teacher may well be made the basis of school policy. Many enlightened teachers can do little under the supervision of an unenlightened and phlegmatic principal or superintendent; still others might in spite of them. This argues for enlightened supervision. The administration of the attendance function should be just as enlightened and human. Guidance and counseling services, properly organized and functioning adequately, will require cooperation with all the school's special services or the community's social agencies where necessary. A reclaimed youngster should find an environment diffusing encouragement when he returns to school.

Specifically, there are several suggestions to improve attendance within the school itself. Satisfactory attendance should be encouraged, if not rewarded, by intangible means; tangible rewards and contests for perfect attendance are of doubtful value. Children should feel a sense of belonging in the class and school. Opening exercises and the school program should be made attractive. Punishment in the form of detention rooms for tardiness or absence may, perhaps, be questioned. Suitable publicity given to those with perfect attendance should be extended to those who have good attendance records with legitimate reasons in case of absence. Whatever administrative plans are set up, care must be taken to carry them out with discrimination and justice to all concerned.

Responsibility of the Pupil. Whatever may be done by the home and the school to improve attendance should find some response within the pupil himself. Children should be gradually taught to assume responsibility for their own acts. Acts of deception, as in forged excuses, forms of defense, as in pride or shame, or willful absence, as in truancy or pupil strikes, need suitable treatment. Adolescence, both of boys and of girls, brings its own problems, which can be helped toward solution through understanding teachers or parents. Sometimes it may be difficult for a child to rise above his own environment; but he can be helped in so doing. If education is to become a continuous process, he should be taught that even a day lost breaks the harmony of his educational progress.

Responsibility of the Community. Those causes of non-attendance found within the community may be classified as remediable and unremediable. Parental or patron's disapproval of the school, its teachers, or its administration should not be aired before pupils, either in the home or before community gatherings. If it need go that far, legal remedies should be sought in the proper way. Children's attendance at community celebrations ought to be considered in the light of state control of school attendance; the same applies to vaccination or quarantine requirements. The existence of seasonal occupations may require school cooperation in certain instances. Religious or racial attitudes or disputes ought not to interfere selfishly with the child's greater good. Assistance rather than obstructive influences should characterize the proper enforcement of attendance laws. Child labor restrictions should likewise be viewed in the interests of a strengthened manhood and womanhood, rather than in the light of immediate selfish or questionable economic return. Nothing is more desirable in any community than a friendly, cooperative attitude toward the school.

Acts of God humanly unremediable may be annoying. Here there is little one can do unless the cause be wholly or partially within the community's power to prevent. Inclement weather is beyond our control, although we may presage its coming and circumvent its annoyance. In these situations a little foresight may be worth a great deal.

Remedies for Truancy. Since truancy is usually associated with aggravated cases of non-attendance, certain specific approaches to the problem are suggested. The remedies for truancy lie in (1) its prevention, (2) its relief, along causal lines indicated above, and (3) the studying of each child who presents himself as an individual truancy problem in the light of a more adequate adjustment to his home, school, and community, together with the correction or alleviation of those physical, mental, or other handicaps which bring about the maladjustment. Within the school itself lies, for the most part, the initiative for adjustment. Adequate guidance and sympathetic counseling are its principal factors. The administration of attendance should be along lines suggested in the previous chapter. Youth-serving organizations can help orient the child to his social group. In the last analysis, the program of adjustment must be fitted to each child. If all these remedies are of no avail and the child fails to make adjustment, removal from the group is the only solution in the interests of the social whole. Since he may sooner or later become a court and possibly an institutional case, social workers having to do with these procedures should be consulted and their advice acted upon.[13]

Before closing this section the reader is referred to the section on the visiting teacher in the preceding chapter. Much of what has been said there should assist in bringing about an improvement in school attendance. It might be added that many school services referred to in later sections find application in improving school attendance.

TARDINESS

Importance. Definitely related to the administrative problem of maintaining regularity in school attendance is the insistence upon a scrupulous regard for attendance *on time.* Punctuality is a *character trait* to be developed in children, as important as honesty or morality. Tardiness is the form of its violation. It is a breach of faith with those to whom keeping the faith is due. Equally annoying with the absent pupil to the teacher is the tardy one, in a sense perhaps more so.

Classification. There are available many studies of the causes of tardiness and its remedial administration. Lockwood,[14] for example, indicates the following causes in order of frequency: (1) work, (2) clock wrong, (3) started late to school, (4) accidental or some unusual cause, (5) automobile trouble, (6) sickness, (7) no reason at all, and (8) overslept.

These and all other reasons for tardiness, real or assumed, may be classified as (1) excused and (2) unexcused. The exercise of discretion as to the reason given for tardiness is the prerogative of the school. Excused reasons, in most cases legal, include illness, accidents, working under certain circumstances, inclement weather, and certain home conditions beyond the control of the parent or the child. While the reason assigned may seem excusable on its face, in some cases there may be doubt as to its authenticity. Unexcused reasons

---

[13] L. C. Halberstadt, "High School Truants," *Nation's Schools,* April, 1938, p. 33; Paul Fleming, "Truancy—When and Why It Occurs," *Nation's Schools,* November, 1930, p. 31; James S. Hiatt, "The Truant Problem and the Parental School," *Bulletin No. 29,* Washington, United States Bureau of Education, 1915.

[14] L. A. Lockwood, "Causes of Tardiness," *School Review,* September, 1930, pp. 538 ff.

include faulty timing because of either the clock or loitering, keep-ing late hours, oversleeping, and failure on the part of the home to cooperate, part of which could have been overcome by the child. Numerous other reasons may be given, many of which are scarcely excusable.

Devices for Improvement. Although it is too much to expect that tardiness as an attendance problem will ever be eliminated, numer-ous devices are available for its reduction. There are two approaches to the problem: (1) penalties and (2) guidance. Most of the schemes advanced are a curious combination of both. As to penalties, the following have been tried with varying degrees of success:

1. Detention room
2. Making up time and lessons missed by other means
3. Black lists (varying forms of unfavorable publicity)
4. Requiring pupil to come to school early for a while
5. Assigning a definite responsibility
6. Attaching stigma in some tangible form
7. Using complex system of records and procedure causing annoyance to pupil and parent
8. Calling chronics on telephone, usually early in morning to insure promptness

A close study of these devices reveals a negative rather than a positive approach. Emphasis seems to be on annoyance and punish-ment rather than on correction and the formation of the proper habit of punctuality. Moreover, while the proposed device may be used with the intent of positive improvement, the pupil may view it as punishment. Outward compliance to "get it over with" may all the while hide an inner resentment. Of course, children differ in this respect. Success is a criterion of judgment.

Of greater value because of their positive approach are certain guidance activities. These may include:

1. Building up morale in both pupil and school
2. Competitive devices, as tournaments
3. Rewards, as plates on doors, positive publicity, letters to the home
4. Emphasis upon vigor and personality of principal, teachers, or other pupils as ideals of emulation
5. Student council responsibilities for tardiness
6. Activities of pupil committees, as in home rooms, placing pressure on tardy individuals

The modern school program because of its complexity may contain features which aggravate tardiness. In larger schools tardiness may be due to inaccessibility of lockers, crowded halls, one-way passages, a faulty excuse system, congested offices at certain periods, activities, interruptions of classroom work through a faulty schedule, and an imperfect signal system. Bus schedules may be interrupted because of inclement weather, bad roads, breakdowns, and similar difficulties. Trains or trolleys may be late. The management of the school may be lax in permitting interruptions of classroom work through activities, extra duties, or just plain dillydallying. The problem should be attacked at the point of existence.

Home Cooperation. In the last analysis, tardiness is usually a home and parental problem. At many points it has a direct relation to the degree of home cooperation with the school. Hence, every effort should be made to secure that cooperation, toward which end the following suggestions for parents are offered: (1) send children to school on time; (2) keep clocks accurate; (3) see that required chores, if any, are completed in time for school; (4) get children to bed on time; (5) break up habit of oversleeping; (6) understand fully the rules of the school; and (7) get better acquainted with the school and the teachers. There may be occasions for home visitation by either the principal, the teacher, the visiting teacher, or the school nurse. These occasions should be utilized in the interests of punctuality where necessary.

Many schools refer cases of tardiness to the guidance counselor. Much help can be secured from this quarter. One may be led to observe finally that punctuality is usually the reflection of a well-managed school as well as a well-ordered home.

QUESTIONS AND PROBLEMS

1. At what points do breaks in the educational continuity of each child occur?
2. Make a study of the incidence of non-school attendance in a selected school district.
3. Compare statistics in selected states and cities as to variations in non-school attendance. Try to account for these from several standpoints.
4. What is an educable child? Check carefully figures on the unenrolled children in your state or community. How can you account for their absence from the enrollment sheets? What other provisions have been made for their education?

5. Make a study of the causes of non-attendance by the examination of literature in the field. In the light of your study appraise the classifications outlined in the chapter.

6. To what extent are Bermejo's findings in 1923 invalid in 1940?

7. What is the greatest single cause of non-school attendance? Contributing cause? Cause most easily removed? Cause most difficult of removal?

8. Evaluate the sections in the chapter in which definite responsibility is allocated *within* the school system for the alleviation of non-school attendance; *without* the school system.

9. Make a study of the literature on truancy. What other causes for truancy can you indicate? What other remedies?

10. Make out a case for or against each of the following: (*a*) the detention room, (*b*) black lists, (*c*) other forms of stigma, (*d*) make-up work—in case of absence or tardiness, (*e*) forms of pupil pressures, (*f*) competitive devices, (*g*) systems of rewards, (*h*) building up morale; how? (*i*) cooperation with the home; how?

11. Make a study of the visiting teacher movement. What is its chief value? Outline the qualifications for home and school visitors in any state. What states have such qualifications? What school districts within your state have developed the visiting teacher plan?

12. In what respect does tardiness differ from truancy as an attendance problem? Study the causes and treatment of tardiness by (*a*) an analysis of the literature, (*b*) writing to several schools for their plans.

13. By reference to actual cases, show that truancy is the first overt act leading to delinquency.

14. Study a selected school system to point out how poor administration is a contributing factor to (*a*) non-attendance, (*b*) truancy, and (*c*) tardiness.

SELECTED REFERENCES

1. Broom, Eustace, and Trowbridge, Bertha, "The Visiting Teacher's Job," *Elementary School Journal,* May, 1926, pp. 653–661.

2. Cornell, Francis G., "Public School Attendance Changes," *School Life,* February, 1946, pp. 20–22.

3. "Education for Family Life," *Nineteenth Yearbook,* American Association of School Administrators. Washington: National Education Association, 1941, chaps. iii, iv.

4. Fleming, Paul, "Truancy—When and Why It Occurs," *Nation's Schools,* November, 1930.

5. Fornwalt, Russell J., "Toward an Understanding of Truancy," *School Review,* 55 No. 2, February, 1947, pp. 87–92.

6. Halberstadt, L. C., "High School Truants," *Nation's Schools,* April, 1938, pp. 33–34.
7. Heck, Arch O., *Administration of Pupil Personnel.* Boston: Ginn and Company, 1929.
8. "How Can Tardiness and Truancy Be Remedied?" *Nation's Schools,* September, 1945, pp. 41 f.
9. Ingram, Christine P., "Education in Training Schools for Delinquent Youth," *Bulletin No. 5,* Federal Security Agency. Washington: United States Office of Education, 1945.
10. Landis, Paul H., *Adolescence and Youth.* New York: McGraw-Hill Book Company, 1945, chap. xx.
11. Lewis, Russell A., "All Present and Accounted For," *School Executive,* September, 1941, pp. 15 ff.
12. Lindley, A. S., "Reasons for Absence of Junior High School Students," *Educational Administration and Supervision,* January, 1945, pp. 45–52.
13. Ludden, Wallace, "Why Delinquency?" *Progressive Education,* October, 1944, pp. 26 f.
14. Miller, Frank M., *Development, Present Status, and Administrative Relationships of the Visiting Teacher in the United States,* Doctor's Dissertation, University of Pittsburgh, 1942.
15. Myers, Garry C., "How Home and Family Conditions Affect Child Personality," *National Elementary Principal,* June, 1936, pp. 303–310.
16. Otto, Henry J., *Elementary School Organization and Administration.* New York: D. Appleton-Century Company, 1944, chap. ix.
17. Punke, H. H., "Economic Status and High School Attendance," *Social Forces,* March, 1941, pp. 365–368.
18. Richey, Herman G., "Factors of High School Enrollment in Illinois," *School Review,* November, 1940, pp. 657–666.
19. Riebe, H. A., Nelson, M. J., and Kittrell, C. A., *The Classroom.* New York: The Cordon Company, 1938, chaps. vi, vii.
20. "Schools for a New World," *Twenty-Fifth Yearbook,* American Association of School Administrators. Washington: National Education Association, 1947.
21. "Schools and the Problems of Juvenile Delinquency," *Elementary School Journal,* February, 1947, pp. 310–314.
22. Schultz, J. L., "School Medical Service and Attendance Work," *American School Board Journal,* November, 1939, pp. 44–45.
23. Strang, Ruth, *The Role of the Teacher in Personnel Work.* New York: Columbia University Press, 1935.
24. Warters, Jane, *High-School Personnel Work Today.* New York: McGraw-Hill Book Company, 1946.

CHAPTER VII

Child Labor and Education

IT HAS taken society many years to develop a public opinion favorable to the upward extension of the period of school attendance for children and the protection of young persons from unfavorable employment conditions. Not that the child should not be taught to work and learn habits of industrious living, but that he is entitled to the birthrights of childhood, to every means for that growth and development to which nature has entitled him, and to the removal of all restrictions which would tend to rob him of them. Since education is a fundamental part of his development, his school attendance is necessary for the greater part of his immature existence.

Our interest in child labor at this point is to understand more clearly its nature, the fundamental problems associated with it, and its educational implications. We are interested in the distinction between child labor and the right of children to learn to work as a basis for a livelihood and a happy and useful life. This chapter will present state and federal laws, together with the problems associated with their administration as an educational function. It assumes that child labor legislation protects the boy and girl from exploitation during immaturity so that they can complete, as far as possible, an educational program to which they are entitled. It does not take into consideration that developmental function of education which should prepare him for earning a living and supporting himself and those dependent upon him. This is reserved for a later chapter.

CHILD LABOR AND CHILDREN'S WORK

Definition. Simply stated, child labor means the exploited labor of children. Considered as an economic practice, it means the gainful employment of children under legal age limits, so that they are materially contributing to the labor income of the family or of themselves. Considered in the light of later statements in this section, child labor is the employment of children, with or without pay, under another's direction and to his gain in some measure, which deprives the child of his fair share of full development, educational and otherwise. It has the connotation of prematurity. Child labor always implies exploitation, in which the exploiter gains materially to the detriment of the one exploited. Perhaps the thought of children contributing to family support would not have such evil connotations if it were not for the attendant social evils which have sprung up through the years surrounding their employment. Public attitude against child labor has probably been influenced more by these social evils than by the paltry wages children have received or the paltry output of their labors.

During his immature years the child needs opportunities for growth and development, not only physically but in mind and personality, through all of the activities and experiences which properly belong to childhood. When his services as a wage earner or as a contributor to his own or his family's support, either through compulsion or by choice, conflict directly or indirectly with his prior rights of development as a child through education and play, the result is definitely child labor.

Children's Work. Seemingly inconsistent is the universally accepted notion that work is essential to human life and happiness; that it is incumbent upon society to teach its children to work, to learn habits of industry, and to prepare eventually to earn a living. It is important to point out that the function of work in childhood is primarily *developmental,* rather than economic. To this end play is just as important, and if the work interferes with play or with opportunities for growth and development—or contrariwise, let it be added—the outcome is not in harmony with this principle. It is true that one must stress adequate preparation for occupational living through the nature of the work to be done. Throughout there must be a recognition of the *dignity of work,* the right to work, creative effort, and the joy of honest toil and achievement. In no sense do these statements fail to apply to those children who may be economically fortunate. Children's work, then, as a social good is the direct antithesis of child labor as a social evil.

THE CHILD LABOR MOVEMENT

Earlier Attitudes Regarding Children. Several important concepts, some of them conflicting, should be clearly understood when studying child labor and the movement to restrict it. The first of these concerns the prior right of the parent over his own children.[1] Through the centuries this concept has had many connotations. The laws of the state seldom interfered with this right unless it was a matter of life or gross injustice. Many children, especially in the larger families of the poor, were considered economic liabilities, who should be turned into economic assets through the exploitation of their labor. Again, the child, being originally sinful by nature, needed to be kept industrious, even through the liberal application of force. There was a strong tradition against idleness in any form, play and leisure being roundly condemned as instruments of the devil. Especially in the early history of this country, the labor of everyone including women and children was greatly needed; none could be dispensed with. Apprenticeship was the usual form of paternal control of the child's labor especially where provision could not be made for it within the family. Learning the ancestral occupation in his father's shop or bound out to another, the apprentice child worked until young manhood for his "board and keep." In itself apprenticeship has had an honorable history. The industrial revolution with its forms of mass apprenticeship and attendant social evils called for agitation for governmental control and restriction.

Early Restrictions. Early restrictions had to do largely with the education and general welfare of these children, rather than with an attitude against the labor which they performed. Fortunately for childhood, about the middle of the nineteenth century there appeared a new sense of the importance of child life. The discovery of the social worth of children introduced a movement contemporary with abolition and the religious fervor of the fifties. A succession of laws was passed by the various states restricting the labor of children in various ways. By 1909 each of the forty-eight states had passed legislation governing child labor in one or more occupations.[2] These regulations referred to limitations upon types of occupation for employment, age, and other restrictions. Recognition of the prior right

---

[1] See Chapter IV.

[2] William Fielding Ogburn, *Progress and Uniformity in Child Labor Legislation,* New York, Longmans, Green and Company, 1912, p. 53.

of children to an education through school attendance thus emphasized the definite relationship between compulsory school attendance and child labor restriction.

Contemporary Influences. The legal and social restrictions upon
child labor were accomplished through certain noteworthy influences. The first workingmen's associations in the early 1830's pro-
tested against the competing labor of young children. The abolition
of slavery undoubtedly had a moral effect. In 1870, the Census
Bureau of the United States began to collect information regarding
occupations for persons ten years of age and upwards, revelations
that were highly significant. In 1881, the American Federation of
Labor adopted a plank calling for complete abolition by the states
of employment of children under fourteen in any capacity. House
and Senate hearings on child labor were held during the eighties.
Settlement houses, Hull House, for example, did heroic social work
among children. In 1904 the National Child Labor Committee was
founded, an organization of great influence for good in the child
labor movement. Of great significance was the formation of the
federal Children's Bureau in 1912, with duties and responsibilities
covering all aspects of child welfare. All of these revelations of child
labor by the federal census, labor organizations, federal and state
agencies, and individuals and groups interested in child welfare
were none too comforting and contributed immeasurably to continued restrictions.

STATE CHILD LABOR LEGISLATION

Historically, child labor control has been a prerogative of the several states. We have noted that by 1909 each of the forty-eight states
had passed legislation governing child labor in one or more occupations. However, the scope of such control was so limited in many
states as to be almost negligible, especially where the will to enforce
it was lacking.

The best approach to the study of current child labor legislation in
the several states is in terms of the major standards recommended
by the International Association of Governmental Labor Officials for
state child labor legislation and the extent to which existing laws
meet them.[3] These will be analyzed.

---

[3] *Report of the U.S. Department of Labor,* Children's Bureau, Washington, November 1, 1944.

Minimum Age. It is recommended that sixteen years be the minimum age in any employment in a factory and in any employment during school hours, with fourteen as the minimum in any nonfactory employment outside school hours. At the present time fifteen states meet this standard in whole or in part, principally in the northeastern part of the United States.

Hazardous Occupations. For employment in hazardous occupations, a minimum age of eighteen is recommended. The state administrative agency should be authorized to determine occupations hazardous to minors under eighteen. Few, if any, states extend full protection in this respect to minors up to eighteen years of age, although many states prohibit employment under eighteen in a varying number of specific hazardous occupations. Twenty states have an administrative agency with authority to determine which occupations shall be considered hazardous. In many of the states the chief state officers for labor, education, and health together make the decisions.

Maximum Daily and Weekly Hours. In line with the recommendation of an 8-hour day for minors *under* 18 in any gainful occupation, 12 states and the District of Columbia have laws which meet this standard for both sexes and for most occupations. Seven other states meet it for girls up to 18. A 40-hour week for minors under 18 in any gainful occupation is provided for in but a few states. Some permit a 44-hour week. In addition there is a tendency to follow the recommendation to prohibit work during specified night hours for both sexes under 16. This applies to most occupations with exceptions in some states for minors of both sexes between 16 and 18.

Employment Certificates. Employment or age certificates for minors under eighteen in most gainful occupations are required in some twenty-one states. In general, employment certificates are of four types: (1) those furnished children who desire to work before and/or after school and on Saturdays, usually restricted to street trades, as selling papers; (2) vacation permits to work at specified occupations while school is not in session; (3) permits to work during regular school hours under certain conditions, as age or type of occupation, often with the proviso that between certain ages the child shall attend continuation school; and (4) evidence of age or completion of a required minimum education.

The different items required on employment certificates and the number of states requiring them are as follows:[4]

Item Required	Number of States	Item Required	Number of States
Age or date of birth	20	Occupation to be engaged in	5
Residence	10	Statement of physical fitness	4
Place of birth	9	Signature of minor or state-	
Identification of firm	9	ment that the minor appeared	
Sex	8	before the person making the	
Color of eyes	8	certificate	3
Statement of educational status	7	Race	3
Height and weight	7	Signature of parent	1
Color of hair	6	Signature of continuation	
		school representative	1

Summary. From the above brief analysis it will be noted that (1) considerable progress had been made in many states to restrict the exploited labor of children, and (2) in many other states child labor legislation in force is considerably below recommended standards. The administration of child labor laws is principally a state matter. Those responsible for it in each school district must be familiar with all laws and regulations and maintain close relationship with all employing agencies.

FEDERAL CHILD LABOR LEGISLATION

Since the early years of the present century there has been a growing movement for federal control of child labor. It originated in the difficulty encountered in securing controlling legislation in many states, in the general confusion created by a great variation in state laws, and in the fact that no state could set high standards for child employment without driving certain types of industry to other states where there was less regard for child welfare.

Early legislation ran afoul of the Supreme Court. It was not until 1924 that the friends of child labor concluded that further progress on a national scale could only be achieved by means of an amendment to the Constitution. In 1924 a proposed amendment was approved in both houses of Congress and submitted to the states. After

---

[4] A detailed analysis of child labor legislation in all states will be found in "School Census, Compulsory Education, Child Labor; State Laws and Regulations," *Bulletin No. 1.*, Federal Security Agency, Washington, United States Office of Education, 1945.

more than twenty years, the total number of states concurring is twenty-eight, with little immediate prospect of securing the necessary additional eight.

In the meantime the seriousness of the situation in many states necessitated some congressional action. Several laws were passed, most important of which was the Fair Labor Standards Act of 1938. These laws apply to the power of Congress to regulate interstate commerce, and pertain to labor of children employed in producing goods for interstate trade.

Briefly, the Fair Labor Standards Act sets 16 as the minimum age for general employment, and 18 for all occupations which may be found and declared by the Children's Bureau to be particularly hazardous for minors between 16 and 18 years. Fourteen years is the minimum age for employment outside school hours in all occupations other than manufacturing, mining and similar occupations, operating and tending machines, public messenger service, and specified hazardous occupations. All work must be performed outside school hours with a maximum 3-hour day and 18-hour week when school is in session. When school is not in session a maximum 8-hour day and 40-hour week is allowed, with all work performed between 7 A.M. and 7 P.M. Certain exceptions are made for children selling newspapers.

The law regulates employment or age certificates together with certain types of exceptions. Wherever state standards for employment are higher than federal standards, state standards apply.

STATUS OF CHILD LABOR

From an analysis of child labor legislation, both federal as well as state, it is not difficult to observe that thousands of children each year find employment in all sorts of industrial occupations not covered by legal restriction. The best estimate would place the number of children under sixteen years restricted in their educational progress by being gainfully employed between 750,000 and 900,000. Their distribution by occupations is shown in the following paragraphs.

Agriculture. More than half of all children gainfully employed are in agriculture, not including children working at home, doing housework, chores, and odd jobs. There has been an increase in the number of migrant families, especially on the west coast. Many are the victims of dust bowl or similar conditions, or are displaced sharecroppers, unemployed farm and urban workers, and war workers. They keep constantly on the move. Some of their children have never been inside a schoolhouse. They are often used to depress production costs, with a resulting substandard of living. In New Jersey, a study of these migrant children showed that 89 per cent had lost some time in school; 42 per cent were retarded, compared with 19.8 per cent in Philadelphia, whence many of them had come.

Street Trades. About one-third include newsboys, magazine venders, peddlers, and bootblacks. Many of these children work at night in unwholesome social conditions, in all kinds of weather, with resulting dangers to themselves, not a few being under fourteen years of age. Many others are unaccounted for.

Intra-State Industrial Occupations. The great bulk of industrial workers within the states are employed as clerks and errand boys, and do odd jobs in retail stores, bakeries, beauty parlors, barber shops, garages, repair shops, hotels, restaurants, theaters, bowling alleys, and in domestic service. Classified with this group are thousands of children employed in the home with their parents and others in making flowers, clothing, toys, and small goods of all kinds; many are unaccounted for.

Minors—Sixteen and Seventeen Years Old. The employment of children sixteen and seventeen years old must be considered a part of the child labor problem, especially in those instances in which their labor is exploited. Moreover, their employment must be safeguarded from moral and physical hazards and regulated as to hours, types of occupations, and nightwork. Since the laws of many states require their attendance at school, their continued employment during school hours interferes with educational opportunities provided for all children of the same age groups.

CHILD LABOR AND THE HOME

Basically, the responsibility for child labor rests on the home and the parent. The home is the social agency responsible for the education, protection, and welfare of the child. It is the state's duty to recognize this primary obligation and to foster every means for its proper functioning in the interest of all children.

At the same time there are many conditions for which the home would seem not to be entirely responsible. Home conditions causing or contributing to child labor are poverty, broken homes, widowed mothers, employed parents, agricultural demands in which the child is needed or in which his services are found profitable, indifferent parents, ignorance of the effects, and undesirable conditions from which the child feels forced to escape. The community and the state must step in to alleviate any of these conditions which the home seems unwilling or unable to eradicate. On the one hand the home must be strengthened, and on the other, parental freedom to exploit or permit the exploitation of their children must be curtailed. Likewise, the greed of employers to profit by children's labor should be promptly suppressed. It is the responsibility of the home to see that the child is provided with every opportunity to develop as normally and in accordance with the greatest welfare of society.

EDUCATIONAL IMPLICATIONS OF CHILD LABOR

Next to the home, the school has a responsibility in making provision for each child's educational and social welfare. This responsibility is specifically provided for in the educational laws, and, by implication, in the general oversight which the school has over the child during school hours.

Attendance. The child's first protection is the compulsory attendance laws which require his attendance during the days school is in session. This protection may be vitiated in the case of many children through (1) inefficient enforcement of the law; (2) shortening of the school term due to the urgency of farm work; (3) parental indifference or connivance; (4) community attitudes; (5) distance factors and lack of transportation facilities; (6) migrant children who may not be enrolled in school, and if enrolled move out of the jurisdiction of one school district to another where their presence is unknown or disregarded; and (7) connivance of employers to prevent the school from knowing when children are employed, or to interfere with the enforcement of the law.

There is a definite relation between poor school attendance and retardation among child workers, retardation being usually twice as great as among children regularly in school. Thus a child who is retarded in school is less likely to want to remain in school very long and may seek early withdrawal. Tardiness and indifference to school are also related. Moreover, there are thousands of children whose work outside of school, in addition to their daily schoolwork, gives them a working day of ten to twelve hours, even more. Where recreation is denied, or where unhealthful or poor social conditions prevail, normal child growth is seriously hampered.

Health Factors. Health as the first educational objective is the birthright of every child. Child labor is definitely an anti-health factor. Tuberculosis and other diseases are the direct outcome of long hours of overwork by children under unhealthful conditions, especially where there is an insufficiency of nourishing food. Irregular hours for meals and sleep have their effects. Exposure, the rush and excitement of street trades, the drive of piecework, and nagging overseers tend to produce heart conditions, nervous instability, and stunted growth. Moral conditions are directly related. Removal from these circumstances and placement within a well-planned and administered school health program should be the natural substitute.

Amount of Education. Child labor cuts short the amount of education children may receive. There is a direct relation between the length of the school term and the extent of child labor in certain states and in rural areas. Curtailment of educational privilege results in a proportionate number of citizens ill fitted for the responsibilities of society. Children who leave school early or who are irregular in attendance lack drill in fundamentals and tend to forget much that they have learned. Child labor must be recognized as contributing to the illiteracy of the nation, to sub-standard levels of living, to delinquency, and to anti-social attitudes.

No child in America should be without the opportunity for free public education for a continuous nine-months school term each year up to at least age sixteen, perhaps seventeen or eighteen. To accomplish this objective federal aid may be necessary. Any compensating economic adjustment due to the elimination of child labor is far preferable to the price we now pay for the toil of America's heritage.

Improvement of Conditions Within the School. Within the school itself are many conditions contributing indirectly to child labor. A dull, monotonous routine inspires in a child the desire to escape. If there is a lack of interest in his schoolwork, an ill-adapted curriculum, or a teacher without understanding, his mental conflict becomes intensified. Children who are retarded or who have been absent do not fit easily into a fixed schedule of work. Quite often a child's mind is distressed by pressures of nagging parents, irascible teachers, and non-social children. Unhealthful home conditions unknown to the school may contribute to his mental anguish.

The first task of the school is to create a pleasing environment and plan an educational program adapted to the needs, interests, and abilities of the children. Each boy and girl should be inspired with a will to learn. Back of the successful program is an understanding teacher who helps the child to help himself.

Guidance. The school can play an important part in pointing out to boys and girls the dangers to health and morals of child labor and the importance of a lengthened span of education. The entire structure of the organization for guidance should be built with the purpose of giving each child every possible advantage and assistance in making decisions affecting his life at school, at home, and in the economic world. The hazards of child labor must be pointed out and attractive, wholesome work tasks provided in the school. Visits to the home should bring about understanding of conditions there and amelioration wherever possible. Moreover, at the proper time and place the child must receive vocational adjustment and placement. Work is the natural right and responsibility of every person, including children, who must be properly prepared for it and eventually find their place in a workaday world.

The Continuation School. Part-time education for minors between certain ages is required by the laws of half the states. Underlying these schools is the principle that the child who must be gainfully employed for specific reasons allowable by law may continue his education while thus employed. In order to be effective, it is necessary that the attendance department keep a careful check on all children, follow up permits when issued, and otherwise ascertain the whereabouts of all such children at all times. Teachers of these children should be carefully selected, the program adapted to their individual needs, and every effort made to keep them interested in further education. It is important that cooperation be secured with the home and with employers. When the child leaves his employment, he should be returned to the day school at once, unless other employment is secured.

Specific Administrative Aspects. Much of what has just been said must become the task of the school administrator. In the first place, all responsible for the administration of child labor should be thoroughly familiar with state laws and regulations, as well as with forms used or recommended. The schools should cooperate with labor and welfare departments of the state or other agencies similarly

responsible. Attendance officers should make complaints and prose-
cute cases in which child labor laws are violated if theirs is the responsibility. Secondly, public school authorities, as well as labor
department representatives, where they have the power to do so,
should inspect factories, offices, and other places where children
might be employed and examine employment rolls. The nature of
the occupation should be noted, especially its hazardous or unhealthful aspects. This may require the cooperation of social welfare agencies. In the third place, all employment certificates should include all
required data. They should be carefully followed through when the
child leaves employment or moves from the district. Proper evidence
of age should be established. Above all, the spirit of insisting that
all children secure every educational advantage should characterize
the administration of child labor. The child's educational birthright
should not be taken away from him.

QUESTIONS AND PROBLEMS

1. Find and compare several definitions of child labor. What points
   are (*a*) in agreement; (*b*) inconsistent? Formulate your own definition.
2. What sharp line of distinction can you draw between child labor
   and children's work? Indicate values in each.
3. Examine the following statement: "Child labor is both a cause and
   effect of illiteracy, ignorance, low wages, unemployment, sub-
   standards of living, and sub-standards of family and community
   life." Wherein do you agree or disagree?
4. Strict child labor laws tend to relieve dependency, reduce poverty,
   improve the schools, and develop better parental and civic attitudes.
   To what extent is this statement true? Can you prove your point by
   reference to actual situations?
5. Assign definite reasons for the failure to have the proposed child
   labor amendment adopted. Be specific.
6. In what types of occupations are the greatest evils of child labor
   found?
7. Make a study of child labor conditions within a specific school
   system. What conditions within the schools are contributing to
   child labor?
8. What should be done within the schools to make school more effective and to improve conditions of work for all children?
9. Analyze the continuation school as to effectiveness. What states have
   this institution?

10. Give an evaluation of the White House Conference program as to child labor.

SELECTED REFERENCES

1. *American Child.* 419 Fourth Avenue, New York: National Child Labor Committee.
2. "Counseling, Guidance and Personnel Work," *Review of Educational Research,* April, 1945, vii.
3. Dillon, Harold J., *Work Experience in Secondary Education.* New York: National Child Labor Committee, 1946.
4. Fuller, Raymond G., *Child Labor and the Constitution.* New York: Thomas Y. Crowell Company, 1923.
5. Heck, Arch O., *Administration of Pupil Personnel.* Boston: Ginn and Company, 1929, chaps. iii, iv.
6. Ireland, Tom, *Child Labor as a Relic of the Dark Ages.* New York: G. P. Putnam's Sons, 1937.
7. Knopf, Adolphus S., *Child Labor and the Nation's Health.* New York: The Christopher Publishing House, 1937.
8. Lumpkin, Katherine D., and Douglass, Dorothy S., *Child Workers in America.* New York: Robert M. McBride and Company, 1937.
9. Merritt, Ella Arvilla, and Hendricks, Flay, "Trend in Child Labor 1940–1944," *Monthly Labor Review,* United States Department of Labor, April, 1945, pp. 756–775.
10. "School Census, Compulsory Education, Child Labor, State Laws and Regulations," *Bulletin No. 1,* Federal Security Agency. Washington: United States Office of Education, 1945.
11. "Study Employment Plans versus Child Labor," *School Review,* October, 1946, pp. 447 ff.
12. Taylor, Florence, "Uprooting Child Labor," *Journal of Home Economics,* October, 1945, pp. 483–486.
13. *Thirty-fourth Annual Report of the Secretary of Labor,* fiscal year ending June 30, 1946. Washington, Government Printing Office, 1947, pp. 69–105.

PART III

Providing for All Pupils

CHAPTER VIII

Admission of Pupils

IN PART II our attention was directed to the attendance function as the first perquisite of pupil personnel administration. Several chapters will now be devoted to administrative measures which will place all pupils in a fitting position to receive instruction and enable them to profit by the learning situations provided. Admission is the first step in classification of pupils. Once admitted, the pupil should be assigned to some space presumably adequate to his ability and needs in order to progress. If he is ill fitted in any way in his original assignment, adjustment must be made to provide, both temporarily and ultimately, for more adequate school progress. Since promotion and non-promotion are measures of that progress, it is important to understand the factors that influence promotion in any way. This chapter will discuss the first of these steps to progress, namely, admission procedures.

LEGAL ASPECTS OF ADMISSION

Regulations. Although all states require the school attendance of all children within certain age limits, provision must also be made for the attendance of children outside these limits. Local boards of education are given authority to prescribe and enforce reasonable rules and regulations in regard to admission within the framework provided by law.

Legally, children within certain age limits may be admitted to school at the opening or during the school term. Varying interpretations of these age limits may be made. Entrance, health, or other examinations may be required, and children excluded who fail to pass them. Boards may exclude children who fail to meet such specific state requirements as residence, or children who are immoral, physically unfit or unclean, or who may be unfit to associate with other pupils. The compulsory attendance regulations apply to those listed on the school census who are legally required to attend school within the specified periods of time. In administering the regulations those responsible for admission should be thoroughly familiar with child labor laws with their restrictions, provision for part-time education through continuation schools, re-admittance after illness or quarantine, residence requirements or restrictions, situations in which the payment of tuition is required, and any other legal phase bearing on the admission and retention of the child.

Age of Admission. The public schools are generally open to all children and youth between the ages of six and twenty-one. Usually, this is a constitutional provision. In many states the period of compulsory attendance is from seven to sixteen years.

Twenty-four states designate age seven for entrance to their public schools. Most of the others place the lower limit of compulsory attendance at age eight. Ohio law, however, reads from six to eighteen. School boards make their own regulations, and with pressure from parents to take children as soon as possible, many schools permit entrance of children who will be six at various specific dates during the school year, a fairly common one being before January 1 of the next calendar year.

It is interesting to note certain comparisons between the compulsory ages and the school census ages. In 45 states the minimum census age is less than the minimum compulsory attendance age, and in 4 states it is the same. In 39 states the maximum census age is higher than the maximum compulsory attendance age, and in 9 it is the same. In 22 states the census ages are the same as the legal school ages. In 33 the minimum census age is the same as the minimum legal age for admission to school, in 11 it is less, and in 4 it is greater. In 31 states the maximum census age is the same as the maximum legal age for school attendance, in 15 it is less, and in 2 states it is greater.

ADMISSION TO PRE-PRIMARY SCHOOL

Admission to the Nursery School. The nursery school, originally developed as a school for youngsters from one or two to six years of age, was an effort to provide for young children of working mothers, more especially those who were suffering from neglect and abuse as a result of social and industrial conditions. Its early leaders conceived it as an establishment which should provide physical care and training in desirable social habits for the little ones of the working classes. It was soon observed that *all* children of these tender ages could easily profit by the opportunities provided.

Admission to nursery school has been influenced by the type of the school itself. Forest has identified six types, which indicate somewhat the various groups of children served: (1) the research-center nursery school; (2) the cooperative nursery school; (3) the private-school nursery group; (4) the philanthropic nursery school; (5) the nursery school conducted as part of a teacher-training program; and (6) the federal relief nursery school.[1] Some children need primarily physical care, as children of working mothers; some are largely in need of observation because of their naïveté; some have nervous, mental, or social maladjustments; and some are the children of mothers who feel ill-adapted to raising them or who wish to use their time for matters of seemingly greater importance. Out of the admission practices in use has grown an institutional pattern in which all children from the ages of two to four or five years can easily profit. Unfortunately, however, these benefits are extended to comparatively few.

Kindergarten Admission Practices. Quite the reverse of the nursery school, kindergartens when first introduced into this country were organized privately for the benefit of the children of the well-to-do. Gradually their advantages to all children came to be realized, especially as public school systems began to incorporate them within the school organization. The fact that kindergartens are both publicly and privately controlled is some indication of the types and social status of the children attending.

Otto[2] has given us perhaps the best information on current admission practices to the kindergarten. Chronological age is the most frequently used basis. Provision is usually made for admission between the ages of four and six years, the median age being about five years. Within these age limits many interpretations are needed. Children

---

[1] Ilse Forest, *The School for the Child from Two to Eight,* Boston, Ginn and Company, 1935, p. 43.

[2] Henry J. Otto, *Promotion Policies and Practices in Elementary Schools,* Educational Monograph No. 5, Minneapolis, Educational Test Bureau, 1935, p. 5.

are usually admitted once a year, although provision is made in some districts to admit them twice a year, and, more rarely, at any time. Opportunities for admission vary usually with the number of children to be accommodated and the facilities available. The length of the kindergarten period is also a factor. This varies from one-half (usually one) year to two years.

Pre-Primary Groupings. Much experimentation is proceeding at the pre-primary level in order to adapt the nature of the instruction to the specific needs of the child. A form of organization is sought to provide for a better integration of needs at this level. This is indicated in a study of selected school systems reporting some type of pre-primary organization and instruction made by McIlhattan[3] in 1941. Out of 280 school systems reporting, he found that the term *kindergarten* was used in 176 (62.8 per cent), *pre-primary* in 39, *junior-primary* in 15, and *five-year-olds* in 10. A total of 38 different designations of pre-primary groupings was found, among them being *junior first grade, reading readiness group, first grade "B," pre-first grade, pre-school, pre-reading group, five-year primary, beginners, transition class, entering group,* and *play group.*

The name of the grouping is a general indication of the nature of the admission requirement. It is assumed that each of the designations bears some relation to the needs of the child admitted and the work of the group. In view of the fact that these forms of organization are definitely associated with public elementary schools, one can note the trend toward inclusion of various forms of pre-primary groupings within the framework of the public education.

ADMISSION TO THE ELEMENTARY SCHOOL

First-Grade Admission Practices. The age for admission to the first grade of the elementary school is commonly identical with the usual legal age of admission, namely, six years. However, in practice there are many interpretations of this age requirement. Otto[4] reports thirteen different interpretations based on an annual promotional basis, such as becoming six years old before September 1, or other specified days. Where promotion is made on a semi-annual

---

[3] William H. McIlhattan, *Factors Associated with Admission to the Work of the First Grade,* Doctor's Dissertation, University of Pittsburgh, 1941.

[4] Otto, *op. cit.,* p. 7.

basis, ten different interpretations are noted. Later admission to the first grade due to the health of the child, parental or school neglect, or for other reasons may result in retardation and should be guarded against carefully, except where the interests of the child may be favored.

Thus, while chronological age is the basis of admittance to the first grade, exceptions are constantly made to the general rule. Some of the most frequent are: the child moves in from an outside district; his birthday falls a few days on either side of the specified age date; he has been tutored; he has had previous kindergarten training; variations in ability are shown by tests; special board action has been taken; the child gives evidence of advanced maturity; and any combination of factors and circumstances may call for an exception.

The practice of annual admission to the first grade on the age basis, with the exceptions that take place in many school systems and the high percentage of children who fail to be promoted at the end of the first year, has resulted in a wide range in ages of first-grade children—from 4½ years to 9½ years, with children occasionally older. Recently there has been an earnest effort to associate other factors in admitting children to the first year of the elementary school. Probably the best study of preferred factors has again been made by McIlhattan,[5] who secured data from 280 selected school systems. The different factors reported, including chronological age, are indicated in Table 7.

The table shows that there is a definite tendency to regard factors other than chronological age for admission to the first grade. Perhaps the outcome of experimentation along these lines will be a merging of all pre-primary and primary groupings into a definitely identified elementary school organization in which children will be admitted at ages considerably under six years. Within this school organization will be arranged groupings which seem to fit the varied needs of the children, physically, mentally, emotionally, socially, as well as their ability to profit by the elementary skills. Thus, many factors will need to be taken into consideration in admitting, as well as assigning, the child in order for him to profit most by his environment and instruction.

---

[5] McIlhattan, *op. cit.* The 280 school systems studied were those reported as engaged in preferred administrative practices. Nearly all states were included.

Additional Admission Requirements. Evidence of successful vaccination against smallpox is demanded in most states. Some states require serum injections for certain diseases, as well as freedom from contagious disease at the time of admission. There is usually a residence requirement. Non-educable children may not be ad-

TABLE 7. FACTORS ASSOCIATED WITH ADMISSION
TO FIRST GRADE IN 280 SELECTED SCHOOL
SYSTEMS

Factor	Frequency of Use
1. Chronological age	255
2. Reading readiness	128
3. General ability	128
4. Mental age	109
5. General health	100
6. Social maturity	92
7. Emotional development	78
8. Physical maturity	78
9. Desirable habits	54
10. Test results	51
11. Parents' attitude	46
12. Home environment	31
13. Motor control	8
14. Vocabulary	4
15. Attendance at kindergarten	4
16. Teachers' judgment	3

mitted, and hence must be provided for otherwise as the law allows.

Thus, although chronological age is the chief factor in first-grade admission, being perhaps the only accurate measure we now have and quite easy to administer, other factors are being taken into consideration as experimentation shows their value.[6] Since the conditions surrounding the admission of the child to the educational processes are so important in his school progress, every effort should be made to develop a combination of all those factors which will assure his *continuous progress.*

In view of the fact that group instruction is characteristic of most elementary schools, now organized as a year to a grade, admission

---

[6] Compare P. R. Mort and W. B. Featherstone, *Entrance and Promotion Practices in City School Systems,* New York, Teachers College, Columbia University, 1928.

is generally on an annual basis. If it were possible to provide adequately for individualized instruction, admission to first grade could be arranged at any time as is done when pupils of later grades move into or within the school district.

Some authorities state that the mental age of a child should be 6½ years to permit successful achievement in the average first grade. If one considers normal I.Q.'s to extend from 70 upward, normal children of six years' chronological age would vary from approximately 4¼ years to 7¾ years in mental age.[7]

These considerations indicate that according to some authorities mental age is a better criterion for entrance to school than chronological age. However, readiness, social adjustment, health, economic background, and motor coordination may be effective factors in the success of the first-grader.

Admission to the Secondary School

The Incidence of Adolescence. The monumental studies of G. Stanley Hall on adolescence[8] may be said to indicate the basis for the modern differentiation between elementary and secondary school. Perhaps we are indebted to Inglis[9] more than any other person for an exhaustive analysis of the nature and traits of the secondary pupil upon which the modern secondary school program could be organized. It is interesting to note that his work appeared about the same time that the Commission on the Reorganization of Secondary Education (1912–1922) issued its famous report on the Cardinal Principles of Secondary Education. Inglis not only examined traits and characteristics of secondary school pupils but formulated principles and aims which have profoundly influenced the administration and program of the secondary school. He conceived these aims to be the preparation of the individuals (1) as a prospective citizen and cooperating member of society, (2) as a prospective worker and producer, and (3) as one who will make use of those cultural activities which enrich leisure time and encourage the development of personality.

As an outcome of these influences, the secondary school has come

---

[7] R. W. Edmistan and C. E. Hallahan, "Measures Predictive of First Grade Achievement," *School and Society,* April, 1946, p. 268.

[8] G. Stanley Hall, *Adolescence,* New York, D. Appleton Company, 1904.

[9] Alexander Inglis, *Principles of Secondary Education,* Boston, Houghton Mifflin Company, 1918.

to be considered principally as an *institution for the education of the adolescent* selected according to his ability to profit by these aims, and gradually eliminated if such ability was lacking. The four-year high school consisting of grades nine through twelve became the typical form of the secondary school seemingly best adapted for the accomplishment of these aims.

The Junior High School. The movement to reorganize secondary education began to make itself felt in the emergence of the junior high school. The benefits of secondary education were extended downward to include children of the seventh and eighth grades, many of whom were adolescent or moving into adolescence. It was believed that the needs of these children, when joined with the children of the ninth grade, could be realized far better in a separate institution known as the junior high school. Koos[10] in 1927 made a careful survey of available literature and characterized the junior high school as having eleven peculiar functions, all of which center around providing a better type of education as well as environment for the early adolescent. Ten years later, Pringle still characterized it as "an organization of the seventh, eighth, and ninth grades into an administrative unit for the purpose of providing instruction and training suitable to the varied and changing physical, mental, and social natures and needs of immature, maturing and mature (adolescent) pupils."[11]

It was Morrison,[12] however, who endeavored to give us a clear-cut distinction between the elementary and the secondary school, with the differing functions of each. He held that a pupil is ready to enter the secondary school when he has attained the four primary adaptations, namely, handwriting, number, reading, and social, and that he completes the secondary school as soon as he becomes capable of pursuing self-dependent study and of utilizing the instructor as one would ordinarily use the library, the laboratory, the occasional public lecturer, or the office consultant.

The Tendency. These purposes and distinctions serving to characterize the work of the secondary schools, both junior and senior,

---

[10] Leonard V. Koos, *The Junior High School*, Boston, Ginn and Company, 1921, p. 17.

[11] Ralph W. Pringle, *The Junior High School*, New York, McGraw-Hill Book Company, 1937, p. 68.

[12] Henry C. Morrison, *The Practice of Teaching in the Secondary School*, Chicago, University of Chicago Press, rev. ed., 1931, chap. i.

indicate the *basis of admission* to them. This would seem to include all adolescent children who could profit in any manner by the instruction provided, especially as compulsory ages were extended upward, and more and more adolescent youth came into the secondary school. The reorganization movement to embrace the junior high school has brought and retained more pupils in school. Enrollments have grown until today the secondary schools enroll approximately 80 per cent of all youth of high school age. Some state laws specifically provide for the extension of school facilities and opportunities up to the age of twenty-one years. As a result, admission requirements have become so simple as to allow entrance to any person of secondary school age (adolescent), usually from twelve or thirteen to eighteen or nineteen years, who can profit by the opportunities offered and who will not, because of physical, mental, moral, or social handicaps, become a menace to other pupils. Upon admittance, it becomes the problem of the secondary school to classify and place him so that he can benefit by the instruction offered. Thus, the tendency is definitely toward liberal admission requirements with wider adaptations to all abilities and needs through different forms of school organization and classification.

Private secondary education is much more selective. Many private schools admit on the basis of examination, ability to pay, parental tradition and influence, promise of success, specific college entrance needs, and other specific requirements.[13]

QUESTIONS AND PROBLEMS

1. Compare by reference to earlier chapters and contemporary literature progress made in procedures for admission to elementary and secondary schools.
2. Evaluate the scientific basis of admission standards set forth in this chapter.
3. Evaluate the grade-a-year policy in admitting pupils.
4. Study and report on the admission practices in your state as set forth by law or regulation.
5. Construct a formula for admitting children to (*a*) kindergarten, (*b*) elementary school, based on a combination of factors as found by McIlhattan.

---

[13] The student is referred to Porter Sargent, *A Handbook of Private Schools,* published by the author, Boston, 1946–47.

6. To what extent are teachers' judgments a reliable index in admitting pupils to the (*a*) elementary, (*b*) secondary school?
7. Set up defensible criteria for admittance to (*a*) junior high school, (*b*) senior high school, (*c*) other types of high schools.
8. Indicate essential records to a preferred admission plan.
9. Make a report on one or more school systems to determine admission practices.

SELECTED REFERENCES

1. Espy, Herbert G., *The Public Secondary School*. Boston: Houghton Mifflin Company, 1939, chaps. iii, xiv.
2. Forest, Ilse, *The School for the Child from Two to Eight*. Boston: Ginn and Company, 1935.
3. Hildreth, Gertrude, "Age Standards for First Grade Entrance," *Childhood Education,* September, 1946, pp. 22–27.
4. Landis, Paul H., *Adolescence and Youth*. New York: McGraw-Hill Book Company, 1945.
5. Lane, Robert Hill, *The Progressive Elementary School*. Boston: Houghton Mifflin Company, 1938.
6. Main, Zilpha, and Horn, Ellen A., "Empirically Determined Grade Norms as a Factor in the Educational Adjustment of the Average Child," *Journal of Educational Research,* November, 1937, pp. 161–171.
7. McGaughy, J. R., *An Evaluation of the Elementary School*. Indianapolis: The Bobbs-Merrill Company, 1937, chap. vii.
8. McIlhattan, William H., *Factors Associated with Admission to the Work of the First Grade,* Doctor's Dissertation, University of Pittsburgh, 1941.
9. Mort, Paul, *The Individual Pupil*. New York: American Book Company, 1928.
10. Otto, Henry J., *Promotion Policies and Practices in Elementary Schools*. Minneapolis: Educational Test Bureau, 1935.
11. *Planning for American Youth*. Washington: National Association of Secondary School Principals, 1944.
12. Reeder, Ward G., *The Fundamentals of Public School Administration*. New York: The Macmillan Company, 1941, chap. xx.
13. Sargent, Porter, *A Handbook of Private Schools*. Published by the author, Boston, 1946–47.
14. Wiley, George M., Jr., *The Redirection of Secondary Education*. New York: The Macmillan Company, 1940, chaps. iii, iv.
15. Wrinkle, William L., *The New High School in the Making*. New York: American Book Company, 1938, chap. iii.

CHAPTER IX

Classification of Pupils—
Assignment and Grouping

PROVISION having been made for the child's admission to school in accordance with legal and other requirements, he must now be properly assigned to an educational space and within an appropriate educational pattern which will allow him to make the greatest educational progress possible for him. Ideally, assignment should be made to an educational environment such that instruction can be readily adapted to his individual progress.

This chapter sets forth the fundamental principles and practices associated with the assignment of children. After a consideration of certain functional concepts, the evolution of grouping is discussed. Present practices and newer tendencies in assignment and grouping constitute the larger part of the chapter.

FUNCTIONAL CONCEPTS

In classifying pupils, two functions of education must be kept clearly in mind, namely, the integrating and the differentiating functions. These apply to all levels of education. In their application, the student should always keep in mind that the different units of the school system are to be considered in accordance with the integrating functions they perform, rather than as divisions made up of so many separate grades, groups, or years. Within each group, the emphasis should be upon the greatest possible educational and social maturation and advancement of each pupil, considering the educational objectives to be attained.

The Integrating Function. Man's responsibility to man demands the acquisition of many knowledges, skills, and appreciations, most of which must be acquired through the school. The integrating function must recognize this fundamental social objective. The school should teach common understandings, common ideals, common attitudes, and a body of common knowledges and skills such as will enable all men to live together with full recognition of their mutual responsibilities and obligations. These facts should be taken into consideration in classifying pupils, and should apply on all levels of education.

The Differentiating Function. The differentiating function is based upon the well-known fact that children differ. The existence of individual differences is a normal condition of nature. They cannot be eliminated even though it be thought desirable to eliminate them. When one examines the scores of any test, however simple, he is impressed with the wide range of achievement and abilities revealed. Individuals are unlike not only physically but in abilities and many other characteristics. While it is true that one may tend to display superiority in one direction, he may be less proficient in another.

Provision for individual differences must be considered as an important part of the educational function. Each pupil's varying abilities and characteristics must be studied if he is to develop as he should in the direction of a balanced life. At the same time education tends to increase rather than decrease certain divergences among individuals. This is shown in comparing cultures and civilizations as well as persons.

EVOLUTION OF GROUP INSTRUCTION

Individual Instruction. In an earlier chapter we pointed out that individual instruction characterized many early schools, the pupil coming to the teacher's desk to recite his lesson learned by rote. Some attempts were made to classify children into groups according to reading ability by assigning them a particular reader or speller. However, instruction and recitation were largely individual. As more and more children came to be educated, especially poor children, group instruction came into vogue. Children were often grouped according to the potentialities of their future careers and sent to appropriate schools and classes. For the most part, however, early schools were ungraded, with individualized instruction predominating. These continued to exist even to a generation or so ago, especially in rural areas. Similar situations will not be difficult to locate in many present-day rural schools.

Introduction of Grading. We have noted how the idea of grading children—a year to a grade—was first introduced in Boston in 1848, and was widely advocated by Horace Mann and Henry Barnard. By 1870 most public elementary schools were organized to include eight grades. Pupils were classified according as they fitted into, and were able to meet, grade requirements. Perhaps the graded reader and speller have been the most significant instruments in determining classification in each grade. Modern textbooks are still organized and written according to this principle.[1] Many other factors have recently been introduced to determine grade placement.

FACTORS IN ASSIGNMENT

Group Instruction by Grades. The concept of the graded school, with a year to a grade, has come to be the chief factor in the assignment of pupils, with group instruction as the primary characteristic. In the elementary school, largely because of necessity, group instruction is well established. Since the cost of individual instruction for every child is prohibitive, mass teaching offers the only satisfactory procedure. Through group instruction, it is argued, children's needs can be better ascertained; group discussion becomes more stimulating; social needs are better taken care of; failures are reduced; irregular progress is discouraged through group action; and leadership and initiative are developed through competition. Moreover, pupils' attitudes toward the whole educational process are improved, discipline can be maintained en masse, and costs are materially reduced.

Assignment of pupils should consist in so placing them that the fullest opportunities for educational growth occur, considering also teachers, rooms, facilities, locations, environment, and other factors.

Advantages of Individual and Group Instruction Compared. At this point it is appropriate to summarize the advantages of individual and group instruction so that the reader will be able to see both sides of a still controversial question. As a matter of fact any teacher may use both forms in the course of her daily teachings. The

---

[1] The reader should review early methods of classifying pupils as found in Chapter III.

controversy centers around the prevailing method used. The advantages claimed for each are as follows:

A. Advantages of Individual Instruction
   1. It permits the slow child to go at his own rate and thus gets better and more thorough results.
   2. It prevents the child from overestimating his progress.
   3. It concentrates the attention upon the work of individuals rather than upon the average work of the class.
   4. It allows the more gifted to go ahead and use his extra power upon the work of his own choice. It thus prevents him from falling into habits of idleness.
   5. It permits the teacher to catch little glimpses of the child's interests and possible vocational tendencies.
   6. It gives the teacher an opportunity to develop diagnostic skill in ascertaining just how a child's mind works as it finds its way through a problem.
B. Advantages of Group Instruction
   1. It makes better provision for the social aspects of education, because there is opportunity for cooperation, speech, social and political participation.
   2. It assists in motivation, because it appeals to the desire for the good opinion of others, and to the interest in group-discovered problems.
   3. It is economical, because it saves duplicate preparation and explanation.
   4. It permits the slow learner to get something from the more rapid learner.
   5. It also enables the fast learner to learn his material better through the experience of explaining it to the slower pupil.
   6. It reduces the amount of preparation that the teacher must make for her daily work and simplifies the problem of management and discipline.[2]

Ability Grouping. The significant discovery that children differ plays an important part in their classification by ability. Although the subject of ability grouping is controversial in certain respects, the significant evidence will be presented in order to indicate its relation to the classification and progress of pupils.

---

[2] Clapp, Chase, and Merriman, *Introduction to Education,* Boston, Ginn and Company (1929), pp. 466–467.

Rankin[3] has summarized the most significant studies dealing with ability grouping in the following statements:

1. Evidence slightly favored homogeneous grouping as contrasted with heterogeneous grouping, especially where adaptations of methods and materials are made.
2. Most teachers prefer to work with homogeneous rather than heterogeneous groups.
3. Evidence regarding the relative merits of various bases of grouping is inconclusive.
4. Data adequate for evaluating various types of adaptation of materials and methods are not available.
5. Homogeneous grouping is most effective for dull children, and least valuable, at times harmful, for bright children.
6. The particular grade levels and subjects in which homogeneous grouping is most effective have not yet been fully determined.
7. Data regarding the effect of homogeneous grouping upon characteristics of pupils other than skills and knowledge are subjective and inconclusive.

As indicated above, ability grouping has many opponents. Significant arguments advanced against it are:

1. An adequate basis for grouping has not been scientifically determined.
2. Ability grouping does not approach real life situations in any respect.
3. Ability grouping develops class distinction—a sense of inferiority in the lower group and a feeling of superiority in the upper group; a stigma is attached to the lower group.
4. Ability is specific, therefore it is impossible to form groups that are homogeneous in each of the various subjects, with a single general classification.
5. Grouping on the basis of special ability is not practical from an administrative viewpoint.
6. The curriculum is not adjusted to the different levels of ability represented by the groups.
7. Ability grouping causes jealousy and resentment on the part of pupils and parents.
8. Teachers are not trained to teach effectively groups at the various levels of achievement.

[3] National Education Association, "Internal Organization of School Divisions," *Review of Educational Research*, October, 1934, pp. 382–389.

9. Ability grouping causes an undesirable competitive spirit between pupils, and in some cases between teachers and patrons.[4]

The principles of ability grouping have been adapted to many forms of school organization and pupil classification, on both elementary and secondary levels. In a sense, ability grouping is an attempt to approximate more closely individual instruction while retaining the group instruction principle.

CLASSIFICATION ON THE ELEMENTARY LEVEL

Current Procedures in Classifying Elementary Pupils. Perhaps the most significant survey as to classifying pupils for instructional purposes was made by Otto. He identified four policies:

Policy 1. The pupils of any one grade of the elementary schools of a system are not divided on the basis of intelligence or other measures into groups or sections for instructional purposes. The pupils are arbitrarily assigned to one or more rooms to obtain classes of convenient size.

Policy 2. The pupils of any one grade of the elementary schools of a system are divided on the basis of intelligence or other measures into two distinct sections. The pupils in each of the two groups are organized into classes for instructional purposes.

Policy 3. The pupils of any one grade of the elementary schools of a system are divided on the basis of intelligence or other measures into three distinct sections. The pupils in each of the three groups are organized into classes for instructional purposes.

Policy 4. Miscellaneous practices which could not be classified among policies 1, 2, or 3. Usually this practice refers to the division of the pupils of a grade into four, five, or a number of groups.[5]

In his analysis Otto pointed out that Policy 2 was most frequently used as a method of classification (about 44 per cent). There is a definite tendency to use objective data in some form in classifying pupils.

Bases Commonly Used. In classifying children in the elementary schools, the bases most commonly used are chronological age, mental age, educational age, social age, intelligence quotient, and teacher's

---

[4] J. H. Dougherty, F. H. Gorman, and C. A. Phillips, *Elementary School Organization and Management,* New York, The Macmillan Company, 1936, p. 265.

[5] H. J. Otto, "Current Practices in the Organization of Elementary Schools," *Northwestern University Contributions to Education,* Series No. 5, pp. 32–33.

judgment. While no single basis may be said to be used exclusively, the most common one is the chronological age of the pupil. Although mental age is used to some extent, perhaps the most reliable single measure is the educational age, especially in the middle grades of the elementary school. More recently, attention has been given to the child's social age, especially since each school group reveals a wide range of social maturity. Until more reliable instruments of measure are developed, social age cannot be used as extensively as its value would seem to warrant. Teacher's judgment still remains one of the predominating bases of classifying pupils, although every teacher would admit earnest efforts to utilize impartially all data at hand.

Classification at the Pre-Primary Level. Chronological age has been the chief basis for classification at the pre-primary level. Within the larger group, however, small groups have been organized around the maturity of the child, physical or social attributes, and other factors. As a matter of fact, the smaller numbers of children in attendance in classes at the pre-primary level have tended to allow individual instruction far more than is commonly practiced at the elementary level. A combination of factors should be considered as a basis for pre-primary classification.[6]

Grouping Within the Grade. Grouping of children within each grade is a common practice in the elementary school. It came about through (1) development of a large body of data on individual differences and (2) progress of the testing movement and its application to the field of education. Contributions of Terman and others as to intelligence and results of achievement tests have usually been used as a basis for classification. Teacher judgment is often used. Perhaps the most significant example of this method of classification is the Detroit X-Y-Z plan, in which children are grouped as bright, normal, and slow, respectively. The course of study is modified to meet the needs of these different groups. A much broadened curriculum is provided to meet the needs of the X or bright group as compared with the Y group, while the Z group is expected to complete only certain minimum essentials. Transfer of pupils from one group to another on the basis of progress is possible at stated intervals.

---

[6] Consult McIlhattan's findings, *op. cit.*

A Summary of Bases for Classification. Bringing together the bases that are commonly used in the classification of pupils in the elementary school, one finds a formidable list. Heck[7] reports the following list, which has been rearranged in order of frequency (Table 8).

TABLE 8. FREQUENCY WITH WHICH DIFFERENT FACTORS ARE MENTIONED AS OF CHIEF IMPORTANCE IN GROUPING

Rank	Factor	Frequency
1	Teacher's estimate of intelligence	576
2	Mental age as obtained from group testing	231
3	Teacher's marks	209
4	Intelligence quotient as obtained from group testing	154
5	Teacher's estimate of industry	135
6	Standardized educational tests	67
7	Results of individual intelligence testing	44
8	Previous school marks	32
9	Chronological age	18
10	Health	2

It will be noted that "teacher estimate of intelligence," by which is also probably meant achievement, is ranked first. Chronological age has received a low rank in this table; yet it is one of the chief bases for grouping little children. Until a scientific formula is developed which will take into proper consideration the complex factors necessary to pupil classification and progress, the teacher's estimate with its personal and emotional aspects and bias will probably remain the primary factor in classification.[8]

Scientific Classification. Since the object in classifying the child is definitely to assure his greater progress in the environment which the school offers, whatever valid, reliable, and objective information can be brought to bear to assist in better classification should be carefully considered. This suggests the need of adequate training on the part of all teachers, principals, and supervisors who are concerned with this important function. Where school marks are the

---

[7] Arch O. Heck, *Administration of Pupil Personnel,* Boston, Ginn and Company, 1929, p. 450.

[8] See Philip Boyer, "The Administration of Learning Groups in Elementary Schools," *Thirty-Fifth Yearbook,* National Society for the Study of Education, 1936, part i, pp. 191–215.

basis of assignment, efforts should be made to determine them as objectively as possible through sound statistical procedures. Where test results are used, as in determining mental age, educational age, or intelligence quotients, care should be exercised in their administration. Even teacher judgment may well have some objective basis.

McCall and Bixler[9] have advocated a classification by which pupils are assigned to grades and classes according to grade scores abbreviated as "G" scores. Russell[10] recommends a promotion quotient technique which considers the relationship of the work and status of a pupil compared with other pupils of his own chronological age. The probable rate of growth expected of him may thus be determined.

The use of intelligence and achievement tests is too well known to need discussion here.

Recognizing the need for a more scientific determination of the bases for classification and assignment, we must still be careful not to lose sight of the progress and welfare of the child in the maze of statistical procedures and ponderous data.

CLASSIFICATION ON THE SECONDARY LEVEL

Bases Commonly Used. Many of the principles and practices which have been discussed in the preceding section have equal application to the classification of pupils on the secondary level. Teachers' estimates of pupils gathered largely from previous grades or marks have been the most important factor therein. In fact, grades and marks have become the chief selective agent in the elimination of the "unfit," and in giving character to the secondary school population. Since they have played and now play such an important part, students of education should recall the overwhelming evidence which points out the unreliability of teachers' marks.

Grouping of pupils in the secondary school occurs through selection of, or assignment to, specific courses of study, as academic, scientific, commercial, and vocational curricula. Choices affect assignment, as in elective or college-preparatory courses, one's circle of

[9] W. A. McCall and Harold H. Bixler, *How to Classify Pupils,* New York, Bureau of Publications, Teachers College, Columbia University, 1928; W. A. McCall, *Tables for the T-G-B-F Scale System,* New York, Bureau of Publications, Teachers College, Columbia University.

[10] Charles Russell, *Standard Tests,* Boston, Ginn and Company, 1930.

friends, and economic and social factors of home and community environment. Pupils are classified and transferred as their abilities seem to indicate or predict, or as personal or parental choices dictate.

Some form of homogeneous grouping became necessary when large numbers of pupils came into the high schools and were retained in them through compulsory education laws or socio-economic conditions. In actual practice homogeneous grouping has come to mean classification into bright, normal, and slow groups, although plans are in operation which attempt to provide for certain types of individualized instruction, amounting theoretically to individual placement. In order to place the pupil in the proper group, mental achievement and aptitude tests, teachers' judgments of ability, intelligence, and personality, previous marks, chronological age, sex, and other factors are used.

Summary of Plans in Use. Plans in general use in secondary schools to meet individual differences include (1) homogeneous grouping, (2) special classes, (3) plans characterized by the unit assignment, (4) scientific study of problem cases, (5) variation in pupil load, (6) out-of-school projects and studies, and (7) advisory or guidance programs. Many if not all of these plans are applicable to the elementary school. The first three, homogeneous grouping, special classes, and the unit assignment, are most frequently used. The literature also reveals application of the principles underlying these plans to traditional secondary school organization and grouping, such as unit assignments, library-centered curricula, and project teaching, with accompanying devices such as the school journey.

Summary of Factors in Secondary School Classification. We are now ready to bring together the factors essential to secondary school classification. In general they have equal application to the elementary school. The order of the following is inconsequential.

BASES OF APPRAISAL. The pupil's record should be examined with care. Undoubtedly, teachers' judgments have entered, and will enter, into the record at many points. There is nothing particularly odious about a reliable judgment on the part of any teacher, if he has arrived at such judgment as objectively and impartially as possible. Special attention should be directed to judgments where subjective tests, such as the usual school examination or quiz, are used and where measures of the evaluation of such tests are faulty.

The teacher and principal should have a definite knowledge of reliable objective measuring devices and a reasonable skill in their use. This involves knowledge of statistical procedures and terminology, and the ability to interpret test results. Adequate guidance techniques should be known and applied.

KNOWLEDGE OF THE PUPIL. The pupil should be studied and records kept of his personality characteristics, especially those likely to enhance or impede further progress. Ineffective habits of work, deficiencies in previous education, physical defects, mental disabilities or quirks of any kind, personality difficulties, or emotional or psychological deviations should be noted.[11] Then there are various maturity levels, physical, mental, social, and emotional, which suggest temporary assignment. The child should be studied for those characteristics which may be the outcome of peculiar home and environmental conditions. His attitudes and aspirations are important, as well as his previous and present social behavior. As far as possible he should be kept with the group to which he socially and chronologically belongs. In short, his complete school record should be reviewed, and all data of a permanent nature gathered which will throw any light on his attainments and prospects.

KNOWLEDGE OF THE PROGRAM. In order to assign all pupils properly, the one responsible for this task should have a thorough knowledge of school organization plans, objectives, programs, procedures, and values. Some general knowledge of curricula is essential as well as the content of subjects, the methods used, and the teachers assigned. Above all, he should know the usefulness of each to the pupil, both now and later. Within the school it may be necessary to assign the pupil for temporary adjustment. He should ponder how the school organization can best be modified to meet the pupil's needs, interests, and capacities.

THE EXCEPTIONAL PUPIL. Special consideration should be given when assigning those pupils who vary markedly from the normal

---

[11] Wm. C. Reavis, *Pupil Adjustment,* Boston, D. C. Heath and Company, 1926; Roy O. Billett, "Provisions for Educational Differences, Marking, and Promotion," Survey of Secondary Education, *Bulletin No. 17,* Washington, Government Printing Office, 1932. See also Arch O. Heck, "Contributions of Research to the Classification, Promotion, Marking, and Certification of Pupils," in "The Scientific Movement in Education," *Thirty-Seventh Yearbook,* National Society for the Study of Education, Bloomington: Public School Publishing Company, 1938, part ii, pp. 187–199; A. E. Traxler, *Techniques of Guidance,* New York, Harper & Brothers, 1945; H. H. Remmers and N. L. Gage, *Educational Measurement and Evaluation,* New York, Harper & Brothers, 1943.

groups. Variations may be of a physical, mental, social, or emotional nature. Special classes may be arranged to care for accelerated or retarded groups, gifted children, or any others who come within this classification. Children of similar characteristics may be grouped without too great regard for chronological or mental age achievement. Instruction must, of necessity, be largely individualized. Certain classroom procedures and equipment are necessary for the proper instruction of these groups. A later chapter will discuss exceptional children in greater detail.

LIMITATIONS OF SCHOOL AND COMMUNITY   Since the typical high school in the United States is not large, and since there are still so many small elementary schools, largely rural, it will be difficult, even impossible, to apply all of these principles. A community attitude may be such as to frown upon new methods and procedures. Even the administration or the teachers may not be sympathetic. While these limitations must be recognized, the teacher and principal owe their best endeavors to each child. The greatest problem facing every teacher will be his own limitations; he should free himself from every shade of, and inclination toward, personal bias or favoritism. Perhaps his second greatest problem will be to overcome his own inertia.

QUESTIONS AND PROBLEMS

1. Show by examples that you have a clear notion of the distinction between the integrating and the differentiating function in education.
2. Evaluate the grade-a-year policy of admitting and classifying children.
3. Make a list of the legal requirements in your state in regard to the admission of children.
4. Compare the usual admission practices in (a) nursery school, (b) kindergarten, and (c) elementary school as to objectivity and provision for the progressive development of each child.
5. Construct a formula for admitting children to the elementary school based on a combination of factors as found by McIlhattan.
6. Comment on the statement, "Adolescence should be the chief factor in admitting children to the secondary school, including the junior high school."
7. What is meant by scientific classification? Evolve a plan for the elementary school; for the secondary school.
8. Evaluate the arguments for and against ability grouping.
9. Miss Jones, who has taught for twenty years, states that her judg-

ment in classifying pupils is just as reliable as any so-called scientific plan she has ever seen in operation. Comment on her statement.

SELECTED REFERENCES

1. Bent, R. K., and Kronenberg, H. H., *Principles of Secondary Education.* New York: McGraw-Hill Book Company, 1941, chaps. xi, xii.
2. Drake, L. N., "Administrative Techniques Used for Pupil Adjustment in Junior High Schools," *American School Board Journal,* May, 1940, pp. 21–22.
3. "Five Unifying Factors in American Education," *Ninth Yearbook,* Department of Superintendence. Washington: National Education Association, 1931, part i, "Pupil Promotion Problems."
4. "Grouping of Pupils, The" *Thirty-Fifth Yearbook,* National Society for the Study of Education. Bloomington: Public School Publishing Company, 1936, part i.
5. Helseth, I. O., "On Grouping Children in School," *Childhood Education,* February, 1944, pp. 250–259.
6. Jackson, George T., "Each According to His Ability," *School Executive,* January, 1943, pp. 37–38.
7. Keliher, Alice V., *Critical Study of Homogeneous Grouping,* Contributions to Education, No. 452. New York: Teachers College, Columbia University, 1931.
8. Lindel, Albert, "Upgrading Retarded Pupils," *Journal of Education,* April, 1947, pp. 132–134.
9. Newson, Langfitt, and others, *Administrative Practices in Large High Schools.* New York: American Book Company, 1940, chap. xv.
10. Otto, Henry J., *Promotion Policies and Practices in Elementary Schools.* Minneapolis: Educational Test Bureau, 1935.
11. Otto, Henry J., "Use of Social Criteria in Grouping Children at School," *Childhood Education,* March, 1946, pp. 326–329.
12. "Pupil Personnel, Guidance and Counseling," *Review of Educational Research,* April, 1939.
13. "Scientific Movement in Education, The," *Thirty-Seventh Yearbook,* National Society for the Study of Education, Bloomington: Public School Publishing Company, 1938, chaps. xvi, xvii, xxxii, xxxiii.
14. Stevens, G. D., "Evaluation of Some Methods of Organization of Classes for the Mentally Retarded Adolescent," *Educational Administration and Supervision,* April, 1945, pp. 193–204.
15. Willcockson, Mary, "How Ability Groups Improve Social Climate," *Education Digest,* December, 1946, pp. 28–31.
16. Wofford, Kate V., *Modern Education in the Small Rural School.* New York: The Macmillan Company, 1938.

CHAPTER X

Classification of Pupils—Promotion and Non-Promotion

PERHAPS no other function of school administration is approached more seriously than the promotion of children; nor is there any in which greater individuality and tenacity of opinion on the part of teacher, principal, or superintendent exist. Indeed, one might add that there is not another contact of the school with the parent that is replete with greater emotional effect. Some of the most difficult problems that the school faces may be traced to decisions as to non-promotion. Every child in every part of the school system is affected by it directly or indirectly; every teacher is concerned with it; every principal has to face the responsibilities of having each child under his supervision pass on to the next grade, subject, or unit. Moreover, there is a definite relationship of all associated in promotion, each to the others.

Promotion is so thoroughly associated with the school organization and the pupil's admission to and classification in it that it can hardly be considered apart from them. The theories or notions one holds about the school and its philosophy are definitely a part of those held about promotion. Perhaps all would agree that the child should progress normally through the school organization and procedure, granting, of course, that these are well adapted to his needs, abilities, and interests. Difficulties, however, are encountered immediately one approaches the manner of accomplishing such progress.

It is proposed in this chapter to consider principles and practices underlying promotion to analyze the factors and causes incident to non-promotion, and to offer suggestions for individual and group adjustment as it affects school progress.

THE SIGNIFICANCE OF PROMOTION

Importance of Continuous Progress. On the assumption that every administrative and teaching endeavor should be focused on the natural and continuous educational progress of every child, it becomes a matter of vital importance to provide administratively for the smoothing of that progress through proper step-by-step advancement. To accomplish this purpose in the best interests of the child has been a problem wherever schools have existed. That school may be said to be well articulated where the greatest degree of educational smoothness has been achieved; and, conversely, to be poorly articulated where individual pupil progress is irregular or unnatural to any considerable extent.

Promotion a Stepping-Up. In any graded system, whether on the elementary or the secondary level, in which the goals to be achieved are more or less clearly defined completion of any level implies immediate promotion to the level above. The American school system, being a graded one, provides for the regular "stepping up" of every child, usually annually. The child then is said to have "passed," a truly joyous occasion. If he has not achieved the required goal, he is said to have failed, an occasion of frustration and sadness. Thus, honor and achievement are attached to the one; disgrace and dishonor to the other. While non-promotion is usually meant "to be in the best interests of the child," the accompanying emotional disturbances are not without their subsequent effects.

Promotion Conflicts. Principles and practices come into conflict in the administration of promotion. A human desire to allow the child to go forward with his group is balanced by standards of attainment to be maintained; possible conflict of judgment on the part of principal and teacher; parental factors of home environment, social status, or influence; the grading system; the next term's work; matters of intelligence, achievement, and deportment; strength and weakness in one or another subject; and many others. Then there are contingencies of class size, teacher load, good or poor teachers, the course of study itself, methods of teaching the school's philosophy, and, above all, the influence exercised by the superintendent or principal in regard to promotion policy.

Factors in Promotion. A study of promotion should take into consideration certain factors which must be associated in its administration. Among these are the intervals of promotion, basis of promotion especially in relation to specific school policies, promotion in different divisions of the school, and temporary or irregular promotions of one sort or another. All these must be considered in relation to the different divisions of the school system, as the elementary or the secondary school, and to administrative policies and attitudes in the same system and between school systems, as in the instance of transfer. Anticipated entrance to the work of a succeeding grade upon promotion from the grade below may be barred by examinations or other administrative hurdles.

Intervals of Promotion

Forms. Annual promotion is usual throughout the United States, being used in about half of the smaller cities and generally throughout small districts and rural areas. Semi-annual promotions are typical of larger cities of the United States, being found in nearly three-fourths of the cities with populations of 30,000 or more. Recently, however, there has been a definitely discernible tendency to return to the annual plan. The quarterly promotion plan, having units of work to be completed in nine or ten weeks, was first used in St. Louis. It has not been accepted elsewhere and has been recommended for abandonment in that city in favor of the annual plan.[1] Other promotion plans built around a unit-of-work plan of organization imply a form of promotion upon the completion of each unit.

Advantages and Disadvantages of Annual Promotion. Some eighteen arguments have been advanced, as reported by 555 school superintendents, in favor of the annual promotion.[2] Among these are: feasibility for the small school, longer teacher-pupil relationships, time saved from possible administrative disruptions during semiannual promotions, possibilities of homogeneous groupings, ease of pupil transfer from system to system, smaller teaching force, greater economy, conformity with community tradition and parental favor, elimination of half-grades in rooms, and greater ease in organizing materials of instruction. Outstanding disadvantages of annual promotions may be said to be: loss of a whole year in case of non-

---

[1] *A Report of a Survey of the Public Schools of St. Louis, Missouri,* New York, Bureau of Publications, Teachers College, Columbia University, 1939, pp. 373–374.

[2] "Five Unifying Factors in American Education," *Ninth Yearbook,* Department of Superintendence, Washington, National Education Association, 1931, part i, pp. 65–74.

promotion, tendency to retard superior children, inflexibility, confusion in transferring children, reduction of length of attendance especially in regard to failure, increase of retardation, higher costs, and difficulty in making up subjects.

Advantages and Disadvantages of Semi-Annual Promotion. It is possible to deduce advantages and disadvantages of semi-annual promotion upon careful study of the arguments presented above. One might summarize the advantages of semi-annual promotion as follows: In case of failure only one-half year is repeated; it is logical to repeat that portion of the work missed rather than a whole year; the school organization is made more flexible; acceleration is easier; costs are lower; more frequent evaluation of pupils' work is possible; there is greater ease in accommodating transfer children; fewer extremes of ability and social age occur within the same grade; there is less discouragement to pupils, less retardation, shorter time with a poor teacher; the curriculum is more adaptable; and the children are held in school longer.

Those school systems which have abandoned the semi-annual plan of promotion have been influenced by a combination of the following arguments: There are too many small sections in smaller schools; teacher turnover with pupils is too frequent; homogeneous groupings are more difficult to administer; the work of organization is multiplied; larger teaching force is required; disadvantages of mid-year promotion and graduation exist; and teachers tend to fail borderline cases and to think too much in terms of subject matter completed.

Promotion in the Elementary School

Practice. It has been pointed out that the chief motivating factor in the promotion of pupils at the end of any term is the desire to keep the child progressing regularly, as far as possible, from one measure of attainment to another. In estimating this attainment, account is usually taken of chronological age, scholastic achievement, and social maturity. Adjustment of individual pupils where advisable may be made through promotion at any time during the term.

The bases of promotion are often determined by administrative regulations, agreements among teachers, and community tradition. Otto reports twenty such regulations in the elementary schools (Table 9).

Theories of Promotion. Two theories or policies are held as to promotion in the elementary school: (1) The elementary school is an institution representing certain minimum standards of educational accomplishment for each grade and the school as a whole, the acquisition of which is the duty of every child before he is permitted

TABLE 9. GENERAL REGULATIONS COVERING PUPIL PROMOTION
AS STATED BY CLASSROOM TEACHERS[3]

Regulations	Frequency	Per Cent[a]
No rules..	203	11.92
Retain only those who are sure to profit by retention..	178	10.45
Fail if marks are below passing in two or three majors.	159	9.35
Chronological age should be a major factor..........	128	7.52
Achievement a major basis........................	83	4.88
Promote on 70–75 per cent efficiency..............	75	4.41
Promote on basis of general ability................	73	4.29
Social age.......................................	65	3.82
Minimum standards must be attained..............	60	3.52
Do not retain more than two years.................	57	3.35
Promote on ability to do work of next grade........	55	3.23
Mental age should be a factor.....................	54	3.17
Teacher's judgment...............................	45	2.64
Principal or superintendent decides................	34	2.00
100 per cent promotion...........................	27	1.58
Standard test used as basis........................	26	1.52
Reading ability should be basis....................	26	1.52
Faculty discussions...............................	22	1.29
Promote if possible to reduce failure..............	17	1.00
Warn parents on report card......................	14	0.82

[a] Percentage based on total of 1702 teacher blanks analyzed.

to pass to the next higher grade or school. (2) The elementary school is a school of a certain terminal length and when the child has remained there for the number of years indicated by the length of the course, he should be promoted to the next higher articulated division.

The first of these theories, generally held by large numbers of

[3] Henry J. Otto, *Promotion Policies and Practices in Elementary Schools,* Minneapolis, Educational Test Bureau, 1935, p. 25.

educators, is giving way to the second point of view, which is being accepted by a considerable group. This is especially true in regard to the six-year elementary school with the recognition of adolescence at the age of twelve or thirteen years as the terminal point. Naturally, the completion of any elementary program of study within a six-year period will force attention to more desirable methods of admission, classification and assignment, teaching and learning procedures, and adjustment and promotion within the elementary school itself.

The Primary Division. The heavy rate of non-promotion in the primary division of the elementary school, especially in the first grade, has long been a serious administrative problem. This has been complicated by the discovery of pronounced individual differences among children at the first point of school entrance. Thus, innovations in promotion are probably of most significance at the primary level. The first of these innovations is the use of mental and reading readiness tests to determine fitness to do the work of the succeeding grade. The use of these tests has tended to break down grade distinctions at the kindergarten-primary level. The second innovation is a plan to allow the pupils to remain with the same teacher throughout this period, namely, through the second and third grades, perhaps even through all elementary grades. A third plan is known as the flexible progress group system,[4] in which pupils are permitted to advance flexibly through a series of consecutive learning levels based upon mental maturity and reading ages.

Each of these plans emphasizes the scientific study of the child and endeavors to fit the school and its organization to his needs. Of significance is the fact that the teacher should remain with the child long enough to understand him *as both progress*. There is reason to suggest that the cooperative progress of teacher and group might well extend continuously beyond the third grade through the elementary school.

Proponents of the continuous progress concept point out that many of the administrative devices now attached to the grade-a-year promotional plan automatically disappear. If adapted to the primary unit of three years, it is conceivable that some children may take as many as four years to complete the work. If arranged to include the kindergarten, as some propose, the terminal years may be set

---

[4] Leonard B. Wheat, "The Flexible Progress Group System," *Elementary School Journal*, November, 1937, pp. 175–183.

definitely at eight or nine years of age. It is important to emphasize that pupils must be taught (and teachers likewise) to think more in terms of units of work to be mastered, not necessarily geared to a year's time. Teachers must also be required to assume more responsibility for the mastery of this work. One of the chief characteristics will be the development of objective evaluation procedures. It is conceivable also that the length of term may be increased in the case of some pupils, modified for others, in order to accomplish the desired mastery at its terminal point. We need much experimentation with this principle.

The Intermediate Grades. Efforts to bring about better promotional plans in the intermediate grades (fourth, fifth, and sixth) are centering largely in elimination of subject rather than grade failures, of which the most common are arithmetic and English. Since grade promotion is still characteristic of the intermediate grades, remedial efforts have focused on departmentalization accompanied by homogeneous grouping and diagnostic and remedial treatment. Attention should be directed toward better articulation with the seventh (junior high school) grade.

Much that has already been said about the continuous program principle applies as well to the intermediate grades. By this time, if properly taught, the pupil should have a thorough understanding of what is to be expected of him as he advances. Perhaps the teacher will need more assistance than the pupil. She should have an awareness not only of the work to be accomplished in her unit but of the work in preceding and succeeding units. When a teacher follows through with the pupils for a longer period, six years, for instance, a greater understanding of the continuity of progress should be evident, as has been characteristic of rural schools for many generations. The chief objection to continuous progress over long periods is the possibility that pupils may be subjected to a poor teacher. Perhaps there is no better way to find out about and eliminate her quickly.

The practice of terminal promotion at the end of six chronological years thus throws tremendous responsibility upon the junior high school to take and provide for the child *as it finds him*. Perhaps this is the major obligation of *every* division of the school system.

Problems of Promotion at the Elementary Level. The application of any administrative policy or set of promotion criteria may involve many problems. Many of them center around provision for individual differences, as in dull and gifted children. Double promotions, widely practiced with gifted children, are hazardous, bring eventual problems, and may not be the best answer. Teacher attitudes and varying preparation standards pose many problems. Home environment and attitudes may bring up questions of irregular attendance, social and physical maladjustments, lack of parental cooperation, and transfer. Administrative problems may have to do with curriculum adjustments, over-ageness, lack of standards, the grading system, and absence of pupils' scientific case histories.[5] If continuous progress is selected, it may take time and patience to orient both teachers and pupils. Curricula will have to be studied and adapted with great care and evaluation procedures carefully developed.

Promotion in the Secondary School

Practice. Bases of promotion in the secondary school are marks, final examinations, daily records and examinations, and other combinations with these which may include mental and achievement test scores, chronological age, points earned, total school record, citizenship, and physical and social maturity.

Subject promotion is generally accepted as the *modus operandi* in the secondary school. It has the advantages of permitting rapid advancement, making definite provision for special abilities and disabilities of children, bringing about more homogeneous grouping, and making a closer articulation of work among the different schools. Moreover, units of work offer greater ease in administration.

Subject promotion in itself does not tell the whole story in the secondary school. Sequences of subject matter may be required to be completed before graduation, as first and second years of a language or certain prerequisites for entrance upon a subject. Moreover, there are often course requirements within a curriculum. A specified number of Carnegie units must be completed before graduation, and state requirements must be met.

Both annual and semi-annual promotions are found at the secondary level. Difficulty of the curriculum or subject to be pursued

---

[5] For a good discussion of pupil case histories, see Ruth Strang, *Pupil Personnel and Guidance,* New York, The Macmillan Company, 1940, pp. 199–200.

may be considered as a factor in promotion. Pupils of superior ability are sometimes permitted to carry additional subjects, while pupils of lower ability may be confined to fewer subjects or required to remove "conditions." The promotion of pupils on the condition that they succeed in the next grade or subject is practiced extensively in the secondary schools, while the practice of requiring of failing pupils an additional burden of "conditions" along with their regular classes is happily passing. Then too, the secondary school often has a coaching plan to assist the needy student, largely on a subject matter basis. It is needness to remark that the pupil's work load should always be geared to his ability to progress effectively.

Promotion Remedies at the Secondary Level. Standards of promotion should be carefully studied at the secondary level. Basic to these should be more adequate classification and better adaptation of subject matter to varying needs and abilities. Measures of achievement, as grading and testing scores, should receive attention; so, also, should adequate records considered in the light of more complete case histories, leading to closer teacher-pupil understanding. Combinations of factors to be considered in promotion might well be discussed in teachers' meetings and conferences. Better supervisory techniques enter at this point and may be an important factor quite overlooked.

APPROACHES TO SCIENTIFIC PROMOTION

General Principles. One of the most comprehensive studies of pupil promotion throughout the school system was made by a committee of the Department of Superintendence and reported in the *Ninth Yearbook.*[6] This study has had a profound influence. The following principles were suggested:

1. Promotion should be decided on the basis of the individual pupil.
2. Promotion should be on the basis of many factors. The final decision as to whether a particular pupil should be promoted should rest not merely on academic accomplishment, but on what will result in the greatest good to and the all-around development of the individual.
3. In order that promotion procedures may be more or less uniform throughout a particular school system, a definite set of factors

---

[6] *Op. cit.,* chap. i.

should be agreed upon to be taken into consideration by each teacher in forming a judgment as to whether or not a particular pupil should be promoted.

4. Criteria for promotion must take into consideration the curriculum offerings of the next higher grade or unit and the flexibility of its organization, its course of study, and its methods.

5. It is the duty of the next higher grade or unit to accept pupils who are properly promoted to it from the lower grade or unit and to adapt its work to fit the needs of these pupils.

6. Promotion procedures demand continuous analysis and study of cumulative pupil case history records in order that refinement of procedure may result and guesswork and conjecture be reduced to a minimum.

The committee hastened to point out that promotion cannot be settled on the basis of any one of these principles alone; the six must be taken as a whole. In their application, however, varying local conditions will always have to be taken into consideration in the interests of the individual child.

Newer Tendencies in Promotion. The problems of promotion have always been real to teachers and school administrators. Various promotional schemes have been tried in the past in order to utilize adequately the pupil's capacities, achievements, interests, and abilities. Progressive schools are studying the best ways that this can be accomplished. However, research is limited. Without doubt there is still too much adherence to traditional academic standards.

The new education is looking forward along many lines to provide for the educational progress of each child. Several plans of promotion have been developed which seek to encourage uninterrupted progress. Two plans are mentioned:

1. Ungraded rapid promotion rooms. In this plan maladjusted children are placed in ungraded rooms and allowed to proceed in accordance with their ability and achievement. Instruction should approach individualization.

2. One hundred per cent promotion. Under this plan all children pass along with their group at each period of promotion without regard to subject matter or other achievement. Grouping by social maturity is an essential criterion in order to keep together children having about the same degree of social maturity. The grade concept is abandoned and replaced by such group designations as "first year," "sev-

enth year." Grouping within these years may be provided for as the needs of pupils indicate.[7]

Trial Promotions. Some form of promoting pupils *conditionally* may be found in approximately three-fourths of all school systems. Promotions of this type indicate some degree of uncertainty in the mind of the teacher or principal as to the ability of the pupil to progress with his group. Usually there is some extenuating circumstance, as absence due to illness or accident, change of school system, over-ageness, borderline achievement, or desire to stimulate greater effort.

The trial promotion may depend for its success on the pupil's attitude and effort, his mental and chronological ages, and the ability of the teacher in the next grade to meet adequately his needs. A new environment may work wonders with an indifferent pupil, especially when he realizes the import of the opportunity.

Many administrators are opposed to trial promotions largely on account of the possible effects of demotion, tendency of the teachers to promote every child, parental insistence, and the lack of follow-up efforts. Then too, many feel that a trial promotion merely delays the acquisition of adequate fundamental preparation. On the other hand, studies show that large numbers of pupils promoted on trial have justified this confidence reposed in them.

Summary of Promotion Principles. We are now ready to bring together principles which should be considered in administering promotion. These are:

1. The fundamental purpose of classifying and promoting pupils is to provide them with opportunities to do the things necessary to their growth and maturation, physically, mentally, socially, emotionally, and morally. Promotion techniques will be effective as they provide the best means to this end.

2. The organization and administration of the school itself should be such as to allow the pupil to develop at his maximum rate of progress. Arbitrary grade or subject standards should give way to individual pupil standards scientifically determined.

3. Promotion in point of time, as annual, should be subordinated to

---

[7] See Walker W. Cheyney and Phillip A. Boyer, "Is Non-Promotion a Defensible Policy?" *Elementary School Journal*, May, 1933, pp. 647–651; also H. G. Sackett, "How Is the School Facing Promotion?" *School and Society*, July 31, 1937, pp. 143–145.

promotion in point of individual adjustment or development. This will place greater stress on child study, guidance, and teaching as directing study,[8] and the adaptation of the organization and procedure so that this may be accomplished.

4. The educational program of each pupil should be determined individually in accordance with his particular interests, capacities, and present and future needs. Individual differences will be developed to their logical conclusion.

5. The socialization of each child should be properly provided for. The school program should be adapted to this end.

6. The teacher should remain long enough with the child to enable her influence and understanding to function in the life-growth of the child. This may be longer than one year, even as long as six years.[9]

NON-PROMOTION (SCHOOL FAILURE)

Early Concepts of Non-Promotion. Advancement through the several classes in earlier schools was dependent upon more or less complete mastery of subject matter evidenced by the results of rigid, if crude, examinations. Holmes, speaking before the National Education Association in 1896, asserted what can be taken as a good example of the philosophy of his day: "As regards promotion I do not believe they should be made so long as a student is delinquent in a single subject. No matter if he be delinquent in but a single study, let him sit in a lower grade, promote him and he will be careless about the old study."[10] In accordance with this theory, failure of from 10 to 20 per cent of all pupils was formerly considered proper and defensible. Moreover, it was not thought possible for a good teacher to prepare many more than 80 per cent of the class properly for the examinations to follow.[11] Accordingly, children were failed, and the teacher, proud of the feat, thus upheld the standards of the school and saved the system.

---

[8] Daniel P. Eginton, "Classifying and Promoting Pupils," *Nation's Schools,* August, 1934, pp. 22–25.

[9] See principles of classification and promotion as developed by Reavis, Pierce, and Stullkin, *The Elementary School,* Chicago, University of Chicago Press, 1938, pp. 160–161.

[10] W. H. Holmes, *School Organization and the Individual Pupil,* Worcester, Mass., Davis Press, 1912, chap. ii, "Promotion Intervals."

[11] E. E. White, "The Promotion of Pupils," *Education,* IX, No. 6 (1889), 415–419.

This same attitude has carried over into many modern school systems. Fortunately, however, the philosophy that school failure is always an evidence of maladjustment of some sort, whether of the child to the school or of the school to the child, has been slowly permeating educational thinking. Buckingham expresses the thought in a manner favorable to the child when he declares that, in the very nature of things, there can be no misfit children but only misfit methods and misfit teachers.[12] In reality, where non-promotion exists, the school rather than the child has failed.

Extent of Non-Promotion and Demotion in the Elementary School. Numerous studies are available which indicate the extent of non-promotion and demotion, the latter referring to transfer from one grade to a lower grade. Otto found that 3.8 per cent of pupils in annual promotion schools and 4.8 per cent in semi-annual promotion schools failed of promotion to the next higher grade.[13] Cumulatively for six grades this means that 22 to 28 per cent of the children failed somewhere along the line, i.e., approximately 25 per cent. Duplications, of course, must be taken into account. These figures seem to agree with Mort and Featherstone's study of sixth-graders, which showed that, already in that grade, 27.1 per cent of the pupils had experienced retardation in some form.[14]

All studies indicate that non-promotion is highest in the primary grades, the first grade taking the heaviest toll. The attitude of most teachers seems to be that non-promotion is the most advantageous method of pupil adjustment. All through the grades the number of actual demotions is relatively low. In systems having semi-annual promotion plans, the percentage of non-promotion tends to increase. One will recall that advocates of semi-annual promotion argued that it would tend to reduce non-promotion, which argument does not seem to be borne out by the facts.

The number of non-promotions and demotions steadily decreases as the eighth grade is approached. However, a heavy toll is again taken at the end of the eighth grade as a result of county and other forms of examinations. This excessive retardation at the eighth-grade

[12] R. B. Buckingham, *Research for Teachers,* New York, Silver, Burdett and Company, 1926, p. 299.

[13] Henry J. Otto, *Promotion Policies and Practices in Elementary Schools,* Minneapolis, Educational Test Bureau, 1935, p. 91.

[14] Mort and Featherstone, *Entrance and Promotion Practices in City School Systems,* New York, Teachers College, Columbia University, 1934.

level due to non-promotion has been one of the chief factors in the development of the junior high school movement.

Failure on the Secondary School Level. Earlier emphasis upon subject matter mastery as a basis of promotion has been the principal reason for promotion by subject in the secondary schools. Most of the reported studies indicate failure on this basis. In one junior high school it was found that 38 per cent of the boys and 31 per cent of the girls failed in at least one subject during their junior high school three-year enrollment. In general boys have a higher percentage of failure than girls. As to the subjects failed, the order of frequency as found in fifteen high schools seems to be Latin, mathematics, foreign languages, commercial work, social studies, science, and English, with the special subjects following in no particular order.[15] Mort published a composite table of failures in classical and English high schools which gives figures varying slightly from this order.[16] However, one must warn against assuming any standards of practice from a perusal of these and similar studies. Schools differ as to their standards of grading, teaching, and curriculum materials. Such standards may be faulty at the outset. The desired outcome is a standard not of *failure* but of *promotion* in which every pupil develops at a rate of progress consistent with his ability and capacity.

CAUSES OF NON-PROMOTION

The fact that non-promotion (failure) does occur in school systems, both elementary and secondary to a greater or less extent, leads one naturally to inquire into causes. Failure is expensive to the child in that he thereby loses, at least in theory, that amount of time in his school progress during which he must re-cover known material. Many children feel a loss of status, frustration, and distaste for school. It must not be forgotten that there is a duplication of the instructional costs for the grade which he is repeating. A most profitable study for any school system would be to analyze not only the incidence, extent, and causes of failure of its own children, but the costs of pupil failure and extent of retardation within its own school system.

---

[15] Department of Curriculum and Research, Pittsburgh Public Schools, 1935.

[16] Paul Mort, *The Individual Pupil,* New York, American Book Company, 1928, p. 179.

An analysis of the causes of non-promotion reveals four different groups: (1) causes traceable to the pupil and his individual nature; (2) causes traceable to the teacher and his procedures; (3) causes traceable to the organization and administration of the school system; and (4) causes traceable to the out-of-school environment.

1. Causes traceable to the child himself and inherent in him are (*a*) physical defects, both remediable and irremediable, which interfere with his normal progress; (*b*) mental inability to do the work of his grade, which may be due to improper placement or some form of abnormality; (*c*) the child's social behavior; (*d*) his emotional nature; (*e*) personality maladjustments; (*f*) his general health; (*g*) irregular attendance or truancy within his own control; and (*h*) inertia (laziness).

2. Causes traceable to the teacher include (*a*) personal unfitness; (*b*) poor methods; (*c*) lack of interest in, or misunderstanding of, the pupils and their work; (*d*) false concepts of school standards; (*e*) the marking system; and (*f*) partiality in some form.

3. Causes traceable to the school organization and its administration include (*a*) overloaded teachers or too large classes; (*b*) poorly adapted admission and promotion policies; (*c*) misfit organization; (*d*) maladministration of organization; (*e*) unadapted program of studies, textbooks, or materials of instruction; (*f*) heavy pupil load; (*g*) inadequate attendance enforcement; (*h*) unregulated social and athletic programs; (*i*) lack of cooperation with the home; (*j*) inadequate guidance and counseling programs; (*k*) poor articulation between school units, and (*l*) unattractive school environment.

4. Causes traceable to the out-of-school environment include (*a*) negative parental attitude toward school, teacher, or the child himself; (*b*) unfavorable family conditions; (*c*) unfavorable economic conditions; (*d*) unfavorable community environment; (*e*) juvenile delinquency; (*f*) language difficulties; (*g*) social distractions; and (*h*) lack of home facilities.[17]

---

[17] In William A. Yeager, "Analysis of the Causes of Failure in a Typical High School," *Thirteenth Annual Schoolmen's Week Proceedings,* Philadelphia, University of Pennsylvania, 1926, pp. 131–146, the student will find a technique for analyzing the causes of failure adapted to high schools, with some emphasis on case-study procedures.

Remedial Measures

The Approach. This analysis of causes of non-promotion naturally furnishes the basis for the remedial approach. It would be logical to assume that prevention would begin at those points (1) where failure is the most alarming, and (2) where the ascertained causes indicate some measure of relief or prevention. We have already noted many innovations in school organization and pupil classification portending greater regularity in school progress. Maturation levels of the child at designated points are being studied with increasing care. The significance of maturation as a factor in educational diagnosis and adjustment is well known. The child himself must both understand and be understood. He must be taught to assume greater responsibility as to his own part in his educational development. He must be taught to give close attention to study habits, attendance, and a continuous self-analysis in the light of his own progress.

The Teacher. Initiative for the study of failure as it concerns the individual child may well rest with the teacher since he makes a direct point of contact with each child. The teacher will naturally center his attention on the removal or relief of those situations inducing failure as suggested in the preceding section. Teaching subject matter must give way to teaching the child, with a clear understanding based on data scientifically prepared and utilized. Here the guidance service must function effectively. Moreover, teaching must become more and more individualized, with materials and classroom management being better adapted to this end. Failure should be prevented before it occurs. Attention should be given to all related causes within the disposition of the teacher, especially administrative ones.

The Principal. An examination of the causes of failure reveals many opportunities for administrative attacks on the problem. Educators now frequently hold that the school rather than the child fails. If this is true, those responsible for the management of the school should recognize the causes of failure which may be attributed to a faulty organization and its administration, and use more effective procedures. The principal should work carefully with his teachers to assist them with removing causes of failure with which they are directly concerned. He has a certain responsibility in study-ing the out-of-school environment insofar as it pertains to these problems. In fact he may need to supply the spark of initiative for study all along the line.

Specific Remedies. In recent years attention has been given to the following procedures in order to facilitate the progress of the child where promotion is under consideration.

TRIAL PROMOTIONS. The conditional promotion of the child, where advisable, on a short-period basis has previously been pointed out and appears to be about 75 per cent successful. It is especially valu-able where, in the cases of retarded children, provision is made for some adjustment of teacher, curriculum, or other factors.

STUDY OF PROMOTION PERIODS. In some respects it is unfortunate that semi-annual promotion plans, or plans covering shorter periods, to reduce time lost through failure have not been too successful. Al-though more students fail, the period of retardation is shorter. The average number of years lost per child is about equal to that in the annual promotional plan. Where the plan is in operation, a closer study should be made of conditions inducing failure. More attention to a proper promotion span and the adaptation of administrative procedures and curriculum materials to it would be in order.

CURRICULUM ADJUSTMENTS. Some form of homogeneous grouping in which the curriculum is adjusted to the need of the pupils has assisted in reducing failures. If adjustments were continued through the several divisions of the school system and the progress of the child were smoothed through a study of individual needs, the re-sults would be more hopeful. Otto contends that, in the usual ability grouping, the organized procedures of the school have not been altered in any way; the child has merely been shifted from one place to another in an effort to find a niche into which he will fit better.[18]

Perhaps there is a better attempt at administrative adjustment to the individual pupil of low mental ability in special class situations. There should be an effort to adjust the curriculum and teaching procedures to the different ability groups. Considerable difference of opinion exists as to the effectiveness of the results accomplished.

INDIVIDUAL PUPIL ADJUSTMENT. In attempts to reduce failures by adjusting the work to the individual pupil, the following have been

---

[18] Henry J. Otto, *Promotion Policies and Practices in Elementary Schools,* Educa-tional Monograph No. 5, Minneapolis, Educational Test Bureau, 1935, p. 99.

tried out with some measure of success: (1) dropping a subject and substituting a study period; (2) electing an additional subject; (3) dropping an advanced subject and putting double time on a weak subject; (4) transferring a pupil to another school, as a trade school; (5) repeating a subject for better foundation and better study habits, even though it is an elective; (6) transferring a pupil to another teacher; (7) assigning pupils to a special period for individual assistance; (8) introducing more adequate guidance procedures including study of home conditions.

The normal curve of distribution for promotion is used in many schools. It is supposed to be a check on teachers who (1) fail too many pupils, and (2) fail too few. It assumes, however, that 6 or 7 per cent of all pupils will and should always fail, a questionable assumption at the outset and one that does not fit adequately into any plan of *smoothing* the educational progress of every child. In some schools the grading of pupils has been modified to coincide with some form of ability grouping; in others, there is a tendency to eliminate grades entirely, substituting credit certificates, or even certificates of attendance only. There is a marked inclination to emphasize the qualitative aspects of grading in terms of individual improvement and to provide a composite mark utilizing a wider variety of factors, a procedure in line with child development rather than subject matter mastery, upon which most school marks are based.

Next Steps to a Study of Non-Promotion. Approaches to the reduction or elimination of non-promotion have taken the form of (1) greater recognition of the individual nature of the child with classroom adjustments to fit his particular needs; (2) improvement of supervisory relationships with emphasis upon teaching procedures and curriculum adaptations; and (3) administrative adjustments which, in some instances, may mean complete reorganization of the school. It will be noted in each of these approaches that the typical grade-a-year concept of promotion seemingly remains, for most schools, as the criterion of progress.

Smoothing the educational progress of every child should require a fourth approach, one that may modify, perhaps eliminate, the grade-a-year concept of promotion. Beginning with a classification of pupils on equivalent ability and social levels and a comparable initial achievement basis, such an approach should make provision for as rapid progress of each child as the individual mastery of an adapted environment and program and his own limitations permit. In order to accomplish this result, some reorganization of the general school plan may be necessary. Large general school divisions should replace the graded school plan, organized as follows: (1) primary, including kindergarten and the nursery school where feasible; (2) intermediate; (3) junior high school; (4) senior high school and junior college.[19] Within these divisions most of the pupils will be grouped on the same age levels. Ideally, curriculum offerings and procedures in which there is close contact with the home and community will be individually adapted; practically, it may be necessary to plan for groupings within groups. Each child should be allowed to progress as he achieves certain standards of mastery. A reasonable flexibility should provide for adjustment to individual pupil needs and abilities under guidance.

In closing this chapter, we repeat with emphasis an earlier sentence: Every administrative and teaching endeavor should be focused on the natural and continuous educational progress of every child. Whatever facilitates his all-round development contributes to this common purpose.

QUESTIONS AND PROBLEMS

1. Analyze the different emotional considerations associated with promotion and non-promotion on the part of pupils, teachers, parents, the principal, the school board.
2. Compare the advantages and disadvantages of annual, semi-annual, and quarterly plans of promotion. To what extent is it possible to institute individual progress concepts within the framework of these plans?
3. How do you account for the great variety, as well as tenacity, of theories and notions held by classroom teachers as to promotion and non-promotion?
4. Make a study covering five years of promotion and non-promotion in a selected school system. Analyze your data in the light of desirable principles and practices.
5. Take a position in regard to trial promotion. Test your theories by a study of trial promotions over a period of years in a selected school system. Secure the points of view of at least five teachers.

---

[19] Compare J. A. Lindsay's suggested plan in his *Annual and Semi-Annual Promotions,* Contributions to Education No. 510, New York, Teachers College, Columbia University, pp. 142–143.

6. Carry your study of Question 4 farther by classifying by divisions and analyzing the causes of failure.
7. Make a study of remedial plans to reduce or eliminate failure in selected school systems. Evaluate your findings.
8. What do you consider the most significant educational contribution to reduction of non-promotion? Give reasons for your answer.

SELECTED REFERENCES

1. Butterfield, E. W., "The New Fifty Per Cent," *Clearing House,* January, 1934, pp. 265–272.
2. Carrothers, George E., "Why Do High School Pupils Fail?" *Bulletin of the National Association of Secondary School Principals,* March, 1946, pp. 29–36.
3. Caverly, Ernest R., "Shall the High School Eliminate Its Failures?" *Clearing House,* January, 1938, pp. 259–263.
4. Curtis, Francis D., "Specific Suggestions for Teaching Dull-Normal Pupils," *School Review,* September, 1936, pp. 525–532.
5. Edmonson, J. B., Roemer, Joseph, and Bacon, Francis L., *The Administration of the Modern Secondary School.* New York: The Macmillan Company, 1941, chap. iii.
6. Elsbree, Willard S., *Pupil Progress in the Elementary School.* New York: Bureau of Publications, Teachers College, Columbia University, 1943.
7. Hildreth, Gertrude H., "Hazards of Straight Promotion," *Educational Administration and Supervision,* January, 1946, pp. 19–26.
8. Kandel, I. L., "Promising Innovations in Secondary Education," *Educational Forum,* November, 1936, pp. 29–38.
9. LeBaron, Walter A., "Some Practical Techniques in Developing a Program of Continuous Progress in the Elementary School," *Elementary School Journal,* October, 1945, pp. 89–96.
10. Lindsay, J. Armour, *Annual and Semi-Annual Promotion.* New York: Bureau of Publications, Teachers College, Columbia University, 1933.
11. Meyers, F., "We Experiment with a Non-Failure Program," *Childhood Education,* January, 1942, pp. 205–209.
12. Otto, Henry J., *Elementary School Organization and Administration.* New York: D. Appleton-Century Company, 1944, chaps. v, vi.
13. Otto, Henry J., *Promotion Policies and Practices in Elementary Schools.* Minneapolis: Educational Test Bureau, 1935, chaps. iii, iv, v, viii.
14. "Promising Practices in Secondary Education," *Bulletin of the National Association of Secondary School Principals,* October, 1940.

15. "Psychological Tests and Their Uses," *Review of Educational Research,* February, 1941.
16. "Pupil Personnel, Guidance, and Counseling," *Review of Educational Research,* April, 1939, "B. School Progress," and "C. School Marks." These sections contain many references of value to a further study of this chapter.
17. Reavis, Pierce, and Stullkin, *The Elementary School.* Chicago: University of Chicago Press, 1938, chap. vii.
18. Reeder, Ward G., *Fundamentals of Public School Administration.* New York: The Macmillan Company, 1941, chap. xx.
19. Stroud, J. B., "How Many Pupils Are Failed?" *Elementary School Journal,* February, 1947, pp. 316–322.
20. "The Scientific Movement in Education," *Thirty-Seventh Yearbook,* National Society for the Study of Education. Bloomington: Public School Publishing Company, 1938, part ii, chap. xvi.
21. Wallin, J. E. Wallace, "Teachers' Opinions Regarding Automatic Promotions," *Educational Administration and Supervision,* May, 1943, pp. 295–306.
22. Wheat, Leonard B., "The Flexible Progress Group System," *Elementary School Journal,* November, 1937, pp. 175–183.
23. Wiley, George M., Jr., *The Redirection of Secondary Education.* New York: The Macmillan Company, 1940, chap. vii.
24. Witty, Paul A., and Wilkins, L. W., "The Status of Acceleration or Grade Skipping as an Administrative Practice," *Educational Administration and Supervision,* May, 1933, pp. 321–346.
25. Wrinkle, William L., *The New High School in the Making: the Philosophy and Practice of a Modernized Secondary School.* New York: American Book Company, 1938.

CHAPTER XI

Administering to the Needs
of Exceptional Pupils

AS THE White House Conference so aptly pointed out,[1] a true concern for all children must take into account the fact that many of them labor under heavy handicaps in competition with their fellows. This statement is all the more apparent when one considers the wide range of individual differences among children, and the many factors that are associated in producing them. They are essentially grouped about two basic factors—nature and nurture—with the addition of a third, namely, age, which as Freeman[2] points out consists of the changes in the individual that take place during the process of his growth and decline. Specific factors affecting individual differences are genetics, inheritance, environment, race and nativity, sex, physique, those changes that accompany his age, and circumstance. When one or more of these elements are exaggerated, conditions may occur producing handicaps which affect, directly or indirectly, his educational progress.

We have seen that the public schools are geared largely to the "normal" child. Exceptional children find in the typical school system a lack of suitable opportunities to meet their needs and varying abilities. As a result there is discouragement and frustration because

---

[1] *Children in a Democracy,* General Report of the White House Conference, Washington, January 19, 1940, p. 62.

[2] The student should read Frank S. Freeman's stimulating chapter, "Contributions to Education of Scientific Knowledge about Individual Differences," in "The Scientific Movement in Education," *Thirty-Seventh Yearbook,* National Society for the Study of Education, Bloomington, Public School Publishing Company, 1938, part ii, chap. xxxiii.

of these educational blind alleys, with little opportunity to meet life situations adequately.

It is the purpose of this chapter to indicate the field of special education, that phase which provides for the exceptional child. Four classes of exceptional children are identified and discussed, namely, those who are usually accepted as (1) physically exceptional, (2) mentally exceptional, (3) socially exceptional, and (4) emotionally exceptional. While many writers do not include the last group as a separate classification, certain specific deviating characteristics which these children possess will be pointed out as affecting behavior situations in the classroom and as contributory in specific instances to the first three groupings. Finally, principles and suggestions will be presented for administrative purposes.

AREAS REQUIRING SPECIAL EDUCATIONAL ADJUSTMENT

Any consideration of the exceptional child must begin with the fundamental principle that children differ. At the same time the large majority of children have characteristics and abilities which are sufficiently similar, from the standpoint of education, to enable their needs to be supplied reasonably well through the usual classroom procedures. Many children, however, possess characteristics and abilities superior or inferior to the "normal" or "average" to such an extent that their needs must be studied and educational provision made for their development under special conditions. These children may be said to be exceptional, that is, they deviate from the normal group. On the one hand, they may be deficient (handicapped) in one or more particulars; on the other, they may excel as to physical, mental, social, and emotional abilities and characteristics. Some of the deficiencies may require temporary adjustment; others need special treatment throughout the school experience, perhaps throughout life. Baker emphasizes the important fact that exceptional children are fundamentally similar to normal children.[3]

Perhaps the best estimate of the number and type of handicapped children in the United States available is that of the committee on special education of the White House Conference in 1930. This com-

---

[3] Compare Baker's classification: (1) physical handicaps, (2) mental growth and development, (3) neurological and psychogenic diseases, (4) behavior adjustments, and (5) educational retardation (Harry J. Baker, *Introduction to Exceptional Children,* New York, The Macmillan Company, 1944).

mittee indicated that there were 13,521,400 such children in the United States, as shown in TABLE 10.

TABLE 10. HANDICAPPED CHILDREN IN THE UNITED STATES[4]

Type of Handicap	
Blindness (children under 20)	14,400
Partial sight	50,000
Impaired hearing	3,000,000
Defective speech (5 to 18)	1,000,000
Crippled condition (calling for special education)	100,000
Tubercular condition	382,000
Suspected tuberculosis	850,000
Weak or damaged heart	1,000,000
Malnourished state (school age)	6,000,000
Behavior problems (3 per cent of elementary)	675,000
Mentally retarded condition (2 per cent of elementary)	450,000
Grand total	13,521,400

This table indicates eleven groups of handicapped children in the United States, nearly all of whom may be classified as physically handicapped. It does not include the children who are socially and mentally exceptional and in need of educational adjustment. Many of these are so handicapped that either they are not educable in the public schools or special facilities are not available to give them adequate care. If special classes or appropriate instruction is not available, they must be placed in institutions. It should be pointed out that exceptional children are entitled to an adequate development of their abilities and potentialities in accordance with their specific needs just as normal children are. Only with the acceptance of this ideal can it be truly said that equal (adequate) educational opportunity for all children is being realized.

THE PHYSICALLY HANDICAPPED CHILD

The fact that greater attention seems to have been paid to the physically handicapped child may be the result of greater ease of identification. Heck[5] has classified the following types of physically

---

[4] White House Conference, *Special Education: The Handicapped and the Gifted*, New York, The Century Company, 1931, pp. 5–6.

[5] Arch O. Heck, *The Education of Exceptional Children*, New York, McGraw-Hill Book Company, 1940, pp. 111–340.

handicapped children for which the public schools should make educational provision: crippled children, blind children, low-visioned children, children with defective vision, deaf children, those hard of hearing, children with defective speech, and delicate children.

Crippled Children. A crippled child is usually characterized as one who possesses an impediment to walking serious enough to require some form of special care and attention. The degree of the impediment may determine the nature and extent of the physical care which must be provided and the special facilities needed for his comfort. In addition to his physical handicaps, which may require special physical equipment, the crippled child presents an interesting mental attitude. Quite often his physical imperfection results in psychological or social maladjustment. Ordinarily he is happy in nature, yet self-conscious, at the same time responding to an urge to action within his limitations and possibilities.

Heck points out four principles which should underlie a program of education for the crippled child: (1) equality of opportunity, (2) an educational program that recognizes his handicaps, (3) adequate development of initiative and self-reliance, and (4) retention in school as long as help can be given.[6]

Educational provision for the crippled child should be in accordance with his physical needs and the facilities available. If the child can walk to school or be transported thereto, a suitable environment and adequate individual teaching should be provided. If the number of crippled children is sufficient teaching may be in groups. If the child is a shut-in, instruction should be provided in the home or in the institution in which he may be placed. Medical attention and adequate care should be available at all times. It must be remembered that his growth requires frequent adjustment of all forms of physical correction and assistance. On the whole, his education should depart little from that of a normal child, although its cost is ordinarily about four times the cost of regular elementary education. It has been estimated that there may be as many as 377,000 crippled children in the United States, approximately 2.9 per cent of the total population, about one-third of whom need special school or class instruction.[7]

Blind Children. Mention of and care for the blind can be traced to Biblical times. In this section we are concerned with children who

<hr>

[6] *Ibid.,* pp. 112–113.
[7] *Ibid.,* p. 142.

are either totally blind or whose vision is so limited that they cannot profit by ordinary educative procedures. Bradway's use of the social maturity scale with a limited number of pupils who were blind, deaf, and crippled to determine which kind of disability was the greatest handicap is of great interest to educators. Although the number studied is rather limited for reliable conclusions, the results are significant. She concluded that the blind appeared to be the most handicapped, and the deaf the next most handicapped. However, neither blindness nor deafness constitutes a permanent bar to social expression or performance.[8]

Blind children are educated largely in state schools for the blind and in a few private schools. A few American cities make provision for their education in the public schools. While there are many arguments in favor of the state school, many adherents believe that classes in local public schools are far better socially and psychologically both for the blind and for his seeing neighbor.

Besides special instruction the blind should have a type of elementary and secondary education adapted to normal children. They should be taught to provide for their own physical needs as far as possible and to make themselves vocationally independent. Today there are many vocations open to them. Those able to profit by any form of higher education should be privileged to achieve it through scholarships or other forms of aid. The blind student and his "seeing eye" may be noted in many universities.

The educator's first task is to locate and provide for the blind child. Low-visioned or diseased children tending to blindness should be watched with great solicitude; medical care must be insisted upon. Where local classes are provided, proper attention should be given to adequately trained teachers, equipment, library, curriculum, and home contacts.

Sight-Saving Classes. Children with serious defective vision should be placed in some organization and environment fitted to provide a type of education not available to them in the normal classroom. Table 10 indicates 50,000 children handicapped in this manner, but the number is probably much greater. Most low-visioned children are being educated in special sight-saving classes in our

---

[8] Katherine P. Bradway, "Social Competence of Exceptional Children: III The Deaf, the Blind, and the Crippled," *Journal of Exceptional Children,* December, 1937, pp. 64–69.

larger towns and cities, a few being given institutional care. When the number of such children has been determined through a local census, a sight-saving class should be organized according to the procedure suggested by state law or regulation. The proper glasses should be provided where needed, together with suitably printed textbooks and equipment under the direction of a specially trained teacher. Taught to recognize their own physical limitations and needs, low-visioned children should proceed with their education as normal children do, looking forward to their ultimate place as useful citizens. Part of the school program may be carried out with the regular classes, as in appreciations, contests, out-of-class activities, and social relationships.

Special attention should be directed to proper lighting facilities not only for sight-saving classes but for all children. Probably less than half of our public and private schools have adequate lighting. Every effort should be made to correct the eye defects of the estimated five million children who are now in need of eye attention with the number apparently increasing. In this respect, the responsibility on public education is heavy. If the parents are unable to cope with the problem, social agencies and service clubs should be contacted for assistance.

Deaf and Hard-of-Hearing Children. Perhaps every American child has heard of Helen Keller and her remarkable victory over great sensory handicaps. At the age of eighteen months, she was deprived of both sight and hearing at a single stroke by a severe illness. With these senses there departed the power of speech, leaving her blind, deaf, and dumb.[9] Her life is a testimony to a remarkable spirit and sheer determination which has conquered seemingly insurmountable drawbacks. There is a lesson in it for every handicapped child. To be born deaf or to lose the sense of hearing before speech is attained is a far greater handicap than deafness after speech is attained or a language achieved. For this reason the problem of the "born deaf" child is particularly difficult.

At the outset a distinction should be made between deaf, partially deaf, and hard-of-hearing children, since instructional procedures are differently adapted to each group. Usually, the deaf are classified as

---

[9] The interested reader may find her books intriguing: *The Story of My Life* (1903); *Optimism* (1903); *The World I Live In* (1908); *The Song of the Stone Wall* (1910); *Out of the Dark* (1913).

those born deaf and those who become deaf before they acquire speech. The partially deaf include those with serious hearing defects who fail to make progress in the regular school. The hard-of-hearing may include those who have lost the sense of hearing since they have acquired speech or who hear with various degrees of difficulty.[10]

Factors to be considered in the education of the deaf are: (1) determination of the place and manner of instruction; (2) equality of opportunity for an education, depending upon the nature and degree of the handicap; (3) adequate type of education selected for personal association with hearing persons; and (4) prevention, in that the causes of, and remedies for, deafness are understood and applied.[11]

Both state and public schools have been developed for the education of the deaf. The manual and oral methods of instruction are used, with many schools emphasizing a combination of both. A specially trained teacher is necessary for deaf children, with equipment and curriculum properly adapted. Special classes may be necessary for small groups. The average annual cost of education for the deaf is $300. About one in two thousand persons is deaf, one-third of these being under twenty years of age.

Hard-of-hearing children represent those who hear with various degrees of difficulty. Since these have already acquired speech and a vocabulary, their education follows a somewhat different procedure. Usually, special schools or classes are organized under specially trained teachers. The hard-of-hearing child should be discovered by an audiometer and properly classified according to degree of hearing difficulty. Every teacher should be acquainted with the uses of the audiometer in order to isolate such children and provide for their needs. Moreover, all teachers should be familiar with the causes of poor hearing and urge medical care wherever necessary.

In many states, special provision is now being made for these children. Unfortunately, the educational benefits are not uniformly accruing to all aurally handicapped children, especially in the more sparsely populated areas. The problem is largely one of organization, transportation, and support, together with greater sensitivity to the need.

Children with Speech Defects. Speech defects are usually thought

---

[10] Josephine B. Timberlake, "Children Who Cannot Hear Well," *Phi Delta Kappan,* October, 1940, pp. 61 f.

[11] Arch O. Heck, *The Education of Exceptional Children,* p. 232.

of as variations in speech usage caused by malformation or misuse of organs of speech which render the resulting variation confusing or embarrassing in any degree. Borden and Busse speak of these variations as conspicuous, confusing, or unpleasant.[12] Such defects usually include stuttering, lisping, stammering, dialect, thick speech, baby talk, hoarseness, foreign accent, and any others due to a physical cause. It is important to point out that the psychological and emotional effects of speech defects upon the child may be more significant and more difficult to deal with than the defects themselves.

Proper diagnosis and isolation under specially trained personnel is the first step. The child must realize the helpful nature of assistance being given him to correct his defect, especially since it may be psychological in nature. It is important that confidence be built up in him and retained. If medical assistance or surgery is necessary, every effort should be made to see that it is provided. Special teachers and classes should be formed, with the child under instruction for whole or part time. Larger school systems have one or more speech teachers who instruct children at stated intervals. The home should be contacted and parents urged to cooperate. Only a small portion of the one million children with speech defects are receiving proper instruction, although many states are now giving much needed assistance. As usual, such children in rural and small-town areas are the most neglected.

Physically Weak Children. There are many children of school age, both in and out of school, whose physical condition is such as to require special school organization and instruction. This group includes the tubercular, the undernourished, the cardiac, the anemic, the highly nervous, shut-ins in hospitals or at home, those of lowered vitality, and others who for physical reasons are unable to profit through normal classification.

Since the public schools are responsible for the educational welfare of all children, these children should be provided for in a manner befitting their physical condition. When necessary, special schools or rooms should be supplied, with instructors who are prepared to assume the responsibilities which their special care may entail. The needs may extend to good food, open-air schools, and adequate rest. Remedial care and prevention should be stressed in individual cases

---

[12] Richard C. Borden and Alvin C. Busse, *Speech Correction,* New York, F. S. Crofts and Company, 1925, p. 126.

and their return to normal educative procedures attained as rapidly as possible. It is estimated that there are 8,607,000 physically weak children in the United States.

THE MENTALLY EXCEPTIONAL CHILD

Classification. Since the discovery and application of the Binet-Simon technique for the measurement of intelligence, mental differences in children can be ascertained with some degree of accuracy. Terman[13] in 1916 prepared a classification of children on the basis of intelligence which has been commonly accepted since that time.

Children at the upper and lower limits of this scale may be considered as exceptional, the exact limits being still a matter of difference of opinion. Table 10 indicates the number of mentally retarded children as 450,000, although it may be as high as 2,000,000. The number of gifted children may be as many, depending upon the selected points on the scale.

TABLE 11.   TERMAN'S CLASSIFICATION OF CHILDREN UPON BASIS OF THE INTELLIGENCE QUOTIENT[14]

I.Q.	Classification
Above 140	near genius or genius
120–140	very superior intelligence
110–120	superior intelligence
90–110	normal, or average intelligence
80–90	dullness, rarely classifiable as feeble-mindedness
70–80	borderline deficiency, sometimes classifiable as dullness, often as feeble-mindedness
Below 70	definite feeble-mindedness

The Mentally Retarded Child. Mentally retarded children include those below "normal" classification on the Terman scale. They range from those of low intelligence (dull) through the moron stages to imbeciles and idiots. Definite feeble-mindedness including imbeciles and idiots are institutional cases. These children should be isolated from the school population and placed in institutions as early as pos-

---

[13] Lewis M. Terman, *The Measurement of Intelligence,* Boston, Houghton Mifflin Company, 1916, p. 79.

[14] *Ibid.*

sible. Most morons should be similarly placed, especially when sexual perversion or criminal tendencies are in evidence. However, many high-grade morons can profit by public school attendance.

Public school provision for children of low mental ability probably begins for the majority of children who have an intelligence quotient of 70. These are definitely mentally retarded and become more difficult problems if they also have some physical, social, or moral defect.

To many teachers there is confusion between backwardness and mental deficiency. Gesell has given us such a clear statement of this distinction that he is quoted at some length:

Mental deficiency is something more than ordinary backwardness in studies, and it is something different. Ordinary backwardness is comparatively not very serious. A merely backward pupil will not graduate at the average age, but there is no reason to believe that he will not succeed in life. Ordinary backwardness may even be curable. It may be due to irregular attendance, to poor nutrition, to adenoids, to haphazard schooling, poor teaching, defective vision, lack of familiarity with our language, and a long list of other causes which retard, but do not altogether destroy, normal development.

Now, a mentally deficient child does not even have the *possibilities* of normal development. His retardation is permanent, and it is incurable. He may have poor eyesight and many other defects, but they are not the cause of his deficiency. In perhaps a majority of cases his backwardness is inborn; it is an hereditary or inherent handicap. In three or four cases out of ten it has been an injury from disease or a similar cause which so damages his immature brain that he cannot enjoy normal mental development. Like a plant that has been stunted, he fails to reach a full mental stature. He, therefore, shows a certain lack of mental vigor, and always a kind of immaturity. Unfortunately, we cannot in any way remove such a fundamental weakness and incompleteness. It is because the brain itself is incompletely developed that we cannot make him normal. We must admit, then, that mental deficiency is an extreme constitutional form of backwardness, which dates from birth or early infancy, and which is so serious that it will prevent the child from taking his place either in school, or in the world, on a full par with his normal fellows.[15]

Teachers and administrators should be fully sensitive to the characteristics of intellectual deficiency. Mental retardation may be accompanied by physical retardation. Judgment and common sense are

---

[15] Arnold Gesell, *The Retarded Child: How to Help Him,* Bloomington, Public School Publishing Company, 1925, pp. 13–14. The student should read this little volume in its entirety.

usually defective. There may be certain deficient sensory capacities as well as organic sensations. Emotional and instinctive deficiencies are usually quite apparent, also inability to judge the requirements and consequences of the moment. These inadequacies have a direct bearing on the child's moral and social nature and conduct. His attention span is limited. His motor coordination may be imperfect, affecting bodily movements and responses and producing peculiarities. On the other hand, it has been found possible to develop certain motor controls and skills habitually, so that many of these children can become economically self-supporting and socially useful.[16]

With their limited intelligence and, in some cases, physical or other imperfections, a type of education adapted to their abilities and specific needs should be developed. Competition with members of their own group should inculcate a feeling of confidence. Mastery of fundamentals and elementary skills should be stressed, together with an earnest desire to become good citizens, prepared to do some specific task accurately in order to support themselves and those who may be dependent, wholly or partially, upon them. Usually, special schools and special classes of fifteen to twenty pupils are organized under teachers with training in special education. Handwork should be emphasized. Constructions should be concrete and highly practical, with emphasis on the vocationally useful. Above everything else, there must be adequate emphasis on right conduct, since delinquency may here find its early beginnings.

The problems of the child of low mental ability have definite social implications. Causes lie deep in the social fabric, the effect of both heredity and environment. However, other causes may be pathological and accidental. Few cases are remediable. Sterilization has been proposed for the most deficient and has been practiced in some instances. Medicine and surgery can help sometimes, being responsible for many cures and improvements. Possible improvability of the I.Q. is so small as to affect very little the type of training and the prediction of the child's future.[17] Of course there are always individual exceptions.

---

[16] See Lee Edward Travis, "Intellectual Factors," in "Educational Diagnosis," *Thirty-Fourth Yearbook,* National Society for the Study of Education, Bloomington, Public School Publishing Company, 1935. Chapter II has an excellent discussion of these characteristics.

[17] The reader should be familiar with the discussions on "Intelligence: Its Nature and Nurture," in the *Thirty-Ninth Yearbook,* National Society for the Study of Education, Bloomington, Public School Publishing Company, 1940, chaps. i, ii.

The Gifted Child. Children of superior mental ability as indicated by the upper levels of the Terman scale are classified as gifted. Their I.Q.'s may begin anywhere from 110 to 130. Beginning at the former figure, the number of exceptionally bright children may equal the number of mentally retarded; at the latter figure, namely, 130, the number may be reduced to approximately 50,000. Other elements taken into consideration in designating gifted or talented children may include: (1) ability of the child to do things better than his fellows; (2) scores on tests of specific abilities, i.e., musical, mechanical, and artistic; (3) display of unusual talent in a given situation; and (4) general all-round superiority.

From this group comes the leadership of the nation. The children included in it are the most valuable to society in that respect and, from the standpoint of specific educational opportunities accorded them, perhaps the most neglected. As indicated above, they display, in addition to a high intelligence quotient, certain specific abilities, as in art, music, or academic achievement, frequently in abstractions. Usually they indicate signs of leadership, initiative, and special aptitude at youthful ages, being more inclined toward them than is usual in the activities of children of the same ages.

Connor[18] has pointed out certain problems of gifted children which should be taken into consideration in planning an educational program. These include boredom, isolation, sense of inferiority, negativism, high pressure, meddlesomeness, chicanery, worry over good and evil, worry over social responsibilities, bafflement in social situations, and bafflement with older children. The emotional effect of these situations is difficult to counteract.

Gifted children should receive a type of education specifically adapted to their superior ability. Care must be taken, however, to have them develop normally with the avoidance of maladjustment, socially, psychologically, and physically. Some children tend in early years to become individualists, perhaps somewhat emotional. Their teachers should be highly intelligent and specially trained. Enrichment of materials and variation in procedures has proved of great value.

The special school and special class have been advocated as de-

---

[18] William L. Connor, "The Education of Gifted and Talented Children," *Phi Delta Kappan,* October, 1940, p. 74.

sirable for the education of the gifted child. Heck[19] has stated clearly advantages and disadvantages. Such a social group studying in an environment of enrichment under skilled tutelage would seem to be the proper approach. However, opponents of this plan prefer retaining the gifted child within the normal group, claiming that it is the more democratic plan, prevents intellectual and social aristocracy, and is probably best for the child physically and psychologically. If these able children are retained in the regular classroom, it should be possible under a skilled teacher to provide for the proper enrichment and stimulation needed. At the same time, many normal children may find the leadership of gifted children stimulating and desirable.

The school progress of the gifted child, as well as the child of low mental ability, creates problems of articulation, especially as between units of the school system. Where promotion seems desirable, one should ascertain if there is available in some other community a suitable school environment in which the gifted child may profit, particularly when he is moving from the elementary to the secondary school. Hollingworth[20] in writing on this problem offers the suggestion that the *whole child* should be considered in promotion to the high school. Until he reaches physical and social maturity it is better for him to remain in his social group with an enriched program. Upon promotion to the secondary school, he normally will have enough to do if he follows efficiently an academic curriculum. He should also be encouraged to become proficient in artistic pursuits with emphasis as well along recreational lines. However, pupils above 140-150 I.Q. are in definite need of enrichment and careful observation.

Suffice it to say that the gifted child is a potential genius. He should be discovered and given every opportunity to develop to the extent of his abilities; at the same time great care must always be taken to protect and develop his physical body and to improve his social relationships. In this regard there is without doubt a public angle to consider in his education. Possibly there are between one and two million children in the United States who need this training. Few

---

[19] Arch O. Heck, *The Education of Exceptional Children,* pp. 392–402.

[20] Leta S. Hollingworth, "Problems of Relationship Between Elementary and Secondary Schools in the Case of Highly Intelligent Pupils," *Journal of Educational Sociology,* October, 1939, pp. 90–102.

of them are receiving the attention they deserve. Their education is both a challenge and an opportunity.

THE SOCIALLY MALADJUSTED CHILD

Social Conformity. Social usage determines the standards to which childhood and youth are expected to conform. Most standards are determined by family, school and community, mores and customs, and legal mandates and restrictions. Discipline might be defined as submissiveness to these controls with some means of correction for failure therein. Reasonable amenity to the controls represents acceptance of social restrictions on the part of each child. Refusal to conform on account of willfulness, inability, or for any other cause classifies him as socially maladjusted, and hence in need of a specific type of school organization, education, adjustment, and in extreme cases institutional care. In making these statements, we fully recognize the part that youth plays in social change, small as it may be.

Identification. Certain conditions in our social order have rendered large numbers of children socially maladjusted to some degree. A conservative estimate would be 3 per cent of the elementary school population, altogether nearly a million children, taking into consideration upper age youth. Socially maladjusted children or youth include truants, delinquents, incorrigibles, sex offenders, and all those whose actions class them as "incipient criminals." They may be physically or mentally handicapped or both, or they may be physically fit and intellectually capable. Causes for their condition may be traced to heredity, unhealthy home and community environment, broken homes, low intelligence, physical handicap, frustrated and maladjusted life, emotional instability, or other, more individualized sources. Remembering that a large portion of our delinquents and youthful criminals come from this group, one realizes the importance of the problem from the standpoint of education and society.

Care and Treatment. In caring educationally for the socially maladjusted child it is important to recall that, after all, each child is an individual and entitled to every effort that can be made in his behalf. His present condition may be due to no fault of his own. Social attitudes concerning his treatment have passed through four stages: (1) the penitentiary, (2) the deterrent, (3) the reformatory, and now (4) the socio-educational. As far as possible, an individualistic attitude should be kept on the highest level of approach. Rather than punishment, the child may need adjustment, assistance, education, and perhaps medical care. He should remain in the home whenever possible, if it is a fit place to live, which involves a close contact with the home. In some cases removal to a foster home may be found desirable; sometimes it is mandated by the courts. In extreme cases, removal from the social group to a parental school, reformatory, or other institution may be the only immediate solution. Here the protection of society becomes a superior obligation.

Special Schools and Classes. Ordinarily, socially maladjusted children are isolated from normal groups in the public schools and housed in special schools or grouped in special classes. This is essential since their continued presence in regular classes tends to create confusion and discord. Under a strong but understanding teacher, such a child may be led to discover and correct his own weaknesses and become normally adjusted. Classes should be small, not over fifteen to eighteen. Admission should be by individual placement after careful diagnosis. The curriculum should be adapted to the needs of each child, with the instruction tending toward marked individualization. Much will need to be done both by precept and by example in character building and citizenship. This will mean care in selecting the appropriate type of teacher and environment. Teachers should be chosen for their peculiar fitness, after a careful preparation in special education procedures and philosophy. The form of control should be such that each child learns through self-analysis and self-mastery. There should be a place for wholesome socialization and recreation. Eventually, wherever possible, these pupils should look forward to returning to their own social group, that is, the regular class or their own home if removed from it. In addition to training in skills and good citizenship, progress should be made in vocational adjustment.

Many cities have developed justly famous schools for socially maladjusted children.[21] No stigma should be attached to any pupil of such a school; rather, efforts should be made to develop pride in the type of education appropriately provided. In addition to particular schools, many cities have established a definite program of education

---

[21] Some of these have been well described by Heck, *The Education of Exceptional Children,* chap. iii.

for socially maladjusted youth, among them Cleveland, Chicago, and Detroit.

The Parental School. Where it is not possible to help socially maladjusted children through any form of organization in the public schools while they remain in their own homes, it may be necessary to remove them from their homes and place them in an isolated environment. Such procedure represents a form of social quarantine corresponding to similar isolation for those with contagious physical illness. The child may be removed to a foster home, or he may be placed in a special school, sometimes called a parental or correctional school. From the foster home he may attend the special school facilities provided in the public schools.

Parental schools are usually under public school control, although occasionally they are controlled by municipal authorities. Children are generally committed to them by the courts. However, they may be committed by school procedure. Large institutional plants are giving way to the cottage type of building, resembling a home environment. Citizenship and character building are inculcated through appropriate disciplinary procedures directed in large part by the pupils. Some schools on occasion revert to military discipline. Costs are high, usually three times that of ordinary school instruction.

State Institutions. States generally maintain institutions for the guardianship of those children and youth who must be removed completely from free social intercourse. Most of these children are committed on court order for various non-social acts, usually delinquency in some form. Society must be protected. The purpose of commitment is their social regeneration, and the program is designed to that end. Most of those enrolled are classified in the elementary grades, indicating retardation and low mental ability. Some are even feeble-minded. Perhaps not as much attention has been paid to the quality of instruction, curriculum, or outcomes of education in these schools as should be to accomplish the ends sought. Special concern should be given to social hygiene, medical attention, vocational education, fitting the pupil to make a living, and such other matters as will assist in developing a socially adjusted individual.

State responsibility for oversight of these institutions requires that the state assume leadership and maintenance of a large part of the education of its socially maladjusted children. Costs are high, amounting to about $500 annually for each child. Yet these children are entitled to the best education obtainable consistent with their needs and abilities. Where the problem is probably greatest, namely, in large cities, provision is the most adequate. However, the need is just as great proportionately in smaller cities and rural districts. Here the state should assume a generous leadership and make far better provision than is now the case.

Challenges. The socially maladjusted child and youth offer to society one of its most serious problems as well as one of its biggest challenges. These children and youth tend to become destructive rather than constructive social forces. From their ranks may eventually come society's perversive elements unless proper social adjustment has taken place and physical and other defects are removed in time. Moreover, their educational provision is costing several times that spent for normal youth, a fact consistent with the increased cost of our crime bill, but hardly consistent with the comparative educational rights of all pupils. Society must remove causes of maladjustment at the source. It is not altogether an educational problem, but education must assume its fair share of it.

EMOTIONAL CONTROL AND INSTABILITY

Importance of the Emotions. In adjusting the child to live wholesomely in the world about him, educators are coming more and more to realize the important place that emotions and their control have in the educational process. Underlying proper social adjustment in every individual is a matured and controlled emotional pattern of behavior; and conversely, underlying individual and social maladjustment there is somewhere an immature, disorganized, and uncontrolled emotional behavior.

Recent emphasis upon the importance of the emotions in the developmental processes has come about principally as a result of recognition of their intrinsic relationship to every experience and their importance in all attitudes and conduct. This is a great advance over the narrow concepts of the emotions as directly related to instinctive reactions. Here again is seen the influence of the *whole child* concept as basic to the educational process. The growth and development of the child's personality in relation to his environment is the principal aspect of it.

Human Experience Levels. Human experience may be said to

involve activity on three levels, namely, neuromuscular, mental, and affective. On the whole there is close interaction between these three functioning levels. While each new experience bears some relationship to previous experiences, the affective level may be said to bind all together. The feelings and emotions constitute the affective experiences. At the same time, maturation levels must also be considered, not only physical but mental, social, and emotional. Physically mature individuals may be children emotionally. It is highly desirable that body and emotions develop concomitantly.

We have space in this section to call attention only briefly to the increasing place emotions occupy in the educative processes, hoping that the student will study this intriguing problem at greater length.

Mild Emotions. Consideration is now given to three levels of emotional experience, as Prescott[22] has pointed them out. First are the mild emotions, those simple physical contacts and mental stimuli which produce a moderate increase in all normal physiological functions. Among these are noises, physical contacts, reading, music, decoration, conversation, dancing, games, recreation, all types of aesthetic experiences, and the initial stages of love-making. These are usually wholesome and vivid experiences and should form an integral part of the educative processes. They improve the dull and quite often drab aspects of classroom instruction. Knowledge and skills bathed in a mild emotional experience have a far greater retention value. Appreciations in themselves partake of an emotional experience.

Strong Emotions. Conditions which produce strong emotions have a considerably different effect upon the child and the educational process. These take on the nature of a crisis, the result of serious situations involving the basic instincts—anger, fear, joy, sorrow—and sexual orgasm. They demand or produce vigorous action and are accompanied by the most vivid feelings. Some form of bodily adjustment immediately takes place to meet them adequately, such as physiological and glandular changes which seem to gird the individual for action. The action may be either positive or negative in effect. Positive action induces bodily adjustments, such as increased heartbeat, respiration, and other reorganizations of the bodily economy, bringing about superior strengths, feelings of confidence and

---

[22] Daniel Alfred Prescott, *Emotion and the Educative Process,* Washington, American Council on Education, 1938, pp. 18 ff.

courage, dramatic situations, with disruptions occurring if the emotion reaches too high a degree of intensity. In the latter instance, the subsidence of the emotion is accompanied by enervation and ennui; the interference with the bodily functions may continue, at least for a time. Less intense emotions when past leave the body functioning normally in a short while.

Certain of these bodily reactions are quite understandable when it is pointed out that the consciousness of the individual may have evaluated the situation confronting him as inimical or challenging to his personal or group welfare; hence there is an immediate demand to preserve that interest. Nature rises to the emergency whether the danger is real or imaginary. Such an explanation only partially applies to strong emotions of intense joy or erotic pleasure. Here there is a release of bodily energy accompanied by similar feelings of courage, confidence, and active physical response, and a general all-round feeling of "goodness." Nature rises to the emergency, but in a different manner.

Where the effect of the strong emotion is negative, inaction rather than action may be the outcome. Thus, the emotion may result in grief, despair, defeat, humiliation, or remorse, bringing with it feelings of frustration and moods of depression and melancholy. Such an effect may be directly due to the superior strength of the opposing forces in the emotional experience, and in which the bodily forces seem unequal to the task in hand. Similar experiences, long continued, tend to increase the negativity of the effect and the depths of the depression. The student should observe carefully the striking contrasts of the bodily effects of these two types of strong emotions.[23]

Disintegrative Emotions. On the third level of emotional reactions are the disintegrative emotions, called so because of their seemingly overpowering strength and their unsupportable duration. Illustrations of this type include effects of disaster in some forms, psychoneurosis in any form, and psychosis. Degree of intensity and prolongation of the emotion is the prevailing characteristic, with resulting temporary or permanent disorganization of physical and mental functions. These disorganizing emotions may produce hallucinations, hysteria, and eventual psychosis, requiring psychiatric and psychopathic treatment and institutional care.

---

[23] *Ibid.,* pp. 21–29.

It is important to point out that the incipient stages of the disintegrative emotions may be detected by the discerning teacher in the classroom through recurring phenomena. As soon as detected the case should be referred to the school psychologist or psychiatrist.

Mental Illness. As indicated in the previous paragraph, there are many types of mental deviation which are manifested initially in the child as he comes to school. Ordinarily, concern for these persons belongs to the psychiatrist and the physician. Our interest at this point is to understand something of the nature and manifestation of their illness.

Epilepsy[24] is a well-known deviation. There are several types whose physical characteristics vary from mild attacks to serious convulsions. It may create serious disturbances of classroom routine and affect the personality and general welfare of the pupil concerned. Cases should be identified, and treatment and proper placement provided as early as possible. Pre-psychotic conditions may be manifested early in the personalities of some children. An emotional disturbance may give the first inkling, such as hysteria, fears, tantrums, dementia, and melancholy. Predisposition to psychosis in any form may have a physical basis, as syphilis, drugs, alcohol, or heredity. Writers in this field identify the characteristics of such children as seclusiveness, regression in any form, daydreaming, bizarre behavior, sensitivity to comment or suggestions, physical inactivity, and irritability. Illusions and hallucinations should be observed and reported.

Educational Implications. To refer to a pupil or group of pupils upon classification as emotionally exceptional is to imply that there exists, at least theoretically, the emotionally normal pupil. To refer to the emotionally exceptional pupil as being emotionally maladjusted is also to imply that the pupil of normal, or average, outlook on life is not maladjusted from the emotional standpoint. This implication, of course, is not necessarily true. Normal or average emotional condition may not be the optimum condition, and, as a corollary thereto, the normal child emotionally may be as much the subject of investigation in a study of emotional maladjustment as the emotionally exceptional child. One refutation of this contention might be that school activities are fitted to the child of average emotional configuration; however, this would be an assumption of

---

[24] See Baker, *op. cit.,* chap. xix, for a good discussion.

doubtful acceptability. It would seem, therefore, that a study of the emotional life of all school pupils should be made more properly from the standpoint of emotional maladjustment than from that of emotional deviation.

It should also be realized that there is a very definite cause-and-effect relationship between emotional maladjustment and physical, mental, and social maladjustment. Physical deviations from the norm may, and frequently do, engender emotional disturbances, stammering, for example. Emotional abnormalities are almost certain to characterize the social deviate at some time or other. There may be a whole series of problems resulting in social misbehavior, which represent a lack of personal adjustment. Environmental influences may produce attitudes which in turn influence the personality development. These may or may not have social significance, resulting in socially disapproved behavior.

Such considerations definitely point out that emotional maladjustment does not comprehend the total of personality deviation, although the emotions form one of the major parts of what we call personality. Some writers go so far as to indicate that all personality abnormalities are either maladjustments or disorders, the first requiring unspecialized treatment and the latter, specialized treatment or segregation.

The first consideration for education is the recognition of the profound importance the emotions have in the life of the individual. Wholesome mild emotions can and should play a large part in the instructional process on the appropriate maturation level if correctly understood and directed. Proper control of the emotional experience in the classroom is the important prerequisite. The dangers of giving way freely and habitually to expressions of emotion should be guarded against. Strong emotions should be avoided by suppression of the stimuli that bring them about. This should be accomplished by the use of standard techniques. Proper emotional attitudes should be inculcated and unhealthy attitudes removed, as prejudice, superstition, and fear. The mental hygiene of the classroom should be given the same consideration in the mind of the teacher and the pupils as physical hygiene.

Mental illness in any form is the concern, first of the psychiatrist, and then of the medical specialist. The teacher is concerned primarily with identification, then with administering adequately to those pupils who remain in the classroom situation after study and treatment.

The Place of the Teacher. Much that we have offered in preceding paragraphs refers to the role of the teacher in dealing with emotional control and instability. In summary, certain specific suggestions may be helpful:

1. Prevention involves assistance in the removal of any condition bringing about the emotional tension. This may refer to school and home environment, personality adjustment on the part of the teacher herself, or personal or social relations of each child with other children.

2. Alleviation and cure may require individualized treatment of some cases and necessitate the services of professional workers. Clinical assistance should be available to every child. However, there are numerous forms of assistance of an unspecialized nature which every teacher can give.

3. Specifically for every child, the teacher can assist in building up his physical health, develop right attitudes, adjust schoolwork to his mental and health level, have respect for his personality, help him to realize his own ability to control his behavior and face consequences good and bad, evaluate his behavior in social terms, and consult frequently with his parents and others who may be concerned with this adjustment. The classroom must be without mental strain and the teacher herself must be poised and serene.

4. An adequate knowledge of mental hygiene is a requisite of every properly educated teacher, so that she can both evaluate her own emotional adjustment and understand the problems of the classroom.

Administrative Considerations. It is important then to stress the part that emotion plays in the well-balanced lives of physically, mentally, and socially adjusted children. We have pointed out that physically and mentally handicapped children often acquire emotional disturbances as a result of their disabilities. Mental deviates occasionally lapse into some form of introversion. Back of many socially handicapped children is the controlling factor of some strong emotional experience, perhaps continuous in its action. If not relieved, it may result in a psychotic condition. The problem is to isolate the emotional disturbance, remove it if possible, and balance the whole personality.

Conditions within the school which bear a direct relationship to the study and treatment of the emotions should be studied by the administration. The regimentative aspects of the traditional school may have an unwholesome effect. There may be inflexible time schedules, incorrect placement, harsh discipline, unwholesome physical conditions, and difficult teachers who lack understanding. Associated with every school should be the necessary guidance, psychological, and psychiatric services. Medical care should be provided where necessary. Curricular materials should be better adapted. The role of aesthetic experiences should be studied. Home conditions should be ascertained and, where possible, corrected through an adequate visiting teaching service. The implications of adolescence should be better understood together with the pressures and complexities of life as they loom large in the lives of boys and girls.

Suggestions offered for the consideration of the teacher may be followed with profit insofar as they refer to the administration. Too few administrators, especially in large school systems, are sufficiently cognizant of the atmosphere of the classroom. Wise administrators put first things first.

REVIEW OF ADMINISTRATIVE PROCEDURES FOR EXCEPTIONAL CHILDREN

Through the chapter many suggestions have been offered for the education of exceptional pupils. The first step in dealing with them is their proper identification. The use of available tests, guidance and clinical procedures, and other forms of identification will be necessary to this end. Uneducable children, insofar as the public schools are concerned, should be isolated, placed in the proper institution, or otherwise given suitable treatment. Educable children become the responsibility of the public school unless, in the interests of the individual or the group, some other form of education is more desirable.

Upon proper classification of educable exceptional children, the necessary educational organization and program will need to be worked out. Large cities will be able to provide special classes and schools, and assume more easily the higher costs. Children residing in smaller cities and towns and in rural districts will find few facilities designed for their particular purposes. Where the special class is not possible, provision should be found in the regular classroom or under county and state direction through special schools and classes for groups of districts. As we have indicated, it would seem to be the direct responsibility of the state to make ultimate arrangements for these children.

It is important to stress the place of environment in ministering to the needs of the exceptional child—within the school as well as in the home and the community. The need for trained personnel is most necessary, such as psychologists, psychiatrists, guidance counselors, and visiting teachers. Teachers will need training in special education. Available services of social agencies, clinics, and hospitals should be utilized. One should keep always in mind that the child's best education is to learn to help himself.

There are many problems for which the future holds the solution, problems of prevention as well as of cure. There must be a greater sensitivity on the part of the public to the need, with a corresponding willingness to support the program. The special services of medicine, social case work, and psychiatry need to be expanded. Wherever the exceptional child resides, the help of an adequate education should be extended to him.

QUESTIONS AND PROBLEMS

1. Study your state laws, state reports, and other information available for data bearing on the exceptional child in your state.
2. What type of exceptional child is most handicapped? Why? Prove your contention by citing reliable studies.
3. What are the arguments .for and against institutional training of children? What children now housed in institutions might well be cared for in the public schools? Would it be in the state's interest to do so? Why?
4. Try to secure reliable data supplementing the White House Conference's classification and estimate of handicapped children. Draw up your own classification in accordance with data given in the chapter.
5. Compare present facilities for the education of the gifted and the mentally retarded child in the public schools. What desirable changes would you suggest?
6. Secure data showing that delinquents and criminals tend to come from the socially handicapped groups. What other groups?
7. What reasons can you give for the recent emphasis on the importance of emotions in the educative processes? Explain your answer by illustrations from your own teaching or administrative experiences.

8. Set up an organization to care for exceptional children for (*a*) a city of 500,000, (*b*) a city of 50,000, (*c*) a city of 5000, (*d*) a county-wide system, (*e*) a state-wide system.
9. What specific training should (*a*) every teacher, (*b*) teachers of special classes have in regard to the exceptional child?

SELECTED REFERENCES

1. Allport, G. W., *Personality*. New York: Henry Holt and Company, 1937.
2. Bagby, English, *The Psychology of Personality*. New York: Henry Holt and Company, 1928.
3. Baker, Harry J., *Introduction to Exceptional Children*. New York: The Macmillan Company, 1944.
4. Bradley, C., *Schizophrenia in Childhood*. New York: The Macmillan Company, 1941.
5. Conklin, Agnes M., *Failures of Highly Intelligent Pupils,* Contributions to Education No. 792. New York: Teachers College, Columbia University, 1940.
6. Despert, J. Louise, *Emotional Problems in Children*. Utica, New York: State Hospitals Press, 1938.
7. "Education of Exceptional Children," *Phi Delta Kappan,* October, 1940.
8. "Educational Diagnosis," *Thirty-Fourth Yearbook,* National Society for the Study of Education. Bloomington: Public School Publishing Company, 1935, chaps. ii, iv, v, ix, x, part ii.
9. "Fit to Teach," *Ninth Yearbook,* Department of Classroom Teachers. Washington: National Education Association, 1938.
10. Heck, Arch O., *The Education of Exceptional Children*. New York: McGraw-Hill Book Company, 1940. Contains excellent references at the end of each chapter.
11. "Intelligence: Its Nature and Nurture," *Thirty-Ninth Yearbook,* National Society for the Study of Education. Bloomington: Public School Publishing Company, 1940, parts i and ii.
12. Lund, Frederick H., *Emotions*. New York: The Ronald Press Company, 1939.
13. "Opportunities for the Preparation of Teachers of Exceptional Children," *Bulletin (1937) No. 17*. Washington: Government Printing Office, 1938.
14. Otto, Henry J., *Elementary School Organization and Administration*. New York: D. Appleton-Century Company, 1944, chap. xii.
15. Prescott, Daniel Alfred, *Emotion and the Educative Process*. Washington: American Council on Education, 1938.

16. *Review of Educational Research*: "Counseling, Guidance and Personnel Work," April, 1945; "Education of Exceptional Children and Minority Groups," June, 1941; "Education of Exceptional Children and Minority Groups," June, 1944; "Mental Hygiene and Health Education," December, 1940; "Mental and Physical Health," December, 1946.

17. Rogers, C. R., *Counseling and Psychotherapy*. Boston: Houghton Mifflin Company, 1942.

18. "Scientific Movement in Education, The," *Thirty-Seventh Yearbook*, National Society for the Study of Education. Bloomington: Public School Publishing Company, 1938, chaps. xxxii, xxxiii, xxxiv, xxxv, part ii.

19. Stoddard, George D., *The Meaning of Intelligence*. New York: The Macmillan Company, 1943.

20. Sumption, M. R., *Three Hundred Gifted Children*. Yonkers: World Book Company, 1941.

21. Thom, D. A., "Habit Clinics for Child Guidance," *Bureau of Publications No. 135*. Washington: United States Department of Labor, 1939.

22. White House Conference, *Special Education: The Handicapped and the Gifted*. New York: The Century Company, 1931.

23. Zachry, Caroline B., *Emotion and Conduct in Adolescence*. New York: D. Appleton-Century Company, 1940.

NOTE: The following periodicals contain valuable references which should be helpful: *Journal of Exceptional Children; Journal of Educational Research; Journal of Genetic Psychology; Journal of Speech Disorders; American Journal of Orthopsychiatry; American Annals of the Deaf.*

PART IV

Problems Incidental to a Wider Educational Program
for All Pupils

CHAPTER XII

Administrative Problems and Procedures in Facilitating Adjustment and Growth

ONE can easily agree with Briggs that in organization and administration the schoolmen of the United States have manifested great ingenuity.[1] Our schools may run smoothly, but whether they operate effectively may need to be determined by an analysis of their objectives and the nature of the progress of the product. In the last analysis the individual progress and welfare of each child is the best evidence of a school's efficiency.

In this chapter we shall analyze administrative problems which have become apparent through an effort to provide more adequately for pupils' individual progress. Many of these have been intensified because the schools now provide for all youth, without selectivity. This has brought to notice a great range of abilities and interests with a large proportion of non-college and especially non-academic youth. The first step is one of identification, following which administrative procedures must be as closely adapted to each pupil as is possible under the circumstances.

ASCERTAINING AGE-GRADE DISTRIBUTION

The educational and social growth of each individual child has much more meaning when compared with like growth of some comparable group. A simple measure of that growth is chronological age.

---

[1] Thomas H. Briggs, "The Issues of Secondary Education," *Official Report,* Department of Superintendence, Washington, National Education Association, 1936, p. 39.

Since we have taken advantage of that measure in the grade-a-year concept, a study of pupil placement by ages reveals the status of each pupil in relation to his age group.

Age-Grade Progress. We have seen that the organization of the American system of education on a twelve-grade basis presumes that the child enters the first grade at or about the age of six years and progresses annually through each of the twelve grades until he graduates between the ages of seventeen and eighteen years. Such a child is said to have achieved a normal age-grade status. If, however, he is under six years when admitted to school and has advanced through more than one grade during any one year, he is said to be under-age or accelerated. If admitted later to first grade, or detained in any grade for more than a year, he is over-age or retarded.

Age-grade charts provided usually by state departments of education are prepared to record the under-age, normal-age, and over-age status of all children. For example, six-year-old children are those whose ages fall between 5¾ years and 6¼ years. These ages are taken as of a certain fixed date, as September 1 of any year.

Each school district should maintain a reliable record of its age-grade status and at frequent intervals make a careful study of it. It

TABLE 12. PERCENTAGE OF AGE-GRADE STATUS DISTRIBUTION IN THREE GRADES WITH ANNUAL PROMOTION[2]

Grade		Districts in Northern Illinois	Mort and Featherstone Study
I	Under-age	10	17.3
	Normal-age	85	72.9
	Over-age	5	9.8
V	Under-age	13	15.9
	Normal-age	74	62.5
	Over-age	13	21.6
VIII	Under-age	14	18.6
	Normal-age	73	58.9
	Over-age	13	22.5

[2] For a suggested series of age-grade charts, the reader is referred to Henry J. Otto, *Promotion Policies in Elementary Schools,* Minneapolis, Educational Test Bureau, 1935, chap. iv.

should be checked against a reliable chart indicating proper grade placement, and the extent of over-ageness or under-ageness should be determined. Immediate attention should be given to those pupils occupying extreme positions in the chart. Care should be taken not to justify any condition found demanding improvement on the basis of comparable conditions in other schools. Table 12 gives an example of the range of under-age, normal-age, and over-age pupils in annual promotion schools. The table shows that normal ageness tends to decrease from the first to the eighth grades. Over one-fifth of all pupils are over-age in the eighth grade.

It is also interesting to note that semi-annual promotions do not reduce over-ageness.[3] Moreover, the percentage of under-age children is larger for the advanced or high sections of each grade than for the low sections, and the percentage of over-age pupils is larger for the first half or low sections of each grade than for the advanced sections. The explanation for this fact is that the midyear entering classes acquire a larger accretion of repeaters from the fall entering classes and lose by double promotions a larger number of superior pupils than do the fall entering classes.

In observing these data, one should note: (1) the nature of the promotion policy and its administration within the several buildings and by different teachers; (2) "push" of incoming groups; (3) clashes of opinion, between principals (or superintendents) and teachers; (4) "urges" of parents; (5) adaptability of curriculum materials; (6) rigidity or leniency of teaching standards; (7) abilities of the children; (8) case studies of individual children over a period of years; and many other factors.

Mere figures and percentages, however, do not tell the entire story. A further analysis should be made of both retarded and accelerated children individually in order to discern any factors which impede school progress or assist in it. Here the professionally trained psychologist and guidance counselor enter the picture in order to give assistance to the principal and classroom teachers. The next two sections will treat these variations.

Retardation and Its Significance. A child may be said to be retarded if his school progress is slower than his capacities and limita-

---

[3] *Ibid.*, p. 56; also Paul R. Mort and W. B. Featherstone, *Entrance and Promotion Practices in City School Systems: Standards and Accounting Procedures,* New York, Bureau of Publications, Teachers College, Columbia University, 1932.

tions would seem to indicate. Retardation is usually associated with over-ageness. However true this may be in many instances, not all over-age children can be said to be retarded. As an administrative measure retardation is a direct outcome of non-promotion, the declared purpose being to correct the pupil's obvious difficulties. Most retarded pupils are those of lower mental ability. On an average, about 15 per cent of all children may be said to be retarded in some way.

Retardation thus is closely linked with repetition of a grade or subject. In the judgment of the teacher, the child may need to be retained to acquire mastery of certain subject matter. He may be immature, lacking in industry, ill, irregular in attendance, or in need of further discipline. If a dull child, he may require a lengthened time span for "getting the subject." He may be caught in the failure section of a normal distribution curve used in promotion, a too-common practice. Occasionally a pupil may be retarded for the "good of the system," to maintain a "standard," or to show the class that the subject is "hard" and that not just anyone can expect to pass. Retardation thus becomes associated with failure, although in the minds of many teachers they are not synonymous terms. The retarded pupil often becomes a disciplinary problem and, disliking school and everything connected with it, eventually eliminates himself.

The approach, then, to retardation is (1) to determine its extent and (2) to ascertain reasons assigned in individual cases. A case study analysis should be made of each pupil, which should include a medical examination and study of health records, analysis of psychological and achievement tests, previous scholarship and other records, study of personality and traits, home conditions, and such other data as may be available. If tests show marked deviation from normality, the pupil should be placed in a special school or class adapted to his particular status and needs. If the results show need for corrective measures, as in matters of health, these should be taken. Any adjustment in the light of individual needs should be made; otherwise the child should be placed in the proper grade as the results of the tests and other records show and given such remedial assistance as he seems to require. Above everything, it is essential to remove any stigma of, or resentment due to, failure which he may retain. To the extent that causes bringing about retardation can be corrected, he should be allowed to progress with normal expectation of promotion.

Specifically, the following are offered as worthy of investigation in considering the retarded child: his chronological, mental, and social ages, physical handicaps, language handicaps, home environment, regularity of attendance, extent of effort, interests, nature and extent of previous transfers from school to school, attitude of teachers, quality of previous teaching, size of his classes in previous grades, and achievement record in previous classes. All available records and data should be brought together for the study, which suggests closer attention to the need for and study of records. Schools with a large amount of retardation should recognize that a serious situation exists and immediately do something about it.

Acceleration and Its Significance. At the upper end of the age-grade scale will be found about 11 per cent of pupils who are classified as accelerated. Pupils are considered as accelerated if they have made more rapid progress than is indicated by their age-grade normal status. Thus they may be one, two, or even more years ahead of their normal age group. Acceleration may result from earlier admittance, double promotion usually due to an excellent scholarship record or superior ability, omitting a grade or half-grade, parental insistence, or transfer from school to school. Usually accelerants possess higher mental ability than their fellows and in many cases are definitely gifted children.

Acceleration of pupils is, for the most part, an outcome of a misfit school organization. If the school system were organized to meet the needs of each child, the school program would be so adapted that the child could progress normally in an environment suited to his capacity and ability. Acceleration of any pupil presumes, therefore, that the new environment is suited in all ways to his capacities, an assumption not generally in accord with the true situation. In the absence of an enriched environment for the gifted child, teachers advance as arguments for acceleration that (1) a year saved is advisable, (2) the child should not be allowed to "loaf," (3) the new environment will allow him to proceed at his own rate, (4) he needs more stimulation, and (5) on the whole, more is to be gained through acceleration than normal grade progress.

Acceleration of pupils creates problems of social adjustment, often resulting in serious personality difficulties, as introversion and conceit. Little attention is usually paid to the child's mental hygiene. Often his qualities of leadership become submerged under personalities older and stronger, physically or otherwise. His own physical development does not always keep pace with his mentality. The hoped-for enrichment of environmental opportunities in the next grade proves illusory, being merely more of the same experiences of the grade below on a little higher level, with perhaps poorer teaching taking the place of the excellent teaching to which he may owe a goodly portion of his acceleration.

However, some of these fears may prove unfounded, since studies show that accelerated elementary pupils do make more progress in the secondary school, that little harm results to pupils of one to one and one-half years' acceleration, and that many socially maladjusted pupils do find ways of adjusting themselves socially within groups. This is especially true where definite efforts have been made to forestall this difficulty. One test of superior ability should surely be the capacity to adjust oneself to unusual situations.

The approach then to acceleration, as to retardation, is the determination of its nature and extent. Individual study should be made of each child, his physical, mental, social, and emotional status. If no provision in the way of an enriched program is possible in the present school organization, he should be placed where his individual progress is most probable. A preferable plan would be to organize special classes under skillful teachers, with instruction highly individualized. Some object to this plan because of resulting social inequalities. Enriched programs are usually to be favored over acceleration. The final decision should be made after an analysis of many factors found both in school and out.[4] Some suggestions for enriching any school program for accelerated pupils are: proper grade adjustments, special assignments, adding a subject, additional coaching in the same or additional subjects, outside interests such as music lessons, and encouragement of additional school activities, as school paper and athletics. Suggestions of this type are limited only by the school's opportunities and the nature of the school policy.

---

[4] The student is referred to an excellent discussion of accelerants in Paul A. Mort, *The Individual Pupil in the Management of Class and School*, New York, American Book Company, 1928.

ELIMINATION OF PUPILS

Ideally, the school should provide for not only all educable children within the limits prescribed by law for their attendance but for all children who can profit in any way by such attendance and are otherwise not sufficiently mature to become adjusted socially and economically to independent living in a democracy. Strictly speaking, when any pupil of school age leaves school who ordinarily should be in attendance, he is by that act eliminated.

Elimination may be considered: (1) justifiable, for reasons entirely legal and reasonable in nature; and (2) unjustifiable, in which case it is harmful to the child's interests and should be corrected. Justifiable elimination is dealt with by the laws of the various states, which recognize certain exemptions from attendance, as equivalent instruction, disability, legal employment, completion of given grades, sometimes distance, and in some states extreme poverty. Graduation from school under certain compulsory age limits with failure on the part of the board of education or parents to provide for further education is, in a sense, elimination.

Elimination for unjustifiable causes includes discouragement on account of school failure, distance from school, the teacher factor, retardation, certain subject difficulties, preference for outside work, economic necessity, ill health, and disciplinary causes. Perhaps inability for various reasons to do the work assigned is a contributory factor. Estimates have been made that as high as 30 per cent of high school pupils have insufficient mental ability to achieve anything but failure in the typical smaller secondary school and thus are headed for eventual elimination.

A further classification of the causes of elimination might include: (1) causes traceable to the school, as maladjustment, discipline, dislike for school or teachers, lack of ability to do a particular type of schoolwork, and school failure; and (2) causes traceable to forces outside the school, as economic necessity, mental deficiency, exemption by law, desire for work, and mental and physical defects. Here too might be included broken homes, early marriages, pregnancy, delinquency, foreign influences, and religious cults. Many older high school boys leave school before graduation to enter some branch of national service.

The extent of elimination is a good indication of the educational efficiency and holding power of a school system. Theoretically, every child should remain in school as long as he can profit by its offerings or until he is ready for life's responsibilities. This fact should not relieve the school of the responsibility to provide further opportunities if its present offerings are limited and contribute to elimination. Even those exemptions allowable by law should be viewed in the same light, since retardation, and occasionally acceleration, lead to elimination.

Transfer of Pupils

The mobility of our population, recently aggravated by heavy movements of workers and their families and for various other reasons, has created a serious problem affecting the school transfer of many children. These children enter new school situations, facing new teachers, new work, and a new environment. Few of them exactly "fit into" the new situation.

In meeting the needs of these children, the first step is the matter of placement. In practice no grade is standardized as to material covered. There are always differences of teachers, texts, methods, and materials. There is great variation in this respect among cities and states. Too often the practice of demotion is followed on the assumption that the new work is too difficult and the new pupil must gain time to orient himself. Some teachers have been known to consider no transfer child quite as well prepared as their own. Demotion may be due in part to the results of interviews and placement tests in which the child too often is at a disadvantage because of new situations.

Within the same school system, the problem of transfer from school to school is a much simpler process owing to greater likelihood of standardized grade placement. In any event, proper forms should be prepared which will facilitate transfer with definite instructions to the child and his parents as to the school and grade to attend. Since the determination of proper procedures as to transfer is an administrative responsibility, these should be carefully prepared and definite instructions given to the teachers or clerical assistants who perform the actual service.

Pupils received by transfer should be given just as careful attention. Large numbers of pupils present themselves at school on the opening day or during the term, some with transfers for the same or neighboring schools of similar rank, others from out-of-town schools with no credentials except the word of pupil or parents. Proofs of various kinds should be provided showing age, previous grade attended, vaccination record, and health and other records. Temporary grade and room assignment should be made while tests are given, records verified, or parents consulted. The final placement of the child should be in accordance with those principles outlined in an earlier chapter.

PROBLEMS OF A CHANGING SCHOOL POPULATION

Mentioned in previous sections of this book is the important fact that the population of the public schools has been undergoing marked change. There are two noticeable characteristics of this change. The first includes the extension of educational opportunities to more and more children until it now may be said that most of the children of school age in the United States go to school. For illustration: in public high schools in 1890 only about 2.8 per cent of youth aged fourteen through seventeen years were enrolled. By 1910 the percentage had risen to 16.6, by 1920 to 37.9, by 1930 to 51.1, and by 1940 to about 70 per cent of youth of these ages. For all pupils five to seventeen years of age, the ratio of enrollments in public day schools to the school population is now about 85 per cent. Including those attending private schools of all types, concerning which records are inadequate, one can conclude that but few children of school age do not attend school.

A second characteristic to be noted concerning the school population is the effect of many environmental influences, educational and otherwise, upon their attitude toward and progress in school. There is a certain sophistication about many American youth. Our quiz programs attest to precocious knowledge and skills little dreamed of a generation or so ago.

Pupil Range. This sustained rise in enrollments has brought into the public schools an increased range of pupil abilities, interests, and needs. Formerly, secondary school pupils were a relatively homogeneous group. If one did not fit into the educational pattern of the day, he was quickly eliminated. Today, as Jessen points out, "The present high school population displays an almost complete spectrum of abilities of normal human beings and sounds nearly the entire gamut of interests of young people."[5]

The school enrollments naturally indicate more and more pupils from the lower economic and social brackets especially in the secondary field. Only one out of seven will ever go on to a higher educational institution. Intellectual selection becomes difficult. And yet these tendencies would appear to be healthful and directed toward democratization of the educational program and processes. As a result the offerings of the schools have been greatly enlarged, thus attracting and holding youth, offering a more adaptable program, and enticing their interests through all forms of extra-curricular activities.

Group Designation. It is obvious that a challenging administrative problem exists in classifying pupils, especially secondary. The usual designation of college and non-college groups is hardly sufficient. Butterfield[6] speaks of three types: (1) the professional specialist (25 per cent), (2) the skilled trade group (25 per cent), and (3) those who are destined to fill jobs (50 per cent). Clark[7] classifies them into three groups: the college, the skilled occupations, and the general. Too often the secondary school is judged by what it has done for the first group no matter how little provision is made for the second and third. Within both junior and senior high schools one finds variously named curricula, designed to fulfill the needs of a particular group.

The College (Academic) Pupil

The problems to be discussed in this section apply particularly to secondary youth. Elementary pupils are (or should be) characterized by a greater homogeneity, in that mastery of common knowledges, skills, and appreciations can proceed without great regard for differentiated approach. However, in the secondary field, it is essential that provision be made for the needs of all groups. We have used the term "college pupil" as generally employed to characterize youth

---

[5] Carl A. Jessen, "Trends of Secondary Education," *Bulletin No. 2*, Washington, United States Office of Education, 1939, p. 2.

[6] E. W. Butterfield, "The New Fifty Per Cent," *Junior-Senior High School Clearing House*, January, 1934, pp. 265–272.

[7] R. C. Clark, "High School Serves Three Groups," *Journal of Education*, January 16, 1933, pp. 36–38.

of exceptional abilities and skills who can profit by higher education. It is a matter of common knowledge that secondary schools throughout most of their history have been dominated by institutions of higher learning. This domination has been reflected in both curriculum and method. There is now a noticeable tendency among secondary schools to ignore the demands of many colleges that conflict with what seems best for the larger number of students.

The fact remains that there are and will remain some 20 per cent of secondary youth that should receive a type of education designed to fit them for leadership individually for the professions, government, business, agriculture, and many other walks of life. The problem of the school is to (1) identify pupils of potential special ability and leadership, (2) collect all data concerning such potentialities, (3) provide a school program accordingly, and (4) follow these pupils through high school and college scholastically and financially if necessary.

In the administration of college relations to these pupils, the principal will need to be concerned with a number of important matters. These will be presented in some detail in the next chaper.

While much importance is to be attached to college preparation of academically minded youth, greater attention should be paid to those aspects of secondary training which pertain as well to other pupils. Modern objectives of secondary education furnish the basis of this training. The health of all must be given greater consideration. Social needs must be carefully balanced along with individual needs. Grouping of academically minded youth has tended to establish a kind of snobbery which is inimical to the best interests of the democratic processes. To this end socialization of all youth is essential. Too often there is a tendency to overload the brighter pupils both with additional subjects and with pupil activities. Many individual defects which need attention have often been covered up by pleasing personalities and brilliant prospects. Perhaps the conclusion of the whole matter is the thought that every year of secondary as well as elementary education should be made intrinsically worth while for all pupils and the schools' program adapted to that end.

NON-COLLEGE AND NON-ACADEMIC PUPILS

The Non-College Pupil. The term "non-college" is perhaps misleading. Ordinarily it means all pupils who will not go to college.

But this does not tell the whole story. Many pupils will not go to college because they have not demonstrated the latent ability. Many more are apt to be deprived of a higher education because of economic or social conditions beyond their control. Identification of those pupils who show ability to profit by a higher education should be made as early as possible and conditions adjusted so that they may obtain such education. The potentialities of all other pupils should be similarly discovered and provision made for their realization.

All youth should receive education (1) for citizenship, (2) for family living, (3) in American culture, (4) in mental and physical health, (5) for useful work to sustain themselves and others, (6) in thinking rationally, and (7) in making right decisions when faced with individual and social problems.[8] In giving attention to these needs, it is important to remember that youth are youth *now*. The best education for the future is education to live better each day in the light of these objectives.

Identification of Non-Academic Pupils. Recently the non-college boys and girls, particularly the non-academic group, have been receiving greater attention. The latter have been identified as (1) the handicapped, (2) those influenced by social conditions, as poverty or limited environment, (3) children of the foreign born, especially of lower economic circumstances, (4) pampered children of wealth who lack vision and incentives, (5) those who are occupationally diverted or without occupational direction, and in general (6) those who have reached a plateau of development along one or more lines.[9]

Tonsor[10] has suggested other factors to be used as means of identification of non-academic pupils which in turn might well form the basis for administrative adjustment. These are: (1) lack of organized mental processes; (2) inability to think, tendency to guess; (3) ignorance of methods and values of study, accompanied often by an unwillingness to study; (4) absence of constructive habits of any kind; (5) inability to comprehend and follow simple directions;

---

[8] *Education for All American Youth,* Educational Policies Commission, Washington, National Education Association, 1944, pp. 16–17.

[9] Theophil W. H. Irion, "Non-Academic High School Student," *School and Community,* November, 1938, pp. 322–324; also *Bulletin 23,* Department of Secondary School Principals, Washington, National Education Association, January, 1939, pp. 35–39.

[10] Charles A. Tonsor, "Non-Academically-Minded Child," *High Points,* New York, Board of Education, March, 1939, pp. 59–63.

(6) disinclination to focus attention beyond personal desires; (7) inadequately trained eyes and ears; (8) want of vital interests to motivate mental activity; and (9) lack of a sufficient vocabulary for educational purposes.

It will be readily observed that these deficiencies may well characterize many other pupils of secondary school age. In the case of non-academic pupils, they appear more marked. The remedy is to attack each deficiency at its source, and by careful attention overcome it.

Providing for Needs. For some years the National Association of Secondary School Principals has been giving attention to the needs of these pupils. In 1940, the Association compiled a list of "Promising Practices in Secondary Education"[11] in which a section was given over to the non-college pupil, including the non-academic pupil. Phases dealt with were: (1) classifying pupils, (2) teaching pupils effective study habits, (3) remedial reading, (4) cooperation with out-of-school agencies, and (5) the non-academic pupil in particular. These will be discussed in turn.

1. CLASSIFYING PUPILS. Practices indicated as promising in classifying these pupils include use of placement tests, counseling, guidance services, two- and three-level systems of grouping, use of different teachers for different groups, differentiated curricula, different time basis for completing courses, no failures based upon adaptation of work, and achievement diplomas for those not scholastically able to do college type work.

2. TEACHING EFFECTIVE STUDY HABITS. Inability to study effectively has been deemed one of the principal deterring factors to scholastic success. Secondary as well as elementary schools are giving greater attention to this problem. Administrative devices reported include teaching how to study, individual diagnosis with remedial checks, investigation of out-of-school study environment, group study plan of teacher and pupil, emphasizing success of each pupil, pupil-participation in assignment, planning a better work schedule, and better administration of study halls where they still exist. Experimentation is being made in regard to the place of independent study in specific plans of school organization.

3. REMEDIAL READING. Deficiencies in reading are closely related to

---

[11] "Promising Practices in Secondary Education," *Bulletin of the National Association of Secondary School Principals,* October, 1940.

inability to study, a condition which may have been brought about through no fault of the pupil himself. Improvement in reading abilities has enabled many children to remain with or return to their groups. A careful diagnosis through reading tests and a study of reading difficulties is the first step. Remedial plans are largely individual in nature; hence, each pupil should have built up for him an appropriate reading program with material adapted. Schools are experimenting with specially adapted courses of study, special reading classes—usually small—special teachers, motivation techniques, and cooperative planning among teachers. The microphone is being used to advantage. Specific devices emphasized are conversation, letter writing, telling stories, radio programs, and motion pictures. Improvement is noted by using follow-up tests.

4. COOPERATION WITH OUT-OF-SCHOOL AGENCIES. Out-of-school agencies offer numerous opportunities for school use in the education of the non-college pupil. Many of them are vocational in nature and include housing construction, operating or working in stores or other businesses, participating in community or governmental activities, courses in industries, and activities in social agencies.

5. OTHER SPECIFIC DEVICES. Much emphasis is now being laid on short-unit courses adapted to non-academic pupils. Some western states are using correspondence courses with success. Courses should have a practical aspect, with emphasis on leisure time, social, civic, and vocational problems, and activities. Economic problems should receive a large share of attention. Material is being made easier of attainment with emphasis on that which may be immediately useful. In some schools the special class is giving way to a two- or three-group plan, because of the cost and the declared undemocratic nature of the former. Much attention is being paid to school activities which immediately benefit the school. The primary aim seems to be to develop a personality and correct attitudes which may have become warped owing to previous types of school standards impossible of attainment. Attention should be paid to the profitable use of time, to home and family relationships, to spending money wisely, and to vocational usefulness.

ADJUSTMENT PLANS FOR SPECIFIC PURPOSES

Adjustment Rooms. Many school systems have found it advisable to organize special rooms and groups in both elementary and secondary schools for purposes other than caring for exceptional children. Some of these purposes are: (1) to coach pupils who because of absence or other reasons have been retarded a semester or more, (2) to strengthen pupils in certain subjects in which there is an apparent slowness or failure, (3) to assist pupils who have been accelerated to make up work missed, (4) to assist pupils for whom acceleration is planned to make up the intervening material, and (5) to provide for enrichment opportunities and for college entrance or other examinations.

Difficulties of administration and instruction of these groups are immediately apparent because of their varied nature. Complications are encountered as the children are taken from and returned to their own classes. Too often these children are sent to the special rooms indiscriminately by the regular teachers without due regard to their needs and the problems involved in the change.

Under skilled instruction where the purposes are specific, this plan of adjustment has possibilities. Instruction should be individualized wherever possible, although group teaching may be satisfactory under certain circumstances. The chief advantage would appear to be in placing the individual pupil in the hands of a teacher specialist and allowing time to study him, develop the necessary materials, and make the needed adjustment. Close cooperation among teachers concerned is vital, with close supervision advised.

The time spent by the child in this adjustment will naturally vary with his need. Two plans are proposed: (1) that the child spend all of his time with the adjusting teacher for the period of the emergency and (2) that the child devote a portion of his time to the special work, as a part of a day, or one or two days a week. It is important to point out that the adjustment room should not be regarded as a place to "dump" pupils by those teachers who are always ready to evade their proper responsibilities, and that a child should not be labeled by some reproachful designation because he has been a member of an adjustment room.

Make-Up Adjustments. Short-unit courses have been developed in high schools to adjust certain subject matter deficiencies in pupils due to previous failure, transfer, or other reasons, and seem to be preferable to a complete repetition of the course, if it is possible to administer them. In larger junior high schools, such plans have been found helpful with retarded pupils or those who show marked deficiencies. They may be scheduled in subject matter sequence in order to overcome weaknesses. Pupils who are preparing for college entrance examinations may be organized in short courses with individual or group emphasis upon the subject needed.

The summer high school movement has been an interesting recent development. Short courses, usually of six weeks' length, seem admirably suited to the needs of those pupils who desire to make up work, continue with their classes, or be accelerated in any way. Care must be taken, however, that instruction is of sufficiently high quality. This comment is made because of the growing tendency to man such schools with practice teachers and others often poorly equipped for the work. If it is understood that "everybody passes," the purposes can hardly be described as having been efficiently achieved. Saving time may result in losing it in the end.

Summer camps, which have been in operation for many years, serving the useful purposes of body building, recreation, and out-of-door living, have likewise been useful institutions in providing opportunities for scholastic adjustment needs. The time may have arrived when these advantages should be made available to more and more pupils. In this way, by rotation, both the physical and scholastic needs of all pupils can be provided for and all-year employment can be given to teachers and others. Learning pleasantly under the trees and beside the water ought to be preferable to stuffy classrooms on hot summer days. Such a plan has many possibilities. It will be discussed at greater length in another chapter.

Instruction for Home-Bound Children. An interesting instructional procedure, commonly known as the home-bound program, has been developed in several of the larger cities for both elementary and secondary children. Under this plan, teachers are assigned to visit the homes of children who, because of their physical and other conditions, are unable to attend school. This program includes spastic children, certain types of orthopedic children, epileptics, and other motor handicapped children. In such a program, the child is actually enrolled in the school to which he would, if physically able, be assigned. The teacher visits once or twice weekly, furnishes textbooks, and instructs in the regular courses of study. Of necessity, such subjects as physical education are omitted. Full credit toward graduation is given for the work when completed. Such instruction is of inestimable value to these handicapped children as far as their intellectual progress is concerned; however, they may lose many of the social values which are usually associated with group situations. Naturally, the program is expensive, because of the smaller number of children which can be assigned to any one teacher.

QUESTIONS AND PROBLEMS

1. Compare the age-grade status of a selected school system with (*a*) your own state tables, (*b*) tables in this chapter or selected studies.
2. Study (*a*) acceleration, (*b*) retardation in a selected school system. Trace individual case studies over more than one year.
3. Compare two or more school systems in regard to elimination. Try to account for individual pupils. What remedial suggestions can you offer?
4. Make a study of the progress of transfer cases in a selected system over a five-year period. What suggestions can you offer?
5. To what extent is your school community in a markedly changing population area? What is being done educationally about it? What can be done?
6. Identify characteristics of (*a*) college type, (*b*) non-college (non-academic) pupils by reference to specific cases in a particular school system.
7. Make a list of the suggested plans for meeting the needs of different groups indicated in the chapter. See if you can identify any of these in practice, noting results. Evaluate effectiveness.
8. Should a summer camp be attached to every school system as an educational adjustment device? What are its advantages? Disadvantages?

SELECTED REFERENCES

1. Blair, Glenn M., *Diagnostic and Remedial Teaching in Secondary Schools.* New York: The Macmillan Company, 1946.
2. Briggs, Thomas H., "The Issues of Secondary Education," *Official Report,* Department of Superintendence. Washington: National Education Association, 1936, pp. 39–71.
3. Buckley, H. M., "Children Gain from Cleveland's Plan of Levels Instead of Grades," *School Management,* May, 1946, p. 482.
4. Butterfield, E. W., "The New Fifty Per Cent," *Junior-Senior High School Clearing House,* January, 1934, pp. 265–272.
5. Caverly, Ernest R., "Shall the High School Eliminate Its Failures?" *Clearing House,* January, 1938, pp. 259–263.
6. "Curriculum Adjustment for Gifted Children," *Bulletin No. 1.* Washington: United States Office of Education, 1946.

7. Curtis, Francis D., "Specific Suggestions for Teaching Dull Normal Pupils," *School Review,* September, 1936, pp. 525–532.

8. Edmonson, J. B., Roemer, Joseph, and Bacon, Francis L., *The Administration of the Modern Secondary School.* New York: The Macmillan Company, 1941, chap. iii.

9. Eisner, Harry, "Challenge of the Slow Pupil," *Mathematics Teacher,* January, 1939, pp. 9–15.

10. Everett, Samuel, *A Challenge to Secondary Education.* New York: D. Appleton-Century Company, 1935.

11. Fernald, Grace M., *Remedial Techniques in Basic School Subjects.* New York: McGraw-Hill Book Company, 1943.

12. Fontaine, Andre C., "Why Are We Doing Nothing Constructive for Over Fifty Per Cent of Our High School Pupils?" *High Points.* New York: Board of Education, May, 1938, pp. 22–27.

13. Kandel, I. L., "Promising Innovations in Secondary Education," *Educational Forum,* November, 1936, pp. 29–38.

14. Koos, Hughes, Hutson, and Reavis, *Administering the Secondary School.* New York: American Book Company, 1940, chap. vii.

15. Mort, Paul R., *The Individual Pupil.* New York: American Book Company, 1928, chaps. ix, x.

16. Newlon, Jesse H., "Two Criticisms of the High School," *School Executive Magazine,* January, 1930, pp. 238–239.

17. Otto, Henry J., *Promotion Policies and Practices in Elementary Schools.* Minneapolis: Educational Test Bureau, 1935.

18. "Paths to Better Schools," *Twenty-Third Yearbook,* American Association of School Administrators. Washington: National Education Association, 1945.

19. Pressey, S. L., "Acceleration: Disgrace or Challenge," *Journal of Science,* September, 1946, pp. 215–219.

20. "Promising Practices in Secondary Education," *Bulletin of the National Association of Secondary School Principals,* October, 1940.

21. *References on the Non-Academic High School Pupil* (leaflet). Washington: National Education Association, Research Division, May, 1939.

22. *Review of Educational Research:* "Counseling, Guidance and Personnel Work," April, 1945; "Education of Exceptional Children and Minority Groups," June, 1941; "Psychological Tests and Their Uses," February, 1944; "Psychological Tests and Their Uses," February, 1947.

23. Studebaker, J. W., "Camps as Part of the Regular School Year," *School Management,* September, 1946, p. 17.

24. Tonsor, Charles A., "Non-Academically-Minded Child," *High Points.* New York: Board of Education, March, 1939, pp. 59–63.

25. Wiley, George M., Jr., *The Redirection of Secondary Education.* New York: The Macmillan Company, 1940, chap. vii.
26. Wrinkle, William L., *The New High School in the Making: the Philosophy and Practice of a Modernized Secondary School.* New York: American Book Company, 1938.

CHAPTER XIII

Articulation of Administrative Units

A PROPER articulation of the different administrative divisions of a school system is essential for the continuous forward movement of every child. The fact that these units have grown up independently of one another has given emphasis to this need. Many of the problems to be discussed in this chapter have been intensified because of the changing character of an increasing and varied school population. There is a greater range of abilities and interests with a larger proportion of non-college and especially non-academic youth. We shall take up the significance of articulation, the factors affecting the problems of articulation on the elementary and secondary levels, and the relations of the secondary school units with higher institutions of learning.

SIGNIFICANCE OF THE PROBLEM

Present Need for Study. At no time in the history of the American schools has the need for functional articulation of the several units of the school system been greater than at the present time. Similarly, never has there been more need for adequate coordination and adjustment within these units. Nearly all children of school age are now going to school. There is a greater stream of pupils passing through the elementary schools into the secondary schools and on into colleges. At the same time, this stream is increasingly heterogeneous in character from every angle of analysis. With the American people thus disposed to send their children to school and to provide liberally for their educational support, the responsibility for uninterrupted progress is definitely placed upon those in educational authority. We have seen earnest attempts to develop desirable admission practices and to abolish selection through elimination. On whatever the level of instruction, the school must meet the educational needs of pupils assigned to it.

The achievement of closer coördination of units within the system requires marked changes in the attitudes of many administrators and teachers in regard to the "sanctity" of some particular educational unit or procedure. Thus the high school has all too often been thought of as an institution for the socially or intellectually select. The same is true of certain courses within the high school. Some administrators and teachers have become immersed in maintaining the tradition of a school or college, endeavoring to bar the way to those who seemingly will not fit into the traditional pattern. Colleges have accentuated the tradition by glorifying the success of individual pupils from selected secondary schools, which in turn has been seized upon by the particular school named as justifiable evidence of a good school. Proper coordination and adjustment may be directly concerned with opposition to prejudice and lack of open-mindedness. Teachers on all levels should understand more fully one another's materials and procedures. Attitudes of superiority and aloofness should give way to feelings of cooperation and understanding, which will make for more democratic practice.

Retrospect. One characteristic difference between American and European systems of education is that the former has come to provide a graded ladder system whereby each child, regardless of his social class, may progress through the elementary and secondary divisions even to college without hindrance. In European systems such is not the case. Social and other distinctions determine to a large degree the nature and extent of the education of each pupil. While some progress has been made to permit pupils of demonstrated ability to advance in their education, the old concept is well rooted.

Since the several divisions of the American school system grew up independently of each other and became separate entities, each acquired a definite function and peculiar social and other characteristics. As democracy began to emphasize opportunity, the need for articulation of these units became obvious. Jefferson, who foresaw so clearly the relationship between democracy and education, wrote of the common schools and the university going "hand in hand forever," and added, "Let us keep our eye steadily on the whole system."[1] One must understand the tenacity with which the American people cherish immediate control of their own school systems as well as the education of their own children. One must also understand the educational lag which has operated to hinder articulation. Our ladder system is the immediate outcome of the concept of educational opportunity for all. Constantly improved articulation of the various units is an important means to this end.

MEANING OF ARTICULATION

Articulation means the adequate relationship of part to part which makes for continuous forward movement. In education, good articulation refers to such adjustments between and within school units so as to permit each child to achieve maximum growth at all periods of his school life. Poor articulation may be regarded as evidence of the presence of factors which impede that progress in any way and make it a series of disjointed, unrelated accomplishments.

As early as 1899, Dewey pointed out with imperative clearness the lack of articulation between the units which go to make up the school system of the United States. Said he: "All organization is nothing but getting things into connection with one another, so that they work easily, flexibly, and fully. Therefore, in speaking of this question of waste in education, I desire to call your attention to the isolation of the various parts of the school system, to the lack of coherence in its studies and methods."[2]

Naturally, we have made considerable progress in articulation since Dewey uttered these words. However, educational lag is a powerful deterrent to advancement, and not as much progress has been made in this connection as we would like to believe.

FACTORS AFFECTING ARTICULATION

Many factors affect articulation in our school systems. The attitudes of different groups are reflected in state laws and regulations. These attitudes are in turn reflected in varying local administrative policies and concepts as to the scope and function of each admin-

---

[1] John C. Henderson, *Thomas Jefferson's Views on Public Education,* New York, G. P. Putnam's Sons, 1890, p. 124.

[2] John Dewey, *The School and Society,* Chicago, University of Chicago Press, 1899, p. 78.

istrative unit. Within the same state and even within the same city will be found wide variations. The fact that parents may control the education of their children has resulted in the establishment of private and parochial schools, and even tutorial arrangements at home. Many of these children make contact with the public school system at certain points in their educational careers. The absence of strict regulatory standards in American education, as in European countries, has resulted in much experimentation and produced many types of school organization. The individual differences of children noted in different grades, years, and geographical areas is a factor of considerable importance. For instance, members of a graduating class in one year may exhibit marked abilities and achievements; during another year the situation may be quite the opposite. These factors would point to the necessity for giving closer attention to articulation problems.

Articulation Problems on the Elementary Level

We have noted a gradual but definite trend away from the eight-year elementary pattern of organization toward the six-year pattern, which includes usually the kindergarten and the first six grades. It is unfortunate that the privileges of kindergarten education are not now available to all children of kindergarten age. Here is one of the first problems of articulation, that is, adjustment of children in the first grade with and without kindergarten experiences. The nursery school is now coming to be a recognized part of the elementary school. Sooner or later the reorganized administrative unit for elementary education will include provision for all children from two and three years through twelve or thirteen years.

Problems of articulation on the elementary level pertain to the development of an integrated program and adjustment of all pupils both to as well as within the organization. There is a considerable amount of pre-primary education under private auspices. Children who attend parochial schools frequently transfer to public schools at various times, with accompanying problems of adjustment. Many adjustment situations center around variations in compulsory attendance ages, age of entrance, admission, length of the school term, and length of the school day. Differences in objectives and content of elementary administrative units organized on a six-year or eight-year basis may bring about problems of adjustment in transfer.

Articulation problems on the elementary level may be summarized as follows:

1. Problems dealing with the school organization include the selection of the type of organization yielding the best returns in pupil growth; articulation of pre-primary units with the elementary unit; adjustment of first-grade pupils with and without kindergarten experiences; continuity with reference to grouping; size of classes; adaptability of organization to the abilities of pupils; facilities for exceptional children; and questions of transfer from other school systems.

2. Problems pertaining to administration and supervision include familiarity with problems of units above and below as well as with the work of previous and succeeding teachers; distinction between pre-primary, primary, and intermediate grades; psychological and sociological differences in child nature and needs; promotional procedures and standards; understanding of records of pupils; failures and misfits; maturation levels of children, involving classification; and adequate cumulative records and reports.

3. Problems affecting the instructional processes include need for well-defined objectives; departmentalization questions, especially as to grades included and effects on teachers and pupils; formality of instruction; teaching pupils to study; establishing vertical continuity of subject matter and methods; and personnel problems of teachers, which include variations in training and personality, ability to adapt to teaching situations and needs and capacities of pupils, and substitute teachers.

Properly articulated administrative divisions should provide for the continuous growth of each child, unhampered by artificial barriers. Problems of the home, health, and guidance should be considered at every level. Always the system must be fitted to the child rather than the child to the system.

ARTICULATION ON THE SECONDARY LEVEL

Articulation problems on the secondary level would appear to be far more numerous and significant than on the elementary level, owing to the varied organization of secondary education and the quantity and quality of service offered. The secondary school should be properly articulated with the elementary school for *all* children and with higher institutions of learning for *some* children. The rapid expansion of secondary school enrollments within the past generation coupled with the changing conceptions of the meaning of education have revolutionized the high school and multiplied its functions. Changes in organization have affected both ends of the traditional secondary school, the junior high school on the lower level and the junior college on the upper. Between them has appeared a new institution—the senior high school.

We have noted that the secondary school has been undergoing a process of reconstruction. The introduction of the junior high school is not merely a convenient administrative adjustment; rather it is based upon vital changes in curriculum theory and practice as well as organization. In order to accomplish the purposes of the junior high school and bring about a reasonable solution of the problems which brought it into being, a new scientific spirit has appeared. There is now much study of youth problems at all levels: junior high school, senior high school, and junior college. Nor have these problems been entirely solved. Close observers of secondary education believe that we are just in the beginning of a reorganized program for adolescent and post-adolescent youth.

We may summarize as follows:

1. Problems of articulation with the administrative units above and below include questions associated with homogeneous grouping; home-room situations; specific types of organization and grouping; and admission and transfer of pupils entering from private, parochial, or other high schools.

2. Problems associated with administration and supervision include bases of promotion; bridging the gap from one unit to another in the same or a different school system; overlapping requirements of various teachers; and records of pupils.

3. Program problems include fitting the program to the needs of pupils; sufficiency and variations of offerings; orientation; articulation of individual subjects; provision for individual differences; grade placement of subject matter; time allotments; and departmental teaching.

4. Teacher problems include assignment of teachers; reconciliation of teacher attitudes as between the elementary school and the junior high school, the junior and senior high schools, and the senior high school and the college (perhaps one of the most serious problems of articulation); and teacher and pupil adjustment.

5. Pupil problems include pupil adjustment to the life of the secondary school and needed orientation on the part of pupils as to the school itself, the home, and the community in the educational process. There is always the child's adjustment to the new and more complex activities of the institution he is attending. Transportation of children involves serious problems of articulation. Social adjustment is a matter of concern with many pupils. Closer articulation with the home ought to be placed high on the principal's calendar list for early consideration.

The Secondary School and Higher Education

College domination of secondary education has been the fetish of generations from which there now appear to be possibilities of escape. Unfortunately, the destinies of nearly all secondary youth have been bound up in the crystallized organization, content, and procedures of high schools adapted to the 15 per cent who find their way ultimately into college, scarcely half of whom remain to complete what later has proved to many of them an ill-chosen program.

A satisfactory secondary school program should provide for the needs of all youth under that program. We have pointed out repeatedly the necessity of recognizing ability and scholarship and providing for leadership through selection. Certain youth must be fitted for higher education. At some points their education will be identical with that of all youth; at others, a different educational pattern is essential.

The following are some of the problems which emerge in high school–college relationships.

Who Shall Go to College? The principle just set forth offers a guide. Procedures should be set up to determine ability and leadership. Studies should be made of college and university requirements, requirements and needs of the various professions, provision for financial assistance to promising but needy youth, and attitudes of parents and community. These will demand the best efforts of both faculty and administration.

Methods of Admission to College. Adequate information should be made available to pupils, teachers, and counselors on admission or rejection of students to colleges. Knowledge of the specific unit requirements and activities of the various accrediting associations is essential in order that pupils can be admitted without condition. If examinations are required through the college entrance examination board or other authority, the facts should be known and applied. Necessary records include the certificate of graduation and recommendation, result of tests, health records, and similar data. The college is interested in the amount and quality of preparation, personal qualifications, and other data, under the school's endorsement.

Improving Relationships. In bringing about a better articulation of high school and college the following should receive consideration: (1) contact with regional accrediting associations; (2) joint conferences with institutions represented; (3) articulation of curricular materials and methods; (4) proper relative values of the academic subjects as compared with the fine and practical arts; (5) application of studies designed to improve relationships, as the eight-year experiment (thirty schools) of the Progressive Education Association; (6) anticipation of difficulties in college, as note taking, grading, rapid reading, methods of teaching and study, outlining, and examinations; (7) efforts to understand the nature and problems of the college both as an intermediary and as a terminal institution; (8) college recruitment of high school graduates through scholarships, guidance, trips, and college days, and especially for athletic purposes; and (9) reports of students already in college as a basis of improving secondary administrative procedures.[3]

Emphasis upon these problems and procedures will vary widely. In some schools a large percentage of the pupils may be concerned; in others, a comparative few. Constant care should be exercised that the needs of all pupils receive the attention they deserve. One administrative function should be carried out with much attention: the secondary school follow its graduates throughout their college experiences, profiting by their successes and failures. These should become the concern of the entire faculty.

QUESTIONS AND PROBLEMS

1. Give several reasons, based on investigation of a selected school system, for a study of articulation problems.
2. Give examples of progress in solving articulation problems within a twenty-year period.

---

[3] The student will find an excellent discussion of secondary school and college relations in Edmonson, Roemer, and Bacon, *The Administration of the Modern Secondary School*, New York, The Macmillan Company, 1941, chap. xxiv.

3. Evaluate the factors which affect articulation. Can you add others?
4. Evaluate the problems of articulation on the elementary level. Are all valid? Select a school system and note the extent to which they apply.
5. Evaluate the problems of articulation on the secondary level. Are all valid? Select a school system and note the extent to which they apply.
6. Canvass one or more high schools to ascertain the kinds of records kept with reference to their graduates in college. Evaluate them.
7. Give a report on the eight-year experiment.
8. Comment on the statement, "The secondary school should follow its graduates throughout their college experiences, profiting by their successes and failures," in the light of your own experiences.

SELECTED REFERENCES

1. "American Education in the Post War Period," *Forty-Fourth Yearbook,* National Society for the Study of Education. Bloomington: Public School Publishing Company, 1945, parts i and ii.
2. "Articulation of the Units of American Education, The," *Seventh Yearbook,* Department of Superintendence. Washington: National Education Association, 1929.
3. Barnes, Jarvis, "The Future of the Junior High School," *School Executive,* February, 1945, pp. 43–45.
4. "Children in the Community," *Children's Bureau Publication No. 317.* Washington: Federal Security Agency, 1946.
5. Edmonson, J. B., Roemer, Joseph, and Bacon, Francis L., *The Administration of the Modern Secondary School.* New York: The Macmillan Company, 1941, chap. xxiv.
6. Educational Policies Commission, *Education for All American Youth.* Washington: National Education Association, 1944.
7. Eells, Walter C., "Status of the Junior College in the United States," *School and Society.* April 21, 1945, pp. 250–253.
8. Elsbree, Willard S., *Pupil Progress in the Elementary School.* New York: Bureau of Publications, Teachers College, Columbia University, 1943.
9. Jacobson, Paul B., and Reavis, William C., *Duties of School Principals.* New York: Prentice-Hall, Inc., 1942, chap. xiii.
10. Koos, Leonard V., "How to Democratize the Junior-College Level," *School Review,* May, 1944, pp. 271–284.
11. Koos, Leonard V., "Organizational Relationships of Junior College and High School," *Journal of the American Association of Collegiate Registrars,* July, 1943, pp. 399–407.

12. Lane, Robert Hill, *The Principal in the Modern Elementary School.* Boston: Houghton Mifflin Company, 1944.

13. Lane, Robert Hill, *The Progressive Elementary School.* Boston: Houghton Mifflin Company, 1938.

14. "Organization, Administration and Supervision of Education," *Review of Educational Research,* October, 1946.

15. Saunders, Carleton M., *Promotion or Failure for the `Elementary School Pupil?* New York: Bureau of Publications, Teachers College, Columbia University, 1941.

16. Speer, James B., *Articulation Problems as Judged by Pupils, Parents and Teachers.* Doctor's Thesis. Austin, Texas: University of Texas, 1945.

17. White, Robert, Jr., "Feasibility of 6–4–4. Reorganization in School Systems with Junior Colleges," *School Review,* March, 1946, pp. 140–147.

18. Wiley, George M., Jr., *The Redirection of Secondary Education.* New York: The Macmillan Company, 1940, chaps. vii, x.

19. Witham, Ernest C., "What Size High School?" *School Executive,* June, 1943, pp. 32–34.

CHAPTER XIV

Some Administrative Pupil Problems Affecting School and Community

THE administration of a modern school program having for its principal objective the extension of the benefits of educational opportunity to more and more children has brought many problems involving pupil personnel. They have been immeasurably accentuated by the complex social conditions with which the pupil comes in daily contact. Especially when one realizes the expansion of the educational program within a generation, he is vividly aware of administrative need for attention to problems where more complete child welfare is concerned.

Three groups of problems will be given consideration in this chapter, namely, the transported pupil, the tuition pupil, and the activity program. The reader will observe sharp contrasts with older educational philosophies and procedures. Unfortunately, there are wide variations in attitude as to the extension of adequate educational opportunity to all the children of the nation. Even within the same state, such marked variations occur as to seem almost unbelievable. Immeasurable opportunity exists within every state to bring this common objective into greater realization. Perhaps it cannot be done effectively without federal aid.

THE TRANSPORTED PUPIL

In an earlier chapter school transportation was treated as an aspect of the administration of school attendance. In this section we are concerned with transportation in relation to the extension of educational opportunity. School bus transportation is definitely related to the consolidation movement. One would hardly be possible without the other, nor can one understand and evaluate one without the other.

Advantages. The consolidated school with its transportation facilities has definitely shown the following advantages:

1. It provides rural children with more adequate educational opportunities.
2. It serves to improve the health and morals of pupils through recreation, medical examinations, protection against weather and other hazards, and a health program.
3. It has increased enrollments and average daily attendance, reduced tardiness and truancy, and provided a longer school term.
4. It provides a better educational program adapted to the needs and abilities of pupils, better environment, teachers, and curriculum, and more varied social opportunities.
5. It serves to bring a high school education to more children for a greater length of time.
6. Its greater holding power tends to lengthen total educational opportunities of all the children.[1]

The rapid growth of pupil transportation must be traced to factors other than school consolidation. Among these are the increased desire of the public for better educational facilities, statutory provisions for transportation, development of the automobile, and—of great importance—improved highways. The larger local unit movement has been a factor, together with the popularization of secondary education and shifts in and mobility of the population in general. Approximately equal numbers of elementary and secondary school pupils are transported.

Many administrative advantages accrue to the consolidated school largely because of transportation. Among these are larger and more regularly attending student body, a superior instructional situation, superior instruction at lower per capita cost,[2] and a better-organized

---

[1] M. C. S. Noble, Jr., *Pupil Transportation in the United States,* Scranton, International Textbook Company, 1940, pp. 54 ff.

[2] Ordinarily, the consolidated school does not cost less to operate than the district school.

plan of support. The community thereby receives additional advantages which the reader can easily supply.

Where it has been found impossible or impracticable to transport every pupil residing beyond walking distance from the school, or where school consolidation does not seem advisable, efforts have been made to improve the quality of local instruction. Naturally, these efforts extend first to securing better teachers and improving the school environment. In sparsely settled areas, enrichment of the educational program has taken place through correspondence courses, dormitory schools and boarding of pupils near the school, and through circuit teachers and part-time schools such as traveling schools. In all of these plans, educational facilities adapted to his needs should be brought within the reach of every child to the largest possible degree. Naturally, the most isolated child is placed at a disadvantage. There is a tendency in some states to encourage the removal of isolated children of school age to areas having more accessible educational facilities.

Utilization of school transportation then must be considered in relation to the larger educational opportunities available to pupils transported. Thus it becomes an important instrument for educational and social reconstruction. The social, cultural, and occupational points of view of many pupils are changed significantly by their experiences in larger schools. Their cultural vision is widened. It is true that many boys and girls are weaned from the farms, as has been charged, but this may be compensated for in other desirable ways.

Administrative Problems. The administration of a transportation system creates numerous pupil problems especially in the secondary field. Some of these are: (1) schedule provisions, many consolidated schools building their schedules entirely around the school bus schedule; (2) administration of the activity program, especially where activities—club meetings, school band, athletics, and the school's social and recreational program—are held after school; (3) disciplinary matters, such as behavior in the bus, detention after school, and interruption of school program on account of late bus; (4) time-consuming nature of bus administration which often considerably affects the administrative and supervisory schedules of principals; and (5) need for better public school relations. The public needs education in regard to the advantages of school transportation, pupil safety, and economy.

The Tuition Pupil

Definition. Because of limitations in school facilities, many children lack educational opportunities suitable to their needs in their own districts and must find them in a neighboring school district. For the purposes of our discussion, a tuition pupil is a child of school age whose attendance in a school of a non-resident district entails a payment, legally required, to help defray the costs of his education. Responsibility for this payment may rest in part or wholly on the state, the local school authorities, the parents, or in some instances other local agencies.

Classification. Tuition pupils may be classified as follows: First, there are those who desire the advanced educational advantages of neighboring school districts. The fact that the development of school systems in most states has been from the community outward has resulted in many districts without high school facilities. Children living in these districts and desiring a high school education must become non-resident pupils in the neighboring school system having such facilities. These account for the largest number of tuition pupils. Second, factors of distance to residential schools make it expedient to take advantage of convenient near-by schools in non-resident districts. Pupils affected may include both elementary and secondary children. Third, child inmates of any institution within a district usually attend the schools of that district, frequently on a tuition basis. Fourth, upon proper examination, children of a school district found mentally or physically handicapped may be sent to a proper educational center where their needs are adequately provided for. Fifth, pupils desiring special vocational education may be sent to a non-resident school with tuition provided.

Control. Control of admission is usually vested in the non-resident school, which determines standards and conditions. Moreover, the receiving district may not be obligated to enroll the tuition pupil if it entails additional expenditures. Variations in previous levels of the child's preparation may result in demotion or classification quite often leading to retardation. Frequently non-resident children are segregated in sections which seem to fit their scholastic foundations.

Schedule difficulties accentuated by accompanying transportation problems may seriously affect their classification.

Tuition Legislation. Every state makes some provision for the tuition pupil. The district plan used in twenty-three states binds the local district to pay the tuition if it provides no high school. The county unit plan used in twelve states recognizes the county as the responsible unit. Six states guarantee tuition and prohibit charges. In three states the local-option plan merely legalizes the district agreement. It is important to observe that state provision for high school tuition has made great progress in recent years. This is definitely the outcome of the extension of educational opportunity to more and more children, and the result of compulsory education laws requiring attendance of all children within specified ages.

Tuition Policies. Despite ample tuition legislation, denial of educational opportunity to many children can be traced directly to matters of finance. School districts as well as parents have frequently found it impossible to meet these increased costs when the resident school budget can scarcely be met. Then there are questions of the amount of the tuition and the method of determining rates, who shall pay the tuition, its collection, mutual responsibility of districts, and the responsibility of the state. Numerous cases have come before the courts in which one finds little agreement with respect to tuition controversies.[3]

Perhaps in no other phase of school administration has less progress been made in arriving at a sound and equitable financial basis. Barr found that as many school districts charge less than the legally prescribed rate as charge more.[4] Herlinger's investigation shows that in fifty-four selected districts (Pennsylvania) the annual tuition charges vary from $39.92 to $140.00 per pupil with many school districts charging more than is legally permitted. Moreover, there is a definite lack of agreement as to what should constitute the basis for such a financial agreement.[5]

---

[3] Arthur M. Stull, *Tuition Legislation and Litigation in the United States,* Doctor's Dissertation, University of Pittsburgh, 1934, p. 157.

[4] Charles F. Barr, *Discrepancies Between Charges and Costs for Non-Resident High School Tuition in Four Year High Schools of Third Class Districts,* Master's Thesis, University of Pittsburgh, 1934.

[5] Harry V. Herlinger, *Relationship Between Actual Costs and Tuition Costs for High School Tuition in Four Year High Schools,* Master's Thesis, University of Pittsburgh, 1937.

Six desirable policies have been suggested in order to meet these issues successfully. These are:

1. Assessment of a tuition fee determined by the slight additional expense theory.
2. Assessment of a tuition fee equivalent to a proportional share of the cost to the school.
3. Payment by the state of tuition of all non-residents.
4. Assumption by existing districts of entire cost of maintaining high school.
5. Allocation of all territory of the state to high school districts.
6. Direct assumption by the state of the entire financing of secondary education.[6]

Tuition arrangements involving school districts or individuals are usually haphazard and temporary. In some instances they cannot be avoided. Wherever possible, a long-term policy should be worked out, covering needs of the children as to supplemental education and including present population and trends, nature of existing educational facilities, transportation facilities, financial considerations, and the relative efficiency of the school systems concerned, especially if small and ill adapted.

States are giving the matter of tuition children more and more consideration. The problem is closely allied with transportation. In addition, it is definitely related to scientific redistricting, the tendency toward the larger unit, and efforts to provide greater educational opportunity for all children.

Administrative Problems. The presence of pupils from other districts on a tuition basis creates many problems not ordinarily found in a more homogeneous residential community. These may be classified as follows:

ATTENDANCE. Unless transportation is provided, attendance of tuition children is usually somewhat irregular because of distance, inclement weather, and parental and pupil disinterest. There are notable exceptions. Absence and tardiness are usually more difficult to deal with because of these conditions and a lack of control over the enforcing authority. Often there is no proper coordination between attendance authorities affecting enforcement.

---

[6] John Guy Fowlkes and George J. Skewes, "Tuition for Non-Resident High School Pupils," *School Review*, June, 1936, pp. 425–433.

TRANSPORTATION. For the majority of tuition pupils, especially those living within walking distance of the school, transportation is not provided. Increasingly it is being supplied by the resident district. However, many children are forced to find their own means of conveyance, which are varied in the extreme.

Problems of transportation directly affect the school's program itself. Schedules must be arranged in conformity with bus arrivals and departures. Individual methods of transportation are subject to the hazards of weather, roads, oversleeping or lateness due to other causes, work to do on the farms, and parental or pupil indifference. Then there are many pupils who lack the means of transportation itself or are so situated that it cannot be provided.

ADMINISTERING THE SCHOOL PROGRAM. Most numerous and serious are the problems directly related to the school program, especially where considerable numbers of tuition children are transported. School schedules built around bus schedules do not always furnish the most effective program. The activity program favors pupils in residence. Transportation problems hinder special assistance to individuals or groups before and after school; hence, the tendency toward the lengthened school day. Many tuition children do not mesh scholastically into the present organization, which discrepancy calls for individual or group schedule changes. Special classes and sections are often arranged to provide for varying standards of achievement. Unless this is done, some children may become seriously retarded. In most host school districts the school program is designed to meet the needs of residence pupils and non-resident pupils are expected to fit into it somehow.

Where considerable numbers of tuition children come from rural areas, more complete programs of instruction should be planned, including agriculture and homemaking courses, for example. Where the small high school is typical, the needs of rural children unfortunately are subordinated to the usual academic program. Bored with uninteresting and ill-adapted curricula and procedures and irked by trying conditions at home, many of them, usually the boys, become indifferent and drop out of school. Here and there vocational high schools are endeavoring to cope with this problem.

SOCIAL ADJUSTMENT. Social discriminations among pupils may be found in every school; they are more vivid between town and country pupils. Because they are largely rural as well as from another district, non-resident children often encounter a well-defined prejudice. Social and scholastic adjustments may be hard to make. If a child is handicapped in any manner, the difficulty may become accentuated. Occasionally, rural pupils excel and carry off honors, a phenomenon not always well suited to residential tastes.

The benefits of guidance become imperative in maladjusted pupils. Since adolescents usually have a way of keeping their own counsel, the need is all the more obvious. Satisfactory contacts with the home are the more difficult to maintain because of distance, lack of understanding, lack of parental control of the school's programs, and disinterest. Even where parent-teacher groups assemble, parents of tuition pupils seldom mingle on equal footing. Public school authorities should apply themselves to a betterment of these conditions.

SCHOOL ACTIVITIES. Unless activities are scheduled on school time, tuition pupils are often excluded from them. This is especially the case where practices are held after school hours, as athletics, dramatics, and music and forensic activities. The formation of cliques may tend to bar them from office holding or positions of leadership. Naturally, there are exceptions, but they should not blind one to the total situation. Unless the school maintains a cafeteria, special provision must be made for those children who carry their lunch, and for their supervision during the noon intermission. Then there are questions of early arrival, make-up work, detention, and disciplinary situations, which seem to have some special significance where non-residential pupils are concerned.

A Definite Program. The objective of adequate educational opportunities for all children should require that greater attention be given to the problems of the tuition pupil. The first step is a satisfactory local unit of school administration. Consolidation has tended to eliminate the tuition problem by erasing artificial boundary lines. At the same time, a more adequate school program can be offered to meet individual needs. The next step is toward proper financial support. Where the administrative unit is such that tuition children are inevitable, available state or county funds should provide for the costs of their education. It is doubtful if parents should be required to pay all or a part of such tuition except in a case of personal preference of one school over another.

The maintenance of a democratic and properly adapted school program for all pupils should be the principal aim. The school must take each pupil as it finds him, studying and meeting his individual needs. Every effort should be made to provide a solution to administrative problems so that adequate educational opportunity prevails. The ideal school district is one in which the educational offerings extend from pre-school through a program of adult education sufficiently varied to accommodate all who may want to attend and who can profit thereby.

THE ACTIVITY PROGRAM

Learning by Activities. American elementary and secondary schools have long been dominated by the traditional concept that there must always be lessons to be learned. It has become the duty of the teacher to teach these lessons well and of the child to master them. Methods of mastery are memorizing, gathering the thought, recitation, reasoning, interpretation, problem solving, and rewriting.

Creeping very slowly into our educational thinking is an increasing emphasis upon learning through various types of creative endeavor and activity. While the former type of learning is still dominant and constitutes the more formal aspect of our schools, public as well as private, there has come about a new concept which might be termed learning by activities. Older desirable educational outcomes and many newer ones may be attained as a result of pupil immersion in activities that do not involve formally planned study procedures. Learning takes place during the process of *experiencing* an activity modeled after a life situation. Although interest is an essential accompaniment, it must not be secured at the expense of values in the activity itself.

Learning by activities is essentially the method of the activity program which is now gradually permeating the total school program, both secondary and elementary. In this section we are concerned with learning in terms of the child's progress only as it concerns those activities usually known as extra-curricular. The term itself is misleading, used perhaps because these activities grew up outside of the academic curriculum and in addition to it. There is an increasing tendency to relate activities to a wider school program which touches the community life at many points.

Periods. Three distinct periods seem to have characterized the development of extra-curricular activities: (1) that of ignoring them,

(2) that of condemning them, and now (3) that of recognizing them and controlling them.[7] It is interesting to note that their development in the secondary schools was apart from the curriculum, while in the elementary schools they seemed to grow out of the curriculum itself or were closely related to it. Roemer and Allen have pointed out that in the secondary school the characteristics of adolescents are fundamentally utilized in their organization and administration. Some of these characteristics are impulsiveness expressed by many interests, strong emotions and varying moods, social nature, adventurous nature, changeableness, love of approbation, a certain pride, secretiveness, emerging self-reliance, clannishness, and desire for some form of organized action.[8]

Objectives. Activities have both influenced the objectives of secondary education and been influenced in turn. They have provided for such ideals of secondary education as good citizenship, leisure time, developing responsibility, self-direction, training in leadership, followership and fellowship, cooperation with others, subordination of self for the common good, school spirit, vocational choices, and character building. In thus meeting the needs of adolescent youth and fulfilling the objectives of secondary education, they provide a program of social education needed to leaven the traditional academic nature of the secondary school. At the same time, they assist in solving many of its problems, such as disciplinary, and serve as an outlet for natural instincts, emotions and adolescent enthusiasm, and as a rallying point for school spirit, thus revitalizing what often becomes a dull, drab, academic existence.

Forms of Extra-Curricular Activities. The following list presents the principal activities to be found in secondary schools:

1. Art clubs
2. Assemblies
3. Athletics both inter- and intra-mural
4. Charitable and welfare clubs, as Junior Red Cross
5. Class organizations
6. Debating
7. Discussion clubs
8. Dramatic clubs
9. Foreign-language clubs
10. Hiking clubs

---

[7] Nova A. Smith, *The Organization and Administration of Extra-Curricular Activities*, Doctor's Dissertation, University of Pittsburgh, 1939, p. 1.

[8] Joseph Roemer and C. F. Allen, *Extra Curricular Activities*, Boston, D. C. Heath and Company, 1929, chap. vii.

11. Home-room organization
12. Honor societies
13. Journalistic clubs
14. Literary clubs
15. Musical organizations and clubs, as band, orchestra
16. Parties and dances
17. Photography
18. Public-speaking activities
19. School publications
20. Science clubs
21. Scouting
22. Student council
23. Thrift organizations
24. Vocational clubs

These activities offer a wide variety of experience. All of them may not be found in every school, for the school should be selective as to the needs of its own children in terms of the outcomes to be achieved. Club activities have, in the main, been sponsored by subject matter departments, and their programs pertain to the particular subject division to be emphasized. Care should be taken, however, that these do not constitute just another class. There is an increasing tendency to organize club activities around pupils' avocational interests.

Some Essentials of Organization and Procedure. In organizing the secondary school program in which activities of this nature shall form an integral part, it is important, first of all, that selection be made on the basis of an obvious contribution to the objectives of secondary education in general and the schools in particular. Values must be real, not assumed or theoretical. Activities are means to an end and rarely ends in themselves. They should form an integral part of the whole program, having a satisfying place in the daily schedule. Teacher sponsorship should be calculated as a part of the teacher's total load. It is advisable that activities be graded, that is, adapted to age and group capacity and progress.

Activities should contribute definitely to the growth and development of the individual child. Perhaps this is more essential than that some need of the school be fulfilled through the activity. Care must be taken that the interests of all pupils be served, rather than those of dominant individuals. Active participation is essential. Projects such as athletics should be controlled and administered in the interests of all, as to both participation and observation.

While the development of pupil leadership is necessary, the whole program must have wise administrative direction and wholesome teacher sponsorship and guidance. Finances should be closely supervised. Wherever possible activities should be spontaneous, being eliminated when their usefulness has been served.

VALUES IN SPECIFIC ACTIVITIES

School Assemblies. The school assembly furnishes the principal occasion in which the members of the school community can become group-conscious. Its purposes have changed markedly during recent years. Short daily assemblies are giving way to longer weekly or bi-weekly periods built into the schedule, with special assemblies for special occasions made possible by shortened periods. The achievement of group socialization values may be realized through the following: proper procedure in passing to assembly; seating arrangement; general order and proper attitudes toward principal and teachers, speakers, program performers, and one another; dignity of the occasion and high level of performance; school spirit engineered by musical organizations and group action; not too frequent use of pep meetings as means of motivating school activities; and motivation of individuals and groups by their renditions.

The school assembly offers many values to the individual pupil. Leadership is one of the most important of these in planning and rendering programs and offering solutions to school problems. Values in expression are unlimited. Using initiative and self-restraint, developing good manners, taking part in devotionals, and hearing programs with high cultural or other values are some further benefits. Assembly programs should be meaningful, well planned, properly sponsored, and in accord with sound educational objectives.

Musical Activities. Music is a universal language. It stirs the emotions, restores the soul, begets spirit, occupies leisure profitably, and creates understanding. It forms an outlet for suppressed desires, emotional experience, creative expression, and group participation. Musical interest and ability know no limits of age or grade placement. Values may be in rendition as well as in reception. There is no precise discipline quite like the harmony of a well-directed band or orchestra. Vocal or instrumental expression provides joy in achievement. Music carries over into the community and life itself probably more than any other school subject. Training in it gives a knowledge of voice production, enunciation, attack, rhythm, phrasing, breathing, accent, melody, and harmony. It raises individual, home, and community standards of music and develops the habit of active and continuous listening.

Musical values indicated above, especially cultural and spiritual values, should form an essential part in the school progress of the whole child. Expression is made possible through the various musical organizations, as band, orchestra, harmonica club, glee club and choral groups, and group singing, which touch the community at many points. Individual and group instruction may be provided along vocal or instrumental lines. Care should be taken to give music its appropriate emphasis in the total school program.

Forensic Activities. Forensic activities are closely related to musical activities in values. Much that we have said applies to them. Emphasis should be laid on development of intellectual capacities and interests, good sportsmanship, self-reliance, confidence, and poise. Forensic activities foster fluency of speech, clear logical thinking, and a capacity to appraise modern affairs. Working together is secured through debating; the purpose is to discern the truth and express it clearly, intelligently, and forcefully. Open forum activities are assuming greater significance and should be encouraged. These can and should carry over into the community life in many ways.

Club Activities. Youth enjoy the association of those similarly minded. Common purposes and interests are expressed in many and varied ways through club activities which release children from their inhibitions and furnish an outlet for their energies and talents. Small groups under teacher sponsorship with an adequate organization work together in expressive and constructive activities.

Athletics. Perhaps no single school activity captivates the imagination of the student body and, at the same time, is more time-consuming to the high school principal, especially in the smaller schools, than interscholastic athletics. The chief problems in this respect may be relieved through (1) a competent physical director in charge of athletics, (2) carefully selected coaches, (3) a regulated athletic policy, and (4) a well-managed, school-controlled athletic association.

Scholastic athletic contests have been influenced largely by intercollegiate competitions and rivalries of doubtful concern to secondary education. Having great value in furnishing an outlet for group emotional experiences, they can also become dangerous in that good sportsmanship and good health are lost in unwholesome rivalry. Positive benefits of interscholastic athletics are physical development and recreation, school spirit, friendly rivalry, school loyalty, and an outlet for the emotions and physical energies. At the same time, through overemphasis, winning the game at all costs may turn school spirit into mob spirit and create jealousies and unhealthy situations. A few pupils become the performers and receive the benefits. Championship teams become an educational menace, and their members are likely to devolop harmful rather than desirable traits of character.

Many schools look to athletics to supply the funds for other school activities. The sports program thus becomes big business. Night games swell the receipts. When administered on such a level, athletics are of doubtful educational value. Gambling is not uncommon and dishonesty is occasionally bred in amateur ranks. Large sums are paid out to officials and coaches, with the approval of boards of education who anticipate unexpended balances ultimately to be paid into the school treasury. Even when mindful of these evils, those in control too often fear to stem an influential press and noisy minority, both in the school and in the community. Public school authorities should subordinate the athletic program to its proper place and perspective. There is no need to ape the colleges and universities, many of whom unfortunately have succumbed to an athletic program of doubtful value.

Intra-mural athletics are rapidly supplanting interscholastic contests. These are to be commended highly. Every pupil should be required to have a place in such a program in accordance with his age, size, interests, and conditions of health. Emphasis should be on physical development, good sportsmanship, friendly relation, and group spirit. Fees for admission to contests should be entirely abolished, and the physical education program, including athletics, should be supported entirely with public school funds. When educators really sense the significance of the rounded development of every child, physically, mentally, socially, emotionally, morally, and spiritually, they will produce an educational program adapted to this end, placing physical education, health, and recreation in proper perspective. Here and there such plans are already in operation.

Pupil Participation and Load. The activity and social program should become an integral part of the work of the school to further the all-round development of all the boys and girls. Every effort should be made to extend its facilities and opportunities adequately among them. Unfortunately in practice this is not always done. An examination of the leadership of these activities in most schools reveals that only about one-third of the student body receives the advantages of this training. Leaders are usually selected because of superior ability, scholarship, and physical or other excellencies. Moreover, the same students may be found in positions of leadership in several activities simultaneously, both in the school and in the community. The same situation extends to membership and other forms of followership. About one-third of all pupils fail to participate in any form of activity owing to disinterest or lack of opportunity. A wisely administered school activity and social program should develop latent qualities and abilities in all pupils and balance the total load of each pupil. Providing opportunity for this development should take precedence over the desire to excel. There should be no monopoly on leadership, nor should "a good showing" exceed in importance a wide extension of educational advantage. It may require greater effort, but the outcome is definitely more democratic.

QUESTIONS AND PROBLEMS

1. Make a study of transported pupils in a selected school district (or districts) giving attention to the following factors: (*a*) distribution, (*b*) types of transportation used, (*c*) cost factors, (*d*) schedule relationships, (*e*) individual pupil progress in relation to the group, (*f*) others.
2. Write a paper on the development of school transportation in a given community.
3. Evaluate the significance of the administrative problems growing out of pupil transportation as indicated in the chapter.
4. Point out definite relationships between the tuition pupil and the transported pupil by application to a selected district.
5. Make a report on laws, rules, and regulations in regard to (*a*) transportation, (*b*) tuition in your state.
6. Evaluate suggested tuition policies indicated in the chapter.
7. Rank in order of significance suggested administrative problems of the tuition group. Defend your ranking.
8. To what extent has the tendency toward the larger administrative unit solved the problems of the tuition pupil? Be specific.
9. Study and evaluate the activity program in a selected (*a*) elementary school, (*b*) secondary school.
10. Compare specific activities as to relative values in achieving the purposes of education.
11. To what extent will a sound intra-mural health and physical edu-

cation program eliminate the problems and evils of inter-school athletics?

SELECTED REFERENCES

1. Alves, Henry F., and Morphet, Edgar L., "Principles and Procedures in the Organization of Satisfactory Local School Units," *Bulletin No. 11.* Washington: United States Office of Education, 1938.
2. Edmonson, J. B., Roemer, Joseph, and Bacon, Francis L., *The Administration of the Modern Secondary School.* New York: The Macmillan Company, 1941, chaps. xiv, xv, xvi.
3. Engelhardt, N. L., and Engelhardt, N. L., Jr., *Planning the Community School.* New York: American Book Company, 1940.
4. Fowlkes, John Guy, and Skewes, George J., "Tuition Policies for Non-Resident High School Pupils," *School Review,* June, 1936, pp. 425–433.
5. Herlinger, Harry V., *Relationship Between Actual Costs and Tuition Costs for High School Tuition in Four Year High Schools.* Master's Thesis, University of Pittsburgh, 1937.
6. Lambert, Asael C., *School Transportation.* Stanford University, California: Stanford University Press, 1938.
7. Landis, Paul H., *Adolescence and Youth.* New York: McGraw-Hill Book Company, 1945.
8. Langfitt, R. E., Cyr, F. W., and Newsom, N. W., *The Small High School at Work.* New York: American Book Company, 1936.
9. Lepley, James B., "Tuition of Non-Resident High School Students," *Educational Law and Administration,* April, 1933, p. 39.
10. McKown, Harry C., *Activities in the Elementary School.* New York: McGraw-Hill Book Company, 1938.
11. McKown, Harry C., *Extra Curricular Activities.* New York: The Macmillan Company, 1937.
12. Mort, Paul R., *Principles of School Administration.* New York: McGraw-Hill Book Company, 1946.
13. Noble, M. C. S., Jr., *Pupil Transportation in the United States.* Scranton: International Textbook Company, 1940.
14. "Organization, Administration and Supervision of Education," *Review of Educational Research,* October, 1946.
15. Reeder, Ward G., *The Administration of Pupil Transportation,* Columbus, Ohio: The Educators Press, 1939.
16. Reeder, Ward G., *Fundamentals of Public School Administration.* New York: The Macmillan Company, 1941, chaps. xvii, xxv.
17. "Safety in Pupil Transportation," *Research Bulletin,* National Education Association, November, 1936.
18. "Schools in Small Communities," *Seventeenth Yearbook,* American

Association of School Administrators. Washington: National Education Association, 1939.

19. Sears, Jesse B., *Public School Administration*. New York: The Ronald Press Company, 1947.

20. Smith, Nova A., *The Organization and Administration of Extra-Curricular Activities*. Doctor's Dissertation, University of Pittsburgh, 1939.

21. Stull, Arthur M., *Tuition Legislation and Litigation in the United States*. Doctor's Dissertation, University of Pittsburgh, 1934, p. 157.

22. Williams, L. A., *Secondary Schools for American Youth*. New York: American Book Company, 1944, chap. xv.

23. Wrinkle, W. L., and Gilchrist, R. S., *Secondary Education for American Democracy*. New York: Farrar and Rinehart, 1942, pp. 1–60.

24. Yeager, William A., *Home-School-Community Relations*. Pittsburgh: University Book Store, 1939, pp. 126–128.

25. "Youth Education Today," *Sixteenth Yearbook,* American Association of School Administrators. Washington: National Education Association, 1938.

NOTE: *The Nation's Schools* contains many valuable articles pertaining to the material outlined in this chapter. Consult *Education Index.*

PART V

Adjustment Services

CHAPTER XV

The School Environment

THE educational philosophy of a people at a given time and place is directly reflected in the school environment which they provide for their children. During those days when the district school was typical of schoolhouse construction in the United States, formal education was a consistently abridged process. Unfortunately, the one-room school building with its limited educational offerings and environment is still typical in large sections of the country, especially in rural areas where its removal or improvement is often tenaciously opposed. Where education as a social institution has a more prominent place in the thinking of the people of a community, greater attention is paid to the school building and environment. Urban areas have benefited more frequently in this respect.

We are interested in this chapter in school environment as an influence in pupil growth and development. After reviewing strange contrasts in the nature of the school environment now provided for boys and girls, we will discuss the site and the building in relation to the school program and point out the importance of environment in an educational program. The chapter concludes with a brief discussion of the community school concept.

CONTRASTS IN SCHOOL ENVIRONMENT

Extreme variation in school environment is one of the most noticeable and consistent characteristics of American education. In some communities great progress has been made recently in making the public school the most outstanding building. The site is selected with care, grounds are landscaped, the building is carefully planned and equipped, its walls decorated and hung with appropriate pictures.

Every service is provided to suit a modern program; in fact the whole environment is designed to attract and retain the interests of school children.[1]

Although many communities are recognizing the importance of the school environment, it is sad to relate that many thousands of children are even now going from unlovely homes to still more unlovely school buildings—little unpainted frame or brick structures edged on stony hillsides or projecting corners, with small playground space; interiors smoky from a wood-burning or soft coal stove; undecorated walls; old, torn, obsolete maps; double-rowed, scarred, antiquated desks. Withal an uninviting appearance in and out. Nary a picture or a bit of statuary, and if the child is still more unfortunate in being forced to fidget daily in the charge of an unlovely and unsympathetic teacher, what a school environment. For many an unhealthy school environment can be beautified by the sweet influence of a teacher's radiance and understanding of childhood.

Any degree of equal or even adequate educational opportunity for all children is hardly possible when one considers these great extremes in school environmental conditions still to be found among states and within many states. It ought to be the first duty of a state and of the people of any community to provide an adequate and inviting environment in which children must spend so many important hours of their early, impressionable lives. The school building should contribute to the highest conception of life in a democracy and have a place in achieving the better, the more abundant life.

THE SCHOOL SITE

Materially, the school environment consists of the school site, the building, and the equipment and materials within the building. When these are harmoniously selected, coordinated, and administered, the educational process is enhanced in many ways. The site should be sufficiently large to provide playground space, with the building well situated and landscaped. It should be free from disturbing noises, confusion, odors, smoke, and dust, and have an adequate supply of good water. Sanitation measures are essential.

---

[1] William A. Yeager, *Home-School-Community Relations,* Pittsburgh, University Book Store, 1939, pp. 126–128.

The site should have sufficient light and be easy of access and free from fire hazards. The environment should be socially and culturally wholesome, with definite elements of beauty, and adapted to educational activity. Nothing in the whole educational program is more conducive to a cooperative attitude among the pupils and a love of school than an attractive and wholesome environment.

There is no school activity designed to secure the cooperation of pupils, teachers, and the community of greater consequences than projects for the beautification of the school grounds. This may well be taken care of by classes, school clubs, parent-teacher associations, and community organizations. Special days like Arbor Day and holidays offer an excellent occasion to engage upon these activities. Pupils take pride in their own endeavors. School and community spirit is thereby developed. That community is most fortunate in its schools where there is a delightful feeling of belonging on the part of parents, teachers, pupils, and citizens.

The School Building

Nowadays the public school is often the most outstanding building in the community. It is desirable to employ skilled architects who will work hand in hand with the professional staff in planning an artistic and useful school plant in conformity with the needs of the district, the topography of the land, the funds available, and, above all, the educational philosophy of the enterprise. Beauty and utility as outstanding aims of schoolhouse construction should be applied to the interior as well as the exterior.

The health and safety of the pupils must be assured with adequate illumination, sanitation, ventilation, heating, fire protection, lockers, toilet and lavatory, drinking water, rest rooms, and health services. The building should be flexible in arrangement, usefully adapted to a modern educational program, and sufficient to meet the needs of such a program without hindrance. Every aspect of a good school should be provided, economically arranged and adequately used: classrooms with movable furniture, laboratories and shops, health units, auditorium, gymnasium, administrative offices, conference room, rooms and facilities for activities, custodian's quarters, rest rooms, cafeteria, clinics, library, and storage space. Each instructional area should have such adequate equipment as will facilitate the purposes for which the school and its program exist. Harmony in color and design on walls, windows, corridors, and throughout the building is important.

Aspects of the School Environment Which Affect Pupil Progress

The Pupil and His Needs. There is an increasing awareness of the pupil and his needs in constructing and adapting the school plant. These needs grow out of both group interests and individual differences of pupils and are reflected in modern school activities. They include health and recreational services, guidance, psychological and measurement services, rest rooms, club activities, musical activities, libraries, cafeteria, pleasing corridors, adjustment rooms, and others. Proper care of exceptional pupils requires special rooms and equipment. There are many other suggestions made in this book which might profitably be brought together at this point.

The School Program. Modern school programs demand modern school plants. Constant adjustments are necessary where existing facilities are out of harmony with progressive educational developments. The objectives of pupil personnel administration, being child centered, require that every facility be directed toward their realization. Traditional educational programs of the "sit down" type should give way to activity programs where the pupils engage in learning situations requiring freedom of movement and initiative. Educational policies should be revamped and closer articulation secured between the several divisions of the school system.

The development of these programs has brought about a greater spirit of cooperation among architects, engineers, school superintendents, principals, teachers, pupils, and even community groups. There is a greater tendency to combine beauty with utility, without ornateness or wasteful construction. The school environment should be inviting and profuse with learning situations adjusted to the interests and needs of all the pupils.

The administration of the school program involves much attention to plant adjustment. In the elementary school movable seats are replacing fixed row patterns. Activity programs require movement and suggest larger classrooms and adapted equipment. A school-centered library is essential. A self-contained classroom involves many adjustments in the room environment. Extension of the school age downward calls for kindergarten and nursery school facilities with a type of room, program, and equipment fitted to little children. Classrooms should be arranged so that children can live, work, and play.

In the secondary schools, the basic curricular offerings require many peculiar adaptations and adjustments. English rooms may take on the look of Shakespeare's day, a public forum, or a radio broadcasting studio with furniture and equipment to match. The environment changes to suit the activity. Audio-visual aids, coming into greater prominence require provision for their use. Science rooms become laboratories demonstrating natural processes. Activity is characteristic. Similarly the shops, home economics laboratories, cafeterias, libraries, and commercial departments are arranged to provide learning situations properly adjusted to life situations. Every subject matter department offers its peculiar possibilities and opportunities.

In non-curricular activities great progress has been made in supplying appropriate facilities. Home rooms are common in most secondary schools with their special equipment and programs. The school auditorium with its well-equipped stage provides for varied types of instruction, appreciations, entertainment, and morale. The gymnasium is the focus of the physical training program as well as social activities of all kinds. There are provisions for club activities of all types, glee clubs, school band and orchestra, publications, student council, dramatics, and the health program, including rest rooms. Many of these activities require special construction.

Consolidation is pointing the way to a better school program in rural areas. Everywhere unsafe and outmoded buildings and equipment should be replaced as rapidly as time and funds permit and the school made the social, cultural, and civic center of the community with a program artistically fitted to it.

The Community School

Types of Activities. One of the most noticeable trends in recent years has been greater community use of school buildings. While newer buildings can be adjusted to this end, older buildings are difficult and expensive to adapt and usually fall short of anticipated needs. The term *community school* is receiving greater recognition and indicates extension of educational opportunity to the whole community.

Three types of activities have been classified in which the school building is playing host to the community. These are:

1. Educational—night schools, lectures, civic occasions, clubs and classes, rooms open for quiet games and study.
2. Social—lectures, entertainments, social meetings, clubs and classes, social occasions, cooperative activities.
3. Recreational—entertainments, athletics, rooms open for quiet games and study, dancing, social occasions, cooperative activities.[2]

Engelhardt and Engelhardt have offered another approach to a study of adult activities as now instituted in many schools. Categories suggested by them are:

1. Study of socio-civic-economic problems.
2. Study of their homes, home life, and personal living.
3. Need for recreation and relaxation after their rather mechanized daily work.
4. Vocational adjustment, readjustment, and advancement.
5. Attention to those special groups who also need the fundamental tools for participation in society. Occasionally, handicapped individuals need a specialized type of training which adult classes can provide.[3]

Local provision for any or all of these activities is a problem which must be shared in each community. Ability to finance is of great significance, as are community-mindedness and the attitudes of the school authorities. During the war national defense activities increased unusually the community use of the schools, especially along vocational lines.

The community school should be a center in which the life needs of all the people of the community, children and youth as well as adults, can be met on the basic democratic principles of human living. It is a school designed to provide for the educational needs

[2] Merle Al Stoneman and Knute O. Broady, *Building Standards for Small Schools,* Lincoln, University of Nebraska, 1939, p. 26. The reader will find this little book very beneficial and timely. It contains a splendid bibliography.

[3] N. L. Engelhardt and N. L. Engelhardt, Jr., *Planning the Community School,* New York, American Book Company, 1940, p. 4. This is an excellent analysis of the community school and contains a good bibliography.

of all in order to make for successful living. It can be planned for use by day and evening, and on Saturday. Every citizen can find a satisfaction in his seeking for better things in a harmonious environment.

The Farmville Community School. Perhaps the most significant statement of the community school concept has been published by the Educational Policies Commission.[4] It is a description of the Farmville community school. Intended to apply to rural and small-town areas of the United States, many of the suggestions may well apply to all schools. The emphasis is upon consolidation with a single institution serving the entire period of youth, meeting all educational needs. The pupil's direct experience is broadened as rapidly as possible by extending his activities into the local community. Citizenship thus moves gradually out into the larger scene. Such an approach brings the community itself within the radius of its educational activities and encourages education as a community enterprise. The community school can easily be made the most conspicuous community enterprise. It will combine all of the suggestions outlined in this chapter and whatever else may be necessary to meet the needs of the adult population.

QUESTIONS AND PROBLEMS

1. Study and report on contrasting school environments in two or more communities. What effects can you note?
2. Work out a program to improve the school environment through (*a*) community cooperation, (*b*) school board action, (*c*) school action, (*d*) all three.
3. Show by specific illustration that attention to school environmental services improves the quality of pupil development.
4. Show by specific illustration how a school program can be adapted to a particular school environment.
5. What is the community school? Prepare a program in which it assumes a position of importance. Cite examples from literature in which the community school is the outstanding feature.

SELECTED REFERENCES

1. Educational Policies Commission, *Education for All American Youth*. Washington: National Education Association, 1944.

---

[4] Educational Policies Commission, *Education for All American Youth*, Washington, National Education Association, 1944.

2. Engelhardt, N. L., and Engelhardt, N. L., Jr., *Planning the Community School*. New York: American Book Company, 1940.

3. Jacobsen, Paul B., and Reavis, William C., *Duties of School Principals*. New York: Prentice-Hall, Inc., 1942, chap. xxii.

4. Koos, Hughes, Hutson, and Reavis, *Administering the Secondary School*. New York: American Book Company, 1940, chap. xiii.

5. Lane, Robert Hill, *The Progressive Elementary School*. Boston: Houghton Mifflin Company, 1938, chap. iii.

6. Olsen, Edward G., *School and Community*. New York: Prentice-Hall, Inc., 1946.

7. "Social Background of Education," *Review of Educational Research,* February, 1940, chaps. ii, iii, v.

8. Stoneman, Merle, and Broady, Knute O., *Building Standards for Small Schools*. Lincoln: University of Nebraska, 1939.

9. Wofford, Kate V., *Modern Education in the Small Rural School*. New York: The Macmillan Company, 1938, part iv.

10. Yeager, William A., *Home-School-Community Relations*. Pittsburgh: University Book Store, 1939, chap. vi.

CHAPTER XVI

School Control

SEVERAL administrative services are essential in the proper management of a school. They are necessary in bringing about a better adjustment of the pupil to his environment, both within and without the school. In fact we may go so far as to say that proper pupil development cannot be achieved without concern for these services. They should not be considered as isolated administrative functions useful in themselves, but rather as school services whose purpose it is to permeate the whole school enterprise, bringing proper understanding of the child and smoothing his educational progress.

School Control—An Educational Responsibility

The maintenance of control may be said to be the first responsibility of a principal in his school and a teacher in his classroom. Order is nature's first law and no less that of the school. Control may be defined as the act or power of directing with a view to securing order through the exercise of authority, restraint, suggestion, or regulation. Historically, it always is associated with the concept *discipline,* having the connotations of strict mental, moral, and physical training, requiring for its achievement submission to authority, with proper punishment meted out for disobedience in any form. Thus, it implies something external, that is, conformity to an *external* stimulus or impulse, relaxation occurring when that stimulus is removed. More recently, school control has come to imply something internal, a response to an *inner* stimulus or impulse. Although the end may be the same, compliance is secured because of a reasoned discovery that the situation confronting one requires him individually to conform because *it is the thing to do* under the circumstances; and by so doing, he will help to secure the greater good of the individual or group. This is not to say that discipline viewed as the application of an external stimulus may not result in reasoned compliance; perhaps it may and should. It is to say, however, that discipline (control) functions best where there is a resulting *inner* compliance and action because of either a "self-discipline" or altruistic motive.

Legal Basis

Legally, the teacher stands *in loco parentis* in respect to pupil control. By the act of sending the child to school, the parent thereby delegates to the teacher authority to discipline the pupil for all offenses against the good order and effective conduct of the school. Yet it must be borne in mind that the authority of the parent is broader than that of the teacher, the teacher being restricted to the limits of his jurisdiction and responsibility *as a teacher*. This aspect of teacher control has been determined by numerous court decisions.[1] Jurisdiction extends to all offenses committed against the authority of the school within its legal limitations and school regulations, whether on or off the school grounds.

Boards of education as the agents of the state may make reasonable rules and regulations in order to administer more effectively the state's education statutes and policies. To this end considerable discretion is allowed boards of education in regard to both their expressed and their implied powers.[2] Violation of these rules may be punishable by suspension or expulsion. Moreover, expulsion or suspension may occur even if no rule is violated, merely that the good order and discipline of the school (the larger number) may thereby be maintained.

The administration of rules and regulations together with the maintenance of good order and discipline is vested in the administrative officers and teachers. *In loco parentis* extends to teachers and principals the right to administer corporal punishment if, in their judgment, it is necessary and within the limits of their jurisdiction.

---

[1] *Vanvactor* vs. *State* 113 Ind. 276, 15 N.E. 341, 3 Am. St. Rep. 645; *Stevens* vs. *Fassett,* 27 Me. 266; *Lander* vs. *Seaver* 32 Vt. 114, 76 Am. Dec. 176.

[2] For an analysis of these rules, see Newton Edwards, *The Courts and the Public Schools,* Chicago, University of Chicago Press, 1933, chap. xix.

However, malice must not be present, nor excessive use or abuse of the privilege. Even if slight injury results, there is ordinarily no liability to the teacher if he acted in good faith, used proper judgment, and the act seemed necessary to the end sought.

CONCEPTS AND FUNCTIONS

Historical Approach. Early American conceptions of school discipline may be traced to the attitude that the disciplined and conforming pupil becomes more amenable to direction, hence more industrious and likely to succeed. Prussian traditions, coupled with the idea that congenital evil could best be conquered by the rod applied to the boy's back, anticipated many weird disciplinary techniques in the schoolroom. The hickory switch, the dunce cap, the placard proclaiming the "lazy boy," and smacking the palm of the hand with a ruler were examples of Puritanic severity, although, as Lowry[3] points out, it is difficult to imagine how even a Puritan conscience could justify punishment of such severity. Boys were placed under the teacher's desk, in the corner, on benches, and even compelled to stand on one leg or on their heads for considerable periods for infractions of the posted rules.

Even some of us can recall equally obnoxious "disciplinary" methods. The rubber hose may still be found in many schoolrooms, the principal's office, or the basement, where it is usually applied. Many weary hours have been spent by teachers after school compelling a few culprits held in detention to write spelling words and copy encyclopedia sections, with little reclaim or reason. And if all these have not been enough, principals and teachers alike have spent their time devising demerit schemes, detention room plans, withdrawal of privileges, and rewards and penalties of all kinds. The administration of these devices is time-consuming and probably of little real educational value.

From this analysis it will be noted that tradition and legal authority and responsibility color concepts of school control. Moreover, the teacher's earlier experiences, the attitude of the principal or an older teacher, the exigency of the moment, and the emotional make-up of the teacher may all enter the picture. There may be need for extreme measures requiring immediate decision and relief under ag-

---

[3] Wm. J. Lowry, "Does School Discipline Contribute to Delinquency?" *Phi Delta Kappan,* September, 1936, pp. 5–13.

gravated circumstances. These usually result in an application of the older concepts of school discipline, characterized by prompt obedience, external coercion, soldier-like attitudes and responses, will of the teacher predominant, demerits and detention, pervading feeling of fear, uneasiness and annoyance on the part of everyone, and repressive methods of punishment. These are indicative of discipline as a form of *external* control.

Newer Concepts. Newer concepts of school *control* as contrasted with school discipline in the traditional sense emphasize freedom and naturalness, self-direction, and pupil compliance and responsibility based on an *inner control* and an earnest desire to do the right thing. This desire should be immersed in a feeling of inner conformity in which reason has played a part. Group attitude and action may be associated in some form. Individual freedom, precious as it is, should never extend to that point where it interferes with the rights of others. Constituted authority must always be respected wherever located, even in the hands of a pupil. Proper school control always leads the child to see that the authority of the school and the classroom is something more fundamental than the teacher, and that good discipline is, in reality, proper self-control in the interests of all.

More recently, the new education group has extended this philosophy to a point where the "freedom of the child" becomes fundamental to his natural progress and the development of his personality. There must be a recognition of the child's natural powers and his right to seek expression through self-activity. Hence the environment in which he is placed becomes a matter of major importance. He must learn to meet the problems and obstacles of that environment, anticipating its joys and profiting by its consequences. Such a philosophy means physical, mental, intellectual, and spiritual freedom *just as soon as the child is ready for and attains it.* It breaks sharply with the traditional concept and has been the principal point of issue.

Functions. School control may be summarized as a conditioning process to fit the individual to live with and for others as a useful member of society. Although repressive measures may be necessary under certain circumstances, these should give way to positive steps looking toward pupil and group improvement as rapidly as the child can assume self-directed behavior. Specifically, the following functions should be achieved:

1. To create and preserve the environmental conditions essential to orderly progress on the part of each individual pupil and group.
2. To enable the individual pupil to meet his responsibilities as a member of society on all its levels, balancing his own freedom against social limitations on that freedom.
3. To teach the pupil fundamentals of control and behavior leading to an inner control as a desirable basis for human happiness.[4]

SCHOOL CONTROL IN RELATION TO TEACHING SUCCESS AND PUPIL PROGRESS

Teaching Success. One of the first essentials to teaching success is the teacher's ability to establish and maintain right relationships with pupils. Numerous studies to determine causes of teachers' dismissal rank *weakness in discipline* as the principal cause. While there may be certain contributing factors, such as a poor personality, lack of interest, and poor methods, the ability to maintain proper school control is most essential. This fact is further evidenced by pupils' attitudes toward good teachers. Pupils prefer teachers who can maintain control, especially those who, in so doing, are considerate and sincere, have a good personality, and are *good* teachers. The teacher's most important function is to guide the learning processes so that desirable school progress results. Since proper school control contributes to this end, it must be maintained.

Pupil Progress. Pupil growth in conformity with the ultimate outcome of the educational enterprise, namely, full and complete development as an individual within the framework of a democratic society, requires proper conditioning through mastery of the controls necessary to its achievement. Within the school, control is the "governor" of that enterprise. Its smoothness and regularity is a means to the end that the progress of each pupil is achieved. The curriculum and materials of instruction, the devices employed as vehicles, the personality of the teacher, and all other aspects of the school environment should be utilized to bring about this progress.

---

[4] Compare these functions with those stated by J. B. Edmonson, Joseph Roemer, and Francis L. Bacon, *The Administration of the Modern Secondary School,* New York, The Macmillan Company, 1941, chap. x.

Good order is the necessary oil for a smooth-running school. It has been characterized as "proper attentiveness to the task in hand, self-directed pupil activity, consideration of the rights of others, and a spirit of happiness and good will."[5] Desirable school control is reflected in spontaneity, helpfulness, and enthusiasm. Interest is present and a pleasant feeling of belonging. There is a time for quiet when quiet is appropriate, and a time for the hum of activity when industry is the order of the moment. These eventually become *inner* impulses.

The problems of school control are for the most part individual. Wise teacher action proceeds at all times in the thought that education is a maturing process. Child study should take the place of formalized action by rule-of-thumb procedures, impulse, or "intuition" wherever possible in securing the right relationships. Children are composites of physical, mental, social, emotional, and spiritual entities needing integration, guidance, and maturation. Perhaps there is no better form of school control than good teaching by an understanding teacher.

SCHOOL CONTROL AS AN ADMINISTRATIVE FUNCTION

Administrative Responsibility. School control is definitely related to school policy. A board of education may adopt rules and regulations in regard to pupil control and the superintendent may influence by his attitude and direction the nature of that control, but the principal is responsible for the control of his school. His educational philosophy, attitude toward teachers and pupils, and planning and foresight determine, to a large extent, its nature. Serious disciplinary infractions, especially if continuous, are regarded as evidence of incompetent management. If the principal's time is taken up with disciplinary situations requiring frequent conferences with parents, teachers, and children, one may view his administration with alarm. As one writer puts it, disciplinary difficulties are the thieves of the time of incompetent principals.[6]

Manifestations. Desirable school control should be manifested in appropriate individual and group action when restraint is removed.

---

[5] H. A. Riebe, M. R. Nelson, and C. A. Kittrell, *The Classroom,* New York, The Cordon Company, 1938, p. 82.

[6] Philip W. L. Cox and R. Emerson Langfitt, *High School Administration and Supervision,* New York, American Book Company, 1934, p. 175.

In the halls, basement, toilets, on the school grounds, and on the way to and from school, there should be in evidence a certain morale which tones up the whole student body and creates a desire in every pupil to do the right thing at all times. Moreover, there should be confidence of the teachers in the administration, the pupils in the teacher, and the home in the school. Dignity and reserve are essential characteristics, but never snobbishness on the one hand or base familiarity on the other. Creative school control indicates rapid development on the part of the pupil toward self-control.

A spirit of working together is the key to desirable school control. Teachers should know and understand the principal's policies, and seek the cooperation of the pupils. All should work together with the home. When teachers falter, they should receive the cooperation and support of the principal. Even where it is obvious that the fault lies with the teacher, he should be helped rather than censured. Elimination or transfer, however, is the only ultimate solution in the case of a teacher unable to secure and maintain control, in which there should be no hesitancy.

Instruments of School Control

Offenses. An act that disturbs or interferes with any class or school procedure and throws off balance the control aspect of that school might be termed an offense. Its nature is determined by the philosophy of the teachers and the school in regard to control, and varies widely among schools and even in the same school. One might view an offense as a form of "rebellion" against established routine, or perhaps as a manifestation of immaturity. There is always the problem of degree or level of the offense, one level progressively developing to a higher, as, for example, whispering, talking, impudence, noisiness, boisterousness, complete rebellion, and disorder. Thus offenses requiring action at some point range from minor through serious, generally labeled as such in accordance with the attitude of principal, teachers, and school tradition.

Approaches to Improvement. If we hold that the desirable outcome of school control procedures is the maintenance of desirable individual and group self-control, approaches to its achievement may be secured through three successive levels: (1) conduct based on hope of rewards and fear of penalties involving punishment; (2) conduct conditioned by praise and blame; and (3) conduct given direction by force of ideals rightfully established and sufficiently motivated.[7] We must take the child as we find him, progressing toward higher levels of control to eventual self-control. Problems may emerge at unexpected intervals. Aggravating in the extreme are those serious problems of misconduct growing out of petty thievery, fighting, destruction of property, unruliness, and various types of delinquencies. Much depends on the attitude of the parents, the neighborhood, traditions of the school, strength or weakness of the teacher, and the principal himself. To be avoided are wholesale punishments of large groups, apologies without meaning, detention, demerits, and corporal punishment. More helpful will be found individual conferences, loss of privileges, group condemnation, a sense of humor, and, as a last resort, temporary or permanent pupil elimination or transfer.

Corporal punishment, although still widely practiced, is generally condemned by educational writers. If it is used, care must be taken that the end justifies the means and that no physical injury results. Similarly to be avoided are physical indignities and unkind epithets. Detention, although also widely practiced, is generally condemned because it often results in pupil dislike for school and an infringement on the teacher's time. As a corrective it is questionable. Similar repressive measures should be viewed in the same light and seldom practiced without some proof of their efficiency.

Instruments and Activities. Many instruments and activities have been developed in recognition of the pupils' more active part in the administration of the school. When pupils associate themselves in undertaking to publish a school paper, give a dramatic performance, win a football game, organize a debating club, or prepare an assembly program, these activities become purposeful and worth while to them. They become a means to conditioning and result in an increasing tolerance of varying points of view and behavior. Each is encouraged to put the other before himself and to develop group activity in a common concern. A school's educative philosophy can be partly gauged by the *amount* of student participation in school control. If school is life and life is doing something constructive for the group, these activities assist in that direction.

The school library offers excellent apprenticeship possibilities. Pupils can frequently assist in the cafeteria during the noon-hour

---

[7] Riebe, Nelson, and Kittrell, *op. cit.,* pp. 89–90.

rush. Social program in the high school has increased enormously in importance and scope, offering numerous opportunities for pupil participation and social control. Organized dances, cheering sections at games, assembly exercises, home-room activities and programs, dramatics, musical activities, Hi-Y clubs, national honor societies, debating, school patrols, clubs, and societies, student publications, and athletics offer pupils numerous opportunities to exercise school control and initiative.

Perhaps the most significant instrument for participation in school control is the student council. Compared to its progenitor in Europe, where it was largely an assisting routine device, it has become in America an instrument for the development of citizenship. The student council endeavors to inculcate training in representative government based on the principle that government and school regulation of conduct derive their just powers from the consent of the governed. The critical attitude, typical of adolescents, can by this means receive a suitable outlet and practice. However, too much must not be expected of student council efficiency. Democracy in government is not too thorough either in life or in education. Critics of the student council complain that (1) efficient leadership is not always available, (2) best pupil members are not always chosen, (3) opportunities to participate are limited in large schools owing to administrative policy, (4) students mistake license for liberty, (5) favoritism is occasionally shown, and (6) some pupils object to discipline at the hands of their fellows.

Leadership and Followership

America is a nation where leadership is potential in every boy and girl. The experience of self-control through practice in the school is a means of developing it. Varied school activities offer abundant opportunities for the selection of leaders. Thus the qualities of leadership ought to emerge because of the nature of the school's control and not in spite of it. At the same time, followership is necessary in a democracy. This means followership with a purpose rather than blind followership. In that school in which there is the highest type of school morale is to be found virile and stimulating leadership and purposeful followership of a high order. These are essential aspects of a desirable school control.

It seems a travesty in American education that an institution designed to promote democracy is itself so often controlled autocratically. We refer of course to the administration of education. When we are able to work out in practice the democratic theories we profess, education will become more hopeful of success. Teachers need practice in democracy; pupils need practice in government. We must judge results by practical outcomes.

QUESTIONS AND PROBLEMS

1. What does your state school code say about: (*a*) discipline, (*b*) authority of the teacher, (*c*) responsibility of the pupil, and (*d*) relations of the parents?
2. Study two or more school systems and compare philosophies of school control.
3. Evaluate the sentence, "Good order is the necessary oil for smooth-running school progress." Illustrate.
4. To what extent is it true that the modern school is autocratic in procedure? What is the remedy?
5. Tabulate in parallel columns the characteristics of school discipline as the application of external stimuli, and of school control from an inner stimulus.
6. Make a list of desirable devices and procedures useful in securing control in (*a*) the elementary school, (*b*) the secondary school.
7. Compare several teachers within your experience as to teaching success and school control.

SELECTED REFERENCES

1. Arbuthnot, M. H., "Transitions in Discipline," *Childhood Education,* November, 1938, pp. 101–107.
2. Cobb, Stanwood, *The New Leaven.* New York: The John Day Company, 1928, chaps. iv, xi, xii.
3. Cox, P. W. L., and Langfitt, R. E., *High School Administration and Discipline.* New York: American Book Company, 1934, chap. ix.
4. Crow, Lester D., and Crow, Alice, *Mental Hygiene in School and Home Life.* New York: McGraw-Hill Book Company, 1942, parts iv and v.
5. Dougherty, Gorman, and Phillips, *Elementary School Organization and Management.* New York: The Macmillan Company, 1936, chap. v.
6. Edwards, Newton, *The Courts and the Public Schools.* Chicago: University of Chicago Press, 1933, chap. xix.

7. Harris, Pickens E., *Changing Conceptions of School Discipline.* New York: The Macmillan Company, 1928.

8. Kyte, George C., *The Principal at Work.* Boston: Ginn and Company, 1941, chap. xxiii.

9. Lane, Robert Hill, *The Progressive Elementary School.* Boston: Houghton Mifflin Company, 1938, chaps. i, ii, iii.

10. McKown, Harry C., *Activities in the Elementary School.* New York: McGraw-Hill Book Company, 1938.

11. Newsom, Langfitt, and others, *Administrative Practices in Large High Schools.* New York: American Book Company, 1940, chap. xvi.

12. Riebe, H. A., Nelson, M. J., and Kittrell, C. A., *The Classroom.* New York: The Cordon Company, 1938, chap. v.

13. Schneideman, Rose, *Democratic Education in Practice.* New York: Harper & Brothers, 1945.

14. "Scientific Movement in Education, The," *Thirty-Seventh Yearbook,* National Society for the Study of Education. Bloomington: Public School Publishing Company, 1938, part ii, chap. xviii.

15. Starr, G. G., "Not the Teacher, Not Student Government, but School Morale," *Educational Administration and Supervision,* April, 1938, pp. 282–288.

16. Warters, Jane, *High-School Personnel Work Today.* New York: McGraw-Hill Book Company, 1946.

CHAPTER XVII

The Health Program

HEALTH is universally recognized as a conditioning factor in a successful life. Perhaps no saying of antiquity better indicates the aims of a health program than a "sound mind in a sound body." Vigor in body begets vigor in mind. One's ideal of health should be the highest realization of his physical, mental, and spiritual possibilities, rather than mere freedom from disease and deformities.

There are two great fronts in the preservation of health and the treatment of diseases.[1] One is the application of general measures to prevent people from becoming ill, and the other is the restoration of people to health with limitations on the spread of disease. On both of these fronts medical science has made great progress in recent years, especially in regard to motherhood, infancy, and childhood. Our resources have multiplied and our facilities widened. Schools, clinics, hospitals, health departments, physicians, dentists, nurses, nutritionists, teachers, and social workers, together with local, state, and federal government agencies, are offering knowledge and facilities for the well-being of children.

After examining health as a continuing national problem, this chapter points out the place of education in maintaining the health of the nation's children and youth. The fundamentals of a health program are outlined for which the school has a definite responsibility. Some consideration is given to safety education as a school and community problem.

[1] *Children in a Democracy*, General Report of the White House Conference, Washington, 1940, p. 52.

262

HEALTH A NATIONAL PROBLEM

The nation's health is measured primarily by its mortality statistics. Since 1915 the death rate from all causes has dropped from 13.6 per 1000 to less than 10. Life expectancy has risen to an average of 65 years for men and 70 years for women. The infant mortality rate has lessened with the control of children's diseases, as well as those of motherhood. At the same time there is an increase in illness and death from heart diseases, cancer, brain stroke, diabetes, and other diseases incident to middle and old age. Deaths and injuries from accidents have sharply increased. Many people suffer from malnutrition, faulty mental hygiene, and uncorrected physical defects. The draft rejections of World War II were far too many to constitute an index of a healthy youth. The health picture is still not too favorable. It is worsened by a knowledge of the fact that many remedies are available but unused. The means of health improvement have not yet been extended adequately to all people.

A certain confusion in health terminology has been of some hindrance in developing an integrated program. For instance, the terms *health education, physical education,* and *recreation* carry different connotations as well as different methods of approach, with little attempt at integration. The term *physical fitness* has recently been used[2] to emphasize a certain dynamic quality enabling one to sustain adaptive effort over maximum periods of time and to recover quickly. It assumes health as well as freedom from defects, adequate nutrition, and well-founded enthusiasm. It is only one phase of total fitness. There are four elements in physical fitness: freedom from handicaps and devitalizing drains, pleasurable emotions, health habits, and exercise. Further confusion is a result of conflicting claims of drug manufacturers, articles by popular writers on health subjects, and the restrictions of the medical profession itself on extending its present medical knowledge and services to all, which in turn tends to make for lay therapeutics. Still another factor is the vicious current commercialization of physical education in most secondary schools and colleges, which limits the advantages of physical education to a few individuals.

It is not to be assumed that the school is the sole agency responsible

---

[2] "Paths to Better Schools," *Twenty-Third Yearbook,* American Association of School Administrators, Washington, National Education Association, 1945, chap. ii.

for the health of the pupil. Many factors determine the conditions of health: heredity, home environment, nutrition, personal attitudes, intelligence, information, economic status, accidents, disease, and injury. Ignorance and superstition remain widespread. However, the school has a considerable responsibility, which we shall now examine.

HEALTH AS AN EDUCATIONAL PROBLEM

Although the importance of public health to society has long been recognized, health as an educational objective is of recent origin. When it first entered the school program, it was as an extension of the public health program. Boston was the first American city to provide systematic medical inspection, in 1894. Other cities followed. Definite provisions for health work in the public schools was made by 337 cities in the United States by 1910. As an outcome of this movement and perhaps stimulated by the revelations of physical imperfections among young men during World War I, health became the first cardinal objective of education in 1918, an action confirmed by educational writers since that day and more recently by the Educational Policies Commission.[3] The Children's Charter states the right of the child to receive proper health protection in very specific terms: "For every child health protection from birth through adolescence including periodical health examinations, and where needed, care of specialists and hospital treatment; regular dental examinations and care of teeth, protective and preventive measures against communicable diseases; the insuring of pure food, pure milk, and pure water." As a matter of fact, eight of the nineteen divisions of the Children's Charter are directly or indirectly concerned with the child's health.

In spite of recognition of the need of this objective through prior placement, it is necessary to point out the ineffective health accomplishments in the public schools on the whole, with respect to efficient organization, outlining of specific objectives of the health program in each school, necessary activities for their fulfillment, and efficacy of the results obtained. As early as 1932 Graves pointed out that the program of health service was somewhat casual and chaotic.[4]

---

[3] *The Purposes of Education in American Democracy,* Educational Policies Commission, Washington, National Education Association, 1938, pp. 60–63.

[4] Frank P. Graves, *The Administration of American Education,* New York, The Macmillan Company, 1932, pp. 117–118.

Notwithstanding the many activities in our public schools designed to meet some health objective, which in itself is more or less vague, the health program has been considered a thing apart. It has not generally succeeded. There is need for a better understanding of the health terminology. There is need for an adequate coordination of all activities designated to promote health into a unified program in which it assumes its rightful place of first importance.

BASIS OF THE HEALTH PROGRAM

Specific Objectives of Health Education. In 1930 a joint committee of the National Education Association and the American Medical Association set forth general aims of health education as follows:

1. To instruct children and youth so that they may conserve and improve their own health.
2. To establish in them the habits and principles of living which throughout their school life, and in later years, will assure that abundant vigor and vitality which provide the basis for the greatest possible happiness and service in personal, family, and community life.
3. To influence parents and other adults, through the health education program for children, to better habits and attitudes, so that the school may become an effective agency for the promotion of the social aspects of health education in the family and community as well as in the school itself.
4. To improve the individual and community life of the future; to insure a better second generation, and a still better third generation; healthier and fitter nation and race.[5]

These aims conceive a functional health program extending throughout the school life of the pupil. Health, rather than being a subject to be taught, should become a way of living. Through the development of this program the public schools can point the way to better individual and group health, working in cooperation with public health authorities.

Areas of Responsibility. To this end areas are outlined which become the responsibility of the school. These are (1) provision for a healthful environment; (2) a health guidance program, including

---

[5] National Education Association and American Medical Association, "Health Education," *Report of the Joint Committee on Health Problems in Education,* 2nd ed., 1934, pp. 1–251.

health inspections and inculcation of desirable health habits and attitudes, as a part of the service rendered by lay persons; and (3) a health service in charge of a professional staff consisting of physicians, nurses, dental hygienists, and others as needed.

FUNCTIONAL DIVISIONS OF THE SCHOOL HEALTH PROGRAM

School Environment. More and more we are coming to realize that the first obligation of a public school system is a healthful and stimulating physical environment. The physical condition of the classroom should be hygienic, pleasing, and appropriate to the child's growth and development. There should be adequate illumination and protection from glare, desirable temperature conditions and ventilation, freedom from drafts and exposure, properly adjusted seats, good sanitary facilities, safe drinking water, and protection from fire and other hazards. Experiments have recently been made in regard to varying wall colors in relation to exposure and in adaptable shades of color, with their appropriate effects on the hygiene of the room and the children.

The school is home to the children and the teacher is the homekeeper. All should be taught to keep the school neat and tidy. Beauty of surroundings, both inside the school and out, will stimulate a healthful environment. Children should be seated with respect to their individual needs, especially in regard to defects of hearing and vision, delicacy over-age or under-ageness, or any other condition which may profit by thoughtful placement.

An appropriate and healthful school environment should be reflected in a healthful daily routine. The activities of the classroom immersed in a pleasant atmosphere will reflect the mental health of the teacher. Order and the quiet hum of industry should be characteristic. The daily schedule should be well balanced in both elementary and secondary schools, interspersed with rest and recreational activities, avoiding fatigue. Emotional strain, much of which may be caused by the high-pitched, nervous, and unpleasant voice of a teacher or an ill-managed group, should be removed. Nutrition work may be necessary with some pupils; rest periods may be in order for others. Good posture always begets good health.

There is much to do about the school and grounds in maintaining a healthful environment. The school site should be free from noises, smoke, fire hazards, and unhygienic conditions. There should be harmonious surroundings, comfortable equipment, adequate light, proper ventilation, effective heating, and adequate space for recreation. The school environment should be inviting, even beautiful, with shrubbery, drives, gardens on the outside, and pictures, wholesome activity, and the pleasant warmth and cheer of a happy, contented faculty and student body on the inside. Rest rooms, cloak rooms, a cafeteria, and adequate play space all promote mental hygiene.

Health Guidance and Instruction. In fulfilling the health objective the school's health program should include several services which are the responsibility of the principal, teachers, and other school employees. Routine health inspections should characterize each school day's work along lines outlined by the principal or the health department. Opening periods may be the appropriate time for these in the elementary school and home-room periods in the secondary school. If properly emphasized, these activities lead to good health habits and a desire for a healthy, vigorous body. Close personal inspection immediately reveals any symptoms of communicable diseases, which should be reported to the school nurse or physician at once, or the child should be sent to the principal. The home should be contacted in serious cases. Many state departments provide routine directions for these inspections. Children returning to school after serious illnesses must be carefully observed and given individual attention as to physical examination, assignment of lessons, and adequate rest. Nutrition should be watched carefully by weight and measurement charts against height-weight-age tables and provision made for marked variations, especially if accompanied by other warning symptoms.

The child needs to know much about his own physical condition, and it is partly the responsibility of the school to instruct him. He needs to know how to avoid illness and accidents, how to protect the health of others. He needs to know what good health is and how to acquire it. He needs to know how to combat the constant misinformation of newspapers, radio, and magazines, and how to avoid faddists and superstition. He needs to be taught the importance of cleanliness, proper eating, regular elimination, safety, sanitation, recreation, exercise, and rest including sleep. Most of all, he needs to have a sense of balance—to consider his health while enjoying life's many activities. Although the teacher may follow a program which includes all of these, much of her health teaching—probably the most effective part—will be incidental. In short, the pupil should learn the scientific basis of correct living for himself and in his social relationships.

Health Service. Routine health inspection does not ordinarily extend beyond locating health needs, recording the facts, and reporting to the proper authority. These activities may be classified as a lay service in contrast to a well-organized health service, which must be based on a professional organization. Its members are recognized by some form of state license or certificate and operate under definite standards and ethics.

The public school health service may be said to consist of those health specialists who are specifically assigned to locate and, in part, correct health defects, and who are concerned professionally with the physical well-being of pupils and teachers. These include: (1) health and physical education directors and teachers, (2) the medical service, (3) the dental service, (4) school nurses and dietitians, (5) psychiatrists and speech specialists, and (6) social workers and others regularly attached to the health division. Perhaps it would be proper to include the local or state board of health and other agencies in this relationship, that is, at those points where contact is made with the local public schools.[6]

Turner has prepared a splendid outline of a complete school health program which the student should examine carefully. It embraces: (1) health protection, which includes sanitation of the school plant, physical, dental, and psychological examinations, and communicable disease control; (2) correction of defects and health conservation of defectives, which comprises special classes for exceptional children where any phase of the health facts is concerned, clinics, and follow-up service, both within the school and without; and (3) health promotion, which should take into consideration hygienic arrangements, and administration of the school program for pupils and teachers, physical activities, and health instruction and motivation.[7]

Health examinations for school children should be of three types:

---

[6] These usually include sanitary inspection, control of food and milk, laboratory service for the diagnosis of contagious diseases, community instruction in and prevention of certain diseases, as venereal disease and tuberculosis, collection of vital statistics, certain activities in connection with prenatal care and infant health, and clinical and hospital service.

[7] Clair Elsmere Turner, *Principles of Health Instruction,* Boston, D. C. Heath Company, 1939, pp. 274–276.

(1) daily health inspections by the teacher or school nurse to observe absence of normal health conditions; (2) medical and dental examinations by the school physician and dentist as an inventory[8] of the child's health status, with remedial treatment in certain instances; and (3) medical diagnosis and treatment by the family physician, or hospitalization and clinic treatment.

The range of health service varies widely in our schools. Indeed, the absence of these facilities in many small school districts and in rural areas is travesty on the first objective of education. There are a few districts where superior efforts are being made in this direction. In those districts where the health service consists only of first-aid treatment, immunization, or routine classroom inspection, parent-teacher associations have sometimes added these and other health services to their list of activities, a plan worthy of commendation if well organized and under efficient direction.

ORGANIZATION AND ADMINISTRATION

Source of Authority. In its exercise of police power to protect the general welfare of its citizens a state may, by statute, authorize boards of health to make and enforce all rules and regulations deemed necessary to this end. City councils may also confer certain responsibilities upon this administrative body. Then, too, the local board of education is charged by statute with some health duties, such as sanitation and vaccination. Regulations are set up by state boards of health and other state administrative bodies.

The first approach to the administration of the health program is to have a thorough understanding of state laws concerning it. These include statutes on sanitation, safety, building codes, the state curriculum, health inspections, vaccination, immunization, admittance and inclusion of pupils' reports, quarantine, public health regulation, boards of health, tort liability, and many others. The state department of education may have bulletins in which these legal fundamentals are set forth. It is out of these sources of control and authority that a local organization and its administration should be set up.[9]

---

[8] See Paul Haas, *Analysis of Medical Inspection Forms,* Master's Thesis, University of Pittsburgh, 1938, for an analysis of state forms used in these examinations.

[9] For an interesting discussion of this authority and responsibility, see Newton Edwards, *The Courts and the Public Schools,* Chicago, University of Chicago Press, 1933, pp. 534–549.

Size of School. The organization and control of the school health service should be definitely within the school if it is to function effectively. In smaller school districts, a definite professional organization within the school system is usually either quite inadequate or non-existent. The service generally consists in (1) infrequent and superficial examinations under state or county supervision, (2) some health inspection and instruction, and (3) emergency action by the board of education or health when needed. In larger towns and cities, a more authoritative form of organization begins to emerge in charge of specialists in the various phases of health work. The largest school district should have at least a director of health education, school nurse or nurses, school physician (whole- or part-time), dental hygienist, and a sufficient number of health teachers. Large cities will need to expand their personnel as the needs indicate. The Service should include an adequate program of health along the lines recommended by state and professional authorities. Suitable provision should be made for offices, health rooms, clinics, and equipment. Nutrition should not be neglected, school lunch facilities being provided for all children. Smaller school districts may well combine their resources in order to achieve the benefits of a desirable program.

The Director of the Health Program. It has been pointed out that the organization and personnel of the health program will vary with the size of the district and the emphasis placed upon the program. If organized along the above lines, the service will require the direction of a professionally educated specialist. In larger cities such a director should have the status of a staff officer. He should be primarily an educator rather than a physician, and one who is able to perceive the scope of the health program and the relationship of each personnel member to it. He should have the ability to secure the cooperation of parents, physicians, nurses, dental hygienists, psychologists and psychiatrists, teachers, and all those who may be associated with the program. He should have the educational point of view and fit the health service into the school program as a whole. To him we assign the administration of the first major objective of education. The chief problem will be the realization of this objective in small school districts.

Health Instruction. So far we have been thinking of those activities and services which are performed for the child by the school. If the health objective is to be fulfilled, the child himself must have a definite knowledge of many things pertaining to his own body and its protection, and know them so thoroughly that habits of healthful living result. This is the purpose of health instruction.

Health instruction should be an integral part of the curriculum. Usually taught as a separate school subject, it is also definitely related to other fields of knowledge, as physiology, hygiene, and science. For example, sex education and eugenics may be taught in connection with biology, or sanitation with civics. Integration may be made with other school subjects: nature study, social science, home economics, and reading (with health readers in the elementary grades). Safety education is definitely related to health and should have a conspicuous place in the program. Practice in health activities is accorded through the organization of safety patrols, health and sanitation squads, health clubs, and similar recreation group activities. Curriculum materials should be adequate and receive equal consideration in budgetary allotments with the most favored school expenditure.

The teacher's preparation in, and attitude toward, health instruction is equally important. Every properly educated elementary teacher should be qualified to teach health effectively. On the secondary level, every teacher should have had a basic education in health essentials and their application to secondary youth. The attitude should prevail in every school that health instruction is just as important as the most favored school subject, perhaps more so.

Physical Education and Recreation. Physical education and recreation are definitely a part of the school's health program. The recent tendency to reorganize and conduct them in the interests of the health of all the children is marked and wholesome. Activities of this nature include children's play, whether free or organized, intra- and inter-mural sports and athletics, special health exercises, and various forms of recreation organized under public school direction.

Organization of physical education and recreational activities will take into consideration: (1) a definite program for every child adapted to his needs after a careful physical checkup and (2) an emphasis on intra-mural and a de-emphasis on inter-mural athletics and sports. Indeed, one may pause to remark that commercialized interscholastic athletics, as commonly conducted, may well be eliminated from the school program without great loss. Emphasis in those activities which provide for freedom of movement, mental relaxation, and real enjoyment, all at low cost, with a feeling of accomplishment in the health results obtained is desirable. That others win in their turn should be a matter of just as much enjoyment. Skilled direction should be easily available and not too officious.

Health Records. A complete health record system with the clerical help required to keep it up to date is essential in every school system. The individual pupil record should be orderly, brief, and cumulative of all data pertaining to all aspects of his health. Once installed and followed through regularly as information becomes available, it should be reviewed and interpreted periodically by teachers, medical advisers, and all others who are concerned with the child's health status. Particularly important is this in regard to remediable defects which should be corrected. Answers should be sought to such queries as: Has the advice been followed? Has the defect been corrected? Has the school program been adjusted? Has the child gained weight? Is he maturing as he should?

The health record should be cumulative in character insofar as changes in health and medical history can be recorded. It should not be so detailed as to be cumbersome, yet all essential information must be included. Decisions should be made as to the form—whether on a card, a folder, or in a large individual envelope.

The personal health folder of each pupil should contain the following information:

1. The pre-school examination
2. The school health service examination (history, findings, advice)
3. Correspondence with family
4. Correspondence with clinics and agencies
5. Correspondence with family medical advisers
6. School health service notes: reports from teachers, nutritionists, psychologists, and physicians
7. Nurses' reports
8. Notes of counselors and record of use made of these data for guidance purposes
9. A chronological record of examinations, tests, corrections, illnesses, and observations from all sources[10]

---

[10] "Health in Schools," *Twentieth Yearbook,* American Association of School Administrators, Washington, National Education Association, 1942, p. 55.

Mental Hygiene

The mental hygiene of the schoolroom is now receiving an increasing emphasis in the general health program.[11] The child's mental health and balance are of the utmost importance in relation to his general health. The complexity and stresses of modern living make necessary consideration of his mental hygiene if he is to meet them successfully. This is now definitely an educational responsibility.[12]

Mental hygiene in the public school must be approached positively, that is, from the standpoint of the prevention of maladjustment. The White House Conference suggests five focal points which should be considered. (1) the curriculum, (2) pupil placement, (3) technique of instruction, (4) adequate facilities for social life and instruction, and (5) school organization for efficiency.[13] Each of these should receive careful attention in the organization and administration on any level.

Principals and teachers should be closely concerned with the mental hygiene of each pupil. Nervousness in any form is not to be lightly regarded. It may be manifested in disturbances of motor control, emotional or moral upsets, indications of nervous exhaustion, and associated physical conditions. Hysteria, dementia praecox, St. Vitus's dance, epilepsy, and all forms of suppression frustration, or the symptoms of speech defects or other physical ailments ought to be studied carefully by the teacher with such professional assistance as may be available. Sleep and nutrition have a definite relation to mental hygiene. The individual differences of children offer a fruitful field for observation. Any condition in the school causing or contributing to the mental unhealth of any child ought to be ferreted out immediately and removed.

Community Health Activities and the Public School

One of the most interesting phenomena of the past two decades has been the development of community agencies and organizations

---

[11] "Mental Health in School," *Educational Method*, National Education Association, Department of Supervisors and Directors of Instruction, January, 1935, p. 221.

[12] Thomas D. Wood (chairman), White House Conference on Child Health and Protection, *The School Health Program*, New York, The Century Company, 1932, chap. iii, p. 63.

[13] H. H. Remmers and N. L. Gage, *Educational Measurement and Evaluation*, New York, Harper & Brothers, 1943, p. 78.

seriously concerned with the general welfare and improvement of social living. Many of these pertain to the physical welfare and mental hygiene of childhood and youth. They include recreation centers, parks, libraries, clinics, hospitals, arms of service of the juvenile courts, service clubs, and other organizations. Mention has been made of the local health authorities. To the extent that each of these services can contribute to the school health program, it should be utilized.

The administration of any health program in the public schools requires close cooperation with the home at many points. The parent should have a complete awareness of the total educational scheme especially as it relates to health and the place of his own children in it. Through teacher-parent contacts, made in the home wherever possible, this program can be better understood. One or both parents should be present at medical examinations; or, if this is impossible, they should receive official reports of all such examinations through the school nurse or by letter. In turn, the school should require reports from the home on the results of remedial treatment. Parental pride in school athletics and recreation is often in accordance with their own children's participation. Without doubt, the health program is an important means of bringing about better school-community cooperation.

The Summer Camp

Camping as a school project can be traced to the Civil War period. Among others Ernest Balch should be remembered as a pioneer in the camping movement when in 1881 he established Camp Chocorua in New Hampshire for the right development of boys of well-to-do families. He worked out the essential features of organized camps much as they exist at the present time. While the movement has grown through private initiative, by 1930 at least seven cities had camps, maintained or directed by boards of education, attended by children for short periods of time. Many interesting innovations have been worked out in connection with camp life, such as work experience, agricultural experiments and school gardening, harvest camps, and reforestation. The usual values claimed for these camps include wholesome recreation, body building, out-of-door living, scholastic adjustment, and character building. Many camps provide a means of supplementary care for children on an all-year basis.

Recently school camps have come into national prominence as a substitute for military training of youth. Proponents claim that they give experience in group living away from home, develop toughness, teach youth to be self-reliant and to meet the hazards of outdoor living, improve health habits and work habits, and provide all the values of military service except instruction and drill in military tactics.

A number of cities report operation of camps for youth; more camps are run by social agencies, private schools, individuals and companies as a commercial undertaking, and by municipalities, state governments, and the federal government. In 1944 the state of New York passed the Desmond School Camp Bill authorizing school boards to purchase sites and spend school funds for camps. Camps have been operating in many parts of Europe for several years.

It would seem wise, then, to advocate the establishment of summer camps for youth to serve the following purposes: (1) physical fitness; (2) recreation and out-of-door living, (3) character building, (4) scholastic adjustment, (5) work experience, and (6) citizenship training. They should be an integral part of the public school system, partly supported out of local funds supplemented by state and federal funds and supervised and integrated by state authority. Provision should be made for small districts to pool their resources for the establishment of such camps, as on a regional or county basis. If physical fitness and other values claimed for military training can be developed through the school years, both in day schools as well as in summer camps, a year of intensive military training to secure this development at the age of eighteen or immediately thereafter would appear to be superfluous. Through all-year employment, teachers and administrative officers can improve their own physical fitness and raise their economic status at the same time.

SAFETY EDUCATION

Life has always been an adventure, but it is more of an adventure today than ever before. Some of the old dangers are gone, to be sure; in their place have come others more numerous and more serious. The hazards of modern living have been accentuated through mechanical and scientific discovery and invention, mainly of transportation, communication, comforts of home and community, and the industrial world. Paradoxical as it may seem, scientific discoveries have saved and prolonged life on the one hand while increasing the danger of life and living on the other.[14] Safety to life is substitutional, that is, we are to be saved from something for something else.[15] Its effect is not to impoverish life but to enrich it through an increase in the quality of life's adventures. Thus, safety and stimulating progress go hand in hand. If we are to live adventurously, we must live safely as life is gradually brought under control. Society has the obligation to teach its youth to meet the situations of this highly adventurous and stimulating world safely.

Education in Relation to Safety. Education is directly concerned with whatever serves to enrich life, especially during childhood and youth. Youth must be taught to meet life as it is, and direct and use it to his own health and happiness. Education looks toward an ordered world; accidents disorganize it. Life's forces must be brought under control; it is the task of education to assist in so doing. Thus safety education has become an integral part of the work of the public schools.

There are several approaches to the study of the problem of safety education. In the first place, education must cooperate with community organizations devoted to safety. Outstanding among these is the National Safety Council, which is performing an effective service. Insurance companies, whose interest would seem to be directly economic, are doing much for safety. Other organizations include automobile clubs, federal, state, and municipal agencies, the American Red Cross, youth organizations like the Boy Scouts, industries, and numerous groups of a semi-public nature.

In the second place, safety education has definitely been accepted as a necessary part of the work of the schools. Between the ages of three and twenty-two years accidents kill off more of our young people than does any other single instrumentality. This fact does not consider the numerous accidents causing injury to youth of the same ages. Safety education should become a part of the health and physical education program of the school, which develops

---

[14] Expectancy of life is now above the age of sixty-five years for men and seventy years for women. Human life has been prolonged more than twenty-five years during the past century but principally owing to reduction in infant and child mortality.

[15] "Safety Education," *Eighteenth Yearbook,* American Association of School Administrators, Washington, National Education Association, 1940.

coordination and alertness and at the same time, teaches the principles of prevention and first aid.

The objectives of safety education would appear to be: (1) to prevent accidents and save lives (*a*) by developing attitudes necessary thereto; (*b*) by imparting helpful knowledge; and (*c*) by developing habits and skills which help in safeguarding oneself and others; (2) to fuse these elements into a discipline important in itself as a means to effective citizenship.[16]

Safety education is now written into the laws of many states. As an answer to the need, schools almost universally have organized instructional programs designed to meet safety education objectives. The content for safety education is ample in every community. Some notion of the items of learning to be included may be gathered from the following general topics: animals, bicycles, cuts, electricity, falls, farms, fires (causes and prevention), first aid, gas, guns and explosives, safety in history and geography, holiday safety, industrial safety, poisonous plants and insects, poisons, public conveyances, recreation safety agencies, school problems, street and highway safety, and water transportation.[17]

Program. A program of safety education should be organized around several definite lines of activity. Pupil organizations which might be used are safety patrols, safety councils, first-aid groups, and committees which function in connection with a particular activity, as in shops, laboratories, and hallways. The school program might include a safety pledge, safety films, posters, driver education, a campaign to encourage reading and obeying signs and instructions, ways to recognize the hazards of nature, and demonstrations in the assembly, clubs, newspaper, and other school activities. The administration should be directly responsible for the safety and sanitation of the school buildings and grounds, school bus transportation, preparation and adequacy of teaching and other personnel, fire drills, fire alarm system, and for safe machines, shops, and laboratories.

In concluding this section, it is well to emphasize the fact that, through safety education, youth is enabled to meet more adequately the hazards of his environment, which lie, for the most part, outside

---

[16] *Ibid.,* p. 47.

[17] *Problems and Topics in Safety Education,* Washington, National Education Association, 1940, 32 pp. See also other pamphlets in this series.

of the school's control. As these disorganizing forces are brought more and more under social control, life's opportunities are thereby expanded. Thus safety education and invigorating progress are mutually bound together.

THE TEACHER'S HEALTH

Teacher health is a cornerstone of any effective school health program. The strenuous demands of the modern curriculum require much in the way of teacher strength and energy. The teacher's health is far more than an individual problem since it affects directly and indirectly the health, happiness, and success of the children, and indeed of all those with whom he comes in contact. Hence any discussion of the health program should include reference to the importance of sound physical and mental health on the part of every teacher.

Studies which have been made as to teachers' health indicate that not more than one-fourth of all teachers enjoy what may be termed excellent health,[18] although only about 15 to 20 per cent lack the kind of vigor needed for successful classroom work. Men teachers as a whole have better health than women, and younger teachers than older. However, the average annual loss of time per teacher because of illness is about three days, a record equaled by few other occupational groups. Mortality rates are low.

At the same time, the problems of the physical health of teachers are such as may affect mental health. Leading causes of illness are colds and related common respiratory diseases, digestive disorders including constipation, nervous disorders of various types, heart trouble, menstrual disorders, rheumatism, and abnormal blood pressures. Accidents and operations, too, account for a considerable part of teachers' health deficiencies. In addition to these physical conditions, teachers are especially subject to unwholesome mental conditions which influence their mental health. Among these are retreat from reality, worry, isolation, feelings of inferiority and inadequacy, overemphasis of the trivial, moroseness, and irritability. Since three-fourths of all teachers are women, many of these conditions would seem to be peculiarly related to the female sex.

The importance of a sound mind in a sound body is nowhere re-

---

[18] "Fit to Teach," *Ninth Yearbook, Department of Classroom Teachers,* Washington, National Education Association, 1938, chap. ii.

vealed more strikingly than in a teacher. Physical vigor begets mental health and both of these reveal virile spiritual health and power. He who would teach successfully and be long remembered as a maker of men must order his life by means of a rich balance of all of them in equal proportions. Underneath all is a serene mind, contemplative of the deeper meanings of life and cemented solidly in eternal values.

> So high as a tree aspires to grow,
> So high will it find an atmosphere suited to it.
> —THOREAU

QUESTIONS AND PROBLEMS

1. Examine the statement that there are two great fronts in the preservation of health and the treatment of disease. Indicate the progress we have made on these fronts by direct evidence.

2. How do you account for the fact that health has not yet assumed its rightful place as an educational objective of first importance?

3. Make a study in a selected school system of the influence of a healthful school environment on the physical and mental health of children (*a*) on the elementary and (*b*) on the secondary level.

4. Observe the manner in which health inspections are carried out in a selected school system. Examine your findings in the light of preferred practices.

5. Select five school systems of different sizes and study the nature of the health services in them. Evaluate in the light of preferred practices.

6. What health functions does the board of health exercise in your city or town?

7. Observe health instruction as taught in one or more school systems. Evaluate your findings.

8. What do you understand mental hygiene to mean? Contrast five factors which favor and five which interfere with a proper atmosphere of sound mental hygiene.

9. Make a list of the health activities in your community. At what points do they touch the public schools?

10. Plan an organization and program for a summer camp as an integral part of a public school system.

11. Make a study of the needs for safety education in your community. What program would you suggest to meet them?

12. Read "Fit to Teach." Examine your own health status over a period of years in the light of the suggestions in this excellent reference.

13. Do you have a wholesome philosophy of life? In what way is it related to physical, mental, and spiritual health?

SELECTED REFERENCES

1. Boynton, Paul L., *Psychology of Child Development*. Minneapolis: Educational Publishers, Inc., 1938, chaps. v, xiv, xv.
2. Brown, Francis J., *Educational Sociology*. New York: Prentice-Hall, Inc., 1947, chap. xvii.
3. Brueckner, Leo J., *The Changing Elementary School*. The Regents' Inquiry. New York: Inor Publishing Company, 1939, chap. x.
4. Chenoweth, L. B., and Selkirk, T. K., *School Health Problem*. F. S. Crofts and Company, 1940.
5. Crow, Lester D., and Crow, Alice, *Mental Hygiene in School and Home Life*. New York: McGraw-Hill Book Company, 1942.
6. "Fit to Teach," *Ninth Yearbook*, Department of Classroom Teachers. Washington: National Education Association, 1938.
7. "Growth and Development," *Review of Educational Research*, December, 1944.
8. "Health in Schools," *Twentieth Yearbook*, American Association of School Administrators. Washington: National Education Association, 1942.
9. "Mental and Physical Health," *Review of Educational Research*, December, 1946.
10. Otto, Henry J., *Elementary School Organization and Administration*. New York: D. Appleton-Century Company, 1944, chap. xi.
11. "Paths to Better Schools," *Twenty-Third Yearbook*, American Association of School Administrators. Washington: National Educational Association, 1945.
12. Phelps, Harold A., *Contemporary Social Problems*. New York: Prentice-Hall, Inc., 1947, chaps. vi, vii.
13. Reeder, Ward G., *Fundamentals of Public School Administration*. New York: The Macmillan Company, rev. ed., 1941, chap. xxii.
14. Riebe, H. A., Nelson, M. J., and Kittrell, C. A., *The Classroom*. New York: The Cordon Company, 1938, chap. viii.
15. Turner, C. E., *Principles of Health Education*. Boston: D. C. Heath and Company, 1939.
16. Williams, J. F., and Brownell, C. L., *The Administration of Health and Physical Education*. Philadelphia: W. B. Saunders Company, 1939.
17. Williams, L. A., *Secondary Schools for American Youth*. New York: American Book Company, 1944, chap. xii.

CHAPTER XVIII

Guidance as an Adjustment Service

WHEN viewed as constant and satisfying adjustments to one's environment, the formal process of education involve choices to be made at many turns. Society, on the one hand, determines what is best for the child for his social good. Here choices lie outside his control and hence must be made for him. Within the social framework democratic freedoms permit him certain rights of choice because he is a citizen and because he must assume responsibility for his own acts. Guidance assists in this process. It takes account of his own personality on the one hand and his environment on the other. Since the purpose of the school is constant educational adjustment, guidance-counseling is one form of school service by means of which it can be more adequately brought about. The final test of the school guidance service is the satisfying adjustment to life's demands and opportunities. This chapter presents the elements necessary to the process.

The Guidance Movement

Some form of guidance, whether consciously or unconsciously given, is always present whenever the educational process is in operation. Youth as well as adults have always had to meet certain conditions imposed by society and to exercise personal options which involved: (1) the need for choosing between courses of action; (2) the inability to choose wisely without some assistance; and (3) the possibility of adequate help wisely given.[1] Moreover, these conditions are

---

[1] Arthur J. Jones, *Principles of Guidance*, New York, McGraw-Hill Book Company, 1930, p. 365.

intensified by the varying needs, interests, abilities, and opportunities of the individual, as well as by the scope and intensity of the emergency in which he finds himself.

However, guidance as an organized movement is of fairly recent origin. About 1900 a great wave of social and philanthropic effort to serve humanity better began to sweep over the country, finding expression in many ways, especially in the larger cities of the coast. Organized groups, educational, philanthropic, civic, and business, shared in this movement, each endeavoring to give its sociological and psychological theories some practical application.

The vocational guidance movement was one aspect of these applied theories. Although Boston and New York have been rather generally credited with leadership, a number of cities were pioneering along these same lines.[2] As early as 1908, the Boston Vocation Bureau was formed through the efforts of Frank Parsons and Meyer Bloomfield. Here the term *vocational guidance* appears to have been first used. The movement was recognized by the school authorities of Boston a year later and resulted in the appointment of vocational counselors in every high school in 1910.

The movement spread rapidly to other cities. In 1913 the National Vocational Guidance Association was founded in Grand Rapids, Michigan. A study of the origins in many cities as reported by Reed[3] reveals the influence of organizations and activities external to education, such as consumers' leagues.

Originally conceived as vocational guidance, the idea of guidance has been greatly broadened by the use of "modifiers" indicating some specific area of immediate concern in educational adjustment. Moreover, no sharp line of definition marked off one area from another so that there was considerable confusion in terminology and purpose. Yet guidance as an organized educational service has developed to such an extent that all larger towns and cities have it in some form under trained leadership. In smaller towns and rural districts some of its functions, organized or unorganized, are performed by teachers and principals who have enjoyed some more or less formal training as a part of their professional education.

---

[2] Consult Anna Y. Reed, *Guidance and Personnel Services in Education,* Ithaca, New York, Cornell University Press, 1944, chap. i, for evidence of this statement.

[3] *Ibid.*

CONCEPTS OF THE GUIDANCE FUNCTION

Origins. We have seen that guidance as an organized activity was first conceived as vocational guidance. The purpose was to bring about a more adequate adjustment of the individual pupil with his vocational environment. Even here there were sharp differences of opinion as to how this was to be accomplished. As the functions of education expanded in response to a changing and increasingly complex environment, need for adequate general guidance became greater. Guidance came to be conceived as an adjustment process. Its meanings and possibilities emerged as more and more was learned about the child and his nature through the contributions of psychology, especially the study of individual differences, and more about his environment and home life through the social sciences, with education being thought of increasingly as a child development function.

Broadened Meanings. The functions of guidance have been broadened according to the areas and nature of the services to be rendered. Thus the terms *educational guidance, social guidance, civic guidance, health guidance, recreational guidance, personal guidance,* and *moral guidance* came into prominent use along with *vocational guidance.*

Following recognition of the need for guidance, the more important problem was what should be the position of the school in respect to it. Brewer[4] considered it to be as broad as education itself. The individual was to be guided, as rapidly as his own maturation process allowed, to assume the responsibility for his own development. Jones[5] considered guidance as that assistance given one in making intelligent choices in times of crisis. Between these extremes will be found varying points of view which will determine the attitude and services of the guide toward his subject. Hutson[6] has pointed out that many activities labeled as forms of guidance may well be judged to partake more of the nature of training or develop-

---

[4] John M. Brewer, *Education as Guidance,* New York, The Macmillan Company, 1932, pp. 2–3.

[5] *Op. cit.,* p. 28.

[6] Koos, Hughes, Hutson, and Reavis, *Administering the Secondary School,* New York, American Book Company, 1941, p. 177.

ment than of guidance. He considers guidance as services which contribute to the developmental purpose and consist of (1) the service of distribution, those activities of life desirable to differentiate the training of youth, and (2) the service of adjustment for all development, common and integrated, adjusting the individual and the various elements of his environment toward greater efficiency.

Guidance then is conceived as an educational service having many manifestations, all designed to help the pupil toward self-development and individual growth, and at the same time toward attainment of a desirable and harmonious adjustment with his environment and in complete accord with the democratic way of living.

Guidance should not be thought of as domination unless, because of the immaturity or perversity of the child, this becomes necessary. It should not be conceived as something convulsive and short-lived; rather, it is a continuous process, recognizing greater needs in emergencies and stresses. It is not necessarily a service that takes place at a given time, as nine o'clock, Monday morning, although certain aspects may be realized in this fashion. It is rather a pervading characteristic of the essential teaching and learning processes, performed by individuals with varying degrees of skill depending upon the nature of the function to be performed.

Counseling. Counseling may be defined as the principal technique whereby the entire guidance function is brought into focus. It is a procedure, involving varying degrees of expertness. It implies "consulting together" and assumes deliberative judgment based on an examination of reliable and sufficient data. It opens the way for self-decision on the part of the one counseled. Its ultimate objective is to enable the individual as he progressively develops to make choices and solve problems independently. The interview in some form is an indispensable part of counseling. It is the relationship by which the guidance act is accomplished and implies a certain professionalization and competency.

CLASSIFICATION

Need. It has been pointed out that the function of guidance has broadened with the increasing complexity of the educational function and society's relation to it. One need for guidance grows directly out of individual pupil maladjustments, which determine the form of the guidance objective. Numerous studies have been made pointing out the nature of the maladjustment and the need for a guidance service. Examples are pupil failure, absence and truancy, elimination, vocational misfits, college and university misfits, problems of pupils in industry and business, social, emotional, and personal maladjustments, and health and behavior problems. The alarming manifestations of some youth toward delinquency and crime have heightened the need for some measure of counseling, adjustment, and control. A second need for guidance grows out of the pupil's sincere yearnings for truth, for assistance in solving his problems, and for aid at strategic points in his maturing process. These needs determine the kinds of guidance and the functions to be performed. Under certain circumstances group guidance may be the procedure; however, the guidance principle functions best as an individual pupil concern.

Teacher Classification. Authorities are now generally agreed as to the following kinds of guidance:

1. Health and personality guidance—securing and maintaining the best physical, mental, and emotional health and stability
2. Educational guidance—assistance in choices related to educational progress
3. Civic guidance—enabling the individual to become a useful member of home and community as well as of state and nation
4. Vocational guidance—selection of, and adjustment to, a vocation
5. Moral and character guidance—securing proper adjustment to desirable ethical standards
6. Leisure time guidance—assisting in the proper utilization of spare time for individual progress and happiness
7. Social guidance—enabling the individual to adjust himself properly with others in whatever ways are necessary

Pupil Classification. The kinds of guidance indicated above have been conceived in terms of pupil needs viewed from the standpoint of the teacher-counselor. Pupils thus *acquiesce* in the program. It is perhaps a teacher tendency to distribute all pupil problems within such a classification. In a recent survey of the public schools of Pittsburgh, the staff attempted a somewhat different approach, namely, that of listing problem areas according to problems actually indicated by high school pupils. The following problem areas were classified in order of frequency of mention.

1. School problems—including any type of problem which grows out of schoolwork
2. Concern about the future—not only a job but all types of problems in which the future seems to hold the key
3. Economic problems—financial problems of their own or their families
4. Personal problems—growing out of their own personal adjustments
5. Social problems—relations with each other
6. Home problems—especially where there is some disturbing circumstance
7. Physical conditions—especially those which include some physical imperfection or handicap[7]

Young people point out that problems do not occur singly, a fact not entirely realized by those concerned in guidance-counseling. Adjustment procedures involve complex situations. Study must be made of the *total situation*.

FUNCTIONS OF GUIDANCE

In setting up a program of guidance, several principles must be kept definitely in mind. These include recognition of the individual capacities and needs of each pupil, his immaturity, the increasing complexity of the world about him, varying home conditions and opportunities as well as parental attitudes, strategic position of the school and the teachers, unspecialized nature of the child's abilities, urgency of emergency situations, and the need for progressive self-guidance as the child develops.[8]

The function of guidance based on these principles may be classified as follows:

1. Providing the right information, collecting, classifying, and disseminating data essential to an adequate guidance service
2. Cooperating with other individuals and groups who can assist in any way in planning and carrying out the program
3. Counseling service—individual and group
4. Teaching of guidance in those situations where instruction is deemed beneficial
5. Guidance through teaching and learning situations and experiences

---

[7] *The Report of a Survey of the Public Schools of Pittsburgh, Pennsylvania,* New York, Teachers College, Columbia University, 1940, pp. 236–237.

[8] See Jones, *op. cit.,* chap. iii, for an excellent discussion of certain basic assumptions on guidance.

6. Placement service—with adequate follow-up
7. Research service—especially in relation to problems of child study and educational and occupational data

It is important that proper facilities be provided for these functions and the tasks be properly assigned. The organization chart should show definite provision for each function. At points there may be some overlapping, which must be recognized and provided for.[9]

ORGANIZATION FOR GUIDANCE

Once guidance is recognized as an integral part of every school activity, it is essential that the administrative principle of locating and defining responsibilities be considered. Guidance should be approved as a school policy and its limits of attainment specified. It should be conceived as an integrating or unifying process, both by the teacher and by the pupil. The nature of the organization will vary with the size of the school, divisions of the school, as elementary or secondary, and functional emphasis to be placed on it.

Guidance in the Elementary School. Originating as a secondary school function, guidance has now come to have meaning for elementary school children. Perhaps the greatest source of influence is the increasing concern within the elementary school for meeting the needs of the whole child, his personality development and social adjustment. Many of the problems requiring guidance in the secondary school could more profitably be met on the elementary school level. Moreover, the elementary schools have perhaps progressed farther in recognizing and studying individual differences and in meeting the needs of individual children in the classroom. In the elementary schools guidance has and should become an integral part of the whole educational program.

Wherever child study takes place, guidance is its necessary accompaniment. The little child as he enters the nursery school, kindergarten, and first grade faces new problems and different situations and is in constant need of adjustment and guidance. Here the teacher is the person around whom the organization should be built. Her approach is both group and individual. Her efficiency increases with

---

[9] The reader will find in Richard D. Allen, *Organization and Supervision of Guidance in Public Education,* New York, Inor Publishing Company, 1934, chap. vii, an excellent discussion of the functions of guidance charted and distributed to designated members of the personnel.

her knowledge and understanding of the pupil, his problems, and his environment.

As the child progresses through the elementary school, his need for guidance continues. The teacher remains in a strategic position; she assumes the role of teacher-counselor, being responsible for knowing children as individuals and providing the experiences, information, and counsel they need. Continuity with the group is desirable, or at least continuity of contact in those situations in which previous knowledge and adjustments are helpful. The teacher-counselor avails herself of the services of the principal, the psychologist, the psychiatrist, the visiting teacher, the school doctor and nurse, and others who may be helpful. Advantage should be taken of all school and community facilities and adaptation made of school procedures where advisable. Special consideration should be given to points of articulation, as between divisions of the school system.[10]

Small School Organization. In a small school, the organization for guidance will need to be relatively simple. If responsibility lodges in the principal's office, he may (1) assign the direction to a part-time teacher-counselor, (2) appoint a guidance committee who will have general direction of the service, or (3) distribute functions among several teachers.

As the guidance program develops, it will be necessary to make provision for records and the collection of much information about each pupil, his home, and his environment. These should be properly housed and made available in the principal's office or in each home room. Proper utilization should be made of facilities available within the community itself. Any evaluation of outcomes should be considered in the light of the objectives and activities of the guidance service initially agreed upon.

Large School Organization. The very nature of the junior high school indicates clearly the importance of the guidance function at this pupil level. Emerging adolescence and the varying interests, needs, and abilities of youth of this age make it necessary to provide for some definite form of organization. Here the child is contending with new forces which surge within and about and of which he has a new-found awareness. Nor can it be said that these problems di-

---

[10] Ruth Strang, *Pupil Personnel and Guidance*, New York, The Macmillan Company, 1940, pp. 105–107; 171–180.

minish in any sense as he grows older and enters upon new activities. They may be merely different.

The size of the school will naturally determine the nature of the organization. All guidance in any school system should be administered through the principal as the responsible head of the school. This responsibility may be directly entrusted to a director of guidance or other administrative officer or officers. A faculty committee should be appointed who will be responsible for policies and coordinate the work closely with teachers and all specialized personnel within the school system. Various contacts will be made: with the health department personnel, as doctors and nurses, attendance department personnel, as visiting teachers, psychological and research department, and all other persons serving in any advisory capacity.

The size of the school may determine the number of counselors assigned to duty. These should be professionally prepared and certificated and be assigned satisfactory quarters and equipment for this work. They should be chosen because of a high standard of personality and training, being successful teachers with a wide knowledge of, and contacts with, those aspects of school-community life which will be essential in carrying on their work. Boynton remarks that no one who controls the disciplinary problems of the school should be assigned to the guidance functions.[11] While there may be some merit in this statement, the manner of the performance of the disciplinary function will determine whether such a policy should be followed.

Pupil Records. Since a thorough understanding of the pupil through many forms of measurement and diagnosis is so essential, it follows that records of these data must be collected, classified, and housed, and adequate use made of them. They will vary according to the size of the school and the adequacy of personnel to administer them.

The following basic information concerning all pupils is essential for guidance purposes:

HOME AND FAMILY BACKGROUND. This should include information of a personal nature which identifies the pupil as a person and in relation to his home and family background.

---

[11] Paul L. Boynton, *Psychology of Child Development*, Minneapolis, Educational Publishers, Inc., 1938, p. 439.

PHYSICAL AND MEDICAL STATUS. This should include such information as will be revealed through a thorough medical examination, together with observations of a physical nature which might be made by a nurse or health teacher.

PERSONAL AND SOCIAL DEVELOPMENT. This should include personal interests, achievements, intentions, attitudes, activities, problems, behavior, aptitudes, and similar information.

SCHOLASTIC PROGRESS. This should comprise a complete cumulative scholarship record, including distinctions, failures, scholarship patterns, attendance, tardiness, and schools attended.

TEST INFORMATION. This should include a record of all tests—intelligence, achievement, aptitude, personality, reading, etc.

This comprehensive information about pupils should be systematically organized for use. The intention here is not to duplicate records and other data collected and available through other sources, such as the health folders and attendance records; rather these should form an integral part of the program. The effective use of this information will depend upon the guidance personnel. Naturally, the specialist will make greater use of certain materials, while the teacher will have more need of other types. Of great importance is its housing and availability, especially in relation to the guidance techniques employed.

It is highly important that some measure be provided to test the results of guidance. Such tests as these are significant: (1) holding power of school, (2) wise pupil planning, (3) wise pupil understanding and decision, (4) pupil self-direction, (5) wide pupil range of interests and activities, (6) cordial relationships within school and home and community, (7) success of pupils both in and beyond the school, (8) evidence of character development and leadership, and (9) school morale.

Guidance as an Integrated Function. If one accepts the now well-established principle that the guidance function is an integral part of the whole educational process, guidance will permeate every part of the school organization.[12] A spirit of helpfulness to each pupil will be found in all of its activities. The following features of the school

---

[12] See M. R. Trabue's excellent discussion of this point of view in "The Scientific Movement in Education," *Thirty-Seventh Yearbook,* National Society for the Study of Education, Bloomington, Public School Publishing Company, 1938, part ii, chap. xix.

are fundamental in facilitating the guidance function: (1) program of studies through exploratory courses, flexibility in curriculum organization, and achieving guidance objectives through the several subjects studied; (2) the school library, which should be so organized that the program of studies will center in it; (3) program of activities, which has great potential value; (4) school publications which inform and orient, as handbooks, bulletins, and the school paper; (5) organized collection and study of occupational materials; (6) the home-room program, which should become an integral part of the guidance service because of its strategic location and the peculiar functions of the home-room teacher; (7) measurement and analysis research of pupils, as test scores, marks, results of interviews, and case studies; (8) placement and follow-up of each pupil, including the information gathered and contacts made; and (9) space provision for guidance-counseling personnel, accessible, private, and sufficiently spacious.

Effective leadership should be provided in the administrative organization both within each school and in the central administrative staff. The latter should be adequately organized and coordinated with other staff agencies which can render guidance service. There should be a continuous in-service teacher education program since perhaps no school activity can grow stale as quickly as guidance. If there is a state guidance organization and program, it should be approached for services and suggestions. Finally, every person associated with guidance in any manner will want to keep constantly before him the fact that guidance is a service of educational direction to youth, leading ultimately to his self-direction, and whatever can assist in attaining this outcome is most desirable.

Guidance to Youth in Making a Living

Need. One of the final tests of the school guidance service is whether the youth is thereby enabled to make satisfying adjustments, both individual and social, to life's demands and opportunities as he leaves school.[13] At this point we are interested in that phase of guidance which assists him in assuming his responsibility to make a living and support himself and those dependent on him. This may be termed vocational guidance. The American Youth Commission

---

[13] There may be a point of issue as to how far in the future satisfying guidance projects. Perhaps we need more information before we can answer this intelligently.

estimates that probably less than one youth in four (22.7 per cent)
has received what might be considered vocational guidance from any
source whatever.[14] This seems to agree rather closely with the Office
of Education study which states that guidance service is being received by only 28.7 per cent of the approximately 7,166,000 students
enrolled in the white high schools of the nation.[15] These figures give
some indication of the great need of guidance to bring about a better
occupational adjustment of all youth.

Types. Bell[16] has classified three types of school guidance programs: (1) the laissez-faire program, in which there is little or no
effort to diagnose the youth's needs and capacities and adjust them
to some definite occupational choice; (2) the one-directional program, in which youth are directed toward further academic preparation in higher institutions of learning, despite the fact that only about
15 per cent of high school youth, if they remain to graduate, will
enter such an institution, and a still smaller percentage will graduate therefrom; (3) the two-directional program, in which all youth
are divided into two groups, the academic—usually the brighter,
more interested, and more aggressive—and the vocational—those
who portray a lack of enthusiasm for book learning or who are ad-
judged to be potential workers because of their mechanical ability
or their low economic status.

The Task. Adequate vocational guidance should be built on a
consideration of marked differentiation in all youth and the development of adequate information which will lead ultimately to correct
occupational choices and adjustments. The task of occupational
guidance is to enable the two and one-quarter million American
youth who reach the age of employability every year to enter the
proper vocation suited to their needs and abilities, with the prospect
of continuous employment, and one which will enable them to contribute worth-while service to modern society.

The task properly belongs to vocational counselors. The following list of functions is presented here as being basic to vocational
counseling:

[14] *Youth Tell Their Story,* Washington, American Council on Education, 1938,
p. 74.

[15] Data from Royce E. Brewster and Walter J. Greenleaf, "A Roll Call of Counselors," *Occupations,* November, 1939, pp. 83–89.

[16] Howard M. Bell, *Matching Youth and Jobs,* Washington, American Council on
Education, 1940, pp. 20–22.

A. Helping the applicant to evaluate his vocational assets and liabilities
   1. To review his occupational experience thoughtfully
   2. To examine his education and training critically
   3. To consider his aptitudes and abilities intelligently
   4. To discover certain fields of work to which he is particularly adapted
   5. To discover some of the reasons that have prevented him from gaining greater success in any vocational field in which he has accumulated experience
B. Interpretation of the facilities offered by the community to the unemployed individual
   1. To understand some of the significant changes occurring in various occupations and industries
   2. To learn of professions or occupations in which the successful workers have tastes, interests, and abilities similar to his own
   3. To put him in touch with facilities through which he might prepare himself for an appropriate occupation
   4. To find opportunities to add new skills necessary in his work
   5. To plan avocational activities that would employ and develop special abilities and interests for which his occupation gives little opportunity
C. Broader aspects of adjustment
   1. To work out a life program that would contribute to greater happiness and success
   2. To make contacts that would be helpful in putting his plans into successful operation
   3. To gain a better command over his own life and over the conditions under which he is living
   4. To avoid certain fields in which he is weak[17]

Continuous Process. Vocational guidance must become a continuous process. As the youth reaches various stages of maturation, his needs and capacities unfold. Likewise the world of occupations changes. Most youth change jobs frequently, passing on to more desirable choices and conditions. For these reasons earlier choices must be open to constant scrutiny. Moreover, the responsibility of the school does not cease when the youth leaves its doors and secures employment. He may need further diagnosis, assistance, and perhaps training. Close association should be made with community, state, and federal employment agencies. Every school should have a service

[17] *Ibid.,* pp. 25–26.

which studies these factors intelligently, seeking to bring about the most satisfying and appropriate adjustments.

Learning how to make a living is an essential element in learning how to make a life. Guidance alone cannot alleviate unemployment among youth although it may assist, nor can it always insure against enforced idleness. Rather it assists the youth in overcoming frustration, in discovering himself, and in learning how to gain the most from his schoolwork, his capacities, and eventually his job.

This section on vocational guidance looking forward to occupational adjustment should be closely articulated with that part of this text which pertains to youth as they leave school (Chapter XXIV), to which the reader is referred.

QUESTIONS AND PROBLEMS

1. Consult several authorities for definitions of guidance. Place them in some classification and point out differences.
2. Consult authorities on the development of the guidance movement. Prepare a brief report.
3. Prepare a chart outlining functions of guidance on each age level (6–18).
4. What do you conceive to be the function of guidance in your school? Is it being achieved?
5. Distribute a sheet of paper to the pupils of a selected school and ask them to indicate the problems in which they would like to have guidance. Compare your findings with the program of guidance in effect in your schools. Is the program effective?
6. Plan an organization for guidance in (a) a large city high school (over 3000), (b) a high school of about 600, (c) a small consolidated high school, about 200, (d) a rural high school of 50 pupils.
7. Distinguish carefully between guidance and counseling by studying (a) authorities, and (b) a particular school system.
8. Evaluate the claims of guidance enthusiasts. What would be a fair statement as to the accomplishments of guidance?

SELECTED REFERENCES

1. Allen, Richard D., *Organization and Supervision of Guidance in Public Education*. New York: Inor Publishing Company, 1934.
2. Bell, H. M., *Youth Tell Their Story*. Washington: American Council on Education, 1938.
3. Boynton, Paul L., *Psychology of Child Development*. Minneapolis: Educational Publishers, Inc., 1938, chap. xiii.

4. Brewer, J. M., *Education as Guidance*. New York: The Macmillan Company, 1932.

5. "Clinical Organization for Child Guidance within the Schools," *Bulletin No. 15,* Department of the Interior. Washington: United States Office of Education, 1939.

6. "Contributions of Research to the Development of Guidance in Education," *Thirty-Seventh Yearbook*: "The Scientific Movement in Education." Bloomington: Public School Publishing Company, 1938, part ii, chap. xix.

7. "Counseling, Guidance and Personnel Work," *Review of Educational Research,* April, 1945.

8. Crow, Lester D., and Crow, Alice, *Mental Hygiene in School and Home Life*. New York: McGraw-Hill Book Company, 1942.

9. Davis, Frank G. (ed.), *Pupil Personnel Service*. Scranton: International Textbook Company, 1948. (Excellent reference.)

10. Germane, Charles E., and Germane, Edith G., *Personnel Work in High School*. New York: Silver, Burdett and Company, 1941.

11. "Guidance in Educational Institutions," *Thirty-Seventh Yearbook*: "The Scientific Movement in Education." National Society for the Study of Education. Bloomington: Public School Publishing Company, 1938, part i.

12. Jones, Arthur J., *Principles of Guidance*. New York: McGraw-Hill Book Company, 1930.

13. Koos, Hughes, Hutson, and Reavis, *Administering the Secondary School*. New York: American Book Company, 1940, chap. vi.

14. McKown, Harry C., *Home Room Guidance*. New York: McGraw-Hill Book Company, 1934.

15. Newsom, Langfitt, and others, *Administrative Practices in Large High Schools*. New York: American Book Company, 1940, chap. xvii.

16. "Proceedings of the White House Conference on Children in a Democracy," *Children's Bureau Publication No. 266*. Washington: United States Department of Labor, 1940.

17. Reed, Anna Y., *Guidance and Personnel Services in Education*. Ithaca, New York: Cornell University Press, 1944.

18. Reeder, Ward G., *The Fundamentals of Public School Administration*. New York: The Macmillan Company, 1941, chap. xxi.

19. Remmers, H. H., and Gage, N. L., *Educational Measurement and Evaluation*. New York: Harper & Brothers, 1943, part i.

20. Strang, Ruth, *Pupil Personnel and Guidance*. New York: The Macmillan Company, 1940.

21. Traxler, A. E., *Techniques of Guidance*. New York: Harper & Brothers, 1945.

22. Warters, Jane, *High-School Personnel Work Today*. New York: McGraw-Hill Book Company, 1946.
23. Williams, L. A., *Secondary Schools for American Youth*. New York: American Book Company, 1944, chap. xi.
24. Wrinkle, William L., *The New High School in the Making*. New York: American Book Company, 1938, chap. xv.

CHAPTER XIX

Psychiatric and Clinical Procedures and Research

WHEN men lived the simple life and brought up their children amidst unadorned social institutions, the adjustment of the individual to his environment was a relatively simple process. As society became more complex and affected, problems of adjustment increased almost in geometrical proportion. The stresses of modern living have multiplied the need for expert assistance in bringing about this adjustment.

Many of the sciences have made important contributions to the welfare of society which are being utilized effectively in meeting the problems of a complex civilization, especially among children. Particularly is this true in the fields of medicine, psychology, sociology (social case work), mental hygiene, and religion. Their contributions seem to have been focused on the grossly maladjusted individual. However, there is no reason to assume that their ministrations may not prove equally helpful to all children.

This chapter will discuss the field of psychiatry and the use of clinical procedures in child growth and adjustment now available. A section will be given over to the importance of research for teacher and administrator in improving educational therapy and practice affecting pupil personnel.

PSYCHIATRY AND EDUCATION

The Approach. Psychiatry may be said to be the assembly and integration of the scientific contributions of the fields of psychology, medicine, social case work, mental hygiene, and religion, as they bear on the personality, constitution, and adjustments of the individual to his life problems.[1] The main interest of the psychiatrist may be said to be curative, that is, in discovering and applying remedies for maladjustments, conceived principally as individual cases.

Applied to education, psychiatry assists in understanding all of the problems arising in connection with the child's development and adjustments, and seeking a solution in which principles and applications of the above fields may be of assistance. Psychiatry seeks to integrate the total personality of the individual so that he becomes a well-balanced and properly adjusted member of society. Every worthwhile practice known to medicine, social case work, or psychology should be brought into focus. The philosophy of the school should be taken into consideration, the home and out-of-school environment, health and hereditary factors, mental hygiene, social or other delinquencies, scholastic record, the teacher, and any other information which may assist in bringing about this integration of personality.

Psychiatry in education has usually been associated with problem children, nervous, delinquent, or otherwise difficult children. Certain interferences with their normal life adjustment have taken place which, as Anderson points out, may be "the injurious and unfavorable effect of pessimistic reverie, irrational thinking, mental preoccupations, day dreaming, unhealthy interests, poor work habits and attitudes," as they bear upon the child's responses and adjustments.[2] Although these conditions may be more marked in some children than in others, it is important to point out that occasionally every child may have need for adjustment, although not to the same degree and in the same manner as those considered difficult or problem children. This means that all teachers should have some knowledge of psychiatry and be familiar with the methods of the psychiatrist, perhaps to the extent of securing some appropriate education in the field. Such a knowledge should assist in removing any mental opaqueness in children which may interfere with their clarity of intelligent self-direction. What a great advance the science and art of education will make when subject matter priorities are subordinated to proper child understanding and adjustment!

The School Psychiatrist. Psychiatry defined as the study and treat-

---

[1] V. V. Anderson, *Psychiatry in Education,* New York, Harper & Brothers, 1932, p. xi.

[2] *Ibid.,* p. xiv.

ment of mental diseases and maladjustments is usually considered a branch of medicine.[3] Its very nature associates it closely with biology on the one hand and psychology on the other. Consequently, the psychiatrist is usually a physician with special training in these related fields. The school psychiatrist should have further training in the field of education and a proper understanding of children. His specific educational function is the discovery of the child's mental attitudes and responses revealed in behavior in specific situations.[4] As such he is a specialist who must understand and adjust these mental attitudes and responses with environmental situations.

Within every school system there may be children in need of the school psychiatrist. Larger cities may be able to employ such a specialist full time. In smaller districts, his services may be available on a part-time basis in cooperation with other districts, on a county-wide basis, or through some state administrative setup.

CLINICS AND CLINICAL PROCEDURES

Development. In view of the specialized nature of child study and guidance, particularly in the case of problem children, clinics have been established in which may be assembled suitable equipment and materials in an appropriate environment and under expert direction. Clinics and clinical services have had a phenomenal growth within a half-century. In 1896 the first psychological clinic in the United States was established at the University of Pennsylvania; in 1909 the first psychiatric clinic for children was organized in Chicago. It is estimated that the number of psychological and psychiatric child guidance clinics is now somewhere between 650 and 700.[5] Various names are applied, usually *child guidance clinic, psychiatric clinic, behavior clinic,* and *mental health clinic.*

Scope. The terms *clinic* and *clinical* focus attention upon the individual and his problems. With general acceptance of the *whole*

---

[3] Arthur P. Noyes, *Modern Clinical Psychiatry,* Philadelphia, W. B. Saunders Company, 2nd ed., 1939, p. 17.

[4] The staff of the Institute for Juvenile Research, Paul L. Schroeder, Director, *Child Guidance Procedures,* New York, D. Appleton-Century Company, 1937, p. 129.

[5] "Clinical Organization for Child Guidance within the Schools," *Bulletin No. 15,* Department of the Interior, Washington, United States Office of Education, 1939, p. v. The student will find an excellent chapter on the evolution of psychiatric clinics for children in Helen Leland Witmer, *Psychiatric Clinics for Children,* New York, The Commonwealth Fund, 1940, chap. iii.

child concept as basic in education, these problems become diversified, their implications are interwoven, and the need for expert aid is increased. This means that a larger group of persons, both expert and lay, become concerned in their solutions. These include classroom teachers, parents, school counselors, visiting teachers, school physicians and health workers, school psychologists, school psychiatrists, school nurses, and social case workers. The need of expert service is heightened as increasing attention is given to the whole child.

Procedure. Procedure in all clinics is usually identical, namely, discovery and elimination of those factors causing maladjustment. Exhaustive case study analyses are made, including investigation of the child's physical, mental, emotional, and social status, home background, teacher-pupil relationships, scholastic record, and any other information which will lead to proper adjustment.

Services. The extent of clinical services to education may be indicated by Doll's[6] classification of fields of use. He has pointed out that clinical psychology and its methods may be found useful in the following: (1) educational classification in the public schools, (2) remedial education or diagnostic teaching, (3) educational guidance, (4) vocational guidance, (5) occupational selection and adjustment, (6) child guidance, (7) mental hygiene, (8) mental deficiency, (9) crime and delinquency, (10) insanity and mental abnormality, and (11) social welfare (dependents, such as orphans, the aged and infirm, and those receiving charitable relief). This list is an extensive one and may more appropriately be applied to child guidance clinics in which there are associated physicians, nurses, social workers, psychiatrists, visiting teachers, parents, and others. Strang[7] isolates four types of problems for these clinics, namely, those resulting from (1) home conditions, (2) school difficulties, (3) physical conditions, and (4) feeble-mindedness.

Extent of Services. It has been found that approximately 80 per cent of the services offered by child guidance clinics in cities of more than 150,000 population, whereas the smaller communities, with about 75 per cent of the total population, have but 20 per cent of the service. Moreover, the services in smaller communities are far less

---

[6] See C. M. Louttit, *Clinical Psychology*, New York, Harper & Brothers, 1936, p. 8.
[7] Ruth Strang, *Pupil Personnel and Guidance*, New York, The Macmillan Company, 1940, pp. 304 ff.

effective. It is obvious that in their case guidance clinics should be offered on a county- or state-wide basis and possibly under state direction. In fact, such services might well become a project for federal administration and support. Various centers should be established and psychologists, psychiatrists, and other workers made available where needed.[8] Many colleges and universities have established clinics of various types and offer their facilities to near-by communities.

Plans for the establishment and operation of clinics may be found in an excellent bulletin published by the Office of Education. Every type of clinic is described for different-sized communities with different plans of organization, both public and private.[9]

THE RESEARCH SERVICE

The Scientific Movement. The scientific movement in education dates from about the turn of the present century. Much of the progress that education has made has been definitely a part of it. Indications of this movement have been pointed out in previous sections. The reader by this time has been impressed, it is hoped, with the scope of scientific investigations and their meaning for education. Interestingly enough, many aspects of the movement have been an outgrowth of the child study movement of the closing decades of the last century, which turned attention away from a study of theories of education to a study of children.

Of special significance are the study of individual differences in children with their psychological and psychiatric implications, the measurement movement, school surveys, the determination of efficiency in classroom instruction, and the development of standards which may serve as educational guides or against which various phases of the school and its administration may be checked.

The Teacher and Research. The young teacher approaches his work equipped with an untried array of knowledges, skills, and methodology well sprinkled with his own preconceived ideas. Before long the hard realities of the teaching situation confront him. He is

---

[8] Compare Arch O. Heck, *The Education of Exceptional Children,* New York, McGraw-Hill Book Company, 1940, p. 503. In Witmer, *op. cit.,* chaps. iv to viii inclusive, there is an excellent discussion of state-financed clinics offering psychiatric services for children in public schools.

[9] "Clinical Organization for Child Guidance Within the Schools," *Bulletin No. 15,* Department of the Interior, 1939.

met by a bewildering mass of problems, among which are: (1) the complexity of his teaching duties, (2) the unpredictableness of pupil behavior, (3) the ramifications of the instructional process, and (4) the effects of rapidly moving social changes upon the educational program. To these are added problems of supervision, older teachers, the home and community, and, too often, a faltering confidence in his own ability. He finds that his storehouse of untried knowledges and skills scarcely suffices. In his dilemma, he grasps at the tried but outmoded methods of his own school days, or tries to listen to the confusing advice of supervisors and older teachers.

If the young teacher at this juncture can catch the significance of a scientific study of his problems, either alone or in a group, much may be accomplished. Every question should be studied *where it is* in the light of established procedures and, wherever possible, under kindly supervision.

Similarly, the older teacher needs the stimulation and inspiration of the scientific approach, for quite often older teachers succumb to the pleasant apathy of continuing practices that "work" without regard to their efficiency or adaptability to current situations. It seems easier to continue these methods than to learn new ways of doing things. Research to these teachers, granted the open mind, should prove a revitalizing experience, clearing new pathways and opening new leads in the field of learning. The true teacher desires nothing more than to keep abreast of the latest development in his profession and will make every effort to do so.

The teacher must be able and willing to utilize the findings of research as they apply to his own problems. Teaching should become a great adventure demanding continual contact with the latest developments in the field. Unfortunately, many research reports are so written that the teacher is unable to make practical applications of the findings. This fault should be corrected.

Then again, the teacher himself should become a research worker, as Buckingham[10] long ago pointed out. He aptly stated that education needs the teacher as a research worker, just as the teacher needs to become one. There are so many educational problems that can be solved only within the classroom. Sensitivity to those problems with an adequate knowledge of procedure and a will to carry through

---

[10] C. R. Buckingham, *Research for Teachers,* New York, Silver, Burdett and Company, 1926, chap. x.

will assist both the teacher and the profession. Some can be studied as individual problems; others can be attacked through group action, involving supervisory direction of some sort. In their solution lies the joy of accomplishment plus the knowledge that the profession has been advanced.

The Teacher's Preparation. Higher levels of the professional status of teachers indicate the desirability of some preparation in research. Such education should include a mastery of the techniques involved in studying individual pupils and in recording objective data concerning their needs and growth. It should sensitize the teacher to the significance of current research in the curriculum, the field of method, the area of child development, and classroom management. It is not too much to expect teachers as well as principals to be prepared to conduct classroom experiments involving the use of experimental techniques, and to interpret data and conclusions to other teachers in conference. Above all, the teacher should profit by the acquisition of an open mind, being keenly aware of his own limitations and alert to the possibilities of new evidence, and having a sincere desire to seek it and to improve as it directs.

The Administration and Research. Within the administration are many opportunities for the direction and stimulation of research especially pertaining to pupil development. Some may contend that, in the last analysis, the real responsibility lies here. Be that as it may, there are numerous ways in which the administration may be associated with research in the schools: (1) through dissemination to teachers of timely and appropriate research experiments and information, fully understandable to them, accompanied by suggestions for implementation; (2) through amelioration and improvement of teaching conditions as a result of school studies and research findings; (3) through school or class experimentation in which good research techniques are employed; (4) through cooperative research among groups of teachers with proper recognition of results achieved; (5) through encouragement of teachers who conduct research studies by publication or other forms of recognition; (6) through a sympathetic personal attitude toward research and its findings as well as a personal knowledge of techniques of research, accompanied by a proper dissemination of knowledge to staff and teachers; (7) through personal participation in research by giving information, cooperating with other schools, answering questionnaires, and affiliating with research groups; (8) by organization of a research service commensurate with the size and needs of the school and the funds available.

QUESTIONS AND PROBLEMS

1. Distinguish between psychology and psychiatry. What is the place of each in education?
2. Outline a month's duties for a school psychologist; psychiatrist; research department.
3. To what extent are the services of the school psychiatrist applicable to all children?
4. Indicate different kinds of clinics available for school service. Outline the nature of the service each can render. Visit a clinic and write a report on your observations.
5. What preparation in psychology, psychiatry, and research would you require of every elementary and secondary teacher? Be specific.
6. To what extent is it possible to include (*a*) in large school systems, (*b*) in smaller school systems, (*c*) in rural areas Doll's classification of clinical fields of use?
7. Show how you would organize psychiatric and research service in a county; a state.
8. Make a plan of organized research for the following school systems: (*a*) city of 500,000; (*b*) city of 50,000; (*c*) suburban town (5,000); (*d*) county; (*e*) consolidated school.

SELECTED REFERENCES

1. Anderson, V. V., *Psychiatry in Education*. New York: Harper & Brothers, 1932, chaps. ii, iii, iv, v, vi, viii.
2. Boynton, Paul L., *Psychology of Child Development*. Minneapolis: Educational Publishers, Inc., 1938, Introduction, chap. i, also other selected chapters.
3. Buckingham, C. R., *Research for Teachers*. New York: Silver, Burdett and Company, 1926, chap. x.
4. "Clinical Organization for Child Guidance within the Schools," *Bulletin No. 15,* Department of the Interior. Washington: United States Office of Education, 1939.
5. "Counseling, Guidance and Personnel Work," *Review of Educational Research,* April, 1945.
6. Davis, Frank G. (ed.), *Pupil Personnel Service,* Scranton: International Textbook Company 1948, chap. ii.
7. "Educational Diagnosis," *Thirty-Fourth Yearbook,* National Society

for the Study of Education. Bloomington: Public School Publishing Company, 1935.

8. "Evaluating the Work of the School," *Proceedings of the Ninth Annual Conference for Administrative Officers of Public and Private Schools.* Chicago: University of Chicago Press, 1940, chap. iii.

9. Good, Barr, and Scates, *The Methodology of Educational Research.* New York: D. Appleton-Century Company, 1938, chap. xv.

10. Heck, Arch O., *The Education of Exceptional Children.* New York: McGraw-Hill Book Company, 1940, p. 503.

11. Hildreth, Gertrude H., *Psychological Service for School Problems.* Yonkers: World Book Company, 1930.

12. "Implications of Research for the Classroom Teacher," *Joint Yearbook,* American Educational Research Association and Department of Classroom Teachers. Washington: National Education Association, 1939.

13. *Journal of Educational Research,* contains many helpful articles.

14. Louttit, C. M., *Clinical Psychology.* New York: Harper & Brothers, 1936, chap. i, also other selected chapters.

15. "Methods of Research in Education," *Review of Educational Research,* December, 1945.

16. Noyes, Arthur P., *Modern Clinical Psychiatry.* Philadelphia: W. B. Saunders Company, 1939, chaps. i, viii.

17. "Psychological Tests and Their Uses," *Review of Educational Research,* February, 1947. See also previous issues on same subject.

18. Rogers, Carl R., *The Clinical Treatment of the Problem Child.* Boston: Houghton Mifflin Company, 1939, chaps. i, ii.

19. Rogers, Carl R., *Counselling and Psychotheraphy.* Boston: Houghton Mifflin Company, 1942.

20. "Scientific Movement in Education, The," *Thirty-Seventh Yearbook,* National Society for the Study of Education. Bloomington: Public School Publishing Company, 1938, parts ii, iii.

21. Strang, Ruth, *Pupil Personnel and Guidance.* New York: The Macmillan Company, 1940, chap. x.

22. Witmer, Helen Leland, *Psychiatric Clinics for Children.* New York: The Commonwealth Fund, 1940, chap. iii.

23. Wright, Edith A., *Organization and Functions of Research Bureaus in City School Systems* (leaflet). Washington: United States Office of Education, February, 1931.

PART VI

Evaluation, Recording,

and

Reporting

CHAPTER XX ────────────────────────

Determining Pupil Progress

ALFRED N. WHITEHEAD is quoted as saying that "There is only one subject matter for education, and that is life in all of its manifestations."[1] This constitutes an impressive program. The teacher as the immediate director of that process by which the young child is introduced to life has great responsibilities, in knowing both the child and life itself as well as the most efficient manner of introducing him to it.

Education, then, concerns first the development of the individual himself, which must be such as will enable him to achieve a reasonable measure of success in life and a certain happiness in attaining it. Secondly, there must be brought about a reasonable and satisfying adjustment to life about him. Educational goals may be said to be achieved when a proper relation of the individual to his environment has taken place.

The establishment of a reliable basis for evaluating the outcomes of the educational program and its procedures is necessary to this end. There is wide divergence in patterns in different school systems for achieving it. Whatever the objectives, the pattern, or the procedures, how efficiently is the educational assignment being realized? What useful measures determine that efficiency? How can the work of education be made more efficient?

Teachers' marks, the traditional measure of evaluation, are being supplemented by more objective criteria. Many types of objective tests are found in general use. Study should be made of every reliable measure and service which will help to evaluate adequately the

────────

[1] *The Purposes of Education in American Democracy,* Educational Policies Commission, Washington, National Education Association, 1938, p. 39.

whole educational program and allow its purposes to be more efficiently fulfilled.

This chapter emphasizes the importance of a sound measurement program. It sets forth ways and means of using and improving teachers' marks. It treats the subject of objective tests, including measures of achievement and intelligence, and points out the usefulness of these measures in evaluating pupil progress.

Evaluating the Outcomes of the Educational Program

The Traditional Examination. The concept that some form of test or examination should be applied at various stages in the educational progress of the learner is traditional. Oral questioning is probably the oldest form of testing, dignified by the immortal philosopher in the still commonly used Socratic method. It was the principal test of the medieval university. Formal written examinations, while probably more recent than oral questioning, date back many centuries. Hundreds of years ago in China competitive written examinations as a part of the educational system were held in the capital of each province for those who wanted to qualify for appointment to public office. They continued for three days and three nights, and each student had to remain alone in his little cell, of which there were usually several thousand similarly occupied, closely guarded by proctors to prevent any possibility of receiving information from friends. Written examinations were likewise familiar to Greek and Roman teachers.

In America examinations are probably as old as formal education itself. As early as 1834 Horace Mann urged the use of the written examination as superior to the oral quiz.[2] His arguments and recommendations have an interesting modernity quite disconcerting to modern writers on educational measurements who hasten to ascribe all praise to more recent pioneers.

Importance of a Sound Basis of Evaluation. The true educator conceives a school as an environment in which is provided desirable and adequate educational experiences for all children under proper direction. These experiences must be provided in accordance with sound and satisfying educational objectives. At intervals the results

---

[2] O. W. Caldwell and S. A. Courtis, *There and Now in Education* (*1845–1923*), Yonkers, World Book Company, 1924, pp. 37–46.

must be evaluated in terms of these objectives which requires some adequate form of measurement.

Measurement in the form of judgment takes place frequently in the classroom. Teachers form individual judgments of every paper, recitation, blackboard exercise, test, behavior, and attitude. Unfortunately, many of these decisions are colored by subjective considerations, as personal likes and dislikes, behavior patterns, race or religion, industry or the lack of it, personal health or emotional considerations, and previously formed opinions.

Measurement is necessary in order to learn more of the pupils themselves, their individual and group achievements, their strengths and weaknesses, their proper admission and classification; it is, as well, a basis for promotion. A careful inspection reveals other uses of measurement in both the elementary and the secondary school. Some additional uses are: (1) as a means of motivation, (2) to promote competition between groups, individuals, or with one's own past record, (3) for diagnostic purposes, (4) to determine replacement, (5) to compare a pupil's record with college admission standards, (6) to provide the basis of reports to parents, (7) to determine credits, honors, etc., (8) for guidance purposes, (9) to predict the pupil's success, and (10) to ascertain certain aspects of the school's efficiency, such as rating teachers, comparing methods of teaching, and comparing the measurable outcomes of a particular class, school, or subject.

The home and the public in general need a sound basis for determining the effectiveness of the school's program. Too often public conclusions on school effectiveness are in terms of athletic victories or defeats, forensic contests, school-public displays, individual progress or failure as indicated on report cards, and happenings within or about the school as reported by children or by gossip in the daily press. Unfortunately, these biased judgments often color negatively an otherwise effective instructional program.

Establishing the Basis. It would seem then that to intelligently evaluate the outcomes of the educational program, especially the instructional processes, a more reliable basis is necessary. Factors involved therein might be summarized as: (1) provision for a periodic control on the effectiveness of the classroom as well as the school program and procedures; (2) appraisal of these results in the light of forward-looking educational objectives in which the latter are consistently under surveillance; (3) evaluation of the individual and group progress of every child, with resulting adaptations to his needs, abilities, and interests; (4) substitution of scientific objective measurements, with their resulting security to teachers, administrators, and pupils, for inadequate and ineffective subjective judgments; and (5) provision for a sound basis for critical judgments of the work of the school on the part of the home and the community in general.[3]

Remmers and Gage[4] have called attention to the fact that the major purpose of evaluation is to furnish data for guidance. In this instance guidance is defined as the fullest realization by each pupil of his potentialities. There are six aspects of pupils with which evaluation for guidance must be concerned. These are (1) achievement of instructional objectives; (2) physical aspects; (3) mental abilities; (4) emotional and social adjustment; (5) attitudes; and (6) environment and background.

Evaluating the Whole Child. The basis of evaluation outlined in the preceding paragraph contemplates the child as an integrated personality. Unfortunately, many evaluative procedures have been concerned too largely with mental testing and achievement, to the exclusion, or at least to the neglect, of tests of physical growth, social development, and moral advancement. Tests should be developed which will appraise those aspects of child development and growth not now measured, or measured adequately. A true evaluation plan contemplates measures of total development, physical, mental, moral, social, emotional, and spiritual. Perhaps when we comprehend the significance of total development and integration, we will be enabled to envisage a suitable and adequate testing program which will measure it effectively.

MARKS AND MARKING SYSTEMS

Retrospect. The use of marks to measure progress and determine promotion came into prominent use with the advent of the graded school. Standards in terms of percentages, degrees of mastery, or completion of a grade or subject were evolved to determine fitness

---

[3] Compare Ralph W. Tyler, "The Place of Evaluation in Education," in "Evaluating the Work of the School," *Proceedings of the Ninth Annual Conference for Administrative Officers of Public and Private Schools,* Chicago, University of Chicago Press, 1940, chap. iii, pp. 3–11.

[4] H. H. Remmers and N. L. Gage, *Educational Measurement and Evaluation,* New York, Harper & Brothers, 1943, part i.

to pass to the next grade. Cox and Langfitt[5] are of the opinion that marks in themselves are not a part of the secondary school tradition, being inherited from earlier elementary practices and developed as the American public high school was evolved. Then as now, there was a certain confusion as to the make-up and interpretation of the mark for whatever purpose it was used. Some sort of grade or mark seems to have been universally used for the traditional purposes to which they have been put, namely, to record individual progress, to measure individual progress against the group, to determine readiness for promotion, to inform the parents, and to become a matter of permanent record.

Based on this tradition, teachers' marks have come to play the outstanding role in evaluating the progress of all pupils on all levels, through the college and university. They are given for many purposes, as a score on a paper or examination, as a grade at the end of the term, in fact everywhere a judgment has to be made. Standards of judgment emerge which vary almost as much as the teachers who use them. Nor is it easy to determine the final school marks used for promotion when so many variables enter in, as the nature of the examination, results obtained in standard tests, class recitation marks, pupils' work handed in, the conduct of pupils, and their achievement in relation to ability and effort put forth. When scores are determined individually, there is a matter of individual teacher judgment— whether the grade itself has an arbitrary value or whether it is applied against the normal curve of distribution. In some schools all pupils pass; in others the percentage of non-promotion is high.

Marking systems may also be classified as (1) those based on absolute values, the most familiar being the 100 per cent scale, and (2) those based on relative values, as with the use of ranks or the normal curve of distribution. In the absolute scale, the standard may be said to exist in the mind of the marker. The use of the normal curve of distribution as a determinant of relative values in marking tends to locate the standard of judgment as objectively as possible. Recent attempts to improve the reliability of school marks either for examination or as final grades for promotion purposes center around the use of the normal curve of distribution, standard deviation scores, and credit for quality.

---

[5] Philip W. Cox and R. Emerson Langfitt, *High School Administration and Supervision*, New York, American Book Company, 1934, p. 346.

Any discussion of school marks in relation to pupil progress should take into account the school's educational philosophy. Education has been considered as a procession through certain subject matter materials for the purpose of mastery, to develop intellectual power, and to acquire certain skills. Standards of achievement must be met. This is the older concept. The newer concept, as pointed out earlier, views education as a process of child growth and development of personality. This development must be considered in relation to provision for an environment which is fitted to individual needs, capacities, and interests.[6] Most of our systems of grades and marks have been developed in conformity with the first of these philosophies.

Unreliability of Teachers' Marks. We are interested in teachers' marks at this point because (1) they still play and will continue to play such an important part in evaluating the work of the classroom, and (2) in spite of this, there is now ample evidence of their unreliability as a measure of pupil progress.

Writers universally acclaim the pioneer work of Starch and Elliott[7] in their investigations of the reliability of teachers' marks in English, history, and geometry. Graded by competent teachers according to standards in use in their schools, the papers showed, for English, a marking range of nearly 40 per cent; for history, about the same range; and for geometry, an even greater range. This means, for example, that the same paper in geometry was graded by 115 teachers of high-school mathematics with marks ranging from 28 to above 90 per cent.[8] Later studies have shown that teachers within the same school show almost as marked differences in their gradings as do teachers from different schools. One must conclude that, with such great variability in marks, teacher judgments are, to a greater or less degree, unreliable as measures of pupil progress because of their subjectivity.

Principles Underlying Improvement. Within the past few years,

---

[6] Compare Leo J. Brueckner, *The Changing Elementary School,* The Regents' Inquiry, New York, Inor Publishing Company, 1939, pp. 87–88.

[7] Daniel Starch and E. C. Elliott, "Reliability of the Grading of High School Work in English," *School Review,* September, 1912, pp. 442–457; also XXI, pp. 254–259; also XXVI, pp. 676–681.

[8] For an excellent discussion of these and similar studies see G. M. Ruch, *The Objective or New-Type Examination,* New York, Scott, Foresman and Company, 1929, chap. iii.

much research has been done[9] looking toward an improvement in marking standards and the development of newer types of school reports as an outcome. Many of these studies indicate great dissatisfaction with present marking systems. There is a definite tendency to adapt the child study principle within the formal school organization with a resulting reevaluation of criteria. General satisfaction is apparent on the part of the home with the new type of diagnostic letter in place of the more formal report card. Some schools are experimenting with grading by pupils themselves for comparison with teachers' marks and standardized tests.

In applying the newer concept of education as child growth and development of personality, some systems of school organization developed in accordance with this philosophy have found it advisable to abandon, partially or completely, grades or school marks as commonly understood. The attacks of this group have centered largely on the formal recitation. School marks based on these denote motives external to the child. Instead there should be set up within the child internal motives, as ideals, natural desires for expression, and other forms of inner stimulation by means of approval, challenges, following intellectual interests, reposing responsibility, privileges, and the rewards of work well done. In all of this there is a sense of achievement in approaching the mastery level.

When these principles are put into effect, the nervous strain of the marking system is relieved by an internal desire for self-expression and improvement. Continuous progress of children is recorded by the results of observation, tests, and other data which are reported to the parents in letter form or through personal interview. Complete folders of helpful information gathered in many places make the child study angle more purposeful in creating and maintaining a suitable environment.

Methods of Improving Teachers' Marks. Even with all of this evidence, the fact does remain that teachers' marks are, and will probably remain, the teachers' principal measure of pupil achievement. As a consequence, pupil promotion or failure, exemption from examinations, accorded honors, admittance to higher institutions, eligibility for extra-curricular activities, school records, and reports

---

[9] "Pupil Personnel, Guidance, and Counseling," *Review of Educational Research,* April, 1939, reports eighteen studies on school marks between 1935 and 1939, to which the reader is referred.

to the home are now based on teachers' marks and will probably continue to be.

As a result, every effort should be made, under present circumstances, to bring about greater reliability of teachers' marks. The following suggestions are offered to this end:

1. There should be a constant effort on the part of every principal and teacher to approach ever greater objectivity in giving and recording marks based on judgment, and to reduce subjectivity in any form to an irreducible minimum. As far as is humanly possible, teachers must rid themselves of all bias and substitute objectively determined standards of value and judgment. There should be a common agreement among teachers in the same school and in different schools as to the significance of these standards.

2. The marking system which is used to indicate these standards, including all symbols associated therewith, should be uniform throughout the school as well as the system, with a common understanding as to all values and points of significance. Moreover, such understanding should extend to all those who may have occasion to use these records and form judgments based on them, as counselors, home-room teachers, parents, college authorities, and prospective employers.

3. At intervals, some appropriate comparisons should be made by teachers as to the significance and distribution of their marks and marking standards. These should be discussed in a wholesome, unprejudiced manner, as they relate to the different grade levels and teaching fields. In the discussions, much use should be made of graphic presentations, normal probability curves, and commendable practices of individual teachers. The logical outcome of such group discussions should be the constant approach toward a more uniform objectivity.

4. Objectivity should be approached through a wider use of objective tests. To this end attention may be directed to: (*a*) a wiser selection of subject matter materials based on the aims of the course; (*b*) questions properly constructed, clearly stated, and adapted to the age and grade levels to be tested; (*c*) elimination of catch questions; (*d*) proper directions for the test as a whole; (*e*) proper attention to the time factor; (*f*) development of adequate scoring rules; and (*g*) proper validation and proved reliability. Objective tests will receive more extended treatment in a later section.

5. Teachers should be instructed in the proper use of standardized tests and scales, especially the use of norms and diagnostic features.

6. Since essay-type examinations will still remain a means of testing pupils, greater thought should be given to them. In reading them the teacher should be on guard against bluffing, excessive wordiness alone as evidence of knowledge, garbled and ambiguous statements, and meaningless "filler" facts. Since it has been shown that much of the variability of teachers' markings of examination paper arises from varying practices in penalizing pupils for grammatical, dictional, punctuation, spelling, and other careless errors, greater attention should be given to marking agreements pertaining to them.

7. In concluding these suggestions, we may add that there are many principles of fine teaching not readily evaluated by present usages of objective measurement. Teachers' judgments will probably remain supreme in matters pertaining to character building, discipline, attitudes, habits of industry, and numerous similar traits. Only a teacher with fine discriminatory power and a careful, unbiased understanding of children will be able to render these judgments impartially.

NEWER MEASURES OF PUPIL PROGRESS

The Standardized Test. The development of standardized tests has taken place over a period of four decades. From those pioneer attempts of Rice, Thorndike,[10] Stone, and Courtis, the movement has grown until now many hundred tests and scales are available to teachers and administrators for classroom use. In the absence of reliable statistics, present sales of these tests would indicate a wide general use.

Standardized tests may serve the following useful purposes: (1) to

---

[10] E. L. Thorndike's prophetic words uttered in 1914 may be taken as a statement of the future use of standardized tests; they seem as true today as when they were spoken: "These tests will not replace skill, they will not replace tact, they will not replace kindness, they will not replace enthusiasm, or nobility. On the other hand, they will not in any sense harm us, and they will be useful as helps, no matter how ideal our aims. Our ideals may be as lofty and subtle as you please, but if they are real ideals, they are ideals for achieving something; and if anything real is ever achieved it can be measured. Not perhaps now, and not perhaps in fifty years, but if a thing exists, it exists in some amount; and if it exists in some amount it can be measured. I am suspicious of educational achievements which are so subtle and refined and spiritual that they cannot be measured. I fear that they do not exist." *Proceedings of Indiana University Conference on Educational Measurements,* 1914.

improve the traditional examination through careful selection of materials, timing, directions, administrative adaptability, methods of response, and scoring; (2) to approach greater objectivity of measurement through care exercised in their preparation and validation; (3) to provide standards or norms for individual pupils and groups with which comparisons may be made; (4) to improve the instructional processes.

Several limitations of standard tests are quite evident: (1) Standardized subject matter and norms may not provide for necessary flexibility or adaptation to local conditions. (2) They are useful largely as indicators and must be supplemented by other means of measurement. (3) There is an item of expense, making them prohibitive to some schools and teachers. (4) Values claimed for many standard tests are scarcely acceptable. Ruch goes so far as to say that "If one hundred of the best were selected and the rest destroyed, the loss would be negligible."[11] (5) The psychological implications of testing, such as fear, inhibitions, and frustrations on the part of children, present to a greater or less extent in any examinations, seem to have been somewhat accentuated in their use, largely owing to incompetence in administration. (6) There is too great a tendency to rely implicitly on single results obtained and comparisons made with norms. Diagnostic values are overlooked. Reteaching and retesting are too infrequently practiced.

Great care must be exercised in the use of standardized tests in the measurement of pupil progress. Reeder states the whole matter well when he says: "All that tests can do is to reveal a situation, they cannot per se improve a situation; they merely provide the diagnosis, and the remedy must be supplied by the teacher."[12] Teachers and administrators must understand the purposes and values of standardized tests and their place and function in the educational program. Teachers particularly must understand such statistical measures as will enable them to comprehend fully their significance and practical application.

Objective or New-Type Examination. Some consideration has been given above to the objective or new-type examination as a means of improving teachers' testing procedures. We are interested

---

[11] Ruch, *op. cit.*, p. 23.

[12] From Ward G. Reeder, *The Fundamentals of Public School Administration.* Copyright 1930 and 1941 by The Macmillan Company and used with their permission.

at this point in indicating more definitely its place in the measurement program. Two classes of new-type tests are generally accepted: (1) the recall type, in which the examinee supplies the answer, and (2) the recognition type, in which he chooses the best answer.

Advantages usually ascribed to the objective or new-type tests are (1) greater objectivity in scoring accompanied by greater reliability; (2) more extensive sampling of materials to be tested; (3) economy of time in administration of testing; (4) reduction of pupil guessing or bluffing; (5) greater administrative ease and control; (6) higher diagnostic values; and (7) greater adaptability to local conditions and materials (said with reference to standardized tests).

Disadvantages include (1) lack of provision for language training; (2) constant presence of guessing element; (3) excessive tendency to measure acquired factual information; (4) tendency to demand recall of information disassociated from its appropriate setting; (5) as a result of (3) and (4), a tendency on the part of both teacher and pupil to stress retention of factual information rather than mastery, some writers going so far as to call these tests "unpedagogical"; and (6) denial to some teachers of administrative aspects of test construction and use because of (*a*) inadequate duplicating facilities, (*b*) insufficient funds, and (*c*) amount of teachers' time taken in preparation and use. Naturally, this latter statement raises the all-important question as to where and how a teacher's time is most profitably used.

Diagnostic Tests. In the more recent development of diagnostic tests and scales, there has been a laudable effort to correct one of the marked deficiencies of both standardized and new-type tests. While a general measure of a pupil's attainments may be ascertained by comparison with standards or norms, there is need to study individual needs and deficiencies. Diagnostic tests provide a means for analysis and diagnosis of a pupil's attainments and deficiencies and the basis for remedial treatment. Properly used, they may serve useful purposes in pupil progress, especially as they naturally individualize the instructional processes. Although diagnostic tests and scales for various purposes are readily available in the market, teachers may construct them for their own uses without great difficulty.

PSYCHOLOGICAL MEASUREMENT AND SERVICES

Basic Consideration. Throughout this text we have been stressing the importance of child development and school progress. All of our tests, scales, and other measures of achievement are evidences of some portion of that development. The teacher hopes that it is taking place to the fullest extent of the child's innate capacity and ability.

It is with the child's intellect or mental capacity that teachers appear to be most concerned. The program of the public school has traditionally been built upon progressive steps of "average" mental development and capacities. Perhaps there has always been an awareness of marked variations in mental ability, but until comparatively recently these have been subjectively determined. Accurate measurement of mental ability is an innovation of notable significance.

Development of Intelligence Testing. Intelligence testing, as Symonds[13] has pointed out, is the outcome of five converging movements. Binet's earlier experiments in the field of applied psychology led him to diagnose feeble-mindedness and recommend the treatment of special classes. Experimental psychology and the study of individual differences have been most influential in the development. To these must be added improvement in statistical techniques and the contributions of the anthropologists. The survey movement also provided a means of stimulation. Mental tests were quickly perceived to be of major use in the classroom: to classify pupils, for guidance purposes, for discovering exceptional children, and, when used with various forms of achievement tests, for the study of a pupil's achievement in relation to his capacity.

Indices of Intelligence. Intelligence may have many indices, all essential to pupil progress. It may denote certain native abilities, as judgment, reason, response to new situations, adjustment to environment, originality, initiative, comprehension of relationships, ability to learn more things, or the same things better or more quickly. Intelligence may be viewed abstractly, socially, or concretely. It may denote certain mechanical abilities or unusual extension of exceptional abilities in one or more directions. Its proper measurement is a composite of all or most of these.

Viewed negatively, especially when related to ability to learn, intelligence may be expressed in relation to certain deficiencies of any of the above. Moreover, mental deficiencies may be accompanied by physical or other inadequacies, as sensory, motor, moral, or emotional. Again, special disabilities may be quite pronounced, as perceptional defects. These may be congenital. There may also be any

---

[13] Percival M. Symonds, *Measurement in Secondary Education,* New York, The Macmillan Company, 1928, chap. iv.

number of transient interferences with the intellectual processes, such as conflicts of various types, perseveration, and wandering attention.[14]

Great care must be taken in using intelligence tests, especially in fixing any measure of or attitude to a child's ability or accomplishment with any degree of finality. Recent investigations tend to throw considerable doubt on the constancy of the intelligence quotient.[15]

Uses of Intelligence Tests. Intelligence tests may serve the following purposes: (1) to identify non-educable children, as idiots, imbeciles, and certain types of morons; (2) to identify superior children; (3) to isolate and identify the relation of intelligence and delinquency in any form, since it has been estimated that about one-fourth of criminals have some form of mental weakness; (4) as a basis for classification and grading; (5) to test vocational aptitude and fitness; (6) to study individual differences; (7) for prediction purposes, as in selecting subjects, planning for college entrance, placement, and final school grades; (8) for guidance purposes; (9) to assist in planning programs of instruction, individualized instruction, special classes, and for similar purposes.

Attention should be called to the importance of basing intelligence upon more than one test, discovering all available information before arriving at any conclusion, making all conclusions tentative, and holding all such scores and conclusions confidential.

There is some difference of opinion as to the part teachers should take both in giving and in interpreting intelligence tests. One may say that teachers can and should be prepared to give and score group intelligence tests under direction. Interpretations of these tests should be tentative, and subject to review after further testing and additional data. The administration of individual intelligence testing should be considered the task of one professionally trained for that purpose. It is to be hoped that all teachers eventually will arrive at that educational level where they may participate intelligently in this important educational function.

---

[14] For an excellent discussion of these factors, see Lee Edward Travis, "Intellectual Factors," in "Educational Diagnosis," *Thirty-Fourth Yearbook,* National Society for the Study of Education, Bloomington: Public School Publishing Company, 1935, chap. ii.

[15] "Intelligence: Its Nature and Nurture," *Thirty-Ninth Yearbook,* National Society for the Study of Education, Bloomington: Public School Publishing Company, 1940, parts i, ii.

The School Psychologist. Modern testing instruments and procedures demand the professional services of trained school psychologists. Special training is necessary to give many of the tests, interpret the results, and identify children for placement. The school psychologist brings to this service a background of scientific training and a fundamental knowledge of clinical procedures, invaluable in diagnostic and remedial instruction. He can assist in educating the teachers in all matters pertaining to a better understanding of their children and a more objective appraisal of results. His duties may often be associated with research, guidance, and placement, and he may be considered an educational consultant.

The functions of psychology and psychologist specialists have been studied by many writers. Anderson has outlined several methods of procedure for child psychologists, namely, incidental observation, biography, systematic observation questionnaire, psychoanalysis, case history, direct measurement and simple tests of complex functions, rating, experiments involving random and paired control groups, control by statistical devices, and factor analysis.[16] Hildreth found, in her study of the various kinds of psychological services in the schools of the country, some twenty-nine functions, classified as (1) measurement and statistics, (2) study and guidance of individual pupils, (3) assistance in administration and supervision, (4) assistance in instruction, (5) research, and (6) auxiliary functions.[17]

PROGRAMS OF EVALUATION

The term *evaluation* has come to have a wider meaning than the term *measurement,* being usually applied to a program rather than an isolated skill or area of knowledge. We might say that a series of measurements are required in order to increase the accuracy of the final evaluation. As tests and measurements become more valid, *evaluation* can be applied more justly to them.

State Programs. Since education is a state function, the state should have some concern in the evaluation of its program. State-wide testing and evaluation programs conducted by the state depart-

---

[16] J. E. Anderson, *A Handbook of Child Psychology,* Worcester, Clark University Press, 1933, chap. i.

[17] Gertrude H. Hildreth, *Psychological Service for School Problems,* Yonkers, World Book Company, 1930, pp. 23–26.

ment of education are now in operation in some twenty states.[18] These vary as to level and type of testing. In several other states such programs are sponsored by universities. State high school examinations were originally used for the accreditation of the work done in the high schools, upon which standard diplomas were issued. More recently, this plan has been extended in order to accredit and upgrade the school, and to provide a basis for approved state funds. The New York Regents' examinations date from 1865 and are probably the best-known and most comprehensive measurement program of this type.

State department and accrediting agencies have set up other techniques for evaluating the work of the schools. These include supervisory services run by specialists, programs of instruction, and advice as to organization, administration, and buildings. Numerous rating scales and devices in varying stages of objectivity have been evolved. Many states are using the plan of evaluation developed by the Cooperative Study of Secondary School Standards for all types of secondary schools. State supervisors make frequent appraisals through local visitation.

Local Programs. Local administrative officers, either through state mandate or by the nature of their position, arrange for many varieties of measurement programs. Best known of these perhaps is the time-honored county examination conducted by the county superintendent assisted by a staff of teachers and principals. Despite many criticisms it has persisted, although in much improved form. Many cities conduct city-wide examinations using varying levels of objectivity. Of interest and value are those programs of evaluation sponsored by superintendents and principals meeting as a regional organization. Careful preparation and controls are essential to all these programs.

Desirable Objectives. A distinction should be made between the more comprehensive evaluation program and the measurement program. The former will involve active cooperation of schoolmen within the state or under state or regional leadership. Constant efforts should be made to comprehend the total program and the techniques for evaluation.

---

[18] For a list of these states and their programs see "Pupil Personnel Services as a Function of State Departments of Education," *Bulletin No. 6* Monograph No. 5, Federal Security Agency, Washington, United States Office of Education, 1940.

The responsibility of state departments of education for measurement programs is usually a matter of legal prescription or custom. Testing should be geared to desirable educational objectives, the instruments of measure being objectively determined and adapted to them. While the state is interested in universal standards of achievement, care must be taken that the whole administration and teaching function of local school districts be not warped to achieve a good showing without due regard to the child and to peculiar local problems. Moreover, the program should be a cooperative enterprise. The virility and spontaneity of the local school should be maintained and stimulated, not overshadowed. Testing should always be a means to an end, and not degenerate into a meaningless chore in which the child is lost but the system saved.

QUESTIONS AND PROBLEMS

1. Write a report on different examination methods by consulting histories of education. Can you find instances and extent of present use?

2. Evaluate (*a*) Socratic method, (*b*) oral quiz, (*c*) Chinese examination plan, (*d*) short written test, (*e*) essay examinations, (*f*) objective tests as to effectiveness.

3. Make a report on studies of the unreliability of teachers' marks.

4. Compare the effectiveness of a teacher who uses judgment largely as a means of measurement with that of one who uses objective measures.

5. Compare the value of marking systems based on (*a*) absolute values, (*b*) relative values.

6. Comment on the suggestions offered to improve teachers' marks.

7. Make a case for the abolition of all grades or marks in the elementary school. Is such a plan feasible?

8. Compare the advantages of (*a*) standardized tests, (*b*) new-type objective tests, and (*c*) diagnostic tests. Where should each type be used?

9. What advantage has the individual intelligence test over the group test? What uses do intelligence tests have in the schools? What care should be exercised in using them?

10. Give examples of tests useful in evaluating pupil qualities other than mental and physical. To what extent have these been developed?

11. Outline a month's duties for a school psychologist in (*a*) a system of a selected size, (*b*) a county.

12. What preparation in measurement should be required of every

teacher? What can be done to help teachers in service in using better measurement techniques?

SELECTED REFERENCES

1. Barr, Burton, and Brueckner, *Supervision*. New York: D. Appleton-Century Company, 1938, chaps. vi, xvii, xviii.
2. Douglass, Harl R., and Boardman, Charles W., *Supervision in Secondary Schools*. Boston: Houghton Mifflin Company, 1934, chap. xvi.
3. "Educational Diagnosis," *Thirty-Fourth Yearbook,* National Society for the Study of Education. Bloomington: Public School Publishing Company, 1935.
4. "Educational Tests and Their Uses," *Review of Educational Research,* December, 1938.
5. Greene, H. A., Jorgensen, Albert H., and Gerberick, J. R., *Measurement and Evaluation in the Elementary School*. New York: Longmans, Green and Company, 1945.
6. Greene, H. A., Jorgensen, Albert H., and Gerberick, J. R., *Measurement and Evaluation in the Secondary School*. New York: Longmans, Green and Company, 1943.
7. Hawkes, H. E., Lindquist, E. F., and Mann, C. R., *The Construction and Use of Achievement Examinations*. Boston: Houghton Mifflin Company, 1936.
8. McCall, William A., *Measurement*. New York: The Macmillan Company, 1939.
9. McGaughy, J. R., *An Evaluation of the Elementary School*. Indianapolis: The Bobbs-Merrill Company, 1937, chap. viii.
10. "Measurement of Educational Products, The," *Seventeenth Yearbook,* National Society for the Study of Education. Bloomington: Public School Publishing Company, 1918, part ii.
11. "Methods of Research and Appraisal in Education," *Review of Educational Research,* December, 1945.
12. Nelson, M. J., *Tests and Measurements in Elementary Education*. New York: The Dryden Press, 1939.
13. Noble, M. C. S., *Practical Measurements for School Administrators*. Scranton: International Textbook Company, 1939.
14. Orleans, Jacob S., *Measurement in Education*. New York: Thomas Nelson and Sons, 1937.
15. "Psychological Tests and Their Uses," *Review of Educational Research,* February, 1941; February, 1944; February, 1947.
16. Reeder, Ward G., *The Fundamentals of Public School Administration*. New York: The Macmillan Company, 1941, chap. xxiii.

17. Remmers, H. H., and Gage, N. L., *Educational Measurement and Evaluation*. New York: Harper & Brothers, 1943.

18. Riebe, Nelson, and Kittrell, *The Classroom*. New York: The Cordon Company, 1938, chap. ix.

19. Ruch, G. M., *The Objective or New-Type Examination*. New York: Scott, Foresman and Company, 1929.

20. "Scientific Movement in Education, The," *Thirty-Seventh Yearbook*, National Society for the Study of Education. Bloomington: Public School Publishing Company, 1938, part ii.

21. Traxler, Arthur E., *Techniques of Guidance*. New York: Harper & Brothers, 1945.

CHAPTER XXI

Recording and Reporting

ADEQUATELY kept and properly adapted school records constitute one measure of the effectiveness of a school system. Indeed, one might trace the growth of public school efficiency through a study of school records and reports. Two purposes of records have been consistent through the years, namely, to give the child's attendance and his achievement. The scientific movement in education, together with the rediscovery of the child, his nature, and his needs, has profoundly influenced the importance of adequate records, especially those which will serve as evidences of his growth and development. At the same time, the school has a certain fiduciary trust to maintain with the home and the community it serves. More recently, the states have tried to make more uniform the form of the records and the collection of information upon which appropriations may be based and comparisons made.

This chapter attempts to trace the development of school records and point out the modern purposes and values associated with them. Recent movements to improve records and record keeping are discussed, with emphasis on their proper organization and management. School reports bear a definite relationship to school records since the data so assembled become the basis for the report. We shall take up the nature and values of school reports, and types usually considered, and shall associate their organization and management in relation to those made responsible for them, namely, the superintendent, principal, and teacher. Reports to parents have undergone many changes within recent years, as we shall see. Recording and reporting have administrative value enabling those associated with the educative processes to further the school progress of the child. This should be the point of principal emphasis.

327

EARLY USES OF SCHOOL RECORDS

Few Records in the Early Schools. Record keeping in early schools was a matter of keeping track of the pupils, both as to attendance and as to achievement. One can assume fairly enough that neither task was performed very well. Since attendance was not compulsory and the home was little concerned, there was not much need for the record anyhow. Since the determination of achievement remained so largely a subjective matter, and as the particular school reader the pupil happened to be in could be remembered by the teacher and the pupil, why bother with a record? In those days of teacher procession, it might be lost anyway; if so, pupil standing could easily be determined when he came to school by the simple expedient of "trying him out."

Horace Mann and the Movement to Improve Records. As school systems became better developed, efforts were directed toward improving the attendance register. Horace Mann[1] over a hundred years ago spoke of examining "hundreds of different forms" then in use. Without doubt he crystallized the thinking and practice of his day when in 1838 the state board of education in Massachusetts authorized him to prepare a permanent school register in book form designed for a five-year period for different-sized schools. Its preparation was a cooperative effort, many of the "best teachers and educationists in the country offering suggestions and approval."

Horace Mann was undoubtedly farseeing in his day in his conception of an improved report, as he was in so many other educational matters. In it he saw many values: (1) it efficiently prevented irregularity in attendance; (2) it allowed more accurate statistical reports; (3) it enabled the teacher to note the mental and moral progress of each pupil; (4) it contained the entire school history of the child; (5) it furnished each pupil a means of self-comparison; (6) it became "a powerful incentive to good and dissuasion from evil"; and (7) it fastened "the delinquency of absence upon the particular offenders."

Since he was a state school official, values with which he was directly concerned naturally pertained to the administration of attendance; other values he foresaw as pertaining more immediately to the teacher and the pupil.

---

[1] "Ninth Annual Report of the Secretary of the Board of Education," *Common School Journal,* April 16, 1846, p. 120.

About the same time, Henry Barnard in Connecticut developed much the same type of register. He too considered it important, and lectured on "School Records and Reports" at meetings of teachers. Other state officials and city superintendents applied the same idea. Soon the attendance record became, as Moehlman points out, the "real index of school efficiency."[2] Schools were compared with each other, largely on the basis of school attendance. However, there was no common agreement as to the methods of computing attendance. That was to come later.

The National Education Association, organized in 1857, gave frequent heated consideration to matters of school attendance and child accounting. Schools could not be compared as to efficiency without some measure of uniformity. Committees to achieve this were appointed in 1860, 1874, 1881, and 1891. Little tangible action resulted.

INFLUENCE OF THE SCIENTIFIC MOVEMENT

Defects in Records Revealed by Studies.   Perhaps the most significant stimulus to adequate and uniform school records came about as the direct result of the scientific movement in education. The need for better survey techniques and tests and measurements became apparent, for the study of both school systems and individual pupils. Significant among studies pertaining to pupils in which adequate records were necessary were Thorndike's "Elimination of Pupils from School" (1907)[3] and Ayres' *Laggards in Our Schools* (1909).[4] In each of these, accurate comparative school data were highly essential but in many instances were inadequate and inaccurate. Ayres' study of retardation and elimination in city school systems particularly called attention to the paucity of school records and recommended more attention to them in the following language:

Little or no effort has been made to preserve original records, to reduce duplication, to save time and energy or to secure accuracy and accessibility.

Worst of all, different principals and superintendents have introduced

---

[2] Arthur B. Moehlman, "Child Accounting," *Journal of Educational Research*, April, May, June, 1924.

[3] Edward L. Thorndike, "Elimination of Pupils from School," *Bulletin No. 4*, Washington, United States Bureau of Education, 1907.

[4] Leonard P. Ayres, *Laggards in Our Schools*, Russell Sage Foundation, New York, Survey Associates, Inc., 1909. The reader will find Chapter XIX, "Reform in and through School Records," stimulating.

isolated and disconnected practices from which significant facts for the whole system cannot be deduced. There have been many day books and blotters but no ledger accounts.

If existing conditions are to be bettered and our school systems made more efficient we must have a better knowledge of conditions and their significance. To accomplish this we must have better records.

Dutton and Snedden[5] writing in 1908 indicated four defects of existing records: (1) lack of cumulative record material; (2) undeveloped character of units of measure; (3) duplication of material, much of it unorganized; and (4) lack of uniformity of standards for comparisons.

National Education Association Committees. The results of these several studies stimulated the appointment of a committee by the National Education Association on Records and Reports, which reported in 1912.[6] This report undoubtedly was of much value in standardizing a number of terms and procedures. And yet its chief emphasis remained upon attendance.

The scientific movement in education grew apace during the next dozen years. More and more comparative measures of city school systems became increasingly essential in the development of the measurement and survey movements. One direct outcome was the appointment in 1925 of an additional committee of the Department of Superintendence of the National Education Association.[7] It indicated that an acceptable local system of school records should have the following characteristics: (1) They should make for uniformity and comparability. (2) The amount of data recorded should be no more than is needed and used, with all information exact. (3) The various records of a school system should be coordinated and unified.

The committee recommended the following types of pupil records: (1) teacher's daily register book; (2) pupils' general cumulative record; (3) pupils' health and physical records; (4) guidance record; (5) pupils' psychological clinic record; (6) principal's office record.

The following standards were recommended in order to make the procedure of record keeping and report making easily routinized.

---

[5] Samuel T. Dutton and David Sneddon, *The Administration of Public Education,* New York, The Macmillan Company, 2nd ed., 1916, chap. xxx.

[6] National Education Association, "Report of Committee on Uniform Records and Reports," *Bulletin No. 3,* Washington, United States Bureau of Education, 1912.

[7] National Education Association, "School Records and Reports," *Research Bulletin,* V, No. 5, 1928.

Records should be: (1) cumulative; (2) uniform (when used for comparative purposes); (3) durable; (4) non-repetitive; (5) properly organized; (6) complete; (7) available by those who would use them; (8) visible; and (9) separately provided for elementary and secondary pupils where needed and justifiable.

The report of the committee is replete with illustrations of record cards in use, with special consideration given to census and attendance records and reports to the home. Undoubtedly, this report has had a far-reaching influence on the keeping of records and their administration.

Purposes of Records. By this time the reader will have discerned several definite purposes in keeping school records. These will now be reviewed. In the first place, the legal basis should be complied with. State laws generally provide for some form of record keeping, upon the basis of which reports to the proper authorities may be made. In many states, attendance registers are provided, as well as official state record forms and rules and regulations. A second purpose is archival. School records are necessary for proper reporting, promotion, transfer to college or another school, for comparative purposes, survey needs, work permits, and similar uses. A third purpose is attendance enforcement. This is one of the oldest uses of records and still persistently remains. A fourth purpose is for guidance. In this respect records indicating data peculiar to each individual emerge as of fundamental importance. A fifth purpose is for use in reporting to the home. A sixth pertains to use in pupil progress. This is one of the most important, and involves admission, classification, promotion, demotion, and other factors helpful in determining that progress. Other purposes of records pertain to specific information gathered from, and growing out of, health and physical records, clinical records, delinquency and court records. The nature of each of these reveals some specific intention and they should be useful accordingly.

CUMULATIVE RECORDS

A New Approach. The modern school is increasing its emphasis upon fitting its program to the individual child in the light of his needs, aptitudes, and interests. Both curricular and individual analysis, a two-way procedure, are essential to this process. Modern school organization is such that the pupil passes from one school to another and from one teacher to another. Under this system it is manifestly impossible for teachers to remember all the information essential to adequate and desirable individual and group progress.

The 1925 committee of the National Education Association called attention to the need of a cumulative pupil record—one which follows the pupil as he progresses through the school. The cumulative record system attempts to preserve such data as seem worth preserving and provides at the same time for an adequate organization and administration therefor.

Values. Unique values accruing from cumulative pupil personnel records have been summarized as follows:

1. They are essential to insure the continuity of the guidance program of the school.
2. Provide necessary data for advising parents and suggesting adjustments which should be made in the interest of the school and home life of the pupil.
3. Provide data for diagnosing individual pupil difficulties and application of remedial measures.
4. Provide data to indicate to the school the degree to which curriculum practices meet the needs of the pupils.
5. Provide data to know individual pupils better and adapt measures of adjustment (referring to personality largely).
6. Provide data for research into effectiveness of school procedures.
7. Provide data for higher institutions of learning.
8. Provide data for individual pupil analysis on his own part.[8]

Segel[9] has pointed out that the value of the cumulative record lies in the fact that it brings together successive measures, ratings, and influential items (1) of the same trait over a period of time and (2) of different traits over a period of time. We need to know the values of patterns of combined records in different fields and with different sets of activities.[10]

Items to Include. Suggested cumulative record items are: (1) general items of identification and progress, (2) scholarship, (3) educa-

---

[8] "Cumulative Pupil Personnel Records," p. 7; also David Segel, "Nature and Use of the Cumulative Record," *Bulletin No. 3,* United States Office of Education, Washington, Government Printing Office, 1938, 48 pp.

[9] Segel, *op. cit.*

[10] See also "Pupil Personnel, Guidance, and Counseling," *Review of Educational Research,* April, 1939, pp. 175–176. Note references.

tional and general aptitude test scores, (4) social and character ratings, (5) health, (6) home conditions and family history, (7) extra-curricular activities, (8) vocational interests and aptitude test scores, and (9) other items assisting in the school progress of the individual pupils.[11] Some systems have found it helpful to include the curriculum election record, the transfer card, a pupil self-analysis form, record of home visits, correspondence, conference records, and a record of teacher estimates at intervals. Specific guidance and vocational records should find a place when such information is available.

This variety of items naturally suggests the importance of including data found useful in particular school situations and under given circumstances with individual pupils, in which growth and development is the dominant consideration. These can be determined after careful survey and experience. The contents of cumulative record folders, if properly kept, have a way of growing in size. It is important to point out that this growth should not be haphazard like Topsy's, but rather the outcome of careful planning, selection of materials, and farsighted procedure.

Records on Elementary and Secondary Levels. Specific materials in and uses of cumulative records will show increasing complexity as the pupil advances through the different divisions of the school system. Uses on the elementary level will be much simpler, except in studying specific needs, as of the gifted or the maladjusted pupil. At points of articulation, they will be invaluable. In the secondary field, data growing out of an increasing complexity of activities will be recorded, as well as redirection of educational and vocational goals and the use of leisure time. Adequate records are most essential in advising pupils as to further education on the collegiate level and in the placement problem.

Newer Approaches

A new emphasis on the place of school records in the educational process has been pointed out by adherents of progressive education. The realization of the maximum development of the individual through his growth, study of environment and experiences, patterns of behavior, ability to confront new situations, and evolution of those drives which are essential to that development is hardly possible

---

[11] Compare Arch O. Heck, *Administration of Pupil Personnel,* Boston: Ginn and Company, 1929 (Universal List).

without a careful record of his progress. Moreover, the art of teaching, like the art of human relationships, depends on records for finding the patterns of human behavior and directing them wisely.[12]

Giles[13] has pointed out some twelve devices useful in record keeping. With these one can learn the children's real interests, levels, and individual differences and how to deal with them effectively. About ten hours a week will be needed for adequate record keeping and study for the average class. The skillful teacher will be aware of facts to be used in pupil evaluation, of the pupils' progress, and of aids to analysis and guidance; he will be sensitive to the intangibles of teaching and learning, especially as they relate to the objectives of education.

Zyve[14] has pointed out that many teachers are dissatisfied with the records being used in their schools to measure the newer phases and practices in education. They are discouraged from working on the problem because they lack time and training for the careful preparation of subjective records that are possible in schools where classes are small. The activities associated with the development of human meanings and values require a different type of recording from that necessary for subject matter material. To comply with these newer meanings, record keeping should be continually evolving; it should be viewed in perspective.

Perhaps the most comprehensive set of principles basic to pupil personnel records has been developed by Traxler.[15] Fourteen principles have been outlined emphasizing the recording of data concerning each individual pupil indispensable to the proper functioning of the school and each teacher, as well as to facilitate the growth and development of each pupil. Records are classified as to (1) function, (2) filing arrangement, (3) nature of the centralizing unit, and (4) permanence.

ORGANIZATION AND MANAGEMENT OF RECORDS

Guides to the Approach. As the science of education develops, the need for factual material, accurately secured and properly recorded,

---

[12] Eugene Randolph Smith, "Work of the Committee on Reports and Records," *Progressive Education,* November, 1935, pp. 441–445.

[13] H. H. Giles, "Record Making in an Experimental School," *Progressive Education,* November, 1935, pp. 473–477.

[14] Claire T. Zyve, "Recording the Changing Life of the School," *Progressive Education,* December, 1936, pp. 621–630.

[15] Arthur E. Traxler, *Techniques of Guidance,* New York, Harper & Brothers, 1945, chap. xi.

is increasingly apparent. In this connection it is important to observe guides to approach. First, state laws provide for the collection of data, and usually the form to be used is supplied. In the second place, the record system will need to be fitted to the underlying philosophy and objectives of the school system. Third, whatever record forms are evolved and data collected should be developed with an eye to their usefulness, both immediate and ultimate. It is trite to remark that the record system should be kept under constant surveillance.

Attendance Records. Adequate attendance records demand prior attention. School census information should be properly recorded and kept in duplicate, one set at the attendance department office and the other at the office of the principal of the school attended, public, private, or parochial. Since the continuing census plan is coming more and more into common use, it is important that data be constantly revised. Once the child enters school, he is properly entered in the register and daily attendance data are recorded. Absences should be reported to the principal's office and also noted in the teacher's register. The principal should keep a record of the cases showing dates, causes, and disposition. A simple but effective procedure should characterize relations with the attendance officer or department. Records pertaining to child labor, employment, or other legal status should have a definite place here.

Cumulative Records. The collection and recording of data pertaining to the child as he moves through the school system begin as soon as he enters school. These records follow him from grade to grade and from school to school. The nature of the information to be secured and recorded will need to be determined, concerning which suggestions have been previously indicated. Of primary importance are the pupil's personal history, health record, scholastic record and activities, and psychological data. Into the cumulative record may go reports of all interviews pertaining to the pupil, notes on his home environment, special abilities, interests, and disinclinations, and personal observations.

Many writers suggest that a committee of teachers study the questions regarding what records should be kept, where they should be kept, and the manner of their preparation and use. This would seem to be in harmony with democratic procedure. Thus records may serve to unify a system and keep its personnel in harmony.

Availability. The location of all recorded material should be such that it is accessible to those directly concerned. Ideally, records of a particular building should be available in the principal's office in a place where teachers may enter unobtrusively. It is entirely conceivable that the school counselor may assume entire charge of records housed in his office. If the records are kept, as they sometimes are, in the central administrative office, or the office of the secretary of the board, their usefulness may be materially diminished because of inaccessibility.

The filing system should be safe, easy to operate, and capable of expansion. Although record cards can be secured from reliable publishers, these almost never quite fit the situation. It will be advantageous for committees of teachers to study and prepare the forms to be used and have them printed locally.

Management. The management of the recording system should be largely the responsibility of the building principal. Several steps should be noted which include: (1) initiation of teacher responsibility in regard to the nature of the system to be set up; (2) provision for, as well as distinction between, temporary records and those of a more permanent character; (3) definite distribution and explanation of all forms and their administration to teachers; (4) proper housing; (5) setting up a calendar schedule for the completion of records; (6) checkup of records turned in; also follow-up service if needed; (7) provision for their free use by teachers or others entitled to their use; (8) evaluation procedures in terms of pupil progress as a whole, or for revision of the system; (9) provision for teachers to prepare and enter data on records; clerical service provided wherever necessary. In this connection it is pertinent to point out that the principal should not dissipate his time in clerical pursuits which may better be performed by clerical service provided for the purpose. Professional responsibilities should always take precedence.

These suggestions should aid in the management of a system of records. The effectiveness of such management should be studied in direct relation to the effectiveness of pupil progress as a whole. Adaptation, not imitation, should characterize the management at all times. Tests of good management might be considered in the light of: (1) determining regularity of attendance; (2) answering all questions concerning pupil progress; (3) providing information upon which to base needed adjustment, personal, social, educational; (4) supplying information for guidance and placement; and (5) charting tendencies and predictions. In the last analysis, it is the teacher who will give intelligent direction and guidance to the educational efficiencies of the child. Adequate records will help immeasurably in this process.

USE OF RECORDS IN EVALUATION

Records are not only useful but essential in evaluating the work of the school as a whole. While they should have some uniform characteristics for comparative purposes, a school expresses its individuality in part through the form of its records. Educational objectives in general, and of the school in particular, should serve as the basis for their use in such evaluation. Many kinds of evidence of individual pupil and school progress should be easily available. Diederich[16] has pointed out sixteen. These are records of (1) personal patterns of goals, (2) significant experiences, (3) reading, (4) cultural experiences, (5) creative experiences, (6) anecdotes, (7) conferences, (8) excuses and explanations, (9) tests and examinations, (10) health and family history, (11) oral English-diagnosis, (12) minutes of student affairs, (13) personality ratings, (14) family and personal data, (15) courses and activities, and (16) all administrative data, largely of a personal nature.

Specific examples of records useful in evaluation are in connection with (1) health examinations and services, (2) guidance-counseling services, (3) school surveys, and (4) applications of the cooperative technique to secondary schools. Health records have been discussed in a previous chapter. A complete evaluation of the health services of a school system and the health of each child is impossible without them. Similarly, guidance records have been previously discussed. The guidance program of a school system can scarcely be appraised without recourse to them, nor can the counseling service to each pupil be effective.

The scientific study of a school system through survey techniques is predicated upon accurate data maintained through cumulative records. This text contains numerous references to such data insofar as they refer to the pupil and his growth. The administrator and teacher should apply known techniques through survey procedures in order to have a constant check on the effectiveness of the pupil personnel program. Best known of more recent measures of effectiveness is the

---

[16] Paul B. Diederich, "Evaluation Records," *Educational Method,* May, 1936, pp. 432–440.

Cooperative Study of Secondary School Standards. The several sections of this technique require for adequate study objective data of various sorts, examples of which, pertaining to the pupil, are enrollments, attendance, age-grade distribution, personal pupil data, home environment and health data, occupational status and other guidance information, scholarship, and pupil activities.

Reporting in Relation to Recording

Thus far, the discussion has been concerned with records. Much that has been said about them might well apply to reports. As a matter of fact, a record is of little value until it is put to use, and reporting is one of the uses. Reports are made in large part from recorded material, the shift from a record to a report being only as significant as the nature of the data and the use made of it. Thus, adequate and accurate records are a prerequisite to reporting.

Lack of Interest in Reports. Comparative lack of interest in school reporting generally may be traced to several causes. One of these has been the unsatisfactory methods of recording data. We have noted recent efforts to correct this deficiency. Lacking objective data, school reports have been largely subjective and highly opinionated. Where objective data have been available, they have been presented in statistical form usually uninterpreted or explained in vague generalities. Such statistical measures as were used were unintelligible to most of those for whom they were intended until clear-cut comparisons, graphs, charts, diagrams, pictures, and other illustrative material came into general use. One of the most serious faults of reporting has been in presenting all available material in an unorganized manner without regard to its selection for some specific purpose.

Nature and Purposes of Reports

Reporting a Fiduciary Trust. Reporting should become one of the most important functions of the administrative and teaching processes. Education has a fiduciary trust reposed in it, since it cannot be considered apart from the democracy it serves, nor from the maintenance of the ideas, ideals, mores, and practices of society which it seeks to improve. To society then, and especially to those who are directly concerned with the educational process, administrators and teachers owe a proper accounting of their trust and services. Dissatisfactions of the home and the community with the school may often be traced to lack of understanding of its purposes and procedures. Even within the school many dissatisfactions can be traced to lack of exact comprehension. Proper understanding can be achieved through proper reporting practices both within and without the system.

The Report Defined. A report may be simply defined as an accounting. Webster defines it as "a statement or relation of facts given in reply to inquiry or by a person authorized to examine and make return." Such a definition has a certain official ring with the suggestion that, upon compliance, further obligation ceases. Perhaps this attitude has been the most serious deterrent to the profitable outcome of reporting. Objections to making reports, even recording the data for them, center around their seeming uselessness in that nothing further happens.

From the standpoint of the administration of the pupil, we might define a school report as a meaningful accounting of school or pupil progress to those entitled to a knowledge of it, upon the basis of which a better understanding of the educational work of the school and the progress of the child may result.

Purposes. Many purposes have been stated for school reports. We should note, first of all, the legal basis of reporting as required by law or regulation for the purpose of maintaining permanent records and the proper classification, supervision, and support of the schools. Specifically, the purposes of school reports may be summarized as follows: (1) to convey information to those who are entitled to it, as superior officers, parents, board of education, or the general public; (2) to provide a basis for the educational progress of each child and to focus attention upon that progress; (3) to provide a stimulus for professional advancement, serving to secure thereby greater efficiency; and (4) to educate those who receive it, so that the result is a corresponding knowledge of school, class, or individual achievement, and a support of school policies and programs.

Underlying all of these purposes are the concepts of greater administrative efficiency, better educational procedures, local, state, and national needs, essential data for the organization and administration of the school, and adequate and accurate pupil accounting. In any consideration of fundamental purposes, it seems essential to stress the fiduciary trust reposed in those who are responsible for the school enterprise, as well as the educational progress of each child, for whom the schools exist.

Types of School Reports

In this section only those reports which are of concern in pupil personnel administration are considered. They may be further divided into those which directly and those which indirectly concern the pupil. It would be appropriate to add that we should consider only reports which are directly useful to his educational progress. Doubtless our criteria are insufficient in determining this usefulness.

Perhaps the most satisfactory classification of school reports is in regard to the locus of responsibility for them. Responsibility for reports should be located in (1) the superintendent and his staff, (2) the principal, and (3) the teacher.

The Superintendent. The superintendent's report (used in the singular) is a typically American document which began to develop in the second quarter of the nineteenth century.[17] It stemmed from the board of education rather than the faculty side of the school system, and was essentially a report of the professional work of the schools. It was presented in popular form more descriptive than factual.

The movement to improve the superintendent's report can be traced, for the most part, to influences within the National Education Association and is closely related to attempts to improve records. Recent superintendents' reports have shown a tremendous improvement, largely the result of advancement in the printer's art and better methods of presenting data objectively.[18]

As to pupils, the superintendent's report should include the following data: (1) the policies and program of the schools, (2) enrollment and attendance data, (3) age-grade and progress facts, (4) scholarship, (5) promotion and non-promotion, (6) the health and physical education program, (7) athletics, (8) guidance, (9) the school in operation, (10) attention given to special education, (11) vocational education, and (12) such other facts about the pupils which will

---

[17] David S. Snedden and William H. Allen, *School Reports and School Efficiency,* New York, The Macmillan Company, 1911, chap. ii, an interesting chapter on the beginnings of school reports. See also chap. iii.

[18] William Allison Yeager, *Home-School-Community Relations,* Pittsburgh, University Book Store, 1939, pp. 167–172. See also Harold S. Irons, *Development of Characteristics in Superintendent's Annual Reports to the Board and to the Public,* Doctor's Dissertation, University of Pittsburgh, 1942.

assist in a better understanding of their school progress and what the school is doing to facilitate it.

The superintendent will be responsible for the data needed for all state and national reports, and for requiring data from his teachers and his staff so that these may be compiled. He will want to consider the place and importance of bulletins, handbooks, periodic and supplementary reports, and special reports in connection with special occasions, as anniversaries or financial drives. He will be responsible for the form of the permanent record system from which reports are derived, as well as the form for reporting. He will set up a schedule of reporting, allow time for it, and assist principals and teachers in carrying out instructions pertaining thereto.

Although considerable progress has been made in coordinating a plan of school statistics, records, and reports, a recent committee of the Department of Superintendence indicated much dissatisfaction in this regard. The report says in part: "Present accounting, both fiscal and pupil, is inadequate and inaccurate in local school systems. Greater coordination and uniformity are required in the interests of true pictures of local school systems."[19]

The Principal. The principal's relation to reporting may be characterized as (1) intermediary and (2) terminal. In regard to the first, the principal is responsible for data to be transmitted (*a*) to the superintendent and (*b*) to the state or federal offices. Many of these reports are statistical in nature, the material being indicated on forms provided. Naturally, he must expect his teachers or clerical force to gather this information on schedule and report it accurately. The superintendent's office often requires reports of a special nature, such as supplementary data for superintendent's reports, accounts of disciplinary situations, reports on teachers, transportation, or supplies.

From his teachers, the principal may receive reports whose final destination is his own office. These may concern attendance, pupil progress, discipline, committee work, supply needs, and school plant conditions. Only those should be required which will serve some definite use in relation to school efficiency and the educational progress of the pupils.

---

[19] W. C. Reavis and N. S. Dight, Topic Group H, "A National Coordination of School Statistics, Records, and Reports," *Official Report,* Department of Superintendence, Washington, National Education Association, 1934, pp. 228–229.

The practice seems to be growing rapidly for school principals to prepare an annual report. Murphy[20] has made a study of ninety-three such reports in which there is common agreement that their purpose was to inform the public as well as the superintendent and board of education about the school. Most of them were descriptive in character and contained some statistical data. Over 125 subjects were studied. The primary functions served were (1) development of good will and understanding, (2) maintenance of historical record and perspective, (3) provision of a professional stimulus, (4) accessibility of teaching materials, and (5) development and continuity of policy.

The Teacher. Basically, most of the data in a pupil personnel report system must of necessity be provided by the teacher since he is in direct contact with its origin. There are two main classifications of reports for which the teacher is primarily responsible: (1) those intended for use within the school or system and (2) those intended to denote individual pupil progress or convey information to the home.

Within the school system, teachers' reports may be divided into two groups. In the first are those which are required by law or state or local regulation. These are fundamental to the operation of the schools and have been honored by tradition. They include attendance reports, enrollment reports, periodic reports on enrollments and attendance, age-grade reports, scholarship reports, health reports in certain instances, term reports on failing pupils or failures, accounts of guidance activities, book and supply reports, and others as required by law or developed within the system. As in the case of the principal, the second group contains many reports of a more specific nature which may be required of teachers within the school system. There may be special committee reports, reports of the history and changing life of the school, reports associated with the development and use of cumulative pupil records, personality and attitude reports, and numerous others as the philosophy of the school and the zeal and interest of principals and teachers seem to indicate.

REPORTS TO THE HOME

The second classification of reports for which the teacher is primarily responsible includes those reports to the home intended to

---

[20] J. Fred Murphy, "The High School Principal's Annual Report," *American School Board Journal,* November, 1932, pp. 41–42. The reader will find in this study an excellent summary of ninety-three reports.

account for individual progress or to convey information concerning the pupil or the school. The chief form is the time-honored pupil's report card. Other forms include printed circulars, visits of teachers to the home, visits of nurses, visiting teachers, attendance officers, and school census workers, parent-teacher association meetings, and personal letters.

Why Pupils' Reports. The origin of the pupil's report card as an accounting instrument can be traced to the English common law principle that parents had almost unlimited control over the education of their children. While statutory provisions establishing the American common school have limited this right, parental responsibility has remained to see that children partake of the opportunities provided. Since the state requires attendance, some form of accounting of that attendance and the usefulness of the time expended becomes obvious. This has taken on the official nature of the traditional report card. Thus, it seems to be the outcome of a fiduciary trust and a parental right.

More recently, the school has recognized that the efficiency of its educational program is limited by the amount of intelligent cooperation it receives from the home. As the scope of the educational process enlarges, this cooperation becomes more and more essential. Each must understand the other, and both must understand the child and the nature of his progress, especially since his growth and development are determined by those combined forces, conditions, and agencies that surround him both within and without the school.

Oral communications of some sort largely constituted the manner of reporting in the early schools. Perhaps a short descriptive letter of standing accompanied the pupil who moved from school to school. It would be difficult to indicate the time when the traditional report card as we know it came into general use. Suffice it to say that it has had a long and honorable history, despite the general dissatisfaction which has recently (perhaps always) developed against it.

The traditional report card has been described as a card which provides for marking pupil performance in a number of school subjects, either in percentages or on a scale which recognizes several levels of performance above a passing grade. The list of subjects may also include items on conduct and attitudes, possibly one on effort. Information on attendance and promotion is also given. There is a brief note to parents instructing them to sign and return the report card promptly.

Characteristics and Values of the Traditional Report Card. Since it has withstood the test of time, the traditional report card has many values, whatever may be its shortcomings. Parents have always been interested in the progress of their children. School marks have been devised to indicate its nature. These serve many uses. They indicate success or the lack of it; they furnish a means of pupil as well as teacher motivation; they are used in guidance and promotion; they give satisfaction to the parents in an accounting sense; many of life's counterparts can be discovered in this competitive function. The report card conveys definite information as to attendance, tardiness, conduct, and effort. The parental signature assures fulfillment of the teacher's obligation to report.

Objections. For some years the traditional report card has been subject to severe criticisms, the outcome of general dissatisfaction with this system of reporting to parents. Some critics go so far as to contend that it "represents the most retarded phase of American education."[21] Messenger[22] reports a survey of eighty-three selected articles written in the period from 1917 to 1934 revealing the nature of this general dissatisfaction. In these articles are offered many suggestions for improvement. Along with parents and teachers, administrators seem equally desirous of bringing about an improvement[23] and suggest further research in regard to it.

Deficiencies of the traditional report card seem to center around the use of the school mark as applied to the measurement of scholarship. Among the criticisms offered in this regard are unreliability of marks, use of the comparative rating feature, motivation principle associated with marks, use of marks as punishment, indefiniteness of information, relative values of matters marked and reported, misleading information, and the limitations of marks as a means to effective instruction.[24] Marks, as generally reported, do not convey to

---

[21] Robert O. Evans, *Practices, Trends, and Issues in Reporting to Parents on the Welfare of the Child in School,* New York, Bureau of Publications, Teachers College, Columbia University, 1938, p. 1.

[22] H. R. Messenger and W. Watts, "Summaries of Selected Articles on School Report Cards," *Educational Administration and Supervision,* October, 1935, pp. 539–550.

[23] J. Morris Jones, "Is the Report Card Doomed?" *School Executive Magazine,* June, 1935, pp. 291–294, 312.

[24] Evans, *op. cit.,* pp. 12–13. See also Chapter XX of this text.

the parent the real work of the classroom or the real progress of the child. They may cover up inefficient teaching, become the club of the teacher, and constitute the chief fear of the pupil. The qualitative development of the whole child is not revealed by the report, although the recent effort to appraise personality and character traits is a step in the direction of improvement.

Shortcomings of the traditional report card then are associated largely with: (1) the limitations of marks as a measuring stick, (2) subjective considerations in using it, (3) narrowness of its scope in relation to total pupil progress, (4) its unscientific nature, (5) personal and emotional considerations on the part of both teachers and parents, (6) lack of resulting personal conference situations, (7) urge on the part of many pupils to acquire acceptable marks as a reputed measure of their success, and (8) its primary use as a *copy* of archival records rather than a report to the home.

IMPROVEMENTS IN HOME REPORTING

Improvements in home reporting have taken the following forms: (1) changes in the traditional report card, (2) messages to the home, and (3) personal conferences.

Improving the Traditional Report Card. Many administrators and teachers have felt that the magnitude of the task of reporting to the home, especially where large classes are concerned, has necessitated the retention of the traditional report because of its comparative ease of administration. At the same time, the report card can be adapted to local needs and conditions. More and more space is given to general descriptions and explanations. Specific improvements include: letters as marks, graphic presentations, ranks, and applied simple statistical procedures based on the normal curve of distribution. Intervals are less frequent. There is a constant effort to have the child compete with himself rather than against the whole class, and assume a greater share in his own evaluation. The content of report cards is improved. Attitudes and personality traits are included. Scholarship reporting is made more descriptive and understandable; the special services of the school are included, as health and music. Throughout, positive approaches are substituted for negative ones. Efforts have been made to diagnose the pupils' achievements in terms of the objectives of the school.

There is a voluminous literature on the general subject of reporting to the home, much of which pertains to procedures in determining a fair and accurate evaluation of pupil progress and improving reporting practices to the home.[25]

Messages to the Home. Accompanying the traditional report or in substitution for it is the growing practice of communicating with the parent through individual messages. These are usually personal in nature, individual and diagnostic in character. They may be written in the form of letters by the teacher or principal, or prepared in cooperation with the pupil. Information about the work of the school may accompany the report. Special letters are sometimes sent to the parents felicitating them on a merited achievement. Messages of this character bid fair to greatly modify traditional reporting practices.[26]

Personal Contacts. A third innovation in pupil reporting comprises some form of personal contact: personal conferences, teacher visitation in the home, and visiting days for parents in the schools. Some teachers are experimenting with personal delivery of all report cards, making the occasion a conference of mutual help and interest. In this way difficulties may be analyzed and better understandings achieved. Home conditions which promote or interfere with school progress can be studied. Davis[27] has pointed out that recently constructed report cards for elementary grades are emphasizing the *progress of the child* as most significant.

Personal reporting practices are coming to be considered among the more important educational school services helping to bring about better home-school relationships. Considerations are given to balanced child development in terms of pupil growth. Parents and teachers can now work together more harmoniously in bringing about this desired end.

Criteria for Home Reporting. It is possible to find in current literature several sets of criteria for home reporting. Tibbetts[28] has suggested thirteen criteria for determining the character of a reporting system. A good system (1) has a minimum amount of clerical

---

[25] For a summary of this literature see William L. Wrinkle, *Improving Marking and Reporting Practices,* New York, Rinehart and Company, 1947.

[26] J. C. Moffitt, "A Substitute for Report Cards," *Education,* November, 1934, pp. 147–150; also Ruth Andrews, "What's New in Report Cards," *Parents Magazine,* February, 1938, pp. 18, 19, 72–75.

[27] Mary Dabney Davis, "Pupils' Progress Reports," *School Life,* January, 1936.

[28] V. H. Tibbetts, "Determining the Character of a Reporting System," *Progressive Education,* May, 1936, p. 355.

work, (2) is one in which the community is educated, (3) promotes understanding and good will, (4) informs parents of the child in all phases, (5) states simply the school's philosophy and objectives, (6) adjusts school life and school subjects, (7) sets standards of value of work for its own sake rather than for marks or rewards, (8) is suitable for the appropriate age levels, (9) is understandable to the child himself, (10) is based on objective and subjective records, (11) facilitates progress in cases of transfer, (12) considers the child as an individual as well as a member of a social group, and (13) indicates scholastic achievement, individual adjustment, and social growth.

Bristow[29] has indicated certain characteristics of a pupil reporting system adequately geared to democratic principles in which mutual understanding and whole child progress are emphasized. In 1934, the Educational Research Service[30] of the National Education Association made a significant study of newer developments in pupil report cards and pointed out guiding principles. Emphasis was placed on the growth of the child and the spirit and objectives of the school system. Stressing the place of the report in a public school relations program, Yeager[31] analyzed the shortcomings of the report card in current use and pointed out intrinsic values in accordance with preferred practices in fostering mutual confidence and partnership between parents and the school.

Procedure. The procedure for setting up a plan of home reporting is to apply such criteria as may seem to fit a given school-home situation in the light of the philosophy of the school and its objectives and in accordance with home levels of understanding. In the light of those fundamentals which have to do with school accounting to the home and the fostering of ever higher levels of cooperation, ways and means should be sought to promote the greatest amount of *pupil total growth* in the light of his abilities, interests, capacities, and attitudes through cooperation. Pupil and parental approach should be positive. Competition should be individual. Criteria from many sources should be studied and selected in order to bring about the

---

[29] "Guiding Principles in Reporting Pupil Progress," *Bulletin 88,* Harrisburg, Commonwealth of Pennsylvania, Department of Public Instruction, 1935.

[30] "New Developments in Pupil Report Cards," *Circular No. 4,* Educational Research Service, Washington, Department of Superintendence and Research Division, N.E.A., May, 1934, pp. 8–9.

[31] William A. Yeager, *Home-School-Community Relations,* Pittsburgh, University Book Store, 1939, pp. 178–181.

desired outcome. Of special interest are the suggestions and illustrations of report card procedure reported by Traxler.[32]

PUPIL REPORTS IN RELATION TO HIGHER INSTITUTIONS AND THE COMMUNITY

For many decades the offerings of the secondary schools have been geared to college entrance requirements in spite of the fact that a comparatively small percentage of secondary pupils attend higher institutions of learning. In order to determine fitness for entrance, leading admission devices used by colleges and universities from 1875 to 1925 have been: (1) college entrance examinations, (2) the institutions' own examinations, (3) secondary school transcripts, (4) diploma, (5) personal recommendation of school principal, and (6) private conference and special examinations.

More recently, admission methods have been modified to include: (1) psychological examinations, (2) tests of aptitudes and special abilities, (3) personality ratings, (4) comprehensive examinations, (5) general record of all grades, (6) selection of preparatory school graduates from the upper divisions of the class (rank), and (7) the principal's general appraisal. Some of the earlier practices have been retained, such as conferences.

An analysis of the above methods reveals the fact that the records and reports of the graduating (preparatory) school play an important part in transfer to the higher institutions. Where highly selective processes are used, the cumulative record folder will be found invaluable if it contains data revealing scholarship, personality, activity, and many other records. Secondary schools often prepare college histories of their pupils during their secondary school careers. Counselors usually hold frequent interviews. The pupil may be enrolled in the college of his choice several years in advance and make many contacts before admittance. Much depends on the analytical and appraisal statements of the principal, counselors, or teachers. In all of these it is important to emphasize the whole child nature, development and potentialities, rather than mere scholarship or activity rating. In this respect the secondary school has *its own responsibility* to each pupil, which it must perform without regard to the college. In turn, the higher institution has its task and, upon admittance, should take the pupil as it finds him.

---

[32] *Op. cit.,* chap. xiii.

Many colleges and universities send a report of the progress of their first-year students to the secondary school at the end of the freshman year. This is mainly a scholarship report and usually does not contain evidence of other aspects of the student's growth. Success or failure is thus predicated too much upon the college's grades based largely on examinations or quizzes. Moreover, usually only one report is received, and contacts with the secondary school terminate with it.

Secondary schools should make a practice of requiring complete reports from all higher institutions which their pupils attend—at least one a year during the *entire* period of time they are enrolled. Colleges and universities on their part should provide the proper facilities so that this may be accomplished. These reports should be studied by the preparing school, made a matter of record, and used in improving the school programs and procedures and in counseling pupils. It would be helpful if school and college authorities could sit in conference frequently and discuss the welfare of pupils.

Pupil Reports in the Community. School authorities find it necessary, from time to time, to make reports to different persons and places within the community. There is a growing tendency to accept the school's records and appraisal without question when pupils seek employment within the community. Here again it is important that records be accurately kept and that the appraisal be impartial. Social agencies often call upon the school for data on attendance, scholarship, disciplinary situations, and home conditions. Through addresses, bulletins, the newspaper, and conversations, school authorities are constantly called upon to give an accounting of their stewardship. Feelings of confidence and security are always present where records are well kept and reports truthfully and efficiently made.

QUESTIONS AND PROBLEMS

1. Write a brief paper indicating the contributions of the National Education Association to child accounting.
2. What are the (*a*) advantages, (*b*) disadvantages of cumulative pupil records?
3. Evaluate Heck's Universal List for practical school use.
4. Comment on: "About ten hours a week will be needed for adequate record keeping in the average class."

5. Comment on Diederich's sixteen types of records useful in evaluation.

6. What records should be kept (*a*) in the principal's office, (*b*) in the teacher's room, (*c*) in the central administrative office? Give reasons.

7. Study (*a*) records, (*b*) reports in at least two school systems and evaluate your findings in the light of selected criteria.

8. Find several definitions of (*a*) records, (*b*) reports. Prepare your own.

9. Comment on: "One of the most serious faults of reporting has been in presenting all available material in an unorganized manner without regard to its selection for some specific purpose."

10. What is meant by "Education has a fiduciary trust reposed in it"? Relate to reporting.

11. Comment on the author's classification of records in relation to responsibility for them.

12. Collect a bibliography on improvements in home reporting. Classify them in some definite manner.

13. Draw up a preferred record and reporting plan to be used by a secondary school in its relations with higher institutions.

SELECTED REFERENCES

1. Allen, Wendell C., *Cumulative Pupil Records*. New York: Bureau of Publications, Teachers College, Columbia University, 1943.

2. Ayres, Leonard P., *Laggards in Our Schools*. Russell Sage Foundation. New York: Survey Associates, Inc., 1909.

3. Bolton, Cole, and Jessup, *The Beginning Superintendent*. New York: The Macmillan Company, 1937, chap. xvi.

4. Clark, Zenas Read, *The Recognition of Merit in the Superintendent's Report to the Public*. New York: Teachers College, Columbia University, 1931.

5. "Counseling, Guidance and Personnel Work," *Review of Educational Research,* April, 1945.

6. Cox and Langfitt, *High School Administration and Supervision*. New York: American Book Company, 1934, chap. xix.

7. Davis, Mary Dabney, "Pupils' Progress Reports," *School Life,* January, 1936.

8. Davis, Mary Dabney, "Report Cards of Pupil Progress Recently Constructed for Elementary Grades," *Circular Number 169,* Department of Interior. Washington: United States Office of Education, November, 1936.

9. Diederich, Paul B., "Evaluation Records," *Educational Method,* May, 1936, pp. 432–440.

10. Dougherty, Gorman, and Phillips, *Elementary School Organization and Management*. New York: The Macmillan Company, 1936, chap. xiv.

11. Dutton, Samuel T., and Snedden, David S., *The Administration of Public Education in the United States*. New York: The Macmillan Company, 2nd ed., 1916.

12. Evans, Robert O., *Practices, Trends, and Issues in Reporting to Parents on the Welfare of the Child in School*. New York: Bureau of Publications, Teachers College, Columbia University, 1938.

13. Flory, Charles D., and Webb, James F., "Cumulative Records for Elementary Schools," *Elementary School Journal*, December, 1937, pp. 278–290.

14. Germane, Charles E., and Germane, Edith G., *Personnel Work in High School*. New York: Silver, Burdett and Company, 1941, part ii.

15. Giles, H. H., "Record Making in an Experimental School," *Progressive Education*, November, 1935, pp. 473–477.

16. "Guiding Principles in Reporting Pupil Progress," *Bulletin 88*. Harrisburg: Commonwealth of Pennsylvania, Department of Public Instruction, 1935.

17. Heck, Arch O., *Administration of Pupil Personnel*. Boston: Ginn and Company, 1929, chap. xi.

18. Jones, J. Morris, "Is the Report Card Doomed?" *School Executive Magazine*, June, 1935, pp. 291–294, 312.

19. Messenger, H. R., and Watts, W., "Summaries of Selected Articles on School Report Cards," *Educational Administration and Supervision*, October, 1935, pp. 539–550.

20. Moehlman, Arthur B., *Child Accounting*. Detroit: Friesema Brothers Press, 1924.

21. National Education Association, "School Records and Reports," *Research Bulletin*, V, No. 5, 1928.

22. "New Developments in Pupil Report Cards," *Circular No. 4*, Educational Research Service, Department of Superintendence and Research Division. Washington: National Education Association, May, 1932.

23. "Pupil Personnel, Guidance, and Counseling," *Review of Educational Research*, April, 1939.

24. Reed, Anna Y., *Guidance and Personnel Services in Education*. Ithaca, New York: Cornell University Press, 1944, chaps. v–xii.

25. Segel, David, "Nature and Use of the Cumulative Record," *Bulletin No. 3*, United States Office of Education. Washington: Government Printing Office, 1938.

26. Smith, Eugene Randolph, "Work of the Committee on Reports and Records," *Progressive Education,* November, 1935, pp. 441–445.

27. Snedden, Davis S., and Allen, W. H., *School Reports and School Efficiency.* New York: The Macmillan Company, 1911.

28. Strang, Ruth, *Pupil Personnel and Guidance.* New York: The Macmillan Company, 1940, pp. 82–84, 137–138, 151.

29. Tibbetts, V. H., "Determining the Character of a Reporting System," *Progressive Education,* May, 1936, p. 355.

30. Traxler, Arthur E., *The Nature and Use of Anecdotal Records.* New York: Educational Records Bureau, 1939.

31. Traxler, Arthur E., *Techniques of Guidance.* New York: Harper & Brothers, 1945, chaps. xi–xiii.

32. Warters, Jane, *High-School Personnel Work Today.* New York: McGraw-Hill Book Company, 1946, chap. v.

33. Yeager, William Allison, *Home-School-Community Relations.* Pittsburgh: University Book Store, 1939, pp. 166–187.

PART VII

Achieving Personality

and

Social Adjustment

CHAPTER XXII

Problems of Social and Personality Adjustment

MAN is a social being. The social manifestations of children appear at an early age and in many forms. Naturally there are wide variations in the social tendencies of boys and girls due to environment, early training, inborn tendencies, and opportunities. Probably the most challenging problem confronting education is the maintenance of balance and harmony between the individual as a personality and social living. He must get along with others as well as himself.

Education for social living has assumed far greater significance than formerly. The increased complexity of our social institutions, the multiplicity of social opportunities of all kinds, and the increased availability of leisure time have created perplexing problems for home and school alike. In the community are to be found wholesome opportunities for youth development striving with many unwholesome influences; at times the latter seem to be gaining in mastery.

Recognizing the confusion of social impacts upon children of all ages, more especially upon adolescents, the school has been attempting to do something definite and constructive about social education and social adjustment. One of the principal values of the whole extra-curricular activity movement lies in its opportunities for developing desirable social values. In this chapter it is proposed to discuss certain aspects of the social adjustment program which have become pupil administrative problems. Throughout the discussion there should be noted conflicts in social experiencing in which the individual is trying to find himself. Certain stereotypes associated in the socializing processes, such as mutual aid, honesty, loyalty, obedience, and the inculcation of certain virtues, emerge as definite problems, especially where the interests of smaller groups conflict with those of larger groups or the whole. Youth places much emphasis on group approbation, a sense of security, hoped-for successes, and the relationships of face-to-face contacts in which a certain degree of intimacy prevails. One additional fact should be noted, namely, possible cooperation or conflict which may exist directly or indirectly between desirable social adjustment processes within the school and those to be found in the community. Occasionally, in our efforts to meet and adjust social situations we may unconsciously be creating new problems through the cross-purposes of well-meaning but often misguided ambitions.

The social development of all children and youth is then a fundamental educational objective. The program should be sufficiently inclusive to achieve this objective. If all children developed equally in every way, the administration of such a program could be more easily accomplished. However, the manifestations of individual differences among children and youth and the varied environmental factors are undoubtedly the principal causes of problems which arise out of the schools' social procedures. Several of these problems will be briefly discussed.

Problems of Class and Race

On all levels, problems of class and race emerge as manifestations of social inequalities. Social distinctions based on family, economic circumstances, environment, and various community diversities create barriers within the school itself. In some instances parents insist that their children be placed advantageously in the classroom as to seating, grouping, grading, and other types of preferment. The social program of the school is often seriously affected thereby, as in dances, positions of leadership, assembly programs, and athletics. Racial distinctions are accentuated in certain geographical areas. Private schools flourish principally because of the ability of families to support their children in this type of institution together with a desire to maintain traditions of family and social distinction.

Although these problems exist in many school situations, one of the most encouraging characteristics of public school education is its socializing influence, in which all boys and girls find common interests and opportunities in varied classroom and activity programs. This is as it should be. Every means should be taken to extend educational opportunity to every boy and girl without regard to race, color, family or community tradition, or social distinction.

SECRET SOCIETIES

Secret societies for youth, usually spoken of as fraternities and sororities, differ from common forms of social activities in the following characteristics: secrecy, exclusiveness, and freedom from or evasion of effective administration, supervision, and control. Their perpetuation is based on decision of the membership rather than the free choice of the individual desiring admission.

Secret societies found their way into the public school about 1876. Growing slowly, they began to assume some significance. Restrictions began to be placed upon them about 1900, and in 1905 they received condemnation by resolution by the National Education Association.[1]

Legal Jurisdiction. Stamped professionally as a school evil generally, secret societies seemed to grow in spite of official disapproval. Many states passed laws prohibiting membership in high school fraternities. Many boards of education made rules attempting to forbid or regulate them. The courts have been called upon on numerous occasions to sit in judgment. The general conclusion of the courts is that the legislature may prohibit them and may require boards of education to abolish them and expel the members. Moreover, with statutory authority, boards of education may supervise or prohibit them. There is still some legal question, however, what authority boards of education possess in the absence of specific statutory provision. One may conclude, in such case, that the right of a board of education to direct the operation and control of the school would include discretionary power over secret societies.[2]

Why Pupils Join. Some of the reasons boys and girls organize and maintain membership in fraternities and sororities are: (1) curiosity, (2) imitation of college secret societies, (3) duplication of more mature actions of their elders, as their parents in fraternal organiza-

---

[1] *Proceedings,* National Education Association, 1905, p. 451.

[2] Newton Edwards, *The Courts and the Public Schools,* Chicago, University of Chicago Press, 1933, pp. 449–452.

tions, (4) desire to join in an action that is "taboo," (5) atmosphere of mystery which surrounds them, (6) emerging adolescent feelings and emotions, a feeling of self-importance, desire to control school activities, pride in wearing insignia, and a sense of belonging.[3] Parents often complicate the school's problem by their approval, stimulated largely by the pupils themselves. Alumni members are probably more outspoken and difficult to deal with.

Proponents of Secret Societies. Proponents offer the following in favor of secret societies in public schools: (1) They are useful as a guidance ideal, especially where the society's ideals are lofty in character and in accord with public school ideals. (2) They offer a natural opportunity for the outlet of adolescent characteristics and emotions. (3) A harmony of the social patterns of school and society is entirely possible and desirable under proper leadership. (4) Their recreational possibilities are quite fruitful.

Opponents of Secret Societies. On the other hand, their opponents declare: (1) They are subversive to the principles of democracy which should prevail in the public school. (2) They are selfish and narrow, and snobbish; they dissipate energy and proper ambition selfishly. (3) Standards are not in accord with public school objectives. (4) They inculcate a feeling of self-sufficiency. (5) Secondary youth are too immature. (6) They are expensive and extravagant. (7) They use unwise political methods. (8) They are detracting. (9) All virtues claimed for them can be better secured in a well planned and administered club program.

Administrative Attitude. Ordinarily, school authorities oppose secret societies because of their undemocracy, secrecy, and desire to control school activities. Methods taken to eliminate them are: (1) by substitution, namely, in organizing and encouraging a program of extra-curricular activities which will include all of their virtues and none (at least few) of their vices; (2) by disbandment through school board action or administrative rules; (3) through court action; (4) through statutory legislation; (5) through restrictions and regulations, as debarment from school activities and honors; (6) through suspension and expulsion of members; (7) through public school opinion by means of counterattraction methods and parental cooperation.

Where firmly established, secret societies may present serious ad-

---

[3] Walter G. O'Donnell, "The Problem of High School Fraternities," *American School Board Journal*, October, 1939, p. 50.

ministrative problems. In such cases, the principal must decide whether to encourage, restrict, or eliminate them entirely. To accomplish the latter is hazardous without full cooperation from school board, student body, parents, and community. O'Donnell[4] goes so far to say that their continued existence in public schools is a sign of administrative failure. If the principal elects to accept them temporarily, he might try the policies of substitution or counterattraction, or their utilization for the acceptance of many school responsibilities. Perhaps by the latter means they can be maneuvered into a position of control and usefulness.

BOY AND GIRL PROBLEMS

Adolescent Characteristics. Variations in individual maturation are characteristic of adolescence. When boys reach this period, at approximately fourteen years, their own physical development is accompanied by an awareness of the physical characteristics and behavior of girls, and a tendency to include them in their social life. As the girls' reproductive system begins to develop at about the age of twelve years, they show the same emotional feelings and begin to take a marked interest in boys.[5] In both boys and girls, as well as in different racial groups, there is a marked age difference when these physical and social manifestations occur. Since such age variations do occur, boy and girl problems of adolescence are not confined to any grade or any school division. They have been known to appear in the middle grades of the elementary school; they are characteristic of the junior high school; and they reach their fullest development in the upper high school levels.

Manifestations. There are many manifestations of adolescence. Sex is discovered both in himself and in others. Awareness and imagining take full possession. Somehow these must be expressed. Negative expression may be in notes or penciled on toilet walls; in bodily contact with the same or opposite sex extending from holding hands, linking arms or putting arms about waists, and touching themselves or others in intimate places to real or approximate intimate relationships; and in reading suggestive literature. On the positive side, expression takes the form of "flames" or crushes on members of the same or opposite sex with behavior characterized by

---

[4] *Ibid.,* p. 51.
[5] Consult Esther B. Tietz and Charles K. Weichert, *The Art and Science of Marriage,* New York, Whittlesey House, 1938, pp. 215–220.

giggling, jesting, kissing, furtiveness, advances, desire to attract by action or dress, sociability, and group activities like parties or dances.

When the urge and its emotional response become extreme and unrestrained through lax school, home, or personal control, situations may arise which have serious implications. Secluded corridor corners may hide enamored couples who wish to indulge in bodily contact. A parked automobile, or a building, or woods may afford similar protection.[6]

However, boy and girl attractions for each other under normal circumstances and properly controlled are not undesirable. The *Scholastic* magazine declares, "But broadly speaking we think that high school is the time when boys and girls should be meeting and learning to know a lot of different kinds of people of both sexes."[7] Thus, "puppy love" may be the *status quo* of the moment, as many of us can testify. Such attachments often eventually ripen into happy and lasting marriages. The danger is that individual attachments divert the time and attention from *more important* things of the moment. Moreover, youth can be cruel to each other, and resulting wounds are deep and hard to heal, affecting the individual in his lessons, social life, and attitudes. It would be better if sociability could be directed to the group during early adolescence with general enjoyment and emotional expression *for the group as a whole*.

Social Evils. Perhaps at no time have youth and their well-wishers had to contend with such difficult and disturbing factors as during the present. Sherwood Eddy declares that no other generation of youth was ever subject to the education of such commercialized amusements or to such a circulation of suggestive and obscene literature and periodicals. The Payne Studies revelations in regard to the effects of movies on youth are not to be lightly considered. Our public highways offer enticements to youth by way of the family automobile. It is easy to be persuaded to stop at the attractively lighted roadhouse, from which issue the intriguing strains of a modern dance. Once there, drinks are easy to procure if someone in the party has the price or can borrow it. The spirit of it all seems to provide just the emotional outlet for the immediate occasion, and encourages a desire or a dare to go again.

---

[6] Geraldine Courtney, "Immorality in Our Schools," *Forum*, September, 1937, p. 131.

[7] "Puppy Love—Sequel," *Scholastic*, February 11, 1939, pp. 3–4.

Perhaps the greatest commercialized danger to modern youth is the knowledge and availability of contraceptive devices, as well as narcotics. Birth control devices and literature are readily available to him who desires it. Instillations of fear and taboo in matters of promiscuous relations and their results may be removed through the ample protection of a device at low cost; thus a new experience. The results of certain narcotics, notably marihuana, upon youth are well known; the use of these is declared to be on the increase. Secluded parties of adolescent youth have not infrequently been held in which marihuana smoking and cocktail sipping form an overpowering tandem.

Direct outcomes of social promiscuity are social disease and moral degeneration with which youth may easily be contaminated. Since about one in ten in our normal population suffers from social diseases or their effects, it is easy to glimpse the possibilities of defilement to youth which may affect them, their partners, or their descendants. Adequate knowledge of these evils through desirable sex education is the only solution. Control must be both legal and social.[8]

Methods of Solving Boy and Girl Problems. In meeting these problems, there is no substitute for that school, whether elementary or secondary, which has a strong, capable, and understanding principal, enlightened and discerning teachers, and a splendid school spirit with a form of control that enables the individual to find himself while serving the larger group. Such a school must provide for individual knowledge and expression through guidance and understanding, and for group socialization through activities in which all can participate in accordance with their interests, needs, and abilities. Pervading it all must be that indefinable emotional outlet called the *all-pervading school spirit*. In and about the school there should be an environment conducive to friendship, culture, physical and moral development, and what we may characterize as *tone*.

Guidance and counseling are the keys to needed individual adjustments. Rather than blame the youth, we must seek to understand him, his home, his problems, his desires, and his frustrations. Under proper guidance he will unlock his secretive nature and respond to sensible direction.

The social program should be so ample that there is no place for

---

[8] Lester A. Kirkendall and Mark Flutzer, "The Facts Speak for Sex Education," *Clearing House,* September, 1947, p. 2729.

secret societies. All of the psychological manifestations of adolescent youth should find expression in it, with adequate sponsorship of teachers who are both interested and concerned. High school teachers might do well to recall that, after all, many of the subversive actions of adolescent youth are the outcomes of frustrations and defenses against misunderstandings and hopelessness.

Wholesome counterattractions may be useful as a device against obscene literature. As examples, a Better Magazine Club or greater emphasis on vigorous recreational activities may be helpful. Good school spirit may counteract the tendency to besmear walls, blackboards, and toilets. Removal of places of rendezvous may be necessary.

In regard to commercialized vice and amusements, two approaches are available. Legalized conditions should be frustrated through a well-defined wholesome public opinion within the school and community. Illegal forms may be attacked through student government groups by means of appeals to parents, city council, or state authorities. Perhaps youth themselves should begin an open campaign of direct opposition. As to adults, there is no place for faint hearts where the welfare and protection of youth are concerned.

Problems of Illicit Relations

Illicit Relations and Pregnancy. The biological urges and frustrations seem to create more acute problems for youth and society in an age of difficult and disturbing social situations. Attention has been called to many of these in the preceding section. Although the problem is perplexing for the girl who matures early, it must be said that the pregnancy problem is definitely more serious in the secondary school. The fact becomes shrouded in secrecy and hence is difficult to objectify. Where pregnancy does occur, the occasion becomes magnified out of all proportion to its significance.

It is comparatively easy to indicate the extent of marriage among youth of school age, but the incidence of illicit relations and pregnancy is much more difficult to ascertain. Two decades ago, Judge Ben Lindsey, famous Denver jurist, declared that, of 495 girls he dealt with who confessed to illicit sex relations, only 1 in 20 encountered pregnancy.[9] He held that the percentage of wayward school

---

[9] Ben B. Lindsey and E. Wainwright, *The Revolt of Modern Youth*, New York, Boni and Liveright, 1928, p. 80.

youth is much bigger than the 1 per cent claimed by Denver school authorities. Recent studies indicate that premarital sex experiences among youth of school age are definitely more common than a generation ago.

Problems of pregnancy are given favorable consideration by the courts, especially if the girl marries and later returns to school. However, there may be a question of laxity of morals which may affect the decision, especially if it can be shown that the girl is promiscuously inclined. Boards of education in many states have made rules barring pupils upon marriage, and have expelled girls upon suspicion or evidence of pregnancy or loose conduct. Since legal tests have not been made in many states, there is a serious question whether these rules and resulting debarments could be legally substantiated in the courts of those states.[10] Fortunately, there now seems to be much more human sympathy with this problem. Prudery and "scarlet letter" condemnation are giving way to guidance and sex and marriage education in a spirit of helpfulness for the wayward individual. Medical advice and institutional care are available, which is as it should be.

The Married Pupil. Traditionally, the point has prevailed that the schools are intended for unmarried youth; further, that upon marriage the pupil must withdraw from association with those who remain. Where the married pupil comes within the compulsory age limits or the educational terminus has not been reached, the problem of remaining in school conflicts with this point of view. However, a more enlightened attitude is emerging among those who recognize unusual social situations. Computations from census data would seem to indicate that roughly one out of 150 persons between the ages of fifteen and nineteen inclusive in the United States is a married girl and attending school. Many of these are in the elementary and junior high schools. Chambers[11] states that probably one in every 6000 high-school pupils is a married girl. *Building America*[12] reports that approximately 5 per cent of the girls between the ages of fifteen and seventeen are married. Since Negro youth marry at

---

[10] Reference should be made to the reasoning of the courts in the following cases: *McLeod* vs. *State,* 154 Miss. 468, 122 So. 737, 36 A.L.R., 1161; *Mitt* vs. *Board of Education,* 128 Kan. 507, 278 Pac. 1065.

[11] M. M. Chambers, "The Married Girl Pupil," *Nation's Schools,* February, 1940, p. 27.

[12] "Youth Faces the World," *Building America,* I, No. 8, p. 16.

younger ages, one finds that 17.5 and 30.7 per cent of seventeen- and eighteen-year-old girls are married. The ratio of married youth now in school would appear to be much higher.

Bell[13] reports that about 3 per cent of out-of-school youth gave marriage as their reason for dropping out, and leaving at relatively low educational levels. He goes on to justify this statement by declaring that over half the married boys (52.4 per cent) and nearly half the married girls (42.3 per cent) were found to have received no more than an elementary education. These were Maryland youth; one will find considerable variance in those states with lower legal marriage ages. Many pupils, however, who accept the marital status while in high school leave immediately, and in the majority of the states even though they are under the school compulsory age they are not forced to return. Of interest too in the marriage of minor girls is the mooted question of transfer of parental authority to the husband.

Legal Aspects. Those who would bar the married youth of school age from school attendance base their contention on the following: (1) Marriage emancipates the child from parental control of its conduct, as well as the exercise of such control by the school authorities. (2) The marriage relation brings out views of life that should not be conveyed to unmarried children. (3) Debarment is possible above the compulsory age. (4) Their admission is detrimental to the good government and usefulness of the schools.

However, in the opinion of many courts, marriage in itself is not a legally sufficient reason for barring children of school age from the public schools. The reasons are: (1) Schools are open to all persons between five and twenty-one years of age. (2) Marriage is a relation highly favored by the law. (3) Hence husband and wife relationships are refining and elevating, rather than detrimental as claimed. (4) Pupil association therefore is beneficial. (5) Married persons should be commended for seeking further education. (6) They are subject to the same rules and punishment as other pupils.

SEX AND MARRIAGE EDUCATION

Need. Since most of our present discussion is directly related to sex and marriage education, it is strange to observe that the public

---

[13] Howard M. Bell, *Youth Tell Their Story*, Washington, American Council on Education, 1938, pp. 67–68.

school has done so little about attacking these problems at their source. Perhaps, as Lynd[14] points out, we tend to play safe and do nothing where an adult population maintains a position of official silence about sex. Perhaps we do nothing because we dare not. Most authorities agree with Bell[15] who found that youth had to depend principally on their contemporaries on the streets for sex information. About two-thirds of the boys and girls studied gathered what little they did know from boys and girls their own age. More girls than boys got some information from their parents, but in most cases it was meager indeed. Abundant salacious literature provides information of a doubtful nature to the avid young reader.

And yet youth want this information about themselves openly, fully, frankly. The writer observed the keen interest of numerous youth studying the remarkable diagrams and models portraying the story of life at the New York World's Fair. Much the same can be said concerning information secured from museums, biology textbooks, government and other literature, and sex education classes. Rainey[16] declares that of nearly 50,000 youth interviewed, 85 per cent said that they believed they should get a course in sex in their regular school program.

Reasons for Failure. Several reasons must be assigned for failure of the school and the home to provide youth with needed information about their own bodies. Among these are: (1) prudery from a past generation; (2) feeling that such teaching destroys the innocence of the young; (3) unpreparedness for the task; (4) similar unpreparedness of parents; (5) fear, or difference of opinion among administrators as to who should supply sex education; (6) the pervading opinion that, if it is done at all, the home should do it; (7) general dislike on the part of many teachers for the task.

Suggested Plan. Differences of opinion as to where and in what manner sex education should be taught still exist. Perhaps the best solution is that understanding parents should begin instruction early in the home on levels of child comprehension. This instruction

---

[14] Robert S. Lynd and Helen M. Lynd, *Middletown in Transition,* New York, Harcourt, Brace and Company, 1937, pp. 169 ff.

[15] *Op. cit.,* pp. 40–41. These facts are substantiated in numerous other articles.

[16] Homer P. Rainey, "Youth Problems," *Proceedings of the National Education Association,* 1938, p. 249. See also "Youth Education Today," *Sixteenth Yearbook,* American Association of School Administrators, Washington, National Education Association, 1938, pp. 102–107.

should extend through the elementary, secondary, and college levels in accordance with the child's physical and emotional development and his desire for knowledge. Every parent and every teacher should have a part in this education, although its medical and more technical aspects should be left to the school doctor, nurse, or biology teacher. Teachers of homemaking should be better prepared than they are for their important task. Sex hygiene courses, then, should have a place at all stages beginning with proper instruction of the personnel and an adequate, carefully prepared outline to be followed. Full and complete cooperation with the home at the several stages will prevent many misunderstandings.

Educational Approaches to Marriage. If education for life is to be taken seriously as an educational goal, it becomes the duty of the public schools to assume definite responsibility in regard to this question. We must agree with Dickerson[17] when he writes that education for marriage is as broad as education for life itself. The White House Conference on Child Health and Protection[18] indicated the importance of education for intelligent participation in family life and marriage. There is a close relationship between marriage and the home, and marriage as the vocation. Moreover, there is much to learn about the prerequisites of marriage, such as its physical basis, our bodies, courtship, the establishment of a home, and the meaning of parenthood. Every girl should profit through a thorough course in cooking, budgeting, homemaking, family relations, and child care; every boy should learn his part in making a home in addition to learning a vocation. It is not too much to say that boys should learn simple cooking, budgeting, some aspects of child care, family relations and accompanying problems, and above all, a certain self-forgetfulness in the enjoyment and protection of others. Both should have an appreciation of the home as the fundamental unit of the social order. If the modern public school is to meet the needs of all youth, it must deviate from old academic standards and institute an educational program centering about life, its problems and its needs.

---

[17] Roy E. Dickerson, "Prepare Them for Marriage," *Parents Magazine,* December, 1937, p. 24.

[18] Louise Stanley, "The Family and Parent Education," *White House Conference on Child Health and Protection* (1930), New York, The Century Company, 1931, p. 140.

Juvenile Delinquency and Crime

It is characteristic of any social organization to establish in its members a certain conformity to its ideals and general cultural pattern. The basis for this establishment may be found in the laws, customs, mores, and traditions of the people. Conformity is secured through parental instruction and control in the home, the processes and control of education, social control, and the long arm of the law. Each has its own methods of demanding and securing that degree of management necessary to its own end. We are familiar with the nature of parental and home control. School control has been discussed in a previous section. Social control is secured through means peculiar to itself and varying with societies. As a last resort the legal pattern assumes protective custody of the social order, preserving its status and punishing offenders who deviate therefrom through police power, fines, removal from the fredom of that social order, and even the taking of life.

Education and the Legal Framework. We have seen that one of the principal purposes of education is to bring about the adjustment of childhood and youth to the social environment. In order to accomplish this aim legal mandates surround the educational process. This process purposes to assist the young in character building and citizenship duties and responsibilities. Thus, in statutory law is written, in part, the educational pattern for one's individual conduct and his social responsibilities, with penalties provided for violation.

Education, then, viewed as adjustment is predicated on a legal framework. In one sense non-conformists are designated as maladjusted. Those seriously maladjusted are classified as delinquent; to a greater degree, criminal. Any consideration of maladjustment should be viewed in the light of its nature and the gravity of the situation. Social customs and individual guidance are determining factors, with eventual desirable adjustment as the chief motivating factor.

Juvenile delinquency has been defined "as a violation of law by persons of juvenile court age or conduct on the part of such persons so seriously anti-social as to interfere with the rights of others or menace the welfare of the delinquent himself or of his community."[19] This gives a connotation of *serious* maladjustment, in which the conduct is anti-social in some form, involving serious behavior difficulties, such as truancy, incorrigibility, serious acts of mischief, such as destruction of property, thievery, sex delinquency, drug offenses, and injuries to persons.

From both the definition and the description, these offenses would appear to violate some law and indeed do so. Yet it should be pointed out that the adjustment of the offense may not involve lawful procedure and penalty in the usual sense. In recent years there has been a tendency to deal with these cases outside the usual legal procedure. Even many juvenile courts have become so humanized as to take into consideration matters of home environment, health, mental ability, psychiatry, and the development of proper social attitudes.

Nature and Extent. Numerous studies are available indicating the extent of juvenile delinquency.[20] These indicate that about 2 per cent of all children have unusually severe behavior problems, that 80 per cent of this group become delinquent, and that 80 per cent of juvenile delinquents become criminals. Reports from the federal Children's Bureau from 462 courts serving 36 per cent of the population of the United States estimate that, of 17,000,000 children ten to sixteen years of age, 1 per cent pass through our juvenile courts each year.[21] Six-sevenths of all delinquents are boys. Shaw and McKay[22] point out that juvenile delinquency is highly correlated with such separate factors as (1) population change, (2) bad housing, (3) poverty, (4) foreign birth, (5) tuberculosis, (6) adult crime, and (7) mental disorders. All of these are generally inter-correlated. These factors stem from a common factor, namely, social disorganization in some form, in turn growing out of a lack of organized home and community effort to deal adequately with these conditions. The order of offenses of the delinquent appears to be larceny, burglary, waywardness in some form, running away, truancy, assault, trespass, and sex offenses.

---

[19] Unpublished special report for the National Commission on Law Observation and Enforcement, prepared by Katherine F. Lenroot of the Children's Bureau, October, 1929, p. 8.

[20] H. E. Barnes, *Society in Transition,* New York, Prentice-Hall, Inc., 1939, p. 75.

[21] "Children in the Courts," *Children's Bureau Publication No. 250,* Washington, United States Department of Labor, 1937, pp. 6–15.

[22] Clifford B. Shaw and Henry D. McKay, *Juvenile Delinquency and Urban Areas,* Chicago, University of Chicago Press, 1942.

Crime as a Youth Problem. Thirty years ago the criminal was an adult somewhere in middle life. During the past decades his age has been steadily reduced until at present most criminals are under thirty years of age and many are youth still in their teens. Indeed, crime statistics reveal that thousands of young men and women enter upon careers of crime while still of school age. Carr[23] points out that from 50 to 85 per cent of all prisoners begin their anti-social behavior in childhood. Maladjustment in early life becomes serious and leads to delinquency in some form, which in turn assumes criminal proportions.

That youth now predominate in crime is shown by prison and reformatory records. Of these over 50 per cent have arrest records and 75 per cent have delinquency records that brought them in conflict with the police before reaching the age of sixteen. Warden Lawes reported that a survey of 1000 consecutive commitments revealed that 25 per cent were delinquent before the age of sixteen, and 24 per cent between the ages of seventeen and twenty, a total of 49 per cent before the age of twenty. In addition to these facts, the records of the Federal Bureau of Investigation reveal that in one year 35 per cent of the arrest records examined were for persons under twenty-five and half of these for persons under twenty-one. With the largest single age group nineteen years and younger, youth lately in school, the implications for education are inescapable.

Approach to a Study of Causes. These alarming facts have led to a study of the causes of juvenile delinquency in relation to crime and criminal tendency. Initial assignment of causes may be from some particular point of view. The eugenist is inclined to place the blame upon defective heredity; the euthenist blames the home and an inadequate environment; the physiologist suspects abnormal functioning of the ductless glands or parts of the body as a sufficient urge to crime; the psychiatrist finds the cause in mental maladjustments; the physician looks into bodily malformations or lack of proper functionings; the educator finds the blame largely in educational deficiencies; and the religionist looks to irreligion and a decadent morality. All of these may at certain times and under certain conditions incite some individuals to delinquency. However, the careful

---

[23] Lowell Juilliard Carr, *Delinquency Control,* New York, Harper & Brothers, 1941, p. 36. See also Chapter III.

student will regard no single one as the sole cause of delinquency and criminal behavior.

Causes for delinquency can be placed in two categories: (1) personal and (2) social. Personal factors include: (*a*) sex, i.e., larger number of boys; (*b*) racial, as larger proportional number of Negroes; (*c*) nativity, as larger proportion of foreign born; (*d*) parentage; (*e*) intelligence, as great majority of low mental ability; and (*f*) physical status, large numbers showing some physical defect. Social factors include: (*a*) home environment affected by abnormal home life, broken home, poor parental supervision, parents with criminal records; (*b*) employment factors such as unemployment, nature of employment, vocation dissatisfaction; (*c*) truancy; and (*d*) influence of motion pictures and radio. Associated with these factors are influences of older associates, character of neighborhood, mobility of population, conflict in school, and frustrations.

In view of the fact that the community pattern sets the tone of social compliance, or in this case non-compliance, of its youth to the pattern itself, it is to the community that we must look for causal factors and hence their alleviation. Residential communities of higher economic and social status stand in sharp contrast as to delinquency and crime with those of lower economic and social status, whose youth become disorganized, maladjusted, and anti-social. If the opportunities to be and become a success are not provided through legitimate channels, youth tend to find a way through channels declared socially illegitimate. Hence the approach is definitely a community one and includes a cooperative program embracing all citizens, individually as well as collectively organized. The home is of outstanding importance in this program. Education must definitely assume its share of leadership.

In the community the conditions breeding delinquency and crime must be removed. Wholesome recreational facilities must replace unwholesome rendezvous. Bad housing must be replaced. Social cesspools must be eradicated. The community must provide those opportunities which instill in all youth the feeling of having an equal chance to succeed and fair sportsmanship in doing so.

Educational Treatment. The problem of treatment of delinquency has two aspects: (1) its prevention, especially in regard to the potential delinquent, and (2) its correction, or the rehabilitation of the delinquent. Types of organization within the school for treatment of delinquents are: (1) guidance and counseling units, (2) clinics, including behavior and psychiatric clinics, (3) special classes, (4) parental schools, and (5) training schools for delinquents under special state or local supervision.

Types of administrative adjustment within the school might include: (1) a strong attendance department based upon sound modern procedures, (2) a vitalized curriculum meeting especially the needs of maladjusted children, (3) provision for pre-vocational and industrial education, (4) a friendly interest on the part of all teachers in maladjusted children, (5) development of a sex hygiene program, (6) a good library, (7) a well-adapted social and recreational program, (8) closer cooperation with the home.

In addition to these suggestions, there must be a closer cooperation with various agencies and institutions in the community which are dealing with the problems of youth. The youth's expanding energies must be vitally directed. He must be kept busy doing constructive things in a character-building environment. Moreover, he must feel that somebody believes in him, and that he has a chance for good companionship, a good home, and eventually a job.

In extreme cases, there must be close cooperation with the juvenile courts and their widening facilities. Perhaps if we would reverse the expenditure of nearly seven times as much for crime as for education, we might have some financial basis for an enlarged program for better adjusting all youth to a democratic way of living. Such a concept implies an educational approach that recognizes the proper place of education in the prevention of crime and delinquency. Warden Lawes[24] pointed out that this will require: (1) a higher standard for teachers, (2) smaller classes to permit attention to individual differences, and (3) a new concept of the social and scholastic goals of education. In addition, modern education must look forward to a program which includes all youth until the ages when they can be gainfully employed, perhaps to nineteen or twenty years, which extends to all areas, urban or rural, and which disregards social, economic, or racial status. The program should be broad enough to provide for each young person's needs and extend by cooperation through all his waking hours.

---

[24] "A Warden Looks at Education," *New York Times Magazine,* July 31, 1932, pp. 12–13.

THE COURTS AND THE SCHOOLS

Wards of the Court. Children coming before the court for any occasion involving broken homes, loss of parents, delinquency, or through other legal action may become wards of the court. The court makes disposition of the child, placing him in an orphanage, a private home, a reformatory, or in some cases returning him to one parent who is to provide for him. In all such instances, education must be furnished, usually a certain school being designated. The school may be reimbursed and transportation provided, together with maintenance either by public expense or by the family concerned.

Delinquent children returning from detention, county, or state schools must be returned to the public school. It is usually advisable to absorb these children in their former school unless a new environment is deemed better adapted. Parental attitudes often color the situation, especially in regard to broken homes.

Children who are mentally deficient or otherwise handicapped quite frequently come before the courts for disposition. They are usually placed in state or other institutions where a type of education suited to their needs is available. Unfortunately, many state institutions are filled; usually the capacity is quite insufficient and there are long waiting lists. Temporary disposition of these children is often a hardship to them; in some instances it is dangerous to the child and his environment.

Cooperation Between Courts and Schools. In the interests of the child, there is much that can be done to bring about a spirit of cooperation between the courts and the schools. In the first place, the age limits of juvenile court cases should correspond with the school ages, at least with those of compulsory attendance. It is very important that the school have a representative at the court hearing of the child. The school should receive advance notification by the court in case of release of a pupil in detention, so that his return to the school can be provided for. The school should receive such information as notice of official and unofficial hearings to conserve the time of school representatives, notice of commitments, and reports of interest to the school.

LEADERSHIP

Importance. Much stress has been laid on the importance of leadership among boys and girls in order to guide current life situations and point toward future successes.[25] Such leadership should be able to interpret life to young people and give impulse in the direction of desired adult goals toward which youth are striving. It should be able to function under conditions as they are. These become challenges to youth leaders everywhere.

Youth organizations, clubs, activities, and groups, both within and without the school, provide numerous and varied opportunities for training in youth leadership, now so essential in the democratic process. Leadership may be defined as that quality which enables a person to come into some degree of prominence through commanding the loyalty, respect, and obedience of others. However, it is more than this. It involves action, accomplishment, and followership in others. Directly involved also is a strong personality, usually depending on a certain popularity, although not necessarily so.

Qualities. Earlier writers like Galton and Woods took the side that leadership was hereditary. An opposing school including Ellis, Odin, and Cattell has indicated that the forces of leadership must be sought in the environment of the individual. More recently, numerous researches[26] have reported on qualities of leadership in youth. Bellingrath pointed out the importance of home life. Page and Halsey believed that installation of a feeling of self-confidence increased the possibilities of leadership. Eichler showed that leadership qualities can be taught and pointed out over fifty of them which included as basic scholarship, social intelligence, height and weight, individuality, intelligence (general), ascendance, vitality or health, social adaptability, self-control, and persistence. Rohrbach in an earlier study agreed with Bellingrath and showed office-holding chances were favorable to normal or over-age children, taller children, upper grade children, and those of good scholarship and behavior, with little variation for sex or participation in other activities. Fleming too classified character traits of leadership under eight descriptive terms, namely, entertaining, brilliant (athletic, attractive, social), good fellow, cultured, talented, just, good neighbor, and diplomatic. Ability to lead is dependent on the possession of a majority of these. Courtenay indicated another important char-

---

[25] "Youth Education Today," *Sixteenth Yearbook,* American Association of School Administrators, Washington, National Educational Association, 1938, chap. ix.

[26] The reader is referred to "Pupil Personnel, Guidance, and Counseling," *Review of Educational Research,* April, 1936, and April, 1939, for a review of these researches.

acteristic, namely, the persistence of leadership ability in later life.

It would also appear that the interests and available time of pupils for leadership are essential, although ofttimes the busiest are chosen. Other important qualities mentioned are richness of experience, activity in participation, planning of time constructively, and a certain social philosophy. Perhaps previous achievement is an important factor since success begets success.

Program. Identification of leadership qualities among boys and girls and provision for development of those who manifest them is a most significant educational function. It must not be left to chance. Pupils make many mistakes in their choices of leadership. The "gang" often desires to take control without regard to the welfare of all. Affable personalities may easily be misplaced in positions of leadership, causing teachers and principals no end of embarrassment and difficulty.

With so many opportunities provided for leadership in the modern public school, competent direction should be given to the problems involved. Development in leadership is essential to personality. Such direction might well include: (1) a program of youth education in the qualities and importance of leadership in and out of school, as well as in after-school life; (2) the assignment and direction of competent youth leadership in the faculty and community along lines leading to fulfillment of educational objectives for youth; (3) creation of a sufficient number and variety of activities in which youth leadership may be exercised, with opportunities for some appraisal of the services rendered.

THE INTEGRATED PERSONALITY

Nature. Perhaps the chief end of education is the development of rich and many-sided personalities properly adjusted to happy and efficient social living. The term *personality* is generally used to indicate the organization and integration of a large number of human traits. An individual's personality represents a complex picture of his physical appearance, his mental capacity, his emotional and social behavior patterns, his attitudes, and the manner in which he responds to the daily stimulations of his environment. Although he may inherit certain potentialities of personality development, much of what he is to become at any time in his life is the expression of learned patterns of behavior. As he becomes stimulated by environmental forces he learns to respond to them in a way that molds him into the individual he now is and is to become.

The school has a definite role to play in personality adjustment. Sears[27] has called attention to the influences that the learning process, motivation, and environmental conditions have in determining personality. Much emphasis must of necessity be laid on the individual's social experiences and relationships. Here are to be found such influencing factors as class distinction, insecurity, frustration, and assertive behavior. Temperaments must be taken into consideration, as introversion and extroversion, attitudes, and emotions.

The personality adjustment proceeds as an educational objective from the birth of the child. However, many of the problems appear as the challenge of adolescence; at least they appear more pronounced during those years. With each emerging generation comes a new way of looking at life and its relationships. The youth yearns to find himself, but he wants to find himself in his own way. Antagonisms often raise their unlovely heads when the philosophies of one generation clash with those of another; hence these adjustments require the recognition of change as the natural accompaniment of life itself.

Approach. The principal approach to personality adjustment of individual children should be that of the "emerging chrysalis." Gradually their inmost aspirations emerge, all of which seem to need attention, some almost immediately.

Germane and Germane have indicated ten areas of human experience in which pupils need most help. These may easily serve as the basis for an educational personality adjustment program. These are:

1. How to work and study effectively
2. How to get along with others (success in human relationships)
3. How the emotions and feelings are affected by conditioning factors of the environment (area of mental health)
4. How to choose a vocation
5. How to develop a wholesome philosophy of life (area of ethics, religion, character)
6. How to insure a happy home life (area of family relationships)
7. How to be more charming (aesthetics, culture, and charm area)

---

[27] Robert R. Sears, "Growth and Development," *Review of Educational Research,* American Education Research Association, December, 1944, p. 368.

8. How to choose wisely one's recreation (hobbies, leisure activities)
9. How to become more intelligently tolerant and interested in world problems (racial and class prejudices, prevention of war)
10. How to improve one's physical health and endurance[28]

While these are areas suggested as pertaining more particularly to adolescent youth, it is evident that many of them apply equally to younger children. Every child desires to get along, to experience the successes of life as his fellows do. All about him are new challenges and vistas, which he yearns to explore. Frustrations are deep and meaningful and quite often insuperable. Youth is fickle and dislikes restraining. A physical imperfection may produce a psychological inhibition, and a mental frustration an emotional reaction.

The Integrated Personality. The integrated personality then is the resultant of a careful balance of the whole self. Its formation begins with the dawn of life and continues throughout. To be happy, to be creative, to be disciplined, to be unselfish are all a part of it. But an individual's personality and usefulness can only be viewed in social relationships. He can become a useful member of society only to the degree that this integration and balance are being brought about. When this is done, he will have the desire to further the group and advance the existing pattern of culture.

While every personality by virtue of certain hereditary predispositions has certain natural tendencies, into every personality the culture pattern builds its values, goals, ideals, and standards. These become the social expectations by which personality is judged. The extent to which the unities built into a man become integrated with these social values determines to a large degree social acceptance; contrariwise, when these clash at any point, either the individual rises above the social and cultural pattern or he is submerged through social censure in some form. The desirable outcome is the perfected adjustment of each to the other for the constant betterment of both.

QUESTIONS AND PROBLEMS

1. Make a list of problems of class and race that emerge as manifestations of social inequalities. Which of these have educational significance?

---

[28] Charles E. Germane and Edith S. Germane, *Personnel Work in High School,* New York, Silver, Burdett and Company, 1941, p. 29.

2. Make a comparative study of boy and girl problems on different grade levels beginning with the sixth grade.

3. Make a report on secret societies. Evaluate your report and findings in the light of suggestions offered in the chapter. What is your personal opinion of their value in the educational program?

4. Show how a sound system of social activities can assist in solving boy and girl problems.

5. How valid are the arguments that married youth should be barred from the public schools; the college? What policy would you recommend?

6. Prepare a program of (*a*) sex education for a particular school; (*b*) marriage and homemaking. Should both be fused? How?

7. Study those social evils inimical to youth to be found in your community. What can be done to offset or remove them? In which of these is the school directly concerned?

8. Make a report on the extent of juvenile delinquency (*a*) in your community, (*b*) nationally. What is being done to meet these problems?

9. Make a study of youth leaders in a selected school. What unusual qualities do they possess? Can these be developed in all youth? Explain.

10. Make a list of possible opportunities for youth leadership which might be found in an elementary school; a secondary school.

11. Indicate the extent in which Germane and Germane's ten areas of human experiences are receiving adequate attention in a selected school.

12. Why has education for social living assumed far greater significance than formerly?

SELECTED REFERENCES

1. Baker, Harry J., *Introduction to Exceptional Children*. New York: The Macmillan Company, 1945, part v.

2. Bell, Howard, *Youth Tell Their Story*. Washington: American Council on Education, 1938.

3. Chambers, M. M., "The Married Girl Pupil," *Nation's Schools*, February, 1940.

4. Courtney, Geraldine, "Immorality in Our Schools," *Forum*, September, 1937.

5. Eddy, Sherwood, *Sex and Youth*. Garden City, N. Y.: Doubleday, Doran and Company, 1929.

6. "Education for Family Life," *Nineteenth Yearbook*, American Association of School Administrators. Washington: National Education Association, 1941.

7. Germane, Charles E., and Germane, Edith G., *Personnel Work in High School.* New York: Silver, Burdett and Company, 1941.

8. Gillette, John M., and Reinhardt, James M., *Problems of a Changing Social Order.* New York: American Book Company, 1942, pp. 23, 27, 28.

9. Heaton, Kenneth L., and Weedon, Vivian, *The Failing Student.* Chicago: University of Chicago Press, 1939.

10. *High School and Life,* Report of the Regents' Inquiry. New York: McGraw-Hill Book Company, 1938.

11. Kirkendall, Lester A., and Flutzer, Mark, "Facts Speak for Sex Education," *Clearing House,* September, 1947, pp. 27–29.

12. Landes, Paul H., *Adolescence and Youth.* New York: McGraw-Hill Book Company, 1945.

13. Lynd, Robert S., and Lynd, Helen M., *Middletown in Transition.* New York: Harcourt, Brace and Company, 1937.

14. *National Conference on Prevention and Control of Juvenile Delinquency.* Washington: Department of Justice, 1947.

15. O'Donnell, Walter G., "The Problems of High School Fraternities," *American School Board Journal,* October, 1939, p. 50.

16. *Parents Magazine* contains pertinent articles.

17. Phelps, Harold A., *Contemporary Social Problems.* New York: Prentice-Hall, Inc., 1947, chap. xviii.

18. Stanley, Louise, "The Famliy and Parent Education," *White House* Conference on Child Health and Protection (1930). New York: The Century Company, 1931.

19. Strang, Ruth, *An Introduction to Child Study.* New York: The Macmillan Company, 1938.

20. Tietz, Esther B., and Weichert, Charles K., *The Art and Science of Marriage.* New York: Whittlesey House, 1938.

21. "Youth Education Today," *Sixteenth Yearbook,* American Association of School Administrators. Washington: National Education Association, 1938.

CHAPTER XXIII ─────────────────

The Home and Community
as Social Forces

FROM an educational point of view the world of the child is his greatest teacher. The impressions formed in childhood and youth leave lasting remembrances. The school is a part of that world, perhaps a small part to many children. Its work may be to implement, supplement, and counteract other influences, depending upon their nature and the operation of properly formed educational objectives. Its job is to give force and direction to life for the child out of materials gathered from the past, gleaned from the present, and geared to a developing future.

Many of the problems discussed in the previous chapter bear a definite relationship to home and community life. The school can do and has been doing something about them. The complexity of modern society has brought in its wake other problems affecting childhood and youth, the solution of which lies outside the control and direct influence of the school but in which the school should have a definite interest. Many of these grow out of the child's immediate environment, the result of conflicting social forces.

At the outset the student should have a realization of the nature of the home and the community as social forces. Within our social fabric are many influences both helpful and disorganizing to home and community life. Paradoxical as it may seem, disorganizing forces often grow out of the very elements designed to bring about the greater happiness and well-being of society—recreation and leisure, the movies, and the radio. Numerous organizations have emerged to fulfill the social needs of youth. Modern society is made up of migrating and mobile people. Since formal education requires a certain fixity of residence, the education of thousands of children and youth is interrupted. All of these problems and movements have educational significance. One of the greatest challenges of education is to realize its expanding community responsibilities.

HOME AND COMMUNITY

The Home. Nothing human is older than the family. The home became a biological necessity without which mankind would have disappeared from the earth. The young could scarcely have survived without the protecting care of the parents, who have always provided the means of sustenance and physical growth. During the lengthening period of infancy and social helplessness, the responsibilities of the home have been essential to race survival.

However, the family has become more than a social necessity. It is the basis of community life itself. In it the personality of the child begins to develop. Here are learned the aspects of the social pattern to which conformity is expected—the language, folkways, mores, ideals, and many social adaptations. Religion, laws of the race, and often the vocation have become a part of this training. The home has been looked upon as the chief source of moral training. The family gives the child a name, a feeling of belonging, an ancestry, and an inheritance.

It is evident that modern home life is changing. New social forces are undermining the family's once strategic position. And yet its cultural and moral influences will probably always remain. The home is and will continue to be the place of sleep, sustenance, and health restoration, the source of the mores, family traditions, morale, and the base for many occasions for recreation, readaptation, and regeneration. Homemaking is and still will be an art. Efficient home life is reflected in the community life and in the school. The proper education of the child must be predicated upon a happy, durable, sufficient home life.

The Nature of the Community. Communities are formed when the varying interests of families and individuals merge. There is a certain activity area embracing functions of protection, culture, and basic service institutions, consciousness of local unity, and participation in religion, education, business, politics, social life, recreation, and other activities common to all. Withal there is a characterizing homogeneity and what might be designated as community spirit.

Community life is best evidenced through its form of expression. There may be a historic past; family relationships, common rejoicings and sorrows, church and political affiliations, feuds, and sentimental attachments are aspects of this expression; so are the patterns of business life, social and fraternal alignments, welfare agencies, and vivid personalities.

Communities are large and small, urban, suburban, and rural, closely or loosely organized, settled and mobile, moral and immoral, rich and poor, varying in the racial and cultural content. At the same time, there is a degree of stability, a certain functioning in what may be characterized as *total experience situations*. Perhaps the most vivid memories and influences of an individual's life are those of his childhood and youth in his community.

Forces Disorganizing to Individual, Home, and Community Living

For centuries Utopian philosophers have sought for the ideal community life in which men will live together in peace and harmony in a cultural environment eminently and universally suitable. Such complete accord has never obtained, owing to the fact that it is completely incompatible with the concept of social change resulting from a rapid cultural advancement. The desires of individuals and social groups conflict, and it is in these conflicts that advancement occurs. As a culture becomes more complex, stresses and strains increase in intensity.

Social disorganization in some form is always present in any society. Whenever the disorganizing forces exceed those making for stability and harmony, social problems arise. Their intensity seems to be directly related to the effectualness or completeness of individual and group adjustment at various stages of the reorganization processes.

Elliott and Merrill[1] have indicated that three points of view should characterize any discussion of socially disorganizing forces: (1) personal, (2) family, and (3) community. Indices of personal disorganization include, in part, juvenile delinquency, crime in all of its manifestations, insanity, prostitution, drunkenness, suicide,

---

[1] Mabel A. Elliott and Frances E. Merrill, *Social Disorganization,* New York, Harper & Brothers, 1934, p. 20.

and mobility. Family disorganization is indicated by such factors as family disintegration in any form, illegitimacy, venereal diseases, and changing moral standards. Community disorganization is best illustrated by poverty, irregular school attendance, unemployment, political or social vice, and crime. It is quite likely that these factors are interrelated, many being contained in all three groups.

It is important to point out that the disintegrating forces of modern society seem to have a particularly devastating effect upon home and family life. This is especially significant to the cause of education in view of the peculiar relationship that the school bears to the home, children, and their parents. It would seem that upon both the home and the school rests the principal responsibility for augmenting socially desirable forces.

PROBLEMS OF RECREATION AND LEISURE

Recreation. Recreation as a necessary part of the experiences of life is of recent origin. It was must less emphasized even a generation ago and in many cases is frowned upon as a waste of time and energy. Only on special days were games and other recreational pursuits enjoyed when there were minutes to spare from an accustomed routine. Even then there was some repression of the spirit, since frank enjoyment was worldly and sinful, and punishment could ultimately be expected as retribution. To work was life and there was much to do.

There are many reasons for the recent increase in recreational and leisure time activities. The rapid advance of an industrialized society with its inventions, labor-saving devices, and rising standards of living not only provided more free time but stimulated an intense desire to use that time for play. There was more money to buy pleasure. The electric light turned the night into day. Public agencies, state, federal, municipal, and the school, provided playgrounds and recreational facilities as a matter of public policy. Even the church felt that there was more to its work than revival meetings and Sunday sermons and expanded its activities to include recreational programs. Industry found it profitable to make some provision for the leisure time activities of its employees.

The necessity for diversion is a direct outgrowth of our modern living with its tensions, its complexity, and its expenditure of nervous energy. Since we have abandoned the simple life, recreation seems one way to return to it. And so parks, playgrounds, athletics, the open road, camps, rivers and streams, and all types of outdoor activities are now within the easy reach of all. But recreation is not confined to the outdoor life. A variety of indoor activities meet the needs of individuals of all ages, capacities, and financial abilities. There is available a multiplicity of hobbies, physical activities, cultural arts, and social diversions which all classes of people may enjoy. These are not confined, as formerly, to special occasions like holidays. Vacation periods, holiday seasons, week ends, even a portion of every day can bring at least some recreation to all.[2]

Leisure should be the occasion for physical and mental, social and spiritual rejuvenation. With the proper use of leisure there is joy in anticipation, happiness in realization. The memory of a happy occasion, an exhilarating experience, and joyous living together is sweet and refreshing. Recreation should be simple, wholesome fun, participated in by all.

Unfortunately, the necessity for recreation has been exploited. Many recreational activities are katabolic rather than anabolic in their effects—the human organism is broken down rather than built up; they leave one mentally and physically fatigued. Recreation often becomes just as demoralizing as labor carried to the fatigue point, perhaps even more so.

Commercialized Recreation. Numerous forms of entertainment have become passive, a matter of vicarious experience. Commercialized recreation is now one of our major industries. Estimates of our annual recreation bill vary from ten to twenty billions of dollars.[3] Children, youth, and adults participate in these activities, together or alone. It is, however, with youth that we are most concerned.

---

[2] The reader will find an excellent selected list of references in "Youth Education Today," *Sixteenth Yearbook,* American Association of School Administrators, Washington, National Education Association, 1938, p. 141; see especially *Building America: Recreation Issue,* New York, Columbia University Press, (April, 1936); Martin H. Neumeyer and Esther S. Neumeyer, *Leisure and Recreation,* New York, A. S. Barnes and Company, 1936; Jesse Frederick Steiner, *Americans at Play: Recent Trends in Recreation and Leisure Time Activities,* New York, McGraw-Hill Book Company, 1933.

[3] Stuart Chase, in the section on "Play" in *Whither Mankind,* New York, Longmans, Green and Company, 1928, pp. 336–337, estimates our annual cost of play at twenty-one billions of dollars. Jesse F. Steiner, "Recreation and Leisure-Time Activities," *Recent Social Trends,* New York, McGraw-Hill Book Company, 1933, is more conservative, setting the figure at ten billions. He does not include, however, many so-called modern luxuries.

Some recreational activities have a socially disorganizing effect upon them and create problems for parents and school alike. These include the cabaret, night club, dance hall, and similar establishments, the burlesque show, roadhouse, movies, radio, and indiscriminate use of the automobile. The problem of the school is to recognize the nature and effect of these commercialized forms of recreation and, by elimination and substitution, seek to develop a more wholesome program. Youth in increasing numbers are attracted to roadhouses and night clubs featuring soft lights, shaded windows, rhythmical dance music, pretty girls, the opportunity to dance, convivial company, plenty to eat and drink, pleasing entertainment, and freedom from restraint. The exhilaration of liquor, sex, and suggestion is strong.

These establishments may be found centrally located in populous areas as well as in out-of-the-way places easily reached by automobile. They are usually open far into the night and early morning. Young people gather in them drinking, dancing, carousing. Sensing the weakening of the will in the presence of physical and mental stimulation, unscrupulous proprietors have often placed the opportunity for sex participation near at hand. Moreover, youth often fall an easy prey to the pimp and the gambler, whose devices for gain are "fixed" in advance. Perhaps the pecuniary loss of their own (more likely their parents') hard-earned money is not nearly as serious as the demoralizing effect upon their own characters.

Commercialized Motion Pictures. Perhaps no modern institution has had such a profound effect upon childhood and youth as the motion picture. Developed primarily for its entertainment features, it has become through its tremendous emotional appeal a powerful influence in shaping attitudes and social values. Movie personalities shape the thoughts and ideals of multitudes of young people, influencing their manners, dress, speech habits, attitudes toward romance, and social customs.

It is estimated that more than one-third of the motion picture audiences throughout the United States are composed of children and youth under the age of twenty-one. Boys spend more time in the movies than girls, about three-fourths of the attendance of both being over the week end. Parents frequently go with their children, although more children go with their friends. Three times as many boys as girls go alone to the movies. On the average, each child in areas where motion pictures are available goes to the movies about once a week, although many children go two and three times a week, even oftener.

Motion pictures can have a wholesome influence on youth. World boundaries shrink before the eyes. Distant peoples become our next-door neighbors. The world of history book and travelogue becomes reality, unfolding in never ending wonder. Screen personalities vividly portray and influence social customs, attitudes, and ideals.

Marked differences of opinion exist as to the exact influence of the motion pictures in bringing about disorganizing behavior of one kind or another. Although the gamut of anti-social behavior is depicted before the eyes of youth, right always triumphs; punishment is always inevitable. Yet there is ample evidence that the specific techniques of disorganizing behavior portrayed in a glamorous situation are imitated by youth and are more likely to be retained. Thus, gangsterism is imitated. There is glamour in carrying a gun, staging a holdup, drinking, indulging in narcotics, imitating sex patterns. Longings to enter the gay life, enjoy fine clothes, ape fascinating ladies or vigorous men, love, flirt, and live in a world of enchanted make-believe are conditioning influences whose effects in many instances are socially disorganizing. More recently, there are charges that subversion doctrines are portrayed on the screen.

Censorship seems not to have provided hoped-for results. The moral tone of states and communities varies. Public opinion is not sufficiently organized, and the forces of commercialized endeavor and strong screen personalities are powerful enough to have their way. The efforts of certain groups to designate desirable pictures for certain age audiences, while helpful, scarcely reach the children who need them most. Box office receipts are still taken as the index of a kindly disposed public opinion.

The Radio. The radio has come to be one of the most powerful influences in molding national life and thought. It ranks with the school, the press, the movies, and the pulpit, particularly in its effects upon the young. The family radio supplies programs without charge, in sharp contrast to the motion pictures, for which one must pay.

With nine-tenths of radio time given over primarily to commercial purposes, educational uses are far from being realized. Many programs are declared to be of educational concern, although the standards by which these may be judged can scarcely be so designated. It should be realized also that numerous worth-while programs of educational or entertainment value are sponsored by companies advertising commodities which produce disorganizing social behavior, blatantly and subtly proclaiming their wares within the home to the disgust of unwilling listeners who have no means of immediate protest.

During the past decade there has appeared a definite tendency on the part of broadcasters to stimulate the interest of an increasing radio audience, including its great number of children, in dramatizations of crime incidents, mystery stories, police episodes involving criminals, and radio serials of an exciting nature. These "consumer demands," coming as they do directly into the home, are interpreted as meeting parental satisfaction[4] since the means of reception are supposed to be under direct parental control. Opinion differs as to the educational value of many other radio programs, especially if commercialized in nature. Strictly educational programs of a superior nature merit larger audiences than they now have. Emphasis should be laid on such accompanying values of radio as improvement in speech habits, and on acquaintance with many personalities, superior musical programs, and world news.[5]

The Automobile. Activity and the urge to go are typical of youth. The automobile seems to have provided an unusual outlet for their expression, reorganizing the recreational life of town and country. Numerous forms of recreation have been brought within the reach of many. Distant places heretofore inaccessible are easily visited.

At the same time problems are presented which were unknown to the past generation. Youth takes advantage of the thrills of speed and freedom from restraint. This increased mobility brings the open road with its fascinating attractions nearer at hand. The family automobile is often available to children for school and social activities. The confines of the parked car favor opportunities for misconduct and delinquency. It would seem that public school youth are still too immature to cope adequately with all of the bewildering situations which a new-found freedom has placed before them. The automobile has frequently created problems for the schools. Some schools have accepted them and are sponsoring safe-driving courses, safety programs, and controls over the use of cars.

---

[4] Lovell Juilliard Carr, *Delinquency Control,* New York, Harper & Brothers, 1941, p. 236.

[5] William A. Yeager, *Home-School-Community Relations,* Pittsburgh, University Book Store, 1939, pp. 219–221.

Relation to the School. The public school has an intense interest in these recreational and leisure time activities. An essential feature of American education is to help childhood and youth to live abundantly. Rich creative experiences assist in this process, and the public school is considering, more and more, a social and recreational program to this end. Maintaining direct control over it, the school can utilize it adequately in order to fulfill educational objectives.

Within the community recreational activities may be divided into three groups: (1) those provided by some form of the public service, public supported and, for the most part, wholesome for childhood and youth, such as parks, playgrounds, and public libraries; (2) those provided by semi-public or private agencies, in like manner for the most part wholesome, such as settlement houses, scout groups, the Y.M.C.A., and church recreation; (3) those classified as commercialized recreation, both wholesome and unwholesome, including what we have described in preceding paragraphs.

Wherever any recreational activity exists within the community whose objectives are in accord with educational aims, it should be utilized, as far as possible, in cooperation with the total recreational program of school and community. Whatever activities are of an unwholesome nature must be opposed as inimical to public school objectives and degrading to its program. The school has definite responsibilities in regard to the *total recreational environment* in which childhood and youth are immersed. Right use of leisure must become habitual. Stirring ideals, satisfying interests and skills, a stanch, wholesome personality, a discriminating understanding of the world about him, and an earnest desire to assist in its improvement must be built up in the child. In all of this there must be unflinching loyalty to ultimate truths and values.

In any community, school policy should be designed to cooperate with the wholesome and condemn the unwholesome. The rounded development of each child requires a school program attuned to this end with the home and the community playing an important part.

THE YOUTH-SERVING MOVEMENT

Youth has been called a period "when all things pleased, for life itself was new, and the heart promised what the fancy drew."[6] The

---

[6] "The Pleasures of Memory," part i, Samuel Rogers (1763–1855).

years of youth are vigorous but undirected, idealistic but often frustrated, socially inclined but lacking the means of socialization, aware of the urge to do and become, but groping too often without guidance or opportunity.

Once submerged and exploited, the powers and possibilities of youth as a great American asset have recently been realized. Young people between the ages of fifteen and twenty-four years constitute nearly a fifth of the total population. Most of them come from families of lower economic and social levels where opportunities have been limited and the drive to do and become is often frustrated. Money has not been plentiful and cultural opportunities have been restricted for the vast majority of youth. On the whole, the environment has been far from ideal. Deep in the heart and soul of many a young person is the desire to escape, to improve his life over that of his forbears, and to fulfill his dreams and desires.

Youth's Problems. Perhaps no one is more conscious than youth themselves of their own problems. In 1934, a group of representative young people met in New York to discuss five problems which they considered most important: (1) preparing for and finding a job, (2) preparing for the best use of spare time, (3) establishing group associations and friendships, (4) developing and following an acceptable philosophy of life, and (5) finding opportunity to bear civic responsibility now. Many other studies have been made, the most significant, perhaps, being *Youth Tell Their Story,*[7] an account of conditions and attitudes of young people in Maryland between the ages of sixteen and twenty-four. This study identified the following pertinent problems of youth: (1) equal educational opportunities, (2) employment, (3) economic security,[8] (4) guidance in making the right choices, (5) proper vocational training, (6) more appropriate secondary education, (7) leisure time, (8) health, (9) citizenship, and (10) community planning for youth.

These problems assume a far greater reality to youth as they leave school and find themselves face to face with them. On the one hand, the educational pattern may have failed to provide the immediate means of solving them; on the other hand, society has not made

---

[7] Howard M. Bell, *Youth Tell Their Story,* Washington, American Council on Education, 1938.

[8] Many youth desire the opportunity to make money, to have their own money, and to buy for themselves in accordance with their own declaration of needs.

itself ready to receive its new members economically and socially. Most youth activities have been planned for those who remain in school. Upon leaving school young people are left largely to shift for themselves.[9] It is especially to these that society owes its best endeavors. Numerous agencies, commissions, organizations, and individuals have been at work during the past decade in attempting to solve these problems. Much progress has been made.

Youth-Serving Organizations. The basis for membership of youth in organizations must be sought both in the nature of the individual and in the conditions which immediately surround him. By nature, youth is a social being. He enjoys the company of others, especially those of like interests. He may oppose the interests of another, if he honestly disbelieves in them. His expanding self radiates initiative, a new-found vitality, a desire to do something constructive. In his environment, he finds a need and with it a frustration. Parental and community forces of control tend to make him secretive, unless he finds in them a warm understanding of his desires and ambitions. He is idealistic and a dreamer; he has problems, but the world is complex. His wants are exceeded by his ability to supply them, unless it be with the help of another. He would rather supply them by himself. He hesitates to venture forth. In an organization, he may find partial or complete personal satisfaction and solution to his problems and frustrations.

The American Youth Commission of the American Council on Education, organized in 1935, endeavored to consider all of the needs of American youth and to develop a program for their care and protection.[10] Among its specific projects was the gathering of information on national agencies serving youth. Data on over 320 such organizations were published as *Youth-Serving Organizations.*

Table 13 is a summary of twenty-one youth-membership organizations reporting over 100,000 members each.

An analysis of this table indicates the varied nature and purposes of the organizations which youth join. Many have very definite character-building and citizenship motives; others are religious. The appeal of a considerable number is to the great out-of-doors. Some

---

[9] Consult H. B. Swanson, "Youth: Education for Those Out of School," *Bulletin No. 18,* Washington, United States Department of Interior, 1936.

[10] The reader is referred to the numerous publications of the American Youth Commission available through the American Council on Education.

TABLE 13. SUMMARY OF 21 YOUTH-MEMBERSHIP ORGANIZATIONS REPORTING 100,000 OR MORE MEMBERS EACH[11]

Name of Organization	Year Founded	Aggregate Membership Reported	Total of Persons on Headquarters Staff
Allied Youth	1931	500,000	8
American Junior Red Cross	1917	8,351,000	23
American Youth Congress	1935	1,600,000	65
Baptist Young People's Union	1891	325,000	3
Boy Scouts of America	1910	1,000,000	281
Boys' Clubs of America	1906	263,013	11
Camp Fire Girls	1912	232,058	32
Catholic Students Mission Crusade	1918	500,000	not reported
Epworth League	1889	612,119	11
Four-H Clubs	1914	1,060,000	not reported
Future Farmers	1928	117,000	not reported
Girl Scouts	1912	400,000	157
Intercollegiate Organizations of America	1933	250,000	4
International Society of Christian Endeavor	1881	4,000,000[a]	not reported
Junior Birdmen of America	1934	413,964	4
National Student Federation	1925	225,000	6
Order of Rainbow for Girls	1922	250,000	5
Sodality of Our Lady	1583	500,000	35
Y.M.C.A., National Council of	1866	1,061,876	194
Y.W.C.A., National Board	1858	407,000	241
Y.M.H.A. and Y.W.H.A. (Jewish Welfare Board)	1917	350,000	42

[a] This figure is the estimated total membership in all countries including the United States. The estimate for the United States alone is not reported. Data from M. M. Chambers, *Youth-Serving Organizations*, Washington, American Council on Education, 1937, pp. 11–12.

of these organizations are terminal for youth; others are feeders into adult organizations.[12]

Youth seem to prefer organizations which do something for them personally. There is little indication that they sense the opportunity to serve others unless it be through an organization in which this

[11] "Youth Education Today," *Sixteenth Yearbook*, American Association of School Administrators, Washington, National Education Association, 1938, p. 261.

[12] Chambers, *op. cit.*, has included a descriptive inventory of the 320 organizations studied, grouped into 20 classifications and treated as to identification, membership, purpose, activities, publications, and support.

motive is hidden in larger social values, or one influenced by strong adult personalities. While religious organizations appear to be valued for recreational or social reasons, there is a discernible tendency on the part of youth to place increasing emphasis on spiritual values. Thus the principal preferences of youth are those of social diversion and personal benefit. By the same token, members do not care for organizations without a well-planned social program or those which contain members they dislike personally. Programs having educational value are preferred.

Relation to the School. Parents are primarily interested in youth-serving organizations for their character-building qualities and for the opportunities for their children to do useful things in leisure hours. School authorities are interested for these reasons and also to the extent that they fulfill other educational objectives. School approval or cooperation is often based on certain stipulations, as sacredness of the individual personality, open membership, wholesome program, reasonable hours, proper sponsorship, and such minor restrictions as would seem in harmony with good administration.

Much has been made of youth movements in foreign countries. Unfortunately, many of these have fallen on evil days through exploitation and misdirection. Intelligent social and education direction of youth would seem to place them in a favorable position to meet their own problems as they arise. And yet who is wise enough to predict the future for youth, or unwise enough to misdirect education to the extent of making them unable to cope with their future problems?

Youth-serving organizations are of inestimable value in society and should be more definitely related to the whole educational program. Thus, one finds within the community a variety of youth services performing the functions of (1) education, (2) vocational adjustment, (3) welfare and relief, (4) health, (5) recreation, and (6) religion, and operated by public, private non-profit, and proprietary agencies. The performance of their functions may be classified as advisory or informational, regulatory or prohibitive, encouraging or subsidizing, and controlling or supporting.

A more comprehensive view of the total educational pattern on the part of both school officials and youth-serving agencies is in order. Three theories have been proposed as a basis for it. The first is that the school should undertake only those functions it has demonstrated the capacity to perform. Such a conception precludes expansion of the educational function. The second theory is that the school should attempt to deal with any circumstance which is now interfering with or which will facilitate the child's effectiveness. The cooperative principle applied to education suggests a third theory, namely, that through a survey of youth needs and available agencies and some effective means of coordination—a council, for instance—a plan be consummated in which a complete educational program for all youth can become operative in a community. The success of such a program depends upon the vision of the leadership and the cooperative spirit of all concerned in the enterprise.

MIGRATION AND MOBILITY

The tendency to migrate has been characteristic of the human race. From the dawn of history, men have wandered from place to place in tribes, clans, nations, or alone. Migration has been particularly characteristic of this country, both to and within its borders. Very real adjustment has taken place wherever these movements occurred. Cultures have been affected and history has been changed.

Within recent times, with some exceptions, migration has become primarily an individual and family enterprise rather than an organized movement. Underlying all such migration is the thought of economic and social betterment by a change of locality. Associated with it are problems of political, family, and economic importance with their peculiar implications for the childhood and youth involved in the movement.

Migration is usually distinguished from mobility. The latter generally refers to changes in an individual's position in space, which bring about new contacts and some form of stimulation. It may involve psychological as well as physical change. Our modern transportation systems have brought about tremendous movements of individuals and families—city-ward, country-ward, or suburban-ward. Mobility is induced by seasonal fluctuations, factors of climate and soil, economic conditions, relief, inventions, improvements, changes in customs, broken homes, the search for health, boredom, adventure, religion, and many other influences.

Of special educational concern are the children of migrating families. It is estimated that a population of over 400,000 children of school age are living in trailers. Possibly the number would be increased to 2,000,000 if the children of migrating workers were included, those individuals of marginal culture who follow seasonal crops. Health and pleasure seekers uproot children from their schools for periods at a time.

As an outcome many education problems emerge. School records become meager. School placement is difficult, often resulting in retardation, usually from one to three years. Guidance becomes next to impossible. Interest in school is lost because of change and the lure of more time away from studies. It is hard to concentrate, especially in a maze of new school situations and experiences. The development of school morale among transients is a difficult task. Often there is much sophistication, more often frustration. Standards of morality tend to break down among transients, which often leads to general laxity in behavior. Health conditions may not be of the best, especially among marginal groups. Sanitary conditions and facilities are frequently very poor; malnutrition and inadequate clothing may be taken as a matter of fact. With many children there is a definite tendency toward carelessness. Mobility becomes a habit and the lure of the beyond a mirage. Until society does something to better the social and economic conditions of marginal migrants, education can do little.

School and Community Cooperation

The task of education is to accept the philosophy that instruction must be centered in community needs and problems, and, further, that the well-being of childhood and youth must be predicated on cooperative endeavor. For too long a time the schools have held aloof from the home and community life, living in ivory towers of past glories. Until education recognizes the problems we have discussed in this chapter (and many more) which affect youth, and builds a program to meet them, we can hope for little headway against social barbarism at home and abroad. If education is life, here is a good introduction to it.

There are many instances of mutual understanding and cooperation within the community pattern, looking toward a better educational program. Community councils have been organized. The parent-teacher association has been growing rapidly and has established branches in many schools. Service organizations have educational programs. Many of the youth-serving organizations mentioned in the previous sections are working closely with the schools. Some municipal authorities are endeavoring to cooperate with the school authorities.[13]

QUESTIONS AND PROBLEMS

1. Make a report on the significance of home life in America. Get in touch with homes socially, economically, religiously, and in other ways. What criteria would you suggest as desirable for home-school cooperation?
2. Give examples of disorganizing social forces in your community.
3. In parallel columns, list examples of leisure time activities that are (*a*) katabolic, (*b*) anabolic in their effects.
4. Report on studies which indicate effects of commercialized motion pictures on youth.
5. Make a similar report as in (4) for radio.
6. Study those social evils inimical to youth to be found in your community. What can be done to offset or remove them? In which of these is the school directly concerned?
7. Make a study of youth leaders in a selected school. What unusual qualities do they possess? Can these qualities be developed in all youth? Why?
8. After a study of transfers within your district or community, comment on the tendency to migrate with resulting educational effect.
9. What youth-serving organizations are available in your community? Develop a set of criteria to appraise them. To what extent do the schools cooperate with their programs?
10. Make a report on the community council idea. Does your district have a community council? Comment on it.

SELECTED REFERENCES

1. Bell, Howard M., *Youth Tell Their Story*. Washington: American Council on Education, 1938.
2. Brown, Francis J., *Educational Sociology*. New York: Prentice-Hall, Inc., 1947, chaps. ix, x, xv, xvi.
3. Cowgill, D. O., *Mobile Home: A Study of Trailer Life*. Washington: American Council on Public Affairs, 1941.
4. "Education for Family Life," *Nineteenth Yearbook*, American Association of School Administrators. Washington: National Education Association, 1941.

---

[13] The reader might be interested in the discussion of "Ten Bridges Between School and Community" in Edward G. Olsen, *School and Community*, New York, Prentice-Hall, Inc., 1946.

5. Elliott, Mabel A., and Merrill, Frances E., *Social Disorganization.* New York: Harper & Brothers, 1934.

6. Elmer, M. C., *The Sociology of the Family.* Boston: Ginn and Company, 1945.

7. Gillette, John M., and Reinhardt, James M., *Problems of a Changing Social Order.* New York: American Book Company, 1942, chap. xxii.

8. Olsen, Edward S., *School and Community.* New York: Prentice-Hall, Inc., 1946.

9. Phelps, Harold A., *Contemporary Social Problems.* New York: Prentice-Hall, Inc., 1947, chaps. xiii, xiv, xv.

10. "Social Foundations of Education," *Review of Educational Research,* February, 1946, chaps. i, vi, vii.

11. Yeager, William A., *Home-School-Community Relations.* Pittsburgh: University Book Store, 1939, chap. vi.

12. "Youth Education Today," *Sixteenth Yearbook,* American Association of School Administrators. Washington: National Education Association, 1938.

CHAPTER XXIV

As Youth Leave School

WHATEVER the problems that face society, each individual must be concerned with them and assist in their solution. Education is concerned in that fundamental social task, to develop the capacity to take an active and constructive part in the economic, social, religious, and political life of the community and nation, as well as to have a growing concern for international welfare. The task of education is to prepare the individual better to meet life's situations with every reasonable measure of satisfaction to himself and a full measure of personal responsibility to others.

This task is not one for education alone. It is too large. The persistent collaboration of all agencies and institutions that are properly concerned with preparing each rising generation to meet the inescapable problems of living is needed. Not only must each youth upon reaching adulthood find himself able to participate effectively in the social life of his community, but he must become occupationally adjusted, performing the kind of work which he is clearly qualified for. He must not only be happy in his work but secure a sufficient economic return to participate effectively in the social world and thereby contribute to his own greater personal happiness and to that of others dependent upon him.

In this book we have followed the child from the school's first contact through the various educational processes until he arrives at the point of leaving school and entering full community membership. For most youth that means a complete break with the school which nurtured him; for others, perhaps, there may be some further points of contact. The young man or woman about to graduate is not unlike the ship upon the ways, ready to be launched. Every effort has been made to make the vessel seaworthy; yet the supreme test is the launching—an occasion both of festivity and of anxiety. This chapter will attempt to characterize that transition.

THE NEEDS OF YOUTH

Needs of Adolescence.[1] First of all, we must recognize that in every community the youth group is composed of those who are in various stages of transition from the dependence of childhood to full community membership as workers, parents, and citizens. Their chief characteristic is adolescence in varying stages of physical maturity, personal, mental, and social adjustment. Girls differ in many ways from boys and both pass through periods of change, frustration, daydreaming, parental misunderstandings, social misgivings, and the craving for physical and mental excitement, approbation, and success. There should be a greater realization of the schools' task in meeting the emerging needs of youth. The problem is especially significant when it is realized that any one of these youth may be forced through circumstances to leave school at any time. More emphasis must be placed in social readiness on maturing levels of adolescence.

As youth approach the time of leaving school, ordinarily at ages sixteen, seventeen, eighteen, or nineteen, attention begins to focus on the adjustments necessary for satisfying membership in a world of *adults.* The world of reality on the adult level suddenly opens up before them. They see in marked contrast the world of immature young people to whom they have been accustomed. This is not to say that all youth approach this reality at one and the same time. As we have indicated, many young people by necessity or choice leave school considerably before they have completed the physical, mental, and emotional adjustment normal to the adolescent period they are facing. Moreover, the realities of adjustment vary with youth. To some, life affords its protective influences perhaps longer than it should; others face stern problems before their time.

Need for Broad Range of Experiences. With all youth there are certain personal needs to be met, in providing for which education has a definite part. The first of these is escape from parental and

---

[1] The writer is indebted to *Youth and the Future,* General Report of the American Youth Commission, Washington, American Council on Education, 1942, chap. vi, for a presentation of several of these needs of youth.

other control. In youth are the stirrings of physical maturity, the urge to be grown up, to do things. They become irked at restraint. They desire to do those things meriting the approval of their fellows. Here is required sympathetic direction on the part of both school and home. Real guidance must be made available to enable the youth to achieve in due time what he hopes. A second need grows out of the adolescent's urge for a broad range of experiences of all kinds. He is active yet shy, bold yet without confidence, and physically strong yet without the means to control his strength. If his experience is limited and inadequate, his personality and behavior can hardly fail to be the same. It is most desirable that all of his adjustments proceed concurrently with the physical and emotional changes of adolescence. The school's purpose should be to secure all-round development of its product.

Vocational Adjustment. The third need is adaptation to vocational life. This means much more than finding a job; bound up in adequate vocational adjustment is finding a mate, establishing a home, and building a life. For most girls the problem is ultimately that of making a home, to be achieved through marriage. However, not all girls will marry although four-fifths of this group will become homemakers. Thus homemaking should become the primary vocational preparation for all girls. In the meantime many of them will need to become wage earners, some continuing as such throughout their careers. For this and reasons related to the vicissitudes of marriage and economic emergencies, every girl should acquire certain skills and knowledges leading to economic self-sufficiency.

Personal Needs. A fourth need is adequate preparation in proper use of leisure time. Unfortunately, commercialized amusements and recreation offer real problems to the young person. He should be taught how to round out his personality, achieve greater individuality, and contribute constructively to society as an outcome of his leisure development. A fifth need concerns matters of personal health and vitality. In spite of youthful vigor, the actual health of young people remains much less satisfactory than it should be. Mental health is just as important as physical health. Here it is to be noted that vocational or social maladjustment tends to affect seriously mental health and attitudes.

Youth is often a time of frustration because of the nature of the transition through which adolescents must pass on their way to maturity and complete social membership. Many of their problems leave an impression in later years. Youth must be given a definite place in the world in which they live. Life must have meaning for them. The strains of post-war reconstruction will intensify their problems, some of which are not now foreseen. Education has tremendous responsibilities and, along with the home and other agencies, must find the better way.

YOUTH AND WORK EXPERIENCE

Work an American Tradition. America has been built on the labor and ingenuity of its people. The terse remark attributed to Captain John Smith of Jamestown fame that he who would not work should not eat has undoubtedly characterized the development of our country. As wealth has increased, the comforts of life have also multiplied, bringing with them a leisure motif with a corresponding release from the burdens of toil. And yet the retention of the work principle must remain characteristic of America if for no other reason than to perform the enormous tasks of the future.

Youth and Work Experience. Youth then must be taught the significance of work. To furnish the direct work experience so necessary in transforming youth into producing members of society has not heretofore been considered a function of the public schools. Ample work opportunities once available within the family circle have dwindled, excepting on the farm or in small family-operated business establishments. In their absence some form of work experience must be provided if young people are eventually to become social producers.

Youth have been similarly rebuffed in attempting to find remunerative work within the community. Society has recently had little use for their productive labor, and hence they flocked to the public schools because there was nowhere else for them to go. Gradually, the strong arm of the law reached out to compel those below prescribed ages to attend school, even where the school obviously offered no educational advantages. Even in their late teens or early twenties they have encountered difficulties of initial employment because they lacked experience, maturity, or were hindered by economic policies and conditions. The problem has been complicated because of the widespread desire to enter white-collar occupations, made more attractive by an academic secondary program which implied that to work with the hands is less socially desirable than to work with the brain.

Kinds of Work Experience. Reeves[2] has pointed out the necessity for two kinds of work experience: (1) experience in work of the type that good citizens perform when they contribute service to their communities without recompense, and (2) experience in learning how to carry one's own economic weight by working for wages. To these should be added two concepts, first, the realization that one or more persons may ultimately be dependent upon one's labor for the necessities of life, and second, that essential work output contributes both to the happiness of the individual and to the general social welfare. Responsibility for work experience may now generally be placed upon: (1) the school, (2) the community, and (3) the government in cooperation with both.

The School and Work Experience. The public school should make provision for both kinds of work experience. There are many opportunities within it and under its control whereby such experience can be provided. Courses can be developed which have practical work application—for example, improving the school grounds, solving definite school problems, and making or repairing equipment. Vocational courses can develop projects directly related to the home, the farm, and the community. Throughout the school there are many jobs to be done both during term time and in vacation periods. The schools can assist in procuring part-time employment with local business and industrial firms and in providing or securing a limited amount of work for pay in connection with the needs of the school or other non-profit public agencies.

Gilcrist[3] has identified five categories of work experience available within the school: (1) construction and maintenance, (2) clerical assistance and service, (3) departmental assistance, (4) semi-professional projects, and (5) special services which the school can render. He points out that stress upon work experiences will place greater emphasis upon the community school, since practice in good citizenship today is the best guarantee of good citizenship tomorrow.

The Community. Many of the suggestions for work experience in

---

[2] Floyd W. Reeves, "Youth in Defense and Post-Defense Periods," *Journal of Educational Sociology,* October, 1941, p. 103.

[3] "Secondary Education and National Needs—Our Part," *Bulletin of the National Association of Secondary School Principals,* March, 1941, pp. 86–87.

the school carry over into the home and the community. There are numerous activities within the community contributing to their welfare in which youth can have a definite part. In the home and on the farm can be found occasions for both kinds of work experience. Community organizations such as the Y.M.C.A., chamber of commerce, service clubs, and religious and labor organizations provide opportunities. Many non-competitive jobs may be available in beautifying and improving community life, in parks and recreation centers, in public offices, surveys, and in assistance in community activities of all kinds, like clean-up week and patriotic celebrations. Youth might well be taught to face community problems affecting their own welfare and to assist in meeting them through their own initiative and industry.

Private business can help provide work experience, although the outlook there is not so hopeful. While most of these activities supply the first type of work experience, youth should be given some opportunity to work for wages with the accompanying feeling of having earned money by honest toil.

Governmental Agencies. Working in cooperation with school and community agencies, the government has made it possible for many youth to work for wages. Three areas for work have been tried out: (1) conservation of natural resources, (2) provision for goods and services for schools and governmental and welfare agencies, and (3) production of those goods and operation of those services which youth themselves and younger children need.[4] A number of these activities have been subjected to severe criticism, partly from political motives but mostly from the paternalistic point of view.

YOUTH AND MAKING A LIVING

Meaning. No young person can be said to be economically or socially adjusted until he has happily located himself in an occupation of constructive use to society which is suited to his abilities and for which he has had adequate training. Not only must youth be impressed with the thought that they *must make a living,* but they must be given the opportunity to do so. Each must find the occupation he is most clearly qualified to perform. Thus he may be said to be oc-

---

[4] *Ibid.,* pp. 105–106. See also *Youth and the Future,* chaps. iii, iv. The reader will find a good discussion of this problem in "Youth at Work," *Bulletin of the National Association of Secondary School Principals,* May, 1941.

cupationally adjusted when he succeeds in matching his aptitudes, abilities, and interests with the requirements and demands of his job. In this adjustment he must see clearly (1) that he has now been transferred from the position of being supported to that of partial or complete self-support, (2) that others may sooner or later be dependent upon him for support, and (3) that the daily output of his labor is worth while for the democratic society of which he is a part.

Social and Economic Changes. As he faces the task of making a living he finds a complex and highly industrialized society. Life has drifted away from the comparative simplicity of a generation or more ago and has become intricate and involved. Rapid social and economic changes resulting from discoveries and inventions often bring about ruthless displacements of labor and disturbed social living, thereby exacting a toll in frayed nerves and human tensions. The controls of labor unions were never more obvious. As an outcome, one may never be quite sure that the occupation for which he has made careful preparation will afford him a living for life, because of the results of scientific discovery or economic dislocations, or denial of the opportunity to work. The young worker seldom rides out the hazards of the economic cycle, even if he possesses the ability to foresee it.

Occupational Choices.[5] Modern youth faces a choice of some 18,000 different occupations, each requiring a specific type of preparation. These may be further classified into job families, each member of which requires skills, dexterities, or knowledge identical or closely related to those required by other jobs in the family. Each job family employs a certain group of workers. Bell reports a 12 per cent sample of the 18,000 occupations in modern business and industry employing about 28 per cent of the nation's gainfully occupied population (48,829,920). This sample included 2216 occupations, employing 13,-650,280 workers. Examples of the 18 job families studied are bakery, business service, clerical, construction, hotels and restaurants, and insurance. Minimum educational specifications for the 2216 occupations ranged from none (mere ability to speak, read, and write English— 47.1 per cent) to college graduation (6.5 per cent). High school graduation was required in 20.2 per cent of the occupations.

---

[5] Howard M. Bell, *Matching Youth and Jobs,* Washington, American Council on Education, 1940.

Training on the job (in-service training) ranged from none (8.5 per cent) to more than six months (9.6 per cent). A training period of one week or less was required in 67.5 per cent of the occupations, which will indicate that workers, once they were assigned to jobs, could reach normal production in one week or less. These data reflect the limits to the amount of specialized training required in modern occupations. It also points out the restricted responsibility of the schools in providing specialized vocational training. However, one must not minimize the months or years of study often required to achieve occupational efficiency in professional, managerial, and skilled labor fields. The indication is only that the basic work of an industrialized society can be done without the benefit of lengthy specific preparation.

Assisting Agencies. Two agencies, then, are necessary to prepare the youth to fit himself into the world of employment. The school, first of all, must enable him to face the realities of the occupational world. Certain initial knowledges and skills may be provided together with exposure to the workaday atmosphere of store or shop, possibly a tryout under actual working conditions. Second, business and industry must provide the in-service training essential to fitting the youth on the job for the task to be accomplished. Schools and communities will differ markedly in regard to these training responsibilities as well as opportunities for occupational adjustment. Community surveys should be made seeking to ascertain the tasks of both in regard to differentiation of function. Vocational schools might do well to concentrate less upon intensive preparation for a single pursuit and more upon developing a sound general knowledge pertaining to a family of occupations.[6]

Getting the First Job. The first job secured by the young person after leaving school is an all-important one for him. Full-time knowledge of the working world is now introduced to him. He feels that he belongs. The thrill of the first pay check is one long to be remembered.

A recent study[7] indicates that only 3.9 per cent of youth in the schools studied secured their first job through school authorities. In-

---

[6] *Education for American Life,* The Regents' Inquiry, New York, McGraw-Hill Book Company, 1938, p. 22.

[7] "Occupational Adjustment and the School," *Bulletin of the National Association of Secondary School Principals,* November, 1940, p. 55.

fluence was predominant with 33.9 per cent getting their first job through the help of a friend or relative, and 17.3 per cent being actually employed by a relative or friend. Through a personal application, 33.4 per cent obtained work, and the remainder through commercial employing agencies and advertisements. These facts indicate that the school contributes little to the placement of youth. It should do more.

The study above referred to points out other interesting facts in regard to placement. These include the importance of a greater realism on the part of the school personnel in the job training and placement program and in inculcating in youth more realism toward the job once attained; and for both there should be increased knowledge as to local labor conditions and their relations to occupational adjustment.

Greater emphasis should be placed upon personality training and especially the need of making a good first impression when applying for a job. Versatility in adapting oneself to different employers' requirements is important. The employer's interests should be kept in mind by being regular, doing the job well, and, above all, maintaining high ethical standards and good behavior. Subsequent recommendation may depend on it.

Appraisal. The school might ascertain of each employed youth the following: (1) Does he cooperate? (2) Does he stand up well under criticism? (3) Is he interested? (4) Can he be trusted? (5) Does he improve on the job? (6) Does his personal interest extend beyond his own immediate job? and (7) Does he consider the job's effects on his personal health?

Homemaking. Thus far much of our discussion has pertained to making a living with monetary return. This applies to both boys and girls. Quite often overlooked is the inescapable fact that approximately 97 per cent of the women in the United States either become homemakers or fit into homes as members or guests of a family.[8] Homemaking is a vocation just as truly as any other, for which there should be a definite preparation. It is important because it deals with every aspect of home and family living. Fitting girls and women for it is a task that must not be left to haphazard methods. Especially is

[8] F. Theodore Struck, *Vocational Education for a Changing World,* New York, John Wiley and Sons, 1944, chap. xix.

this true where children are concerned since approximately two-thirds of all women bear children.

The current trend to include homemaking courses for all girls in the junior high school should be continued in the senior high school, perhaps the junior college. Marriage and sex education and child care are essential aspects of this training. Above all, recognition of the home's importance in a happy and vigorous social order is paramount. This applies to both sexes.

YOUTH AND UNEMPLOYMENT

Economic cycles leading to depression and unemployment often have a devastating effect on youth. For example, in October, 1939, the American Youth Commission declared that the high ratio of unemployment among youth constituted a national emergency. Measures of relief taken at that time did not always meet general approval. A consideration of the problems of employment at this time may assist us to obviate unemployment in the years of reconstruction that lie ahead. Many young people who were sixteen or eighteen when they left school to find a job in 1934 were still unable to find jobs in 1940 at the ages of twenty-two to twenty-four. Large numbers either possess no skills or any job whatever or find no opportunities to use such skills as they have. For some there is almost as much difficulty in keeping a job once gained as in securing initial employment. Youthful workers have been overrepresented in the farm laboring, semi-skilled, clerical, and sales groups, and underrepresented in professional, farm operating, and skilled laboring classes. The largest numbers of youth on relief were classified as unskilled in any particular. In times of economic depression, with sufficient skilled labor available, industry and business are usually not willing to establish training programs. Accompanying continued youthful unemployment is a feeling of frustration, a damaging mental attitude.

Reasons for Unemployment. Reasons for unemployment as discovered in the New York Regents' Inquiry have probably been typical throughout the country. Of those unemployed, it was found that about 9 per cent of the boys and 20 per cent of the girls were not looking for jobs. Of these some were in school, satisfied with part-time jobs, or otherwise satisfied with their present situation owing largely to lack of economic necessity. A few boys and girls did not plan for any vocation, coming either from homes of some wealth or from homes where they were kept busy until married. Isolation is a factor—some were too far removed for any chance to find jobs. Some were marking time, the right job just not having "turned up." Some had returned to school because they could not find jobs. By far the largest number, more boys than girls, stated that economic conditions were the principal cause of their unemployment. Added to these factors may be physical deficiencies and personal reasons and preferences, as lack of sufficient pay, likes and dislikes, and interferences with leisure time.

SUMMARY OF FACTORS AFFECTING YOUTH'S ECONOMIC LIFE

Future approaches to the studies of occupational adjustment among youth should be made from the following summary of factors affecting their absorption into American economic life:

1. Recognition of the fundamental fact that every youth has the right to work and make an essential contribution to the welfare of society. Every community should develop a definite public policy for its youth.
2. Recognition of the changing economic pattern of American life brought about by the exigencies of war, invention, and economic conditions.
3. Recognition of the necessity for constant pre-training and retraining programs for youth.
4. Establishment of employers' agencies in the community, state and nation, working cooperatively toward suitable employment for every youth.
5. Establishment of work programs for youth if and when necessary.
6. Cooperation of labor unions with industry as well as education in the interests of youthful employment.
7. Retention in school as long as possible of all youth unable to fit into a satisfactory individual work program, especially if desirable maturation levels have not been reached.
8. Closer attention to factors of social change, migration of workers, personal and mental health, and factors of race, sex, standards of living.
9. Relation of youth employment to factors associated with family life and personal ambitions.
10. Recognition of the right of youth to making a life as well as making a living.

11. Recognition of the fundamental principle, as the American Youth Commission has pointed out, that "in future years, it will be the major objective of the American people to manage our economic system so effectively that a sustained level of full employment can be achieved . . . we can and should begin work towards that objective without waiting for the return of peace."[9]

HIGHER EDUCATION

Selection Through Elimination. For the vast majority of youth (about 85 per cent) the secondary school offers a terminal education, the next step being some definite vocational adjustment in order to make a living. Pupils leave school at various ages and educational levels, and for various reasons, depending on economic circumstances, the attendance laws, and opportunities for further education. The gradual elimination of pupils during their educational progress is much more serious than is generally realized. For illustration, the New York Regents' Inquiry found that, of every hundred pupils who enter the ninth grade of the New York State high schools, fewer than forty remain to graduate.[10] About half the graduates continue their full-time schooling in some type of higher institution. A number of those who do not go on to higher institutions immediately may enroll at some future time in apprentice courses, part-time vocational schools, or adult education classes. Not including the latter group, eighty out of every hundred pupils who enter ninth grade cannot look forward to any systematic higher education at the end of high school. Moreover, a larger proportion of the graduates of city high schools than country high schools continue their education beyond the high school, and there is as great variance among communities as among states.[11]

Over the country as a whole there has been a steady rise in the holding power of the high school since 1910, when only 14 per cent of those originally in the fifth grade remained to graduate. By 1940, the percentage has tripled. Foster[12] predicted that only 52 per cent

---

[9] *Youth and the Future,* p. 27.

[10] *High School and Life,* The Regents' Inquiry, New York, McGraw-Hill Book Commany, 1938, p. 34.

[11] *Ibid.,* p. 95.

[12] Emery M. Foster, "School Survival Rates," *School Life,* March, 1938. The reader will find an interesting study of school leavers in S. Marion Justice, "Implications of a Follow-Up Study of School Leavers," *Occupations,* May, 1941, pp. 563–566.

of one entering high school class would remain to graduate. This means that, for the nation as a whole, about half of the entering high school pupils are eliminated before graduation for one reason or another.

Who Should Go to College. There are two opposing schools of thought in regard to who should go to college. One view has been expressed by President Angell of Yale: that the function of the college is to raise up a race of intellectual leaders based on rigid selection.[13] The opposing view has been well expressed by Chancellor Lindley of the University of Kansas, who declares that "in a democracy the chief duty of the college is to train for useful and intelligent citizenship the largest possible number of young men and women."[14] Colleges and universities wholly or partially supported by public funds seem, on the whole, to have accepted the latter philosophy, while private institutions insist upon a more rigid selection of their applicants by college entrance examinations and other means. Throughout the United States there is still an honest difference of opinion as to whether higher education should be reserved for superior minds or properly adjusted to all varieties of aptitudes, interests, and abilities.

Methods of Selection. On any basis, some method of selection becomes necessary especially since many more students now apply for admission and enter college than ever before. Limitations of space and a desire to raise standards have caused higher institutions of learning to give careful consideration to more searching methods of selection. Criteria now commonly used are: (1) certification of graduates from an approved secondary school (usually a scholarship record accompanied by a statement by the principal and/or teachers); (2) relative class standing in school; (3) comprehensive examinations under direction of separate examination boards; (4) college qualifying examinations by the admitting college; (5) psychological examinations; (6) Personality ratings largely based on personal interview; (7) Health examinations; (8) Records of maturity, vocational experience, peculiar fitness, or other qualifications (especially in the absence of one or more other criteria). To these individually may be

---

[13] Quoted in "The Development of the High School Curriculum," *Sixth Yearbook,* Department of Superintendence, Washington, National Education Association, 1928, p. 144.

[14] *Ibid., Seventh Yearbook,* p. 292.

added any combination, depending on the purpose of selection, the institution itself, and the number to be selected.

The secondary school should be deeply concerned in this selective process which naturally affects it in so many particulars. For years a large number of principals and teachers have honestly believed that the secondary school is dominated by the colleges and universities. Their competence is seemingly measured by meeting these selective standards successfully, and by the academic success of their pupils, usually during the first college year. As a result, the secondary curriculum has been largely adapted to the needs of the publicized few who look collegeward. Proclaimed liberalization of each from this bondage does not seem to have progressed very far.

The college, on its part, has claimed that some dominance of the secondary school program is necessary at least for those pupils who expect to enter college. At the same time, they point to liberalization, noting changes in the college entrance requirements, curricula, and standards. Perhaps academic strictness in regard to admitting students is balanced in some instances by lenient acceptance of promising athletes. Then, too, colleges in competition with each other are occasionally brought to the necessity of accepting students through waiving prerequisites to admission. Experimentation has also affected the nature of the preparation in some recently "emancipated" secondary schools.[15]

College Success. Numerous investigations have been made of the relationship of secondary school to college success. Strang mentions some forty-two investigators who have attacked this problem in various ways.[16] Many different measures have been utilized, such as marks in general or in particular, studies, credits, subjects taken, and rank in class. Best evidences of success seem to be a high correlation between high school and college marks and rank in high school graduating class. This emphasis upon marks or ranks in class based upon marks leads to invalid conclusions as to the meaning of college success, as the National Society for the Study of Education has pointed out: "A close relation between previous school marks and present marks merely means that 1) grades are being stressed as the

---

[15] W. M. Aikin, *The Story of the Eight-Year Study,* New York, Harper & Brothers, 1942.

[16] Ruth Strang, *Personal Development and Guidance in College and Secondary Schools,* New York, Harper & Brothers, 1934, pp. 92–105.

important factor of school experience, and 2) the methods and materials of each school unit are similar to those of succeeding units. . . . Both of these emphases are subject to severe criticism."[17] Moreover, one should point out that the student who has achieved success in high school as measured by *grades* uses the same means to secure success in college. Other measures of success are not taken into consideration. Then too, high correlation of grades or ranks must not lead to the conclusion that this similarity of pattern is common to all students, nor that correlation in single subjects is the same as correlation of average grades.[18]

Causes of College Failure as a Secondary School Problem. Failure in college, like college success, reflects upon the secondary school. Some causes of failure may be traced directly to the secondary school. Hence, administrators and teachers should have an awareness of these causes in order to do something about them. Perhaps the best analysis has been made by Heaton and Weedon[19] in a study of academic failure in college and its implications for education. The following may be listed as of interest to the secondary school: (1) reading ability; (2) study habits and skills, especially in making the transition from study requirements in high school to those in college; (3) health considerations, as awareness of physical deviations, proper health habits, sleep, care of eyes, etc.; (4) vocational choice and placement especially where loss of time, disinterest, and reduced motivation are the result; (5) mental attitudes toward college work stemming largely from lack of serious purpose, misuse of new-found freedoms, tendency to emotional disturbances, lack of guidance; (6) preparation to live independently away from home and parents, in which inability to make decisions, social adjustment, and other factors are concerned; (7) adjustments to correct deficiencies in preparation. Inadequate academic preparation, an important cause of college failure, has not been stressed since admittance to college presumes adequacy in this respect. These causes may not be ignored in the secondary school, especially in those schools with a large college preparatory group.

---

[17] Alvin C. Enrich and C. Gilbert Wrenn, "Appraisal of Student Characteristics and Needs," *Guidance in Educational Institutions,* Bloomington, Public School Publishing Company, 1938, part i, p. 34.

[18] Kenneth L. Heaton and Vivian Weedon, *The Failing Student,* Chicago, University of Chicago Press, 1939, p. 86.

[19] *Ibid.*

Secondary School-College Articulation. The administrator and teacher should seek to provide for all pupils in such a way that a better articulation of secondary youth with high institutions of learning is viewed in proper perspective. In bringing this about, consideration should be given to the following:

1. The secondary school exists primarily for the benefit of *all the boys and girls* of the community it serves. This emphasizes the distinctive nature of each school community. The common and varying needs of all groups should be studied and provided for. Dominant needs of college preparatory groups should not overshadow similar adequate provision for the far more numerous non-college groups.[20]

2. In working out its own program, the secondary school should not be overshadowed by the preparatory demands of the colleges. Perhaps the college also should take the student *as it finds him.* There is good reason to believe that the colleges of arts and sciences in the past have been the dominating influence over the high school.[21] Most college failures occur in this collegiate division. On the other hand, many of the so-called difficulties involved in college admission, as Smith has pointed out, "exist only in the minds of over-cautious, ignorant, and inert high school principals and teachers."[22] These are hard words. Wherever there is intimidation from college officials, influential citizens, or other sources, secondary school administrators must know what to do and how and when to do it.

3. Recognition should be given to the results of the numerous studies and other reliable material setting forth causes of failure in higher institutions. These should be studied in the secondary school and utilized to the degree consistent with local application.

4. Institutions of higher learning are of a varied nature. Care must be taken that no one type of secondary preparation dominates unduly.

---

[20] Compare *How to Evaluate a Secondary School,* Comparative Study of Secondary School Standards, Washington, American Council on Education, 1940, especially chap. ii.

[21] *Seventh Yearbook,* p. 294.

[22] Herbert W. Smith, "The College Entrance Bugaboo," *Junior-Senior High School Clearing House,* September, 1929, pp. 28–37.

5. Recognition should be given to the following approved practices in regard to better articulation:
    a. Active aid of state departments of education
    b. Active aid of accrediting agencies and associations
    c. Active aid of functional groups interested in better articulation
    d. Meeting needs of individual students where college entrance is concerned
    e. Better reporting on the part of the college to the secondary school concerning individual progress covering the *entire stay* of student in college
    f. Frequent intervisitation of college and secondary school officials
    g. More stress on institutional information and guidance-counseling activities in the secondary school
    h. Greater individual effort on the part of the college to assist failing students, especially the development of techniques detecting the failing student early in his college career
    i. Abolition of specific curricula in favor of a core group of subjects, with sufficient sequential electives to meet individual or group requirements
6. Perhaps we have accepted too listlessly the byword, "You cannot place old heads on young shoulders." Training in the acceptance of responsibilities as the youth matures will do much to promote success. This should become an educational function on any age level.

Before concluding this section, there is much that should be said concerning a growing *rapprochement* between the college and the high school in which the college is taking the initiative. Some colleges now accept secondary school students merely upon the principal's recommendation. Some are adjusting their requirements for graduation to meet the specific preparation of the student and his needs. Survey courses are offered. There are many experimentations on the college level, as at the University of Chicago, Swarthmore, Vassar, Middlebury, and other institutions. Freshman week helps to orient the student; there is better guidance service. Parents' nights are held. Better college teaching is definitely apparent.[23]

---

[23] Adolph Meyer, *The Development of Education in the Twentieth Century*, New York, Prentice-Hall, Inc., 1939, pp. 214-231.

The Junior College. The junior college movement may become the solution for the great majority of students who look forward to some additional education beyond the secondary school, and who will probably not continue beyond one or two years. In reality the junior college has come to be considered an extension of the secondary school. This is especially true in cities where it is made a part of the public school program and is publicly supported. Many students have no intention of going on to college or university. It thereby becomes a terminal education for them. Others are finding it helpful as a preparatory institution either for general culture or for professional schools. The junior college provides a means of further education for those unable to leave home for one reason or another and for those unable to gain admittance into certain higher institutions. It also offers some types of vocational education. However, even while assisting in solving one articulation problem, it creates new problems of its own.

In conclusion, one is led to observe that experiments now in progress may lead eventually to a new type of organization affecting secondary schools, junior colleges, colleges, and universities. It may take the form of the 6-4-4 grouping predicted by Koos many years ago. In the meantime it will be difficult to overcome traditions, prejudices, and community patterns, especially where succeeding generations look to the fathers.

YOUTH AND THE ARMED SERVICES

Whatever may be one's attitude toward military service and the hope of peace, the fact remains that a citizen's first duty is to his country, possibly in the form of its defense in times of emergency. For many youth this may take one or more years out of their scholastic or productive life.

Such a call is received with mixed emotions. It is difficult to face the realities connected therewith in giving up one's education, lucrative employment, leisure time pursuits, and a planned career. More than that, the subsequent adjustments are not easy to make in spite of governmental efforts and often social privileges.

These matters touch education at many points. What can the public schools do to facilitate pre-entry as well as post-adjustment? What guidance and curricular services can be designed to fit individual cases? How can the school best function in making occupational adjustments? How can the secondary school or the college improve its program in order to retain and interest the bored immature youth? How can the public schools cooperate with governmental agencies?

All of these questions do not anticipate the inevitability of war. Peace with its reward should always be uppermost in our minds.

QUESTIONS AND PROBLEMS

1. Evaluate the section on "The Needs of Youth" in terms of (*a*) literature in the field, (*b*) the youth of your school community.
2. What are the opportunities for work experience in your (*a*) school, (*b*) community? To what extent do youth need it? Should community or governmental agencies control the means for work experience for youth? Just where should the school fit in the program?
3. Why is "making a living" fundamental to "making a life"? Prove by contrasting examples.
4. Consult statistics as to opportunities for occupational choice for (*a*) boys, (*b*) girls. Apply your findings to a local situation.
5. Make a study of occupational counseling in a particular high school.
6. What are the school's responsibilities in regard to placement opportunities?
7. Evaluate the reasons for unemployment among youth. What can the school do about any of these?
8. Make a study of the success, or failure, of graduates of any secondary school in institutions of higher education.
9. Write a report on the growth and development of the junior college movement.
10. To what extent is college failure and elimination a secondary school problem?
11. What relationships can you point out between education and youth where the armed services are concerned?

SELECTED REFERENCES

1. Aikin, W. M., *The Story of the Eight-Year Study*. New York: Harper & Brothers, 1942.
2. Bell, Howard M., *Matching Youth and Jobs*. Washington: American Council on Education, 1940.
3. Bossard, James H. S., *Social Change and Social Problems*. New York: Harper & Brothers, 1938, chaps. i, ix, xii, xiii.
4. *Bulletins of the National Association of Secondary School Principals*. Washington: National Education Association: "Occupational Ad-

justment and the School," November, 1940; "Promising Practices in Secondary Education," October, 1940; "Secondary Education and National Needs—Our Part," March, 1941; "Youth at Work," May, 1941.

5. Educational Policies Commission, *Learning the Ways of Democracy*. Washington: National Education Association, 1940.

6. Engleman, L. E., and Eells, W. C., *The Literature of the Junior College Terminal Education*. Washington: American Association of Junior Colleges, 1941.

7. Folsom, Joseph K., *Youth, Family, and Education*. Washington: American Council on Education, 1941.

8. Germane, Charles E., and Germane, Edith G., *Personnel Work in High School*. New York: Silver, Burdett and Company, 1941.

9. Heaton, Kenneth L., and Weedon, Vivian, *The Failing Student*. Chicago: University of Chicago Press, 1939.

10. Magill, Walter H., *Administering Vocational Education*. Minneapolis: Educational Publishers, Inc., 1941.

11. "Minimum Essentials of the Individual Inventory of Guidance," *Bulletin No. 202*, Vocational Division. Washington: U. S. Office of Education, 1939.

12. "Paths to Better Schools," *Twenty-Third Yearbook*, American Association of School Administrators. Washington: National Education Association, 1945, chap. iii.

13. Rakestraw, C. E., *Training High-School Youth for Employment*. Chicago: American Technical Society, 1947.

14. Reports of the Regents' Inquiry. New York: McGraw-Hill Book Company, 1938: *Education for American Life; High-School and Life; When Youth Leave Schools*.

15. Struck, F. Theodore, *Vocational Education for a Changing World*. New York: John Wiley and Sons, 1945.

16. Varner, G. F., "Challenge to the Junior College," *Junior College Journal*, March, 1941, pp. 381–384.

17. "What People Think about Youth and Education," *Research Bulletin*. Washington: National Education Association, XVIII, No. 5, November, 1940.

18. "Youth Education Today," *Sixteenth Yearbook*, American Association of School Administrators. Washington: National Education Association, 1938.

19. *Youth and the Future*, General Report of the American Youth Commission. Washington: American Council on Education, 1942.

PART VIII

The Organizing Function

CHAPTER XXV

School Organization in Relation to the Pupil Personnel Function— The Elementary School

FROM the simplicity of the traditional school in America, the present system of education has enlarged to include an organization extending from the kindergarten and nursery school through the college and university. Broadly speaking, this system is divided into three areas, elementary, secondary, and higher (advanced) education. Ideally, the school organization should be so set up and administered that each child and youth, or adult for that matter, as he comes to school can find a program of instruction in harmony with the purposes of education and readily adapted to his needs, abilities, and interests. At the same time, his maximum educational program must be assured. The efficient administration of an educational enterprise has its basis in an adequate and economical organization.

This chapter points out some essentials of school organization in relation to the pupil personnel function, keeping in mind the important fact that the purpose of any school organization is to provide an environment in which the child can grow and develop to the fullest extent. After discussing our educational ladder system, the chapter points out the characteristics of each division within the system which bear any relation to the pupil's development, with special reference to elementary education.

Our Educational Ladder System

The three areas of elementary, secondary, and higher (advanced) education developed traditionally and independently of each other. Originally, they were not designed to gear one into the other. As the concept of democracy took deep root, there developed simultaneously the idea that equality of opportunity could be better achieved through a system of education that reached out universally, at the same time permitting and encouraging each individual to develop through its different stages.

And so different forms of school organization strove to meet educational needs on different age and group levels and social demands. At different times and under varying conditions certain patterns became definitely stabilized. The common school typified the elementary level; the academy, now the high school, the secondary level; and the denominational college, that of higher education. These independently developed organizations have become welded together into an educational ladder system characteristic of America in which each boy and girl, stimulated by the typical American urge to rise to the top, could at least have the opportunity of educational privilege. As an outcome, the common expectation is that each child will begin his education in the elementary school, sometimes the kindergarten, and will progress through the several grades, the junior high school, to the probable completion of his work upon graduation from the high school.

At this point the chances of his continuing on to college and university are less than one out of five. If he has the ability and a certain economic and social advantage, together with a satisfactory school or examination record and the principal's recommendation, he may enter upon and complete a program of higher education preparatory to a professional career and corresponding economic and social advantage.

America's educational ladder thus provides the opportunity for each boy and girl, at least theoretically, to obtain every educational advantage that democracy has to offer. Thereby the expression of his individuality may be achieved. Three conditions should be noted, however: (1) the limitations of his social and economic environment over which the child or youth usually has little or no control; (2) the larger claims of society which may operate to deter him from his choice, as in war or family or individual necessity; and (3) other factors, such as marriage or personal choice, which may shunt him into other channels of endeavor. Even in these instances it is interesting to observe the zeal of some individuals in achieving a better education in spite of almost overwhelming odds through night schools, correspondence courses, extension classes, and unrelated cultural opportunities. Many of the greatest men and women of America have achieved educational success the hard way.

Organization and Administration

The student of school organization then should have an awareness, as he approaches the task of organizing his schools, that tradition has established certain definite patterns for him. Naturally he will turn to the outlines of established plans as a frame of reference. This does not necessarily mean that he is to be bound by them; rather that, recognizing the good in things as they are, he can proceed to better ways. Then too, the organization of a school, in theory, is the administrative expression of some educational point of view held in regard to objectives, curriculum, and method. It is desirable that the type of organization be in strict harmony with a particular theory. Practically this may not be possible, owing to many obstacles which hinder the achievement of such harmony, including a conventionally minded community, uninterested or unprepared teachers, lack of supplies, equipment, or financial support, and other factors.

Before proceeding farther, let us have a clear conception of organization and administration. School organization may be defined as the structure or framework within which principals, teachers, pupils, and all other factors operate in carrying on the activities of the school. It refers to the creation of a plan or the existing pattern within which the schools operate. It may be characterized as the blueprint. Administration is the act or process of operating the organization. The techniques and procedures employed in the school organization in accordance with legal requirements, policies, and best practice constitute the administrative process. Policies may be defined as the basic principles guiding administrative practice.

Adequate School Organization Necessary to Pupil Progress

Approach. We have seen that the approach to school organization is through the purposes for which it exists and the educational program to be planned in accordance with them. These purposes should bear a definite relationship to the educational function within the democratic state, recognizing factors of community attitude and control, and pupil needs. The limits of the school organization should be taken into consideration, that is, its vertical extension and services to be rendered. In arranging these limits, adequacy of educational opportunity should be provided for every child without let or hindrance. Attention should be given to cooperative relationships with other educational and social agencies within the community. The educational process should be made continuous[1] and free from partisan controls. Legal provisions should be thoroughly recognized; likewise, parental and community interests and attitudes. At many stages, the plan of organization may, of necessity, be determined by economic limitations. Above all, it should be functional and become the means, rather than the end, in the achievement of educational objectives.[2]

Purpose. The primary purpose of the school organization is to plan and arrange the elements necessary to the educational progress of each child with reference to his needs, abilities, and interests. Some kind of organization is necessary in order to secure the maximum return possible on the investment of time, personnel, plant facilities, and equipment, and to plan for the most efficient and economical use of the funds available. Although school organization in itself may imply something fixed, the distinguishing characteristic of a good organization is its dynamic and adjustable nature to provide for the individual disposition and growth of each child.

Growth Through School Organization. It is important to emphasize that a good school organization is not a thing in itself. Through it the rounded growth of each child is achieved. Its strength or weakness is in direct relation to how efficiently this is done. Moreover, a strong organization in itself will not necessarily attain the objectives sought. Strong and enlightened personalities are necessary to its operation. Here good administrative leadership enters the picture, as well as teachers of high quality. In good admin-

---

[1] This applies particularly where district lines limit educational advancement owing to narrow school opportunities.

[2] An excellent discussion of the fundamental principles of school organization will be found in Arthur B. Moehlman, *School Administration,* Boston, Houghton Mifflin Company, 1940, chap. v.

istration, it should be remembered that neither the mechanics of the school organization nor the procedures of the classroom should interfere with the interests of any child or all of the children concerned. A school organization to be effective should be well conceived, clearly articulated, and calculated to stimulate progressive school service in a spiritual atmosphere of cooperation on the part of all concerned in its operation.

ELEMENTS ESSENTIAL TO SCHOOL ORGANIZATION

Scope. Many elements must be considered in setting up an adequate school organization. A proper survey of the educational needs and services to be rendered is the first step. Following this a definite program based on them should be prepared. Authority should be properly reposed within a duly constituted legal framework and distributed through the state administrative setup, local board of education, local administrative and supervisory officers, teachers, and other personnel. Certain responsibilities should be clarified and delegated in relation to this authority and in accordance with good administrative practice. Unless this is done, services rendered by each individual may not be properly evaluated. Personnel should be carefully planned for, selected, placed, and supervised. Services should be outlined with care and arranged with reference to the qualifications of the personnel, functions to be performed, and funds available. Within this framework the specific type of organization is to be applied. The relation it bears to the administrative division above or below, the type of district and the need for coordination with personnel and services within and without the system are essential factors. Care should be taken to balance properly the educational administrative and the business administrative functions. Provision for necessary facilities and allocation of funds complete the process. All of these should be organized in the light of the policies and needs of the school system. Somehow pervading the whole procedure is the guiding philosophy of the educational enterprise under enlightened leadership. It is difficult to say whether it begins or completes the picture.

Dynamic Nature. Apart from achievements in regard to facilities and school support, the dynamic nature of good organization may be revealed in the progress made as to (1) system of grading and grouping, (2) types of schools and special agencies, and (3) means of adjustment and coordination. While specific patterns of school organization are readily discernible in different school districts, that organization is most effective in which constant and definite attempts are made to adapt it to the peculiar needs and conditions within the local area. Such adaptation should take into consideration geographical factors, size and wealth of community, characteristics and needs of all the pupils, personnel, and funds available. An ever present urge for a more efficient school organization should be everywhere apparent.

Appraisal. In addition to planning, provision should be made for appraisal. This function requires an adequately prepared, industrious, and inspiring leadership and the use of reliable techniques. Attention at all times should be focused on the instructional process. Principals and teachers should enjoy freedom to think and act in the best interests of their own development and that of their pupils. A close relationship should be maintained with all governmental authority wherever reposed. Above everything else, adequate school organization should always be appraised as it is attuned to those for whom it is maintained.

The Elementary School

The elementary school is the characteristic institution for younger children in the United States. It is America's traditional school, familiarly known as the common school, and has a meaningful heritage. Organized as a separate unit of eight years with promotion by grades and curriculum materials and experiences adapted to the child's progressive development, it is still typical throughout the country. More recently, it has been discovered that the work of the elementary school can be accomplished in a shorter period of time. Moreover, the education of the child should be begun much earlier than the usual age of six years—perhaps at four or five years, perhaps as early as two.

The problem of the elementary school is to construct an organization which will provide adequately for the needs, interests, and abilities of the child from (two to) six years to about the age of twelve or thirteen years. Within it consideration should be given to the great range of these abilities and interests, environmental factors, cost factors, peculiar local problems, and traditional patterns and concepts of education of long standing, many of which may be difficult to improve and adjust. Within these limiting factors, everything must be done for the educational progress and welfare of the children.

The student of elementary school organization must consider the all-important fact that each school, public and private, is an agent of the state and part of the state's organization for education. We are predominantly a rural nation in the sense that more than half of all elementary children live on farms or in towns of less than 2500 population. Approximately half of the school buildings are one- or two-teacher schools (including high schools). The most common school district is a rural district operating one or more one-teacher or two-teacher schools. The average enrollment is about fifteen pupils per school. Moreover, the typical curriculum is organized into a large number of subjects separately taught on a schedule permitting only a few minutes for each subject. The instructional program, services, supplies, and supervision are limited. The educational advantages, including health programs, available to most children even in the larger urban areas are sadly lacking in many elementary schools. Fortunately, the consolidation movement is making rapid strides in many states.

Redefinition of the Elementary School

The twentieth century brought about a redefinition of the elementary school in terms of the study of the child and his development, with emphasis on the type of education most suitable to the pre-adolescent. The movement is definitely traceable to the philosophy and experiments of John Dewey and his contemporaries. The results of recent studies have focused attention on the fact that the work of the elementary school, traditionally of eight grades, can be adequately completed in an organization of six or seven years, which includes a kindergarten and grades one to six. This newer philosophy and program have called for greater freedom in the classroom for both the pupil and the teacher.

Innovations appeared in school organization. Definite efforts were now made to adapt it to the varying needs and capacities of the pupils. The whole movement was accelerated by discoveries through experimentation in the field of applied psychology, especially of individual differences, and in health and mental hygiene. Even the traditional school was influenced by many features of these newer practices.

INNOVATIONS IN ELEMENTARY SCHOOL ORGANIZATION

The attempt to change the elementary school organization may be summed up in two motivating purposes: (1) the desire to find practical applications of newer educational theories through experimenta-

TABLE 14. VARIATIONS FROM THE USUAL TYPE OF
ELEMENTARY SCHOOL ORGANIZATION, 1862–1932

Plan or Practice	Person Associated with Its Establishment	Date of Establishment
St. Louis	W. T. Harris	1862
Pueblo	P. W. Search	1888
Cambridge	Francis Cogswell	1893
Elizabeth, New Jersey	W. J. Shearer	1895
Portland, Oregon	Frank Rigler	1897
Batavia	John Kennedy	1898
North Denver	J. H. Van Sickle	1898
Santa Barbara Concentric	Frederick Burk	1898
Platoon	W. A. Wirt	1900
Burk's Individual	Frederick Burk	1913
Dalton	Helen Parkhurst	1919
Winnetka	C. W. Washburne	1919
Detroit X-Y-Z Grouping	C. S. Berry	1919
Cooperative Group	J. F. Hosic	1930

tion, particularly where local conditions and support made innovations possible, and (2) the need to find an immediate solution to local problems affecting the school organization. It may be said that each of these began as an experiment—willingness to test new theories is one of the most fortunate characteristics of American education. The various plans are set forth in Table 14. We will examine some of those which have become better known and have influenced practice.

The Winnetka Plan. The widely heralded Winnetka plan was initiated by Burk in San Francisco in 1913. Under the direction of Washburne, it received its greatest development and recognition in

Winnetka, Illinois. Its fundamental objective is the adaptation of instruction to the abilities of pupils. Instruction thus becomes individualized. Operation made it necessary to devise an organization built around the curriculum. Hence, specially prepared materials have been developed and experiences provided through which each child passes in accordance with his abilities and needs, until he has reached a predetermined educational goal and achieved at least a degree of mastery of subject matter. The curriculum is divided into two parts: (1) the "common essentials," consisting of those knowledges and skills which presumably everyone needs to master, and (2) "the group and creative activities," which include development of appreciation of literature, music, and art, assemblies, handwork and projects, discussions, and those activities leading to harmony through group participation and having cultural and social values.

Pupils are classified largely on the basis of age and social maturity and proceed usually grade by grade. Room transfer, however, is easily accomplished. It is emphasized that progress is individual, with an absence of examination and the usual promotional standards. Flexibility is a major characteristic.

Essential features of the Winnetka technique have been widely adopted in several cities, notably Chicago, where it became known as the McDade plan. In this instance, instructional materials were organized into units of such a size that they could be readily fitted into the program of teaching of any child. This plan provides better selection of material for each child, and at the same time meets better the needs of schools which have large classes and which cannot effect a complete reorganization. However, as McGaughy points out, its influence is indirect and not highly important.[3] Perhaps the spirit and philosophy of the Winnetka technique have been of greater influence than its actual imitation or adaptation in other systems.

The Dalton Plan. The Dalton plan of school organization might well have been named the Parkhurst plan after its founder. Here too, is traceable the influence of Burk in regard to provision for individual differences of children in the elementary school. The Dalton plan is built upon this fundamental concept. Each subject in the curriculum is organized by the teacher into a series of "contracts," units of approximately a month's work, to be mastered before advancing.

---

[3] J. R. McGaughy, *An Evaluation of the Elementary School,* Indianapolis, The Bobbs-Merrill Company, 1937, p. 235.

Freedom is given to the child in arranging his time and plan of study. The school environment becomes a stimulating laboratory in which the teacher is a guide to learning rather than a hearer of lessons. Intervals of detailed testing afford the principal determinant of mastery.

As in the Winnetka technique, provision is made for unusual educational opportunities for children in the fine arts, music, and dramatics. Efforts have been made recently to encourage group activities to offset a highly individualized program.

On the whole, the Dalton plan has had little influence on the elementary school organization, although it has been widely adopted on secondary levels. Abroad, it has had widespread acceptance. Its chief advantages are initiative, a certain freedom of choice, an emphasis upon stimulating environments, subject matter mastery under guidance, and attention to individual differences. Its disadvantages lie in the authoritative control exercised by the teacher over the curriculum content, and the lack of group activity. Some writers have condemned its psychological basis as unacceptable.

The Cooperative Group Plan. Of unusual significance because it breaks sharply with the traditional organization of the elementary school is the cooperative group plan developed by Hosic and his associates at Columbia University.[4] His theories are predicated upon certain definite propositions.[5] Under this plan, the school is divided into several groups or platoons. Ideally, five class groups of at least two consecutive grades (in smaller schools three) would constitute a cooperative group. The material to be covered in these five groups is divided into five different parts and each of the five teachers is responsible for teaching that particular part of the curriculum of the five groups of children from the two or three grades of the school. These groups move from teacher to teacher throughout the school day.

Emphasis is placed on a cooperative arrangement of planning on the part of the five teachers in each group under one of their number who acts as chairman. Thus, one becomes responsible for English

---

[4] J. F. Hosic, L. T. Hopkins, and student committees, *The Cooperative Group Plan for the Organization of Elementary Schools,* New York, Bureau of Publications, Teachers College, Columbia University, 1931.

[5] For a summary of these, see Henry J. Otto, *Elementary School Organization and Administration,* D. Appleton-Century Company, 1944, pp. 137–138.

activities, another for number work and science, and another for arithmetic, each working over two grades. In this manner, there is a definite attempt to coordinate the work and educational experiences of children cooperatively, with the accent upon *group* rather than *grade* lines. The appropriate room environment of each teacher specialist with whom the several groups of children remain for part of the day is an outstanding feature.

The chief advantage of the plan is that teacher specialists work cooperatively with children in an environment conducive to learning. Children spend their time with as many as five teachers a day, which for elementary pupils may be of questionable merit. Disadvantages may accrue from the very nature of the cooperative principle itself, which may become perfunctory and superficial.

Other Unique Types of Elementary Organization. It will be of interest to mention, briefly, other types of elementary school organization which have attracted some attention. Los Angeles has been experimenting with a plan of organization based on classification of children into groups based on age, intelligence quotients, and scores on standardized tests in reading and arithmetic. Detroit has developed a plan of ability grouping known as the X-Y-Z plan with curriculum adaptations for each group. Although homogeneous grouping has had many adherents and has profoundly affected school organizations, it is pertinent to point out that its general acceptance is now declining rapidly, largely as a result of its artificiality and undemocratic and faulty philosophy. The all-year school in which the child attends either three or four quarters out of the whole year has been receiving some attention. Many schools have special classes organized for certain atypical groups.

Recently, observation has been directed to the operation of camps both associated with the public schools and organized under private auspices. These have as their purpose some educational function in providing developmental activities not possible in the day school, and in assisting maladjusted pupils to make some progress in their formal studies. A number of writers look optimistically to the time when a camp will be attached to every school as an essential part of the program.

Some school systems have been labeled "progressive." In view of the ambiguity in the use of the term, it is difficult to undertake any description of them as a type. Purporting to be based essentially on the philosophy of John Dewey, these schools exemplify, in reality, modifications of present practice in which the chief characteristics are greater attention to individual differences, stimulation of learning through self-directed purposeful activities, development of group consciousness, a new recognition of the child's personality and its proper development, opportunities for creative expression, and a happier and more responsible relationship with the home and community. One might use the phrase "child-centered" to describe the spirit of the "progressive" school organization.

Without doubt, the chief contribution of the "progressive" group has been its influence on the traditional school as a *leavening process* rather than in effecting a complete change of organization. While the traditional school organization and procedures are deeply rooted, students of the elementary school see marked changes in them as a result of these philosophies and experiments. There is definitely an attempt everywhere to choose the best out of these many plans and adapt them to the peculiar problems of each geographical and social setting. A stabilized elementary school population is assisting materially in the adjustment.

Organization Adapted to Classroom Situations

Departmentalization. One of the earlier attempts to secure improvement both in organization and in the teaching process through specialization is departmentalization. The approach was through existing subject matter, through the better utilization of the abilities of the instructor in teaching those subjects for which he seemed best fitted. Extensively practiced in the upper elementary grades, children move on schedule to different rooms. The advantages claimed are better teaching, better equipment, an enriched curriculum, promotion by subject, improved physical conditions for pupils, interest and stimulus of several teachers, and transition to high school attitude and methods. The arguments against the plan are that it tends to make teachers narrow, overburdens pupils, impairs discipline, overemphasizes knowledges, and destroys the unity of school life for the pupil.

The platoon school concept is an example of departmentalization carried to its extreme. Platoon schools were in extensive use two decades or more ago, but their number has now been sharply reduced.

The Self-Contained Classroom. One of the most significant devices in classroom organization yet developed in order to provide for the broad common interests of all pupils, and at the same time permit exploration of differences in abilities and aptitudes, is the self-contained classroom. Children with approximately the same social maturity are grouped under the continuous guidance of a single teacher. This group lives and works together democratically, just as they do in normal life situations. The school is the home for the children and the teacher is the adviser and counselor as well as instructor. Grouping within the unit is flexible, depending upon the activity at hand. Activities, as far as possible, are planned by the pupils and carried through by their cooperative efforts. Within the larger groups are smaller groups working together according to their needs and interests. Children individually can undertake projects and activities and are encouraged to do so. Promotional plans are directed by and related to the operation of the unit. Mastery is the ideal. Teachers can advance with the group one, two, or three years.

Continuity of Teacher and Pupil. One of the most promising developments from the standpoint of individual pupil progress pertains to experimentation in permitting teachers to progress with their pupils for periods up to six years. The modal practice seems to be three years. One advantage claimed for this plan is a better understanding of the child and his problems. Moreover, the teacher is required thereby to assume greater responsibility for each child's progress. Its chief objection, namely, the continuity of the incompetent teacher, is rather an advantage since it should serve to identify and eliminate her speedily.

FORMS OF SCHOOL ORGANIZATION FOR PRE-ELEMENTARY CHILDREN

The child-study movement of the past few decades, together with new forces and changing conditions, has brought about the extension of the organization of the elementary school downward. Studies in psychology have demonstrated that certain patterns become fixed in the child before the age of six years. The child requires more adequate medical observation and treatment in the years following birth. Home responsibility often does not fully provide for the changing social and economic life patterns.

The Kindergarten. The kindergarten attempts to give the child an education appropriate to his age and stage of development. Its dominant idea is natural but directed self-activity, definitely focused upon educational, social, and moral ends. A healthy body is the first concern. All of the child's natural powers must be developed, so that he is equipped to meet present and new situations adequately. While acquiring pertinent information, he is broadening his interests, improving in skills, learning to solve problems, developing a language, mingling socially, learning to work and share together. Learning to be happy himself, he is happy with others. All the while he learns to care for his own body, needs, and interests, gradually becoming normally self-sufficient.

Normally, the child enters the kindergarten at the age of four or five years and continues from one to two years until the age of first-grade entrance. The transfer from an environment of self-activity to one of rigidity in the traditional first grade has influenced markedly first-grade environment and patterns. The present trend is to co-ordinate closely the primary unit consisting of the kindergarten and the first two or three grades. This is accomplished through continuous teaching personnel and supervision, frequent intervisitation, similarity in equipment and plant facilities, and a merging of philosophical concepts.[6]

The Nursery School. The extension of the early childhood education downward did not stop at the kindergarten. Provision for the care and education of children from one to four or five years of age was taking form in many ways. Nursery schools developed in England as philanthropic endeavors during and following World War I. The importance of care for children of these tender years crystallized in the establishment of the first nursery school in New York City in 1919. The spread of the movement as educational in motive rather than philanthropic has been an interesting development in this country. One must study many influences to understand it.

Most nursery schools are to be found in metropolitan areas. Comparatively few are attached to or sponsored by public school systems, the greater number being sponsored by college organizations, welfare agencies, foundations, or private auspices. It can scarcely be said that the value of a nursery school training has caught hold of the public imagination. Moreover, there are many obstacles to its development

---

[6] Robert Hill Lane, *The Progressive Elementary School*, Boston, Houghton Mifflin Company, 1938, pp. 128–130, lists twenty specific suggestions for providing more continuity in the child's life on the lower primary (kindergarten-primary) level.

other than funds, among them transportation problems and reluctance of parents to permit attendance of such young children. The ages of children enrolled are usually from two years eight months to four years ten months. Besides, unless the kindergarten directly follows the nursery school, there is apt to be a decided break in the systematic habit development and learning experience.

Nursery school education emphasizes, first of all, a full and complete cooperation with the home, which should always remain the central influence in the young child's life. Healthy bodies, desirable qualities of mind and disposition, and acceptable individual and social behavior must be built. The teacher should represent a stabilizing rather than a dominating influence. Absence of formal instruction is conspicuous. Emphasis throughout is on an environment which will provide for right conditions of physical, mental, social, and moral growth adapted to the child's age and needs.[7]

Without doubt, the traditional elementary school with its more formal and rigid program has been profoundly influenced by the outcomes of the nursery school-kindergarten movement. Some aspects of this influence are building of proper personal and social habits, with a new emphasis on the necessary skills, orientation of the child in relation to his environment and cultural heritage, recognition of personality development, and, to accomplish it better, a happier and more wholesome relation with the home and community. The pity of it is that so few children, comparatively, have the advantage of these educational opportunities.

Early Childhood Education

Need for Integration. One of the most challenging as well as interesting current problems associated with elementary education is that of integrating more closely the work of its several units, namely, the nursery school, the kindergarten, and the primary school. Origi-

---

[7] The reader will find helpful information in the following references: Ilse Forest, *The School for the Child from Two to Eight,* Boston, Ginn and Company, 1935; Foster and Mattson, *Nursery School Education,* New York, D. Appleton-Century Company, 1939; Arnold Gesell, "Experimental Education and the Nursery School," *Journal of Educational Research,* September, 1926, pp. 81–87; Harriet Johnson, *Children in the Nursery School,* New York, The John Day Company, 1928; Cyrus Mead and Fred Orth, *The Transitional Public School,* New York, The Macmillan Company, 1934. See also Lane, *op. cit.,* pp. 51–54, for a concise account of a daily program in a nursery school.

nally, each of these units sprang from a different tradition as well as philosophy. The nursery school is definitely the outcome of modern scientific research in the field of child welfare. As its name implies, it endeavors to provide in the best possible manner for those needs of little children incident to that age and condition. As indicated above, it does not attempt any teaching procedures in the usual sense nor anticipate the work of the first grade. Rather, it emphasizes those principles of child growth and care capable of practical application in a suitable environment. The kindergarten grew up as a separate unit with a special function, namely, the development of Froebel's educational theories in the use of his games, gifts, and occupations. The new kindergarten, however, is recognized as a definite unit in the elementary school organization. Built upon a modern child psychological basis, it studies the whole child with a view to his growth and development. Activities, environment, and teaching procedures are adapted to this end. Perhaps its new spirit and environment are now its most distinguishing characteristics. The child's introduction to more formal educational processes becomes the task of the primary school.

A New Administrative Unit. Since the natural growth of the child through the years from two to eight, that is, through the years represented by these organizations, is the first consideration, every attempt should be made to smooth out that progress, through the removal of artificial and unrelated barriers of organization as well as philosophy. Integration of units has been suggested, through an organization designed for early childhood education which would provide for the child from the age of two through the primary school up to the age of about eight.

In order to accomplish this objective, it will be necessary to redefine the objectives of each unit and integrate their work to allow for normal school progress, with continual broadening and deepening of educational experience. Conflicting claims of each unit must give way to provision of those experiences which will contribute most effectively to the growth and development of the children.

Objectives. Attention should be given during early childhood education to the building of right personal and social habits, the acquisition of those skills deemed necessary in daily life, orientation in the environment as well as introduction to ever widening circles of social living, acquisition of such parts of our cultural heritage as the child can comprehend and assimilate, and development of individual talents and abilities.[8]

Characteristics. As we have indicated, the first step must be to break down artificial barriers within the unit. Unified control will facilitate the process. Many "progressive" schools have made rapid strides in this direction. Teachers themselves will need to reevaluate both their philosophies and their teaching habits. Some schools are eliminating the term "grades" as deterring the movement, and substituting "age groups" or other classifications which seem better adapted to growth. Accurate and significant records will need to be kept and continuous child study made on the several age levels. These aspects will become the basis of new guidance procedures and activities.

LATER CHILDHOOD EDUCATION

The education of children from the ages of eight to twelve has tended more and more to follow patterns of subject matter teaching. In the fourth, fifth, and sixth grades departmentalized methods have become more or less characteristic. Gradually, the teacher has tended to forget earlier emphasis upon pupil growth and development and begun to emphasize "progress" measured by "mastery" of lessons to be learned in an increasingly formalized program.

The principles indicated in the preceding section have equal application here. Subject matter concepts should be subordinated to child growth concepts. Grade barriers and fixed patterns of learning should give way to individual and group needs in which personalities of teachers and pupils mingle to the mutual benefit of all. Throughout there should be a building of right personal and social habits, acquisition of useful skills and the culture heritage, orientation in the world about him, and development of innate abilities and personality.

THE RURAL SCHOOL CHILD AND CONSOLIDATION

The Problem. Rural schools are responsible for the early education of slightly more than half the nation's children. These children come largely from the open country or from about 20,000 little villages which are themselves essentially rural in character. With the in-

---

[8] Probably the best reference for this movement is Ilse Forest, *op. cit.* See also Robert Hill Lane, *op. cit.,* chap. iv.

creasing tendency for urban dwellers to move out into the open country and shuttle back and forth to their non-farm occupations, the non-farm rural population has increased. Small school buildings to the number of about 200,000, 85 per cent of all school buildings in the United States, house these more than 13,000,000 children. Most numerous are one-teacher schools. There are nearly 45,000 elementary schools having more than one teacher and about 27,000 combined elementary and high schools and separate high schools. The average enrollment in the one-teacher schools is about seventeen pupils, with one school in four serving less than ten pupils.

The Teacher. Rural schools require the services of about 465,000 teachers, about 53 per cent of the combined rural and urban teaching staff. These teachers are the lowest paid and poorest prepared, hold the lowest forms of teaching certificates, have the least experience, stay in one teaching position the shortest length of time, and give perhaps the least satisfactory teaching service, with the poorest supervision, of any group of teachers. These are startling indictments, reflections not so much on the teachers as on our states, which permit the continued neglect of the educational birthright of the country's children.

Deficiencies of Rural School Education.[9] And yet there is still more to the story of neglect. These rural children are denied the share of proper school support to which they are rightfully entitled along with their city cousins. Lack of it has resulted in bleak, unattractive school buildings which are often menaces to health and safety; insufficient and unsuitable equipment and supplies; short school terms; absence of library facilities; lack of health services and other remedial care of the children; meager school programs largely confined to traditional academic exercises; insufficient number of high schools; absence of any attempt to relate the work to the interests, needs, and experiences of the children; and instruction by relatively untrained, immature, inexperienced, and underpaid teachers, many of whom are waiting for the first opportunity to secure a teaching position in a near-by town or city. Of course, there are bright spots in the picture and much work has been done to improve rural education, but these conditions are still typical.

[9] For a more complete analysis of present conditions in the rural schools, the reader should consult "Progress in Rural Education," *Research Bulletin,* National Education Association, XVIII, No. 4, September, 1940.

Several other factors are of importance in improving rural education. Rural children usually enter school later than city children owing largely, because of their immaturity, to the distance factor. They have not had the facilities for any form of pre-school education. Their attendance is less regular (by about 3 per cent). They attend for a school term of 163.9 days as compared with 181.6 days for city children. More than 18 per cent of all rural children are not enrolled in school at all. A smaller percentage (by 7.4 per cent) attend high school, and a larger number leave as soon as the compulsory age limit permits.

Consolidation. Perhaps the most significant movement for the betterment of the education of the rural school child is consolidation. It is estimated that consolidation has reduced the number of rural school buildings by over 21,000 between 1930 and 1940. From 1930 to 1934, the number of one-teacher schools declined about 10,000 while the number of two-teacher and other forms of consolidation increased by 2850. The movement has gone forward most rapidly in the northeastern and southeastern states and least rapidly in the northwestern states. There are limits to it, especially as it refers to conditions of topography and population. Coupled with the school consolidation movement are other administrative improvements, such as larger administrative units, merging of districts, creation of larger attendance units, and, above everything, the rapid advance of school transportation.

Advantages of Consolidation. It should be to the advantage of our nation to maintain the permanent quality of our rural population, more especially our rural school children. The educational advantages of consolidation aid in bringing this about. These advantages are better instruction through better grouping; better teachers and teaching conditions; more adequate school facilities and supplies, textbooks, and equipment; broader curricular offerings; more effective supervision; richer cultural and activity offerings; improved attendance; and better health measures and sanitation. Moreover, consolidation broadens the social relationships of children, makes possible library, science, and other school facilities, provides a more attractive school environment, gives greater opportunities for a high school education, and equalizes educational opportunity among all children. Communities are brought together in widening areas. Rural life is improved and maintained through the many other educational and social opportunities available as a result of the improved school program.

Hindrances. The chief hindrances to consolidation are community jealousies and rivalries, poor roads, natural barriers, sparsity of population, and public indifference. Transportation as a hindrance has been largely overcome.

Every person interested in childhood should be concerned with the betterment of rural life, and with making education contribute to the welfare of all its children. Consolidation of schools offers one of the principal means to this end.

Improving the One-Teacher School

In spite of marked improvements to rural education through consolidation, noteworthy as they are, it is essential to point out that comparatively little has been done when one considers that the one-teacher school is still the typical school building in the United States. For instance, in thirteen states, in 1936, more than two-thirds of all the public schools were of the one-teacher type.[10] Of greater significance is the fact that nearly all of these will continue as one-teacher schools because of distance, topography, race, disinterest, and lack of support. In areas served by these schools birth rates are high and ability to support is low. The problem then is to do something about the one-teacher school as an institution.

Considerable improvement has been brought about in recent years as to classroom procedures, courses of study, condition of school buildings (largely with the use of federal funds), better transportation, better public relations, improved health and sanitation programs, and free textbooks. Efforts are being made to secure better-educated rural teachers, pay them adequate salaries, provide better supervision, and improve social conditions in order to make life more attractive. Better instructional supplies are being made available to teachers. The rural school is becoming better adapted through libraries, practical arts, socializing activities, adaptation of individualized programs, and parental relationship. These movements are proving conclusively that excellent teaching is possible in a one-

---

[10] W. H. Gaumnitz, *Are the One-Teacher Schools Passing?* Federal Security Agency, Pamphlet 92, Washington, United States Office of Education, 1940. See also G. A. Works and S. O. Lesser, *Rural America Today,* Chicago, University of Chicago Press, 1942.

teacher school. Assuming adequate teaching, the chief problem is to develop an adequate curriculum harmonized with a comprehensive school program and geared to the social environment of that particular school situation.

ELEMENTARY EDUCATION, THE PARENT, AND THE COMMUNITY

At the most, the child spends not more than 11 per cent of his time in school. Most of the remainder is spent either in the home or under parental influence and control. Formerly, about the only contact which the school had with the home was through reports of various kinds. The home manifested little concern in the educational process. The modern school program presents a marked contrast to its prototype. The modern parent is becoming more and more an interested and intelligent partner with the teacher and administrator in the education of the child. Formerly shunned, the parent's partnership and actual participation are now welcomed, especially as the functions of the educational process are broadened.

Aspects of Parental Partnership. There are several aspects of this partnership. First, parental cooperation is essential in regard to the general education aspects of the school's program such as health, moral training, recreation, and the various activities in the home. Where home assignments are concerned, the parent needs enlightenment, and his cooperation must be sought. Second, modern education becomes a real cooperative process. The school needs to be concerned as to the place of the home and the parent, while the parent must recognize the place of the school. Moreover, the school needs to know the techniques used in the home for child rearing and the relationship which they bear to those used in the school. Problem cases need a specific and sympathetic kind of cooperation. Most important is that movement which has as its objective the study of the child in partnership, in order to bring about a better understanding of the services each is trying to perform. In many communities parents are taking a direct hand in the educational processes in an organized way, insisting upon desirable and adequate educational procedures, philosophies, and facilities. In other communities they are actually establishing their own schools, or are otherwise actively influencing the school through direct participation.

Parent Education. Two vital aspects of this movement may be indicated as parent education and child study. Both have for their purpose a better understanding between parents and child. Parents need to learn from their children just as much as children learn from their parents. Mothers and fathers, too, are eager to know how to bring up their children right. Parent education deals more specifically with this aspect. The child must be studied. Fundamental relationships must be understood, the parent's own life, personality, and experiences reviewed and interpreted, and the child considered in the light of his whole environment. Throughout, there are parent-parent relationships, parent-child relationships, parent-teacher relationships, and those relationships which the child may have within the family group and the community. Parent education may be conceived as family adjustment to the many facets of the environment in which the family finds itself. Just as the child is better understood, so is the parent better adjusted. The result is a better basis for a successful partnership.

Plans for Achieving These Purposes. Recently, plans have been developed for achieving proper cooperation among those concerned in the education and welfare of the child. Possibly the most significant is the parent-teacher association, now common in most school systems. Some have felt that this organization, although possessing considerable merit in achieving these objectives, does not provide for that intimate association which seems so necessary in parent-child-school relationships. Other forms of organization have come into being: In parent councils, organized around a home room, grade, or small group, parents and teachers are brought together in small groups for friendly discussion and counsel. Occasionally, representative groups of the home and school assemble for similar intimate study. Both mothers' and fathers' clubs and councils have been used with success. Some communities utilize an already successful organization, as a Women's Club or Grange, which provides a means for closer association in the interests of the child. Neighborhood groups, either already formed or brought together for the occasion, can be utilized. Informal gatherings of parents around the teacup bring about a better understanding concerning childhood where the interest is child-centered and the spirit of the occasion is helpful and cooperative.

Community Child Welfare Activities. Community emphasis on child welfare has extended to many other services of interest and value to the school and the home. These include pre- and post-natal care for mothers, infant centers for the teaching of child hygiene to young mothers, clinics for medical care and instruction, free information on child care, day nurseries, and availability of the facilities of numerous institutions, organizations, and agencies for the care and protection of childhood. Usually found in urban centers, these services touch the schools at many points.

QUESTIONS AND PROBLEMS

1. What is meant by the sentence, "An adequate school organization is essential to continuous pupil progress"?
2. In your judgment, do state laws and regulations help or hinder the development of a good school organization?
3. What are the chief points of excellence in the traditional elementary school of eight grades; its deficiencies? To what extent is an elementary school of six grades a more satisfactory organization?
4. To what extent do any of the newer forms of school organization meet the needs of elementary pupils?
5. Point out the chief characteristics of each of the forms of school organization indicated in the table.
6. What possibilities do you see for the future of the Winnetka plan? The Dalton plan? The cooperative group plan? Would these plans succeed in your own school community? Explain your answer.
7. What is the chief weakness in the progressive school concept?
8. Compare older and newer conceptions of the kindergarten movement.
9. How do you account for the slow progress of the nursery school movement?
10. What reeducation, if any, is necessary for a teacher who is assigned to a different type of school organization?
11. What future possibilities do you see for a form of school organization which will smooth out the educational progress of all children from the ages of two to eight?
12. What are the chief objectives of parent education? Indicate some of the ways in which they are being realized. Indicate some writers and speakers in this field.
13. Point out the educational disadvantages of the rural child. To what extent is the consolidation movement solving these problems?
14. Review the principles of the Children's Charter. To what extent is it possible to plan a school organization on the elementary level to meet these principles and objectives? To what extent is it being done?

SELECTED REFERENCES

1. Brueckner, Leo J., and others, *The Changing Elementary School.* The Regents' Inquiry. New York: Inor Publishing Company, 1939, especially part i.
2. Caswell, Hollis J., *Education in the Elementary School.* New York: American Book Company, 1942, chaps. ii, x.
3. Elsbree, Willard S., *Pupil Progress in the Elementary School.* New York: Bureau of Publications, Teachers College, Columbia University, 1943.
4. Forest, Ilse, *The School for the Child from Two to Eight.* Boston: Ginn and Company, 1935. In addition to being an excellent reference, this book includes an ample bibliography.
5. Foster, J. C., and Headley, N. E., *Education in the Kindergarten.* New York: American Book Company, 1936.
6. Foster, J. C., and Mattson, M. L., *Nursery School Education.* New York: D. Appleton-Century Company, 1939.
7. Johnson, Harriet, *School Begins at Two.* New York: New Republic, 1936.
8. Lane, Robert Hill, *The Principal in the Modern Elementary School.* Boston: Houghton Mifflin Company, 1944.
9. Lane, Robert Hill, *The Progressive Elementary School.* Boston: Houghton Mifflin Company, 1938, chaps. i, ii, iii.
10. Lewis, Charles D., *The Rural Community and Its Schools.* New York: American Book Company, 1937, chaps. iv, vi, ix, xi.
11. McGaughy, J. R., *An Evaluation of the Elementary School.* Indianapolis: The Bobbs-Merrill Company, 1937, especially chaps. iii, vi, vii, ix.
12. "Organization, Administration, and Supervision of Education," *Review of Educational Research,* October, 1946.
13. Otto, Henry J., *Elementary School Organization and Administration.* New York: D. Appleton-Century Company, 1944, chaps. ii, iv.
14. "Progress in Rural Education," *Research Bulletin,* National Education Association, XVIII, No. 4, September, 1940.
15. Reavis, William C., Pierce, Paul R., and Stullkin, Edward H., *The Elementary School: Its Organization and Administration.* Chicago: University of Chicago Press, 1938.
16. Riebe, H. A., Nelson, M. J., and Kittrell, C. A., *The Classroom.* New York: The Cordon Company, 1938, chaps. i, iv.
17. "Schools for a New World," *Twenty-Fifth Yearbook,* American Association of School Administrators. Washington: National Education Association, 1947.

18. "Schools in Small Communities," *Seventeenth Yearbook,* American Association of School Administrators. Washington: National Education Association, 1939, chaps. ii, ix.
19. Wofford, Kate V., *Modern Education for the Small Rural School.* New York: The Macmillan Company, 1938.

CHAPTER XXVI

School Organization in Relation to the Administrative Function— The Secondary School

THE American secondary school grew out of the early Latin school, traceable to English origins, and the academy. The public high school made its appearance in 1821 in Boston and by 1860 was rather common in the New England states. It was not, however, until the famous Kalamazoo decision in 1874, which paved the way for its public support, that the high school became definitely a part of the public school system. This decision is an important milestone in that public responsibility for the secondary education of all youth was now assumed to be implemented by public funds. By 1890, the high school was accepted in every state as a part of the state school system, being provided by law in most states. Thus, the rising high school came to supplant the declining academy in supplying secondary education. It is the purpose of this chapter to discuss the nature of the organization of the secondary school and its facilities as an institution for the education of adolescent youth.

REORGANIZATION OF SECONDARY EDUCATION

The Traditional High School. By 1890 the American high school had come to assume a definite pattern, that of a four-year institution, enrolling adolescents from thirteen or fourteen years of age who continued their education for approximately four years. Its dominant offerings were dictated largely by the colleges whose academic patterns were still characteristic of their liberal arts heritage. The very nature of these academic offerings in both public and private secondary schools made entrance to and retention in these institutions a highly selective process. Selection functioned at the point of entrance through examinations and at various points in the youth's educational progress through elimination in one form or another. In 1900 one in ten young persons of the age group from fourteen to seventeen years was enrolled in high school.

Changing Conditions. After the turn of the present century the secondary school broadened greatly in scope, functions, and enrollments. Naturally, increased enrollments brought many different types of secondary youth, differing as to ability, characteristics, social status, and educational needs. The very apparency of these differences called attention to them and stressed the need for closer study.

Scrutiny of the Elementary School. As secondary school enrollments grew, the eight-year elementary school began to be scrutinized with great care. Its upper grades disclosed large numbers of adolescent and retarded children. Larger numbers upon graduation were not attracted to, or could not be absorbed into, the high schools. Moreover, it seemed that the repetitive exercises of the seventh and eighth grades were not fitted to the needs of these youth, who were bored with an ill-adapted curriculum and a stern discipline. Their minds were elsewhere. The farm and industry called, perhaps also new-found leisure. Educators began to sense these imminent problems. Could not the work of the elementary school be accomplished just as well in less time? Should not the objectives of the elementary school be redefined? After all, nature had marked off a line of demarcation at about twelve years of age which, it seemed, should logically terminate one's elementary education. The elementary school could not possibly provide for a school population growing rapidly because of a heightened birth rate and the larger families of immigrants.

The New Secondary School Pattern. Meanwhile, existing high school facilities could not adequately take care of the large numbers already seeking entrance. How could the high schools provide for the additional youth who would be transferred from the elementary schools? The answer seemed logical. Construct a new form of school in which should be housed all children now ready for the seventh grade, as well as all adolescent children who might well profit by a revised curriculum, method, and environment better adapted to their needs.

Thus, secondary education was reorganized to absorb the seventh and eighth grades of the traditional elementary school and now comprised six years—grades seven through twelve. The nature of the secondary school organization varied, of necessity, according to the peculiar needs, conditions, and plant facilities of the community. Definite dividing patterns began to emerge, prominent among which was the junior high school of three years—grades seven, eight, and nine. In many places, the old high school building was used to house the assorted groups who were collected therein, and a new building was erected for the senior high school, now composed of grades ten, eleven, and twelve. Where new junior high school buildings were erected, earnest efforts were made to provide new facilities to fit the needs of these newly formed groups. Where sufficiently large enrollments were not available, as in many smaller communities, the new pattern took the form of a six-year high school, composed of grades seven through twelve, organized through the simple expedient of transferring the seventh and eighth grades with their teachers to the high school building and placing them all on a unified schedule and administration. Here and there, new buildings or additions to the old ones provided the needed housing facilities. Occasionally the old high school became an elementary school. Quite often, owing to geographical or other factors, secondary schools came to be made up of various combinations of grades, sometimes including the sixth grade.

Classification of Secondary Schools

Classification by Organization. High schools are usually classified according to the number of grades included. Through the years the standard secondary school of the United States has been a four-year high school consisting of grades nine to twelve, corresponding very closely to the chronological ages of adolescent children from thirteen or fourteen to seventeen or eighteen years.

The typical junior high school, as it developed, came to include grades seven to nine. However, other combinations appeared, as seven and eight, seven through ten, and six through eight. A popular movement in smaller school districts has been to attach the reorganized seventh and eighth grades to the high school, which then included grades seven to twelve and became known as the junior-senior high school. After grade nine was attached to the junior high school, the abbreviated upper organization became known as the more dignified senior high school.

It is important to emphasize that population and geographical distribution have often necessitated high schools of smaller size. The majority of American high schools (about 65 per cent) have enrollments of less than 200 pupils, and about 40 per cent have less than 100. One may find many variations in organization and type in smaller communities and rural areas. Consolidation and transportation are pointing the way to more advantageous reorganization in these districts. However, the high school should remain small enough to permit the unfolding of the pupil's personality in an environment suitable to his needs and interests, yet be large enough to provide a program of variety and high quality. The very large high school can scarcely be said to accomplish the former purpose.

Classification by Type. High schools have been classified into three groups: those that provide (1) general education, (2) special types of education, and (3) a comprehensive program, both general and specialized.[1] General secondary schools include the older types of public and private schools, whose major functions are preparation for college and provision for a terminal general education. Usually these schools have a long academic tradition. Schools of the second type are those whose organization and curriculum provide: (*a*) vocational training, as commercial or trade schools, and (*b*) specialized training for particular needs, as for the blind and deaf, delinquent youth, or others. There is an increasing tendency in these schools to emphasize the vocational aspects of secondary education.

The comprehensive secondary school representing the third type is becoming more characteristic, especially in the smaller cities and towns. It combines the general and specialized types of education, attempting to provide for the educational needs of all children. Recent efforts to substitute a single core curriculum with wide freedom of elective choices for the more restricted multiple curriculum have resulted in a program admirably adapted to the varying needs

[1] E. D. Grizzell, *American Secondary Education,* New York, Thomas Nelson and Sons, 1937, pp. 228 ff.

of youth of secondary school ages, especially in typical schools. *Classification by Control and Support.* A third basis for the classification of secondary schools is by control and support. Two groups are noted. The first includes high schools supported entirely by public funds and controlled by local boards of education under state direction. Most high schools are in this group. All non-public high schools are included in the second group, which is composed of privately supported secondary schools controlled by religious denominations, higher institutions of learning, and private individuals, groups, or corporations. Many of these schools are of long standing and have commendable traditions. Some have developed because of religious preference, such as parochial high schools under control of the Catholic church; others, such as country day schools, have developed because of dissatisfaction with "mass education" in the public high schools.[2] Without doubt, experimental schools, as many of the latter group are declared to be, have a definite place in an organized scheme of American secondary education. At the same time, the state cannot exercise its police power to the extent of prohibiting private schools altogether,[3] since this directly interferes with the liberty of parents and guardians to direct the upbringing and education of children under their control.

The Evening High School. The evening high school is now an established institution in larger urban centers. There are public evening high schools, regularly organized and meeting in school buildings operating under the auspices of the local school authorities, as well as private evening schools with varied offerings. Public evening high schools may be standardized or non-standardized; the former conform to state standards and may be fully accredited. It is important to point out that, obviously, many smaller towns having some form of evening high school opportunities have not been included in United States Office of Education statistics, possibly because they are not standardized. In addition it should be noted that the pupil turnover is much greater in the evening high school than in the day school; that the typical evening school enrollment is for a shorter duration of time; and that the typical subject offerings are fewer than in the typical day school.

[2] E. D. Grizzell, *op. cit.,* pp. 232–233.

[3] *Pierce* vs. *Society of the Sisters of the Holy Names of Jesus and Mary,* 268 U.S. 510, 45 S. Ct. 571, 69 L. Ed. 1070, 39 A.L.R. 468.

Non-Public Schools Offering Secondary Education

Formerly, the concept of free public school education did not extend to secondary education. The academy, the symbol of secondary education in the United States, for many years was privately controlled and operated. Back of this tradition is the long line of celebrated English "public schools," in reality privately controlled academies, as well as many other schools offering secondary education, similarly controlled. In America, the private academy took the form of (1) the New England college preparatory school; (2) the academy, both college preparatory and offering a terminal education; (3) the military school, found largely in the south; (4) the church school, usually under the direct control of a religious denomination and attached to a denominational college; (5) commercial schools, sometimes designated as colleges, offering extensive training in various forms of business education; (6) the parochial high school; or (7) a miscellaneous group of schools offering various types of education to secondary youth, principally vocational and cultural, among which might be mentioned music conservatories, art schools, and trade schools.

Varied Types. The student of these forms of secondary education is struck by the great changes that have taken place with respect to educational facilities for adolescent youth. Numerous college preparatory academies have disappeared before the developing high school movement until now comparatively few such strong institutions remain. Many of them are endowed and operate for youth of certain social and economic groups. Most of the earlier academies were transformed into high schools. The military schools seem to have survived in sections where social and racial distinctions are pronounced. Both the military school and the academy appear to have their place under special conditions such as loss of parents, broken homes, family traditions or disturbances, disciplinary exigencies, or preference for the particular form of training provided. Perhaps a love of the uniform should not be overlooked. Church schools, largely preparatory and attached to denominational colleges, have largely disappeared, but a few remain here and there.

Commercial Schools. Although not as numerous as formerly, when they provided an intensive course of business education for an expanding industrial era and guaranteed a position upon graduation, commercial schools have played an important role not generally taken on by public high schools. As public high and evening schools provided more effective commercial courses without tuition charges, the weaker commercial schools were gradually eliminated. Those that survived strengthened their courses, offering a type of training suited to the needs of high school drop-outs, high school graduates, and those who wanted specific intensive training in one or more phases of business education.

The Catholic Parochial High Schools. The number of and enrollment in parochial high schools have steadily increased owing largely to the policy of the Roman Catholic Church to extend upward the education of children under religious control. Parochial education is also provided by other denominational groups, as the Friends and Seventh-Day Adventists.

Purposes of Non-Public Schools Offering Secondary Education. It is important to point out that the private secondary school offers types of educational service either not available in the public high schools or more adequately fitted to the needs of certain groups. The principle of parental preference may operate in the selection of the particular school. Family tradition is a factor. Dormitory life may be more expedient, especially where there is an absence of desirable home and parental environment. In some instances, the quality of instruction is admittedly superior. Many schools provide intensive instruction for college entrance or other examinations. Sometimes employment is provided, especially for older young men and women.

Control. Most states exercise some form of control over non-public high schools, extending to incorporation, inspection, compulsory education enforcement, standardization, and in some instances supervision. On the whole, however, it may be said that the control is more nominal than actual. These schools are largely supported by tuition, fees, gifts, and endowments. Attempts at partial or complete state support have met with little success.

Reorganization of Secondary Education on the Upper Levels

Colleges generally have welcomed the junior college as a selective agency for its hosts of applicants, excepting, of course, where it has become a competing institution. Opportunity is offered for at least a partial college education to thousands of young people to whom the advantages of a higher education would not otherwise be available because of expense, distance, or other reasons. Many junior colleges have assumed a definite vocational nature, preparing their students for professions and trades, at the same time retaining a definite liberal training. Pre-professional training is offered to those who de-sire to profit by it. Perhaps the greatest value to the parent lies in the fact that the son or daughter can remain under the parental roof during those later adolescent years for closer parental oversight. The cost of a college education is thus so reduced that its opportunities can be extended to a larger number of young people.

Proponents of the upward extension of secondary education have proposed that the junior high school, based on an elementary pro-gram of six years, be extended to include the tenth grade, and that a four-year senior high school-junior college be superimposed on the junior high school. This is known as the 6-4-4 plan. Reorganization of the educational program is then made within both institutions. For this plan it is claimed that problems of articulation inherent in the 6-3-3-4 plan of organization are largely relieved; that the sopho-more year, which is typically early adolescent, *ought* to be joined with the junior high school; that the eleventh and twelfth (high school) grades are better coordinated with the thirteenth and four-teenth (junior college) grades in a single unit dealing with problems of middle and later adolescence. Moreover, organization, personnel, and curriculum are better adapted and administered in a system of this type. The recent proposals of the Educational Policies Commis-sion with reference to the community institute give an example of this movement.

FUTURE PLANNING

The typical secondary school is still dominated by an educational pattern far removed from the concept of a school for all American youth, whose purpose is to fit them fundamentally for desirable com-munity living and understanding. Much educational planning and action need to be done in order to accomplish the true purpose of secondary education in a democracy. In its accomplishment there must be brought about as never before an integration of every avail-able human and social resource. To a considerable extent the re-sponsibility rests with the secondary school teacher.[4]

---

[4] William A. Yeager, "New Horizons for the Teacher," *Bulletin of the National Association of Secondary School Principals*. March, 1945.

There are several points where adjustments should be made in the secondary school program to meet changing conditions. (1) Increased enrollments due to a great influx of adolescents in the secondary schools will bring in their wake a great variety of individual adjustment problems. These should be reflected in a modified school organization. An excellent example of what can be done is the adapted school organization and program which has been developed to meet the needs of service men and women. (2) The secondary school must give more consideration to older youth, those with peculiar problems as well as those who present marked deviation in any form. This may require adjustments in organization and program to provide more individual attention, and adaptation of materials and methods of instruction earlier in the school life of the adolescent. Other suggestions are: (*a*) more differentiated curricula based on pupil needs and community living and including short-unit courses; (*b*) longer school days; (*c*) summer schools, including camps; (*d*) greater development of late afternoon and evening courses; (*e*) district vocational high schools, especially in rural areas. (3) In order to provide for vocational opportunities the work-experience program, both in school and in the community, should be developed. (4) A well-organized counseling and placement program should have a conspicuous place in the secondary school. (5) There should be a marked development of the health, physical education, and recreational programs. It is a matter of general agreement that the physical conditioning of American youth should proceed apace. (6) If a new world order is to have a stable international basis, the secondary school must have an important place in its development.

QUESTIONS AND PROBLEMS

1. Make a list of as many different groupings of secondary school organizations as you can locate in practice. What appear to be the effects of these different types on school progress?
2. Make a chart indicating several types of individual differences of secondary youth, and point out corresponding school provision for each.
3. Select a high school of appropriate size and evaluate it as an optimum institution for the education of adolescent youth.
4. Evaluate the theories on which the non-public secondary school is defended.

5. Compare the advantages and disadvantages of the 6-3-3-2 plan as compared with the 6-4-4 plan. What is the outlook for the junior college?

6. What are the contributions of accrediting agencies to secondary education? Select *one* such agency and study its standards. What are the contributions of the Cooperative Study of Secondary School Standards? To what extent is an evaluation through this procedure helpful?

7. What controls are exercised in your state through the state supervisory function?

8. Plan a type of organization for secondary youth which seems best to provide for continuous educational progress.

SELECTED REFERENCES

1. Bent, Rudyard K., and Kronenberg, Henry H., *Principles of Secondary Education.* New York: McGraw-Hill Book Company, 1941, chap. iv.

2. "Changing Conceptions in Educational Administration," *Forty-Fifth Yearbook,* National Society for the Study of Education. Washington: National Education Association, 1946, parts ii, iii.

3. Edmonson, J. B., Roemer, Joseph, and Bacon, Francis L., *The Administration of the Modern Secondary School.* New York: The Macmillan Company, 1941, chaps. iv, xxvi.

4. Educational Policies Commission, *Education for All American Youth.* Washington: National Education Association, 1944.

5. Kyte, George C., *The Principal at Work.* Boston: Ginn and Company, 1941, chap. vii.

6. Moehlman, Arthur B., *School Administration.* Boston: Houghton Mifflin Company, 1940, chap. xxiv.

7. Mort, Paul R., *Principles of School Administration.* New York: McGraw-Hill Book Company, 1946.

8. *Planning for American Youth.* Washington: National Association of Secondary School Principals, 1944.

9. Rice, G. A., Conrad, C. C., and Fleming, Paul, *The Administration of Public High Schools Through Their Personnel.* New York: The Macmillan Company, 1933, chap. ii.

10. Struck, F. Theodore, *Vocational Education for a Changing World.* New York: John Wiley and Sons, 1945.

11. White, Robert, Jr., "Feasibility of 6-4-4 Reorganization in School Systems with Junior Colleges," *School Review,* March, 1946, pp. 140–147.

12. Wiley, George M., *The Redirection of Secondary Education*. New York: The Macmillan Company, 1940, chap. vii.
13. Witham, Ernest C., "What Size High School," *School Executive,* June, 1943, pp. 32–34.

Note: The following periodicals should be found helpful in studying secondary school organization (see *Education Index*): *School Review; Bulletin of the National Association of Secondary School Principals; The Clearing House; The Junior College.*

CHAPTER XXVII

Organizing the Pupil Personnel Services

THROUGHOUT this text we have been considering the various elements associated with the pupil personnel function. It should be helpful to review the definition of this function, namely, the provision for those services and activities pertaining to the welfare of childhood and youth, both within the school and within the community, to the immediate end that the abilities, interests, and needs of each child are realized and his greater development and good achieved, and to the ultimate end that all pupils can become happy, useful, and contributing members of ever larger social groups. This is an important assignment for the administrator and indicates the broad approach essential as he begins the task of organizing the function. We want to emphasize here that this text conceives this function to be of broad and far-reaching scope. Its effectiveness can only be realized accordingly.

This chapter proposes to discuss the principles essential to organizing the pupil personnel function, together with elements necessary to effective service. Application of these principles and elements will then be made to types of organizations adapted to school districts by size and function. Procedures in setting up programs will be proposed.

PRINCIPLES ESSENTIAL TO THE ORGANIZATION OF THE SERVICES

Philosophical Approach. Throughout this book we have been indicating the elements essential to the pupil administrative function, together with the principles which should govern the operation of each. Pervading this function there has been the fundamental philosophy[1] that education is a social process in which the child comes more and more to share in the total community consciousness of which he is definitely a part. Each child has his own personality pattern, the development of which is his own natural right and society's obligation. This involves the *whole child* concept. Education has its obligation to develop him physically, mentally, socially, morally, emotionally, and spiritually. To this end the integrative approach is essential, and education must be conceived as a *cooperative process,* not only within the school but within the school community. The school is but one agency in this process, although it must assume the responsibility for directing it. The home also is definitely accountable and must be constantly strengthened. The community has its responsibility. The problem is to coordinate all desirable learning situations with responsibilities for them into an educational pattern so that the stated objectives may be realized.

Since the administrative process begins with the location and assumption of leadership, authority, and responsibility, he who undertakes it must naturally accept a pervading philosophical approach. Having done so, he is ready to plan his organization and create the essential environment.

Principles of Action. The following principles of action are essential in setting up the required pupil personnel function and its administration:

1. Providing for the pupil personnel service is essentially an administrative function. This principle involves acceptance of the leadership responsibility. It assumes understanding of the task at hand and a determination to fulfill it. It assumes a sympathetic acceptance of a liberal attitude toward the child and his problems, bathed in the *whole child* concept.

2. A democratic form of organization must be set up in order to achieve the best results, and must be administered according to democratic principles.

3. Selection and assignment of personnel should be approached in a spirit of cooperative endeavor. Naturally, the lines of administrative authority and responsibility must be maintained in ac-

---

[1] For a more thorough treatment of this philosophical approach see William A. Yeager, *Home-School-Community Relations,* Pittsburgh, University Book Store, 1939, chap. xvi.

cordance with good practice. Everyone associated with the educational function has his place; the task is to find and develop it.

4. The organization for the pupil personnel services should be geared to the general school organization and should be in harmony with it. This involves a clear conception of the *total* educational function and the relation of pupil personnel to it. Overlapping functions may be difficult to dispose of. In some cases they may not be too important.

5. The plan of organization should be adapted specifically to the school community. At the same time, it should be flexible, avoiding the fatal tendency toward smugness and indifference to change.

6. Every plan of organization should include *all* elements necessary to the service somewhere in the total educational pattern. This does not mean that each local district must make provision for all elements within it. In smaller districts a larger area, as a county or state, must supplement local initiative. The point is that every child should receive that personnel service to which he is entitled.

7. Personnel should be chosen for peculiar fitness in order to make the greatest contributions to the program as a whole. This applies to both specialists and regular teachers. There should be no fear or favor in effecting change in personnel where the greater development of boys and girls is concerned. In fact, this should be one effective way to isolate incompetence. As education becomes more and more a profession, the competence of its staff members should increase.

8. Duties and responsibilities should be definitely assigned to each member of the staff. The assignment of these duties should be, in part, a cooperative process.

9. Development of the staff in service is just as important as that of the pupils. If the staff members do not develop on their own initiative, adequate forms of stimulation should be provided by the administrator to bring about the necessary action.

10. State laws and regulations should be thoroughly understood and applied in practice. State services should be geared to local services and every advantage taken locally to implement them.

11. Since education is a service, it is natural that its several functions should be scientifically approached. This applies no less to

pupil personnel. The service should be stimulated constantly through research and practice.

12. The pupil personnel service may necessitate higher costs for its installation and operation. This fact should not be a deterrent in the organization and administration; rather the outcome as determined and later realized should be considered a better investment of the pupils' time and the taxpayers' money.

13. The program, as it is placed in operation, must be adapted to the particular and peculiar needs of all pupils, without injustice to race, color, or social or economic status. No individual has a prior right where the cause of democracy is conceived.

14. Some plan of evaluative procedure should be set up to scrutinize the administration of the pupil personnel function. Everyone associated with the function should view this aspect as an essential part of his own job.

Elements Essential in the Organization and Administration of the Services

With the acceptance of an adequate philosophical approach to the organization and administration of the pupil personnel function, and a knowledge of the essential principles of action, the administration is now ready for the next step, namely, a review of the elements essential to the program. These elements have been developed throughout this text and will now be reviewed.

1. *The Attendance Function.* The attendance function includes an understanding of the relation of social responsibility and the school, and of the significance of state laws and regulations, the school census, local administration of attendance, including the better methods of enforcement, and the problems associated with those peculiar conditions to be found in each community.

The administration of the attendance function extends to problems definitely associated with non-attendance—its causes and their elimination. There must be identification of non-attendants and an emphasis upon improving the situation so that each child can profit to the fullest extent by regularity in attendance. Tardiness in any form must not be overlooked.

Finally, the administration of the attendance function includes an understanding of child labor, federal and state laws relating thereto, and its educational implications as well as local administration.

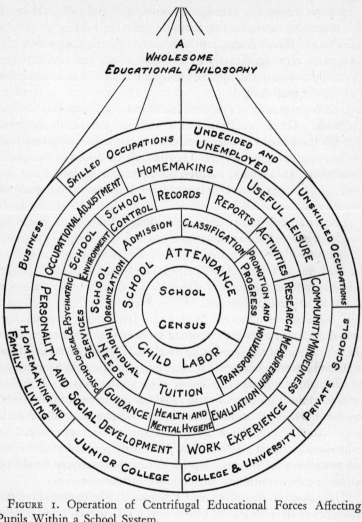

FIGURE I. Operation of Centrifugal Educational Forces Affecting Pupils Within a School System.

2. *Providing for All Pupils.* Admission of all pupils to school is predicated upon legal requirements and regulations. Assignment and grouping for effective progress, both in the elementary and in the secondary school, are essential in order that continuity of growth and development may be realized. Promotion must be administered as a *step progress* in growth.

Promotion should be scientifically determined and failures reduced to a minimum or eliminated. Since the individual differences of all children are characteristic, provision should be made especially for those who vary significantly from "normal" children, such as the physically handicapped, mentally exceptional, and those emotionally and socially maladjusted.

3. *Administration of Problems Incidental to a Wider Educational Program.* Those problems which arise as the pupils progress through the school years are of direct concern in the administration of the pupil personnel service. They include questions of age-grade distribution, elimination, transfer, and adjustment, with plans for meeting the needs of varying types of pupils in the changing school population.

A better articulation of the several administrative units should be sought in order to assure continuous progress of all pupils. Provision should be made for the transported and the tuition pupil, as well as for academic and non-academic types. The administration of specific activities to meet the needs of all pupils is definitely under the scope of the pupil personnel service.

4. *Adjustment Services.* Within the framework of pupil personnel administration are important services which are essential to the adjustment of the pupil as he develops. The school environment is of fundamental consideration, since every child should be provided an adequate environment conducive to his greater progress. It should present stimulating control patterns which can serve as his frame of reference. Here are included the health services with all of their implications, the guidance and counseling services so essential in constant adjustment and direction, and finally psychiatric and clinical procedures for the maladjusted. All of these services should be studied as they contribute to continuity and development.

5. *Evaluation, Recording, and Reporting.* The evaluation of the outcomes of the educational program as it affects each pupil is definitely a function of the pupil personnel service. Such administrative procedures as marks, tests, examinations, measurements, and the services associated with them should be included within the framework. Effort must constantly be made to improve both the nature and the effectiveness of the evaluative procedures as well as the efficiency of all those associated with it.

The keeping of records is a necessary accompaniment of the evaluative process, and of many of the adjustment services indicated in previous sections. Procedures should be developed for the proper construction and management of records and for their use in promoting each pupil's growth. Important also, and dependent upon records is an adequate report to whom the report is due—parents, community, and state. Since home reporting looms largest in this area, it is evident that major attention should be to a form of reporting which secures both better understanding and the greatest degree of cooperation. Pupil reports to higher institutions of learning and to other agencies must not be overlooked as a part of this service.

6. *Achieving Personality and Social Adjustment.* Fundamental to the organization and administration of the pupil personnel service is provision for those problems which pertain to pupils' individual and social personality adjustment. Here, among others, one may include secret societies, boy and girl problems, especially those which lead to serious consequences, juvenile delinquency and crime, and contact with the courts. Provision should be made for sex education and its implications, and for those character-building activities which lead to moral and spiritual uplift. Leadership should be identified and developed.

Many of these activities and problems radiate out into the home and community. The school and the home are twin institutions for childhood development and as a consequence have much in common. Desirable relationships with the home should be fostered. Many of the problems of youth are to be found in community disorganizing forces which should be understood and eliminated wherever possible. There are many necessary contacts to be made with youth-serving community organizations and activities. Learning to cooperate effectively with them and the home is a part of the program. Children affected by the migration and mobility of the population bring many educational problems which belong to the pupil personnel service.

7. *As Youth Leave School.* It would seem at first glance that the task of the school has been accomplished when its boys and girls leave the school. However, this is the time for reflection, and for reviewing procedures which have been presumed to fit the youth for his next step in life. His needs should be reviewed at this point and he should be appraised in the light of their fulfillment. The program in operation should constantly be re-evaluated and readjusted as these

conditions are studied. There are many opportunities for contact with the community's industrial and business pattern to ascertain whether youth are able to make the proper initial occupational adjustment. For most girls there will be homemaking responsibilities after a brief interlude of gainful employment.

Of major concern to the pupil personnel service is the transition to institutions of higher education on the part of those who are admitted to them and can profit by their offering. The sending school has an obligation to "carry through" and examine returns in the light of the needs of subsequent entrants. Finally, there are the armed forces, to which every youth owes his potential service as a citizen. These touch the school at several points.

8. *The School Organization.* There may be some difference of opinion as to the relation which responsibility for the school organization bears to the pupil personnel function. The reader will have already noted throughout this text that the administration of the pupil personnel function touches the school organization at many points. One may conclude that, if line responsibility does not exist in the school system to coordinate the direction of the school organization function with that of pupil personnel, some plan should be developed to bring about this coordination either on a staff basis or through committee conferences or direct teacher contacts. The point is to recognize that the two functions are inseparable and must be in harmony to further the principle of continuous pupil progress.

To this end those responsible for the pupil personnel function should have an understanding of the nature of school organization and the traditional patterns of elementary and secondary school organization. They should understand recent developments in organizing the elementary schools, as to both school and classroom procedures. The idea of kindergarten and nursery school should be grasped, as well as recent proposals to reorient the young child in an organization better designed to smooth his educational progress. There are many problems peculiar to each community, best illustrated in the rural and sparsely settled areas. In this age group, parents should be closely associated with the child's progress as he matures.

The traditional secondary school pattern is now widely modified by means of various forms of school organization and procedures which show promise of accentuating individual pupil progress. These should be studied with great care and their several features utilized where advisable in adapting a plan of school organization to a given situation. Such a plan may break sharply with current practices. It may be more costly, especially if extended upward or outward. State and regional contacts should be understood and applied. Always, the pupils' welfare and progress should be paramount.

STATE ORGANIZATION AND ADMINISTRATION OF THE PUPIL PERSONNEL SERVICE

Since education is a function of a state, its primary responsibility is to develop administrative procedures to implement the educational program of that state. For the most part, the tendency has been to

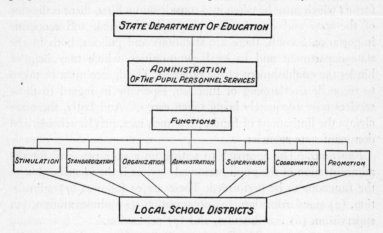

FIGURE 2. Distribution of the Functions of the Pupil Personnel Services in a State Department of Education.

place the emphasis of state school administration on matters pertaining to business management and finance, taxation, state reimbursement, school district organization, school board relationship, school plants, licensing of professional groups, agriculture, and the curriculum. Administrative policies and procedures pertaining directly to the pupil have extended principally to school attendance, the school census, and child labor. Practices and policies among states in regard to these have differed widely. In many states they have been conceived largely as matters for local administration.

In view of the numerous demands made on education in recent

years, its scope has been greatly enlarged, and, as a consequence, many other pupil personnel services have been added to a state's educational responsibility. Among them are guidance, the health service, exceptional children, transportation, and measurement and evaluation. The state has been concerned here in extending educational opportunity adequately to all children because of the limitations of the small school district so typical in the United States. For this reason these services have been gradually extended stateward. The principal task now is to set up a state program which comprehends the scope of the problems in the state and endeavors to meet them.

In applying the plan suggested, it is necessary to point out several factors which must be taken into consideration. First, there is the size of the state and questions of geographical, social, and economic importance. Second, there are traditions and policies, both in the state department and in local communities, which may help or hinder the establishment of the program. Third, care must be taken to reconcile overlapping of function, especially in regard to those services now adequately being taken care of. And lastly, there are always the limitations of funds, personnel, race, private schools, and dominant state agencies.

Functions. The approach to setting up a state program for the administration of the pupil personnel services is the identification of the functions to be performed. These are as follows: (1) stimulation, (2) standardization, (3) organization, (4) administration, (5) supervision, (6) coordination, and (7) promotion.

1. STIMULATION. The first responsibility of a state is to acquaint local school communities with state laws and regulations in regard to pupil services. Supplying information as to desirable practices and procedures, as well as standards, in all fields pertaining to the pupil personnel is a part of this function. Studies in local communities can be made and workshops set up to facilitate the state program. Clinics can be fostered and personnel prepared. Addresses can be given, conferences conducted, and inspiring leadership undertaken. The principal task is to stimulate local school districts to do more for their individual pupils.

2. STANDARDIZATION. The state should set up desirable standards for the pupil personnel services, for example, care of exceptional children, class organization, class size, equipment, and health pro-

grams. Preferred instructional programs and procedures can be outlined. Teacher education and certification are most important, especially where specific requirements are necessary, as in the cases of health, physically handicapped children, and guidance counselors.

3. ORGANIZATION. The state department of education should have a twofold approach to organization. First, the department itself must be adequately organized to administer pupil personnel functions. Figure 2 indicates a suggested approach to such an organization. In the second place, organization as applied to these services includes (*a*) setting up centers, clinics, and workshops demonstrating desirable practices, (*b*) identifying such specific centers in practice and encouraging visits to them, and (*c*) participating in organized means throughout the state or in other states designed to further the pupil personnel function. Teacher education and other state institutions should be visited to locate information as to needs and better practices, and efforts made to disseminate what is learned. This may take the form of bulletins and mimeograph material. Conferences in the state department as well as in the field may require a heavy time expenditure.

4. ADMINISTRATION. While some of the functions indicated in the previous paragraph may be in part administrative, state administration should also include oversight of classes for exceptional children, clinics and child guidance centers, educational diagnosis, surveys, psychological and psychiatric services, transportation, and tuition. Provision must be made to administer the allotment of state funds where provided, as based on pupil units. To this end child accounting procedures should be carefully attended to, as school census, compulsory school attendance, and child labor. The administration of visiting teachers may come under state direction. Health services are here included as well as guidance-counseling. Some state departments have developed measurement programs based principally on testing and examination, as, for example, in New York State. A growing tendency is the development of the more comprehensive evaluation programs which involve a series of judgments and measurements each based on all available evidence. These include ratings, interpretation of test scores, and anecdotal records. Such an evaluation program is definitely a function of a state department of education. A rather well-developed evaluation plan is the cooperative study used for the evaluation of secondary schools, which a state may use

to classify schools. Some states have evolved similar comprehensive rating forms for elementary schools. The administration of a state program involves both measurement and evaluation at many points.

5. SUPERVISION. The functions of administration and supervision may overlap at some points. Supervision may extend to demonstration centers, visitation and conferences, ratings, collaboration with local administrative and supervisory officers, and in-service improvement of teachers and other personnel.

6. COORDINATION. There are many opportunities in the administration of the pupil personnel services for coordination with other state departments which have some educational oversight, directly or indirectly. These include, in part, the health department, library, highways, welfare, agriculture, finance, and the courts. There are many opportunities for collaboration with federal and state agencies having to do with employment, child labor, school buildings, and rehabilitation. Private schools and colleges offer contacts, as well as state schools, such as those for the mentally incompetent or socially maladjusted. Coordination with all of these agencies involves tact and insight if the welfare of the pupil is to become paramount.[2]

7. PROMOTION. While the state is fundamentally concerned with the administration of those functions which guarantee a state-mandated program based on minimum requirements, it has a further responsibility to upgrade these standards wherever possible. To this end a state department should not only make known legislation in effect regarding pupils but seek by legitimate means to promote more desirable legislation. It should make available results of studies and contributions of leaders in the various fields. It should study the laws and practices of other states. It should study and make available the facilities of the federal government in this area; similarly for best practices within the state and other states. In short, the best test of a state department in administering the pupil personnel services is the degree of educational leadership it manifests.

TYPES OF ORGANIZATION OF THE PUPIL PERSONNEL SERVICES IN THE SCHOOL DISTRICTS

Approach. In every school system the proper administrative organization must be developed which will provide for the several ele-

[2] "Pupil Personnel Services as a Function of State Departments of Education," *Bulletin No. 6,* Monograph No. 5, Washington, United States Office of Education, 1940, part iii. This is a helpful bulletin.

ments essential to the pupil personnel function. This organization should fit the size of the system and the needs of the children. With an eye to the state's over-all pattern and within the legal framework provided, each school community must cut and fit its own pattern. Although the school must assume responsibility for leadership, we cannot emphasize too strongly the fact that many aspects and problems of pupil personnel administration radiate out into the home

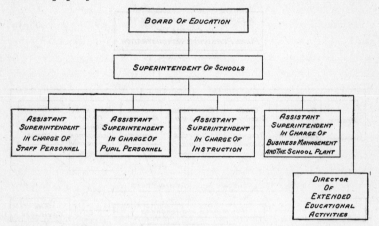

FIGURE 3. Suggested Plan of Organization for a City School System to Include Its Administrative Functions.

and community life. To this end the organization must make provision for activities within the community and develop cooperative relationship with them.

It is also important to emphasize that *all* essential elements of a desirable pupil personnel service need to be supplied to all children. In larger cities, this is fairly easily accomplished. As the district becomes smaller in size, provision on a similar basis is obviously impossible. Here a local organization should be set up which will furnish the elements as far as possible through limited staff and community cooperation. Larger units such as administration areas and counties must make supplementary arrangements for additional services as the needs and occasions arise. That community will indeed be fortunate if, through strong community cooperation, further supplementation becomes desirable and effective.

Before proceeding to an outline of a proposed functional organization for pupil personnel services, it is essential to comprehend organization of a school system to include all its administration functions. Figure 3 shows the major functions to be four in number, namely, staff personnel administration, pupil personnel administration, instruction, and school plant and business administration. In a large city, each function should be in charge of an assistant superintendent of schools. The additional function, namely, extended educational activities, is in charge of a director attached to the superintendent's

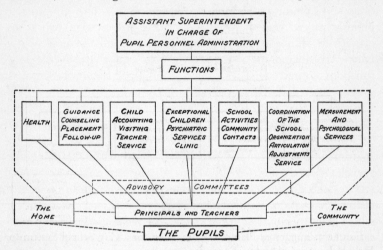

FIGURE 4. Organization for Pupil Personnel Services for a Larger School System.

office. The scope of this function naturally depends on the nature and extent of the educational services offered. However, there are many points of contact with the other functions of a school system.

Preferred Organization. Figure 4 shows how the pupil personnel services may be organized functionally in larger school systems. Seven functional areas are indicated, namely, health; guidance-counseling, placement, and follow-up; child accounting; exceptional children; coordination of school organization, articulation, and adjustment; school activities and community contacts; and the psychological and measurement services.

Each of these seven areas should be in the charge of a director responsible to the assistant superintendent. The personnel in the several divisions will need to be selected and their duties outlined in accordance with the scope of the division and the needs and problems. Vital services must be given first consideration, with gradual extension to activities embracing the total services. At the same time, care should be taken that the whole service be not too centrally directed. Not only should policies with schools, principals, teachers, pupils, and community agencies be cooperatively arrived at, but the administrative procedures should be deeply rooted within each school and community situation.

Each director must have a knowledge of state laws and regulations and administer his division in line with sound educational philosophy and general school policy. He will need to work cooperatively with other division personnel, especially at those points where coordination is essential. Naturally, there are overlapping functions at some points, which will require time for adjustment and assignment.

FUNCTIONS ASSIGNED. The functions assigned to each of the seven divisions are here outlined:

Health function involves knowledge of state laws and regulations, coordination with state and local health authorities and community agencies and activities,* health examinations, medical service, dental service, school nurses, dietitians, psychiatrists, speech and similar specialists,* sanitation, health guidance and instruction,* oversight of school plant to stimulate health essentials,* mental hygiene, sex education,* physical recreation,* health records and reports,* summer camps,* safety education,* teacher health.

Guidance-counseling functions involve the guidance-counseling services and activities, home-room guidance, vocational information, adjustment and placement, contacts with community industries and businesses as to vocational opportunities, follow-up, reference documents and materials,* coordination with federal, state, and local placement services, work experience, relation with higher institutions and private schools,* minor disciplinary problems.*

Child accounting includes responsibility for administration of the school census and school attendance, with knowledge of state laws and regulations associated therewith, child labor, work permits,* exemptions for school attendance, visiting teachers,* transportation in relation to attendance, truancy, ascertained causes of non-attendance,* improving school attendance,* tardiness,* state and other reports pertaining to child accounting, court contacts.*

The function dealing with *exceptional children* involves knowl-

---

* These are overlapping functions and will require coordination with other divisions. This should accentuate the cooperative principle.

edge of legal aspects associated with exceptional children, contacts with state and other organizations having to do with the function, provision for physically handicapped, mentally exceptional, emotionally and socially maladjusted children, court contacts involving these children,* adaptations in school organization and attendance affecting seriously maladjusted children,* psychiatric services, clinics both within and without the school, serious disciplinary problems, supervisory relationships affecting these children.*

School activities and community contacts involve policies pertaining to all school activities, including athletics, school clubs, musical and forensic activities, dramatics, parties and dances, honor societies, secret societies, sex education,* boy and girl problems,* juvenile delinquency,* school and community recreational activities,* coordination with community youth-serving organizations, coordination with director of extended educational activities to promote supplementary educational needs of pupils,* pupil load, summer camps,* parent-teacher associations and similar groups, stimulation of pupil leadership. In addition to these functions, it is suggested that the public school relations might well be administered through this division.

Coordination of school organization, articulation, and adjustment involves knowledge of legal aspects of admission, admission and classification procedures, including pre-school examinations and clinics,* grouping,* studies of pupil progress,* promotion and non-promotion policies, age-grade tables, and reports,* transfers, retardation, transportation in relation to pupil progress, tuition pupils, migration and mobility problems,* remedial plans and adjustment procedures involving school organization, articulation of school units, oversight of school building and site to stimulate pupil progress,* college contacts and reports, contacts with private schools within the community.*

Measurement and psychological services include the measurement services, identification of pupil characteristics, contacts with state and other agencies, cumulative records,* marks and marking systems, pupil reports, coordination of records and reports in other divisions,* surveys, psychological services, case studies of pupils, coordination with state and local programs of measurement and evaluation, and research services.

This preferred organization can be placed in operation in large cities and in counties where consolidation has reached sufficient proportions as to pupil enrollment and services. An advisory committee is indicated on the accompanying chart. It may be composed of the directors, selected principal, teachers, parents, and advisers selected from within the community. Direct and indirect contacts with the home and the community are definitely within the scope of the organization.

Modified Organization. Figure 5 shows a modified plan of organization for a medium-sized school system in which the number

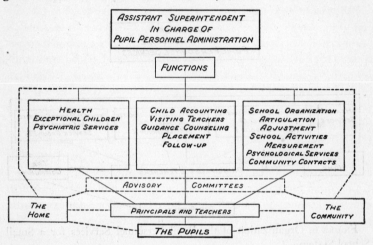

FIGURE 5. Modified Organization for Pupil Personnel Services for a Medium-Sized School System.

of divisions is reduced to three. These include (1) health services and exceptional children; (2) child accounting, guidance-counseling-placement, and follow-up; and (3) coordination of school organization, articulation, school activities and community contacts, and the psychological and measurement services. The several functions associated with each of these have just been outlined. This reduced plan assumes that no function may be omitted; rather that provision should be made for each under reduced staff personnel. The scope of each service will be considerably cut down as the system gets smaller in size. Each functional division will cooperate with a functional principal-teacher committee[3] with advisory and perhaps some administrative relationships. Constantly, the cooperative principle

---

[3] May include parents or other advisers as indicated above.

characterizes the whole organization and its administration. This plan of organization may be placed in operation in the larger county school systems. Directors in charge may serve on a part-time basis in smaller systems.

Small School Organization. As the school system decreases in size, the staff personnel in charge of specific service divisions diminish in number. However, the position of the director of pupil personnel remains. The director may be a specially assigned person, or

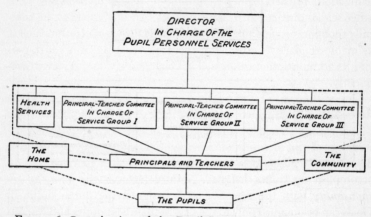

FIGURE 6. Organization of the Pupil Personnel Services for a Small School System.

the function may be carried out by the superintendent himself. The health services should continue as a specialized service; however, the remaining services should be combined as best suited to conditions which pertain within the school system. The suggested plan is to organize three principal-teacher committees to be in charge of selected functions and services ascertained and assigned after a complete survey of the situation. These should be known as Service Groups I, II, and III, whose functions should be assigned. They should be carefully selected, being representative of the various school communities within the district and competent for the tasks assigned. An advisory committee from within the school and community can function as suggested for larger school systems.

Whatever the size of the school, the primary functions remain, although now sharply reduced in scope. Provision should be made for needs and problems as they arise. The cooperative principle remains.

Implementing the Program

As a part of the policy, the board of education should approve the plan of school organization, additional personnel, transfer of personnel, budgeting considerations, equipment and materials, and new regulations. The plan adopted may affect the local school organization, teachers' time, community policies, or relations with other school districts, as in joint services. All of these must be carefully thought through and full information disseminated. It is well if as many elements as possible of the proposed plan of organization and its administration be arrived at cooperatively, and reviewed frequently.

One of the major responsibilities of a superintendent of schools is the selection of competent personnel to head up the various services. Those chosen should be adequately educated for the task. An in-service program of education may be necessary at strategic points of deficiency. In addition to *competence,* personnel must have *time* to accomplish the duties assigned. A third factor is the *fixing of responsibility* with the person who is assigned the duties outlined. Goals can be obtained only to the degree that these duties and responsibilities are clear. A fourth factor is making available suitable equipment and materials, as well as conditions of work.

In all of this the cooperative principle must not be overlooked, the working together for the best interests of all the boys and girls. The advisory committee can become a real asset if properly selected and administered.

Beginning in a small way through attacking the urgent problems of the school system, the program should grow as it feels the thrill of its own accomplishments. An enthusiastic personnel is one aspect of this development. More important is the progress and development of the boys and girls within the system. The program must be constantly evaluated with this end in mind through procedures as objectively determined as possible. The ultimate criterion of success should always be the degree to which the program of education provides for the continuous growth and maturation of the childhood and youth for whom the schools exist.

QUESTIONS AND PROBLEMS

1. Evaluate, by consulting authorities, the principles suggested for the organization of the pupil personnel services in the light of good administrative practice.
2. Study a selected school system in order to apply one or more of the suggested plans for organization. Make suggestions for improvement.
3. Study the organization of the pupil personnel services in one (or more) states. What suggestions do you have to improve the services in that state?
4. In reviewing the suggestions made in this text for administering the pupil, what generally needs to be done in the typical school system? Be specific in your answer.

SELECTED REFERENCES

1. American Youth Commission, *Youth and the Future*. Washington: American Council on Education, 1942, part iii.
2. Cook, Katherine, "Pupil Personnel Services for All Children," *Planning Schools for Tomorrow* (Leaflet No. 72). Washington: United States Office of Education, 1944.
3. Educational Policies Commission, *Education for All American Youth*. Washington: National Education Association, 1944.
4. Germane, Charles E., and Germane, Edith G., *Personnel Work in High School*. New York: Silver, Burdett and Company, 1941, chap. iv.
5. Heck, Arch O., *Education of Exceptional Children*. New York: McGraw-Hill Book Company, 1940, part iv.
6. Heck, Arch O., "Pupil Personnel Work—II. Effective Organization," *Nation's Schools,* July, 1941, pp. 53–55.
7. "Pupil Personnel Services as a Function of State Departments of Education," *Bulletin No. 6,* Monograph No. 5. Washington: United States Office of Education, 1940.
8. Reed, Anna Y., *Guidance and Personnel Services in Education*. Ithaca, New York: Cornell University Press, 1944, Part V.
9. Wiens, David J., "Are Your Pupil Personnel Services Effectively Organized?" *American School Board Journal,* August, 1942, pp. 9–11.
10. Wiens, David J., *Organization of Pupil Personnel Services in City School Systems,* Doctor's Dissertation, Western Reserve University, 1941.

INDEX